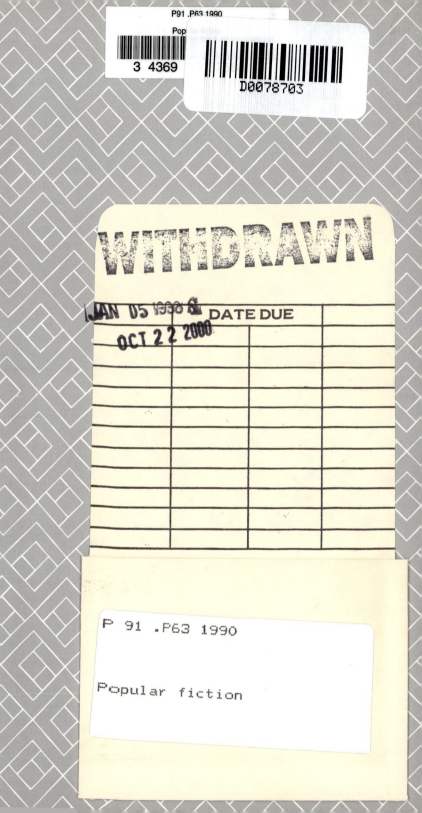
P91 .P63 1990

Popular fiction

3 4369

D0078703

WITHDRAWN

JAN 05 1998

OCT 2 2 2000

DATE DUE

P 91 .P63 1990

Popular fiction

POPULAR FICTIONS SERIES

Popular Fiction

Technology, ideology, production, reading

Tony Bennett

Routledge: LONDON AND NEW YORK

Popular Fiction

How are popular fictions produced, received, and made sense of by their readers or viewers? What role do they play in organizing our conceptions of gender, sexuality, class, and nationhood? How do popular fictions order and regulate our sense of ourselves and our relations to others? How do they inform and structure our daily lives?

These are among the questions examined in this lively collection. Representing the most innovative and challenging work in the field, the contributions look at popular fiction in its literary, filmic, and televisual forms. They range across the main genres of popular fiction: science fiction, soap opera, detective fiction, the spy-thriller, the western, *film noir*, and comedy. Grouped into sections, the essays explore major themes in the study of popular fiction: the functioning of popular fiction within technologies of cultural regulation; the relations between popular fiction and nationalism; the connections between popular fictions and relations of power and knowledge; and the social and ideological factors moulding both the production and reading of popular fictions.

Designed especially as a student text, *Popular Fiction* will be invaluable to students in many areas – English and literary studies, media studies, film and TV studies, communications studies, and cultural studies.

POPULAR FICTIONS SERIES

Series editors:

Tony Bennett
Associate Professor
School of Humanities
Griffith University

Graham Martin
Professor of English
 Literature
Open University

In the same series

Cover Stories
Narrative and ideology in the British spy thriller
by Michael Denning
Combining cultural history with narrative analysis, Michael
Denning tracks the spy thriller from John Buchan to Eric
Ambler, Ian Fleming and John Le Carré, and shows how
these tales tell a history of our times, and attempt to resolve
crises and contradictions in ideologies of nation and empire,
of class and gender.

Lost Narratives
Popular fictions, politics and recent history
by Roger Bromley
Explores the ways in which certain popular cultural forms –
narrative fictions, autobiographical writings, television
productions – contribute to the social production of memory.

Popular Film and Television Comedy
by Steve Neale and Frank Krutnik
Explores the nature of comedy, relating its diverse forms and
conventions to their institutional contexts. The authors
discuss a wide range of programmes and films, looking in
particular detail at slapstick and 'screwball' comedies and TV
programmes such as *Monty Python*, *Hancock* and *Steptoe
and Son*.

Forthcoming

John Caughie on **Television Drama**
Colin Mercer on **Popular Narratives**

282906

First published 1990
by Routledge
11 New Fetter Lane, London EC4P 4EE

Simultaneously published in the USA and Canada
by Routledge
a division of Routledge, Chapman and Hall, Inc.
29 West 35th Street, New York, NY 10001

© 1990 Tony Bennett
Typeset in 11/12 English Times by
Mayhew Typesetting, Bristol
Printed in Great Britain by
The Guernsey Press, Channel Islands

All rights reserved. No part of this book may be reprinted or
reproduced or utilized in any form or by any electronic,
mechanical, or other means, now known or hereafter invented,
including photocopying and recording, or in any information
storage or retrieval system, without permission in writing from
the publishers.

British Library Cataloguing in Publication Data

Popular fiction: technology, ideology
  production, reading. — (Popular
  fictions series).
  1. Popular culture
  I. Bennett, Tony   II. Series
  306'.1

  ISBN 0–415–02517–6
  ISBN 0–415–02518–4 Pbk

Library of Congress Cataloging-in-Publication Data

Popular fiction: technology, ideology, production, reading / edited
by Tony Bennett.
    p. cm. — (Popular fictions series)
    Bibliography: p.
    ISBN 0–415–02517–6. ISBN 0–415–02518–4 (pbk.)
    1. Mass media. 2. Popular culture. 3. English fiction – History
and criticism. 4. Popular literature – History and criticism.
5. Motion pictures. 6. Television broadcasting. I. Bennett, Tony.
II. Series.
P91.P63 1990
302.2'34–dc19   88-14865

Contents

Series editors' preface

There are many good reasons for studying popular fiction. The best, though, is that it matters. In the many and varied forms in which they are produced and circulated – by the cinema, broadcasting institutions and the publishing industry – popular fictions saturate the rhythms of everyday life. In doing so, they help to define our sense of ourselves, shaping our desires, fantasies, imagined pasts and projected futures. An understanding of such fictions – of how they are produced and circulated, organized and received – is thus central to an understanding of ourselves; of how those selves have been shaped and of how they might be changed.

This series is intended to contribute to such an understanding by providing a context in which different traditions and directions in the study of popular fiction might be brought into contact so as to interanimate one another. It will thus range across the institutions of cinema, broadcasting and publishing, seeking to illuminate their respective specificities, as well as the relations between them, with a view to identifying the ways in which popular film, television and writing interact as parts of developed cultural technologies for the formation of subjectivities. Consideration of the generic properties of popular fictions will thus be situated within an analysis of their historical and institutional conditions of production and reception.

Similarly, the series will represent, and coordinate a debate between, the diverse political perspectives through which the study of popular fiction has been shaped and defined in recent years. Feminist studies of the part popular fictions play in the production of gendered subjectivities and relations; Marxist perspectives on the relations between popular fiction and class formations; popular fiction as a site for the reproduction and contestation of subordinate racial and national identities: in encompassing contributions from these often sharply contrasting traditions of thought the series will explore the complex and intertwining web of political relations in which the production and reception of popular fictions are involved.

It should be clear, though, that in all of this our aim is not to transform popular fiction into something else – into literature, say, or art cinema. If the study of popular fiction matters it is because what is ultimately at stake in such analysis is the production of a better popular fiction as well as of better, politically more productive, ways of reading it.

Tony Bennett
Graham Martin

Preface

The study of popular fiction has expanded remarkably over the past twenty to thirty years. In the early 1960s, the subject had no more than a precarious toe-hold on the curriculum in a handful of English departments and was sustained by a roughly proportionate amount of critical work. Moreover, much of this was more concerned with the study of popular fiction as both symptom and cause of a generalized social problem – a decline in standards, whether moral or aesthetic, or, in the British context, the threat of Americanization – than with the specificities of its sub-genres or the peculiar determinations of its production and reception.

By contrast, there are now few tertiary institutions where popular fiction is not accorded some space in the curriculum, and there are many where it constitutes a significant core of full programmes of study. Yet the pattern of its development has also been a dispersed one, for the subject has entered into the curriculum through a variety of routes (often determined by local institutional considerations), so that it is now available within a somewhat bewildering array of curriculum contexts: communications and media studies, cultural studies, film studies, television studies, women's studies, literary studies and so on. At the same time, the study of popular fiction has also been shaped via the contributions of a multiplicity of disciplinary and theoretical inputs – Marxism, semiotics, feminism, psychoanalysis and discourse theory to name but a few – and has, indeed, provided one of the more influential meeting points for the concerns of these different traditions of theoretical inquiry.

No doubt the subject will continue to be developed along a number of different trajectories, shaped by a diversity of both institutional contexts and criss-crossing theoretical and disciplinary inputs. However, my purpose in this collection has been to compensate for some of the shortcomings this pattern of development has produced. My primary aim has been to bring together a selection of critical writings which will give some sense of the shared concerns which underlie the study of popular fiction across the different media of writing, film and television while also according due respect to the specificities of debate relating to each of these. I have thus avoided the obvious choice of dividing the collection into separate sections on popular writing, film and television, preferring instead an organization which works in terms of themes which cut across these different media. For the same reason, I've avoided organizing the relations between the readings in term of clearly demarcated theoretical traditions in order to explore the areas in which the interests of different theoretical positions have productively overlapped.

In contrast to the situation which obtained in the 1960s, there is now a wealth of material – as rich in empirical detail as it is in theoretical sophistication – from which to choose. It may help the reader, therefore, if I spell out the criteria which have guided me in making this selection. Put in the most general terms, popular fiction is now increasingly studied with regard to its role in the formation and regulation of the aptitudes, capacities and subjectivities of extended populations, a role which is conceived as being dependent on the particular ways in which popular fictional texts are deployed within the developed social apparatuses or cultural technologies of cinema, television or publishing. This entails that attention be paid not merely to the form and content of popular fictions themselves, but also to the properties of the cultural technologies which regulate both the conditions of their production and reception.

While all the essays selected contribute to this conception of popular fiction and the modes of its social operation, each of the sections focuses on a different aspect of either its constitution, so understood, or the forms of its social articulation. The readings comprising the first section thus seek to illustrate the respects in which popular fictions are appropriately regarded as parts of cultural technologies which – in contrast with earlier Marxist assessments of cultural forms being determined by the economic and technological conditions of their existence – are assessed as being simultaneously economic, technological, social and ideological in their conditions and effects. The next three sections then examine the functioning of these technologies in relation to different sets of social relations while also highlighting the specific concerns of those bodies of theory which have contributed most influentially to the study of popular fiction in recent years. The essays collected in the second section, in examining the role of popular fictions in the processes of 'nationing' populations and territories, thus also exemplify the logic of those Marxist approaches to popular fiction which owe a debt to Gramsci's writings on the subject of hegemony. Similarly, Section 3, focusing on the relations between gender, sexuality and pleasure, particularly in the cinema, also exemplifies some of the distinctive concerns of contemporary feminist criticism, particularly in its (critical) relations to psychoanalysis.

The fourth section is somewhat differently organized in that it orchestrates a debate between different understandings of the relations between popular fiction, power, knowledge and ideology by means of different readings – Marxist, Foucauldian and feminist – of nineteenth-century detective fiction. Finally, Sections 5 and 6 return to the themes of the first section, but in more detail and with more specialization, in investigating, respectively, the conditions of the production and reception of popular fictions and their ideological effects.

Where possible, the readings collected in each section include a consideration of popular fiction in its literary, filmic and televisual forms. However, the pressures of space have meant that a certain degree of specialization has been unavoidable. Section 3 thus has a predominantly cinematic flavour whereas Section 4 – given its focus on nineteenth-century detective fiction – is exclusively literary. I have also sought to include discussions of as wide a range of genres as possible, and have been reasonably successful in doing so. Between them, the essays collected here encompass a consideration of soap operas, situation comedies, TV science fiction, the Western, crossdressing films, *film noir*, the thriller, the sexological novel, detective fiction and others. Inevitably, though, there are some omissions while, for the sake of the other advantages to be derived from doing so, some genres receive more attention than others, detective fiction, for example.

For the rest, I have aimed throughout to include essays in which theoretical arguments are developed by means of detailed and specific examples rather than being stated abstractly. I have also sought to ensure that, whatever their national origins, the popular fictions discussed have been sufficiently international in their distribution for it to be likely that most British, Australian and American readers will be familiar with them.

While most of the readings selected speak clearly enough for themselves, I have provided a short introduction to each section in order to outline the relations of the readings to one another and to place them in an appropriate theoretical context. These introductions also serve the purpose of specifying the perspectives from which the readings have been edited. Many of these have been substantially reduced from their original versions – partly because of the obvious limitations of space imposed on a collection of this kind, but also to emphasize their contributions to the themes I have highlighted by excising their engagements with other issues. Although this has entailed an inevitable reduction in the scope of many of the readings, I have sought, while accentuating particular lines of argument, not to distort their overall theses or to impose my own views upon them. The only editorial liberty I have allowed myself is that of reducing the range of notes and references accompanying some of the contributions where I have judged these to be of interest only to specialists in the field of study concerned. Apart from this, all contributions appear here as they were originally published except for Laura Mulvey's 'Afterthoughts on "Visual pleasure and narrative cinema"' which contains some revisions proposed by the author.

Finally, I have provided a bibliography which, while it does not pretend to comprehensiveness, will allow the reader to pursue the avenues of inquiry opened up by the readings collected here.

It remains merely to thank those who have contributed to this collection, even if often without knowing it. To Graham Martin, a very special thanks for his helpful comments at all stages in the project, and especially for reading through the collection with a keen and experienced editorial eye. My thanks to colleagues at Griffith University who have helped to shape the ideas governing this collection in the course of many conversations – usually on other matters, but invariably rewarding – and especially to Pat Buckridge, Ian Hunter, Colin Mercer, David Saunders and Dugald Williamson. To Sue, my thanks for everything and more, and to Tanya, Oliver and James my thanks for just being there.

Tony Bennett
Brisbane
January 1987

Acknowledgements

The editor and publisher would like to thank the following for permission to reproduce copyright material: the author and Collins Publishers for Raymond Williams, 'The technology and the society' from *Television, Technology and Cultural Form*; the author and Macmillan Ltd and Indiana University Press for Stephen Heath, 'On screen, in frame: film and ideology' from *Questions of Cinema*; the author and Routledge for John Ellis, 'Broadcast TV as cultural form' from *Visible Fictions: Cinema, Television, Video*; the author and Macmillan Ltd for Stephen Heath, 'When Millicent bucked and writhed . . .' from *The Sexual Fix*; the author and Verso for Benedict Anderson, 'Apprehensions of time' from *Imagined Communities: Reflections on the Origins and Spread of Nationalism*; the author and Yale University Press for Dennis Porter, 'The language of detection' from *The Pursuit of Crime: Art and Ideology in Detective Fiction*; the author and British Film Institute for Colin McArthur, 'Scotland and cinema: the iniquity of the fathers' from *Scotch Reels: Scotland in Cinema and Television*; the author and Unwin Hyman Ltd for Graeme Turner, 'Representing the nation' from *National Fictions: Literature, Film and the Construction of Australian Narrative*; the author and Framework for Laura Mulvey, 'Afterthoughts on visual pleasure and narrative cinema' from *Framework* 15–17; the author and British Film Institute for Janey Place, 'Women in *film noir*' from *Women in Film Noir*; the author and Routledge for Annette Kuhn, 'Sexual disguise and cinema' from *The Power of the Image: Essays on Representation and Sexuality*; the author and Shoe String Press for Tania Modleski, 'The search for tomorrow in today's soap operas' from *Living with a Vengeance: Mass Produced Fantasies for Women*; the author and University Microfilms Ltd for Dana Brand, 'From the *flâneur* to the detective: interpreting the city of Poe' from *The Spectator and the City: Fantasies of Urban Legibility in Nineteenth-century England and America*; the author and Verso for Franco Moretti, 'Clues' from *Signs taken for Wonders. Essays in the Sociology of Literary Forms*; the author, Indiana University Press and History Workshop for Carlo Ginzburg, 'Morelli, Freud and Sherlock Holmes: clues and scientific method' from *History Workshop* 9, Spring, and *The Sign of Three*; the author and Routledge for Catherine Belsey, 'Deconstructing the text: Sherlock Holmes' from *Critical Practice*; the author and Macmillan Ltd for John Tulloch and Manuel Alvarado, 'Send-up: authorship and organization' from *Dr Who: The Unfolding Text*; the author and British Film Institute for Paul Kerr, 'The making of (the) MTM show' from *Quality Television*; the author and SEFT for John Ellis, 'Made in Ealing' from *Screen* 16, 1, Spring; the author and SEFT for Paul Kerr, 'Out of what past?' Notes on the B *film noir*' from *Screen Education* 32–3; the author and University of Chicago Press for Neil Harris, 'The operational aesthetic' from *The Art of P.T. Barnum*; the author, Macmillan Ltd and Salem House Publishers for Jacqueline Rose, 'Peter Pan and the commercialization of the child' from *The Case of Peter Pan, or the Impossibility of Children's Fiction*; the authors and Macmillan Ltd for Tony Bennett and Janet Woollacott, 'Figures of Bond' from *Bond and Beyond: The Political Career of a Popular Hero*; the author and Routledge for David Morley, 'Television and gender' from *Family Television: Cultural Power and Domestic Leisure*.

Photograph credits: the National Film Archive, London, for the photographs accompanying 'Scotland and cinema: the iniquity of the fathers'; the British Film Institute for the photographs accompanying 'Women in *film noir*'; and Annette Kuhn for the photographs accompanying 'Sexual disguise and cinema'.

Section 1

Popular fictions and cultural technologies

Introduction

In a recent examination of the development of a range of popular literary and journalistic forms of writing in the nineteenth century, Colin Mercer suggests that the assumptions of reflection theory, whereby cultural forms are to be read as in some way embodying or expressing their social determinations, can in no way come to terms with the real complexity of those forms or the diversity of their social articulations:

> these diverse forms – *feuilletons*, *Gartenlaube*, magazines, the newspaper, serialized novels, 'household words', little books of hints and self-help, all 'entertainingly written' – cannot be taken to be, even in their 'realist' forms, expressive of a totality which might be society, a class, a community or history. On the contrary, they must be understood not as evidence of something to be located elsewhere, something profound or deep underlying them, but as the composite of surface technologies which elaborate and inscribe the relations between class, community, nation and history. Not that there is nothing happening elsewhere – in the economy, in the courts, in the streets – but that these forms cannot be read off against that 'elsewhere'.[1]

Literary forms are not related to society as to a set of external and independent conditioning relations which they then reflect, so that the task of analysis is to decipher the ways in which those relations achieve an expression in the literary work. Rather, Mercer suggests, they are *in* society, a part of it, actively contributing to the shaping of social relations through the ways in which they organize relations of class, community, nation and history – and, one might add, gender – and inscribe their readers in those relations. The task then becomes one of understanding how such forms are imbricated with, and function in relation to, other social institutions and relations – and at the same level, as 'surface technologies' – rather than excavating them to uncover a set of deeper, underlying relations on which they supposedly rest. It is important to be clear, though, that in referring to such forms as 'surface technologies' – or, elsewhere in the same article, as 'technologies of entertainment' – Mercer has in mind something more than an ensemble of the tricks of the literary trade. While the conception includes these, it also encompasses the technical conditions which such forms presuppose, the economic relations which regulate their production, the institutional contexts which govern the modes of their social deployment and reception – this whole nexus of interacting relations forming a kind of 'social machine' which, in its articulation with other technologies, plays a crucial role in the formation and regulation of specific social forms of individuality.

Although his terminology is slightly different, Stephen Heath has a similar concept in mind when he argues that the cinema must be investigated as a fully social technology:

> The process of cinema . . . is that of a process through which in particular economic situations a set of scattered technical devices becomes an applied technology then a fully social technology; and that social technology can, must, be posed and studied in its effects of construction and meaning. That formulation, however, is itself still problematic. . . . Cinema does not exist in the technological and then become this or that practice in the social; its history is a history of the technological and social together, a history in which the determinations are not

simple but multiple, interacting, in which the ideological is there from the start.[2]

The polemical edge of these arguments is directed most obviously against reductive Marxist formulations of the relations between culture and society according to which, in some versions, technology, or in others the economy, constitutes the 'unmoved mover' of the social structure – the ultimate cause and condition of everything else. Marxist responses to the difficulties this view occasions have largely taken the form of seeking to secure some degree of 'relative autonomy' for cultural forms such as popular literature or the cinema by identifying the mediations through which technological or economic forces must pass in order to connect with and influence literary or cinematic representations. In conceiving such representations as parts of developed social technologies – or, as I, following Raymond Williams's usage, would prefer, cultural technologies – Mercer and Heath seek to undercut the terms of such debates in insisting that the technological, the economic and the ideological are inextricably intertwined from the outset, always already knitted together as parts of complexly organized social apparatuses which function as powerful 'social engines' for the regulation of social relations and the placing of individuals within those relations.

However, the argument also has a second cutting edge, one directed against the suggestion of Lacanian psychoanalysis that subjects are formed – and fixed – through an invariant mechanism. In summarizing her objections to this view, Teresa de Lauretis outlines the respects in which cinema, television and the novel might usefully be regarded as organizing their own subjects rather than working on the ground of an invariant subject form that is pre-given to them:

> I keep thinking . . . that a materialist theory of subjectivity cannot start out from a given notion of the subject, but must approach the subject through the apparati, the social technologies in which it is constructed. Those

apparati are distinct, if not disparate, in their specificity and concrete historicity, which is why their co-participation, their combined effect, cannot be easily assessed. Thus, for instance, while the novel, the cinema, and television are all 'family machines', they cannot simply be equated with one another. As social technologies aimed at reproducing, among other things, the institution family, they do overlap to a certain degree, but the amount of overlap or redundancy involved is offset, precisely, by their material and semiotic specificity (modes of production, modalities of enunciation, of inscription of the spectator/interlocutor, of address). The family that watches together is really another institution; or better, the subject produced in the family that watches TV is not the same social subject produced in families that only read novels.[3]

The novel, the cinema and television are interlocking yet also relatively distinct cultural technologies – specific combinations of technical, economic, semiotic and ideological conditions and effects – which, alongside other technologies (religious, educational), play a significant role in producing, monitoring and deploying specific forms of social individuality; while differing in other respects, the essays collected here share this conception and, between them, illustrate its more significant implications. They have been selected with three main aims in view.

First, to exemplify the general logic of the argument: while all the readings contribute to this purpose, it is most explicitly addressed by Raymond Williams in 'The technology and the society'. In this, one of the earliest and most influential statements of the position, Williams examines the interaction between technical, economic and social considerations in conditioning the characteristic form of broadcast television as a set of relations between centralized transmission facilities and the privatized and domestic reception context of individual homes.

Second, they aim to outline both the similarities and the differences, and the interactions, between the three major cultural technologies involved in the production, circulation and deployment of popular fictions: the cinema, television and the novel. Stephen Heath's 'On screen, in frame: film and ideology' addresses the question of cinema with a view to identifying the way in which, in fixing the position of the spectator in relation to the film frame, it also effects a specific social regulation of desire. Using the work of Bertolt Brecht as a critical perspective through which to locate the limits of the conventions of camera work and positioning characteristic of mainstream narrative cinema, Heath argues that such conventions promote a specific ideology of vision. The framing of the cinematic image, Heath argues, places the spectator in a position of knowledge and command over the images projected on the screen. The resulting effect – 'the specularization of reality for the coherence of a subject' (p. 28) – renders the spectator peculiarly receptive to the imaginary fullness of ideological systems, a tendency enhanced by the conventions of narrative, which Heath regards as one of cinema's primary means for containing the spectator within the space of the film frame.

In 'Broadcast TV as cultural form', Ellis attempts to identify the distinctive properties of television by differentiating the television text – and the viewer's relation to it – from that of the spectator to the cinematic text. In doing so, he accords particular significance to the typically domestic context of television and suggests that the small, self-contained segment – rather than the extended narrative of mainstream cinema – constitutes the distinctive signifying unit of television. While this view is advanced as an elaboration of Raymond Williams's earlier arguments concerning the nature of television flow, Ellis goes considerably further than Williams in contending that the segment forms the principal signifying unit *within* as well as *between* programmes, whether factual or fictional.

Finally, Stephen Heath's 'When Millicent bucked and writhed . . .', in illuminating the respects in which the novel can be regarded as a cultural technology with a significant investment in the social regulation of sexuality, serves a third purpose in demonstrating how the functioning of cultural technologies needs always to be assessed in terms of their relations to adjacent technologies. As a sexual regulator, Heath argues, the novel functions in relation to the representations of sexuality produced by scientific and medical discourse and, with these, helps to organize the sphere of the social within which particular sexual capacities and identities are formed. This argument is illustrated by an examination of the transformation from marriage to orgasm as the typical form of novelistic narrative resolution considered in its relations to the discourses of sexuality put into circulation by the emergence of sexology.

Notes

1 Mercer, Colin (1986) 'That's entertainment: the resilience of popular forms', in Tony Bennett *et al.* (eds) *Popular Culture and Social Relations*, Milton Keynes: Open University Press, pp. 183–4.
2 Heath, Stephen (1981) *Questions of Cinema*, London: Macmillan, pp. 226–7.
3 De Lauretis, Teresa (1984) *Alice Doesn't: Feminism, Semiotics, Cinema*, London: Macmillan, p. 31.

1
The technology and the society
Raymond Williams

It is often said that television has altered our world. In the same way, people often speak of a new world, a new society, a new phase of history, being created – 'brought about' – by this or that new technology: the steam-engine, the automobile, the atomic bomb. Most of us know what is generally implied when such things are said. But this may be the central difficulty: that we have got so used to statements of this general kind, in our most ordinary discussions, that we can fail to realize their specific meanings.

For behind all such statements lie some of the most difficult and most unresolved historical and philosophical questions. Yet the questions are not posed by the statements; indeed they are ordinarily masked by them. Thus we often discuss, with animation, this or that 'effect' of television, or the kinds of social behaviour, the cultural and psychological conditions, which television has 'led to', without feeling ourselves obliged to ask whether it is reasonable to describe any technology as a cause, or, if we think of it as a cause, as what kind of cause, and in what relations with other kinds of causes. . . .

It can of course be said that these fundamental questions are very much too difficult; and that they are indeed difficult is very soon obvious to anyone who tries to follow them through. We could spend our lives trying to answer them, whereas here and now, in a society in which television is important, there is immediate and practical work to be done: surveys to be made, research undertaken; surveys and research, moreover, which we know how to do. . . .

Yet all questions about cause and effect, as between a technology and a society, are intensely practical. Until we have begun to answer them, we really do not know, in any particular case, whether, for example, we are talking about a technology or about the uses of a technology; about necessary institutions or particular and changeable institutions; about a content or about a form. And this is not only a matter of intellectual uncertainty; it is a matter of social practice. If the technology is a cause, we can at best modify or seek to control its effects. Or if the technology, as used, is an effect, to what other kinds of cause, and other kinds of action, should we refer and relate our experience of its uses? These are not abstract questions. They form an increasingly important part of our social and cultural arguments, and they are being decided all the time in real practice, by real and effective decisions.

It is with these problems in mind that I want to try to analyse television as a particular cultural technology, and to look at its development, its institutions, its forms and its effects, in this critical dimension. . . .

Versions of cause and effect in technology and society

We can begin by looking again at the general statement that television has altered our world. It is worth setting down some of the different things this kind of statement has been taken to mean. For example:

(i)   Television was invented as a result of scientific and technical research. Its power as a medium of news and entertainment was then so great that it altered all preceding media of news and entertainment.

(ii) Television was invented as a result of scientific and

technical research. Its power as a medium of social communications was then so great that it altered many of our institutions and forms of social relationships. . . .

(iii) Television was invented as a result of scientific and technical research, and developed as a medium of entertainment and news. It then had unforeseen consequences, not only on other entertainment and news media, which it reduced in viability and importance, but on some of the central processes of family, cultural and social life.

(iv) Television, discovered as a possibility by scientific and technical research, was selected for investment and development to meet the needs of a new kind of society, especially in the provision of centralized entertainment and in the centralized formation of opinions and styles of behaviour.

(v) Television, discovered as a possibility by scientific and technical research, was selected for investment and promotion as a new and profitable phase of a domestic consumer economy; it is then one of the characteristic 'machines for the home'. . . .

(vi) Television became available as a result of scientific and technical research, and in its character and uses both served and exploited the needs of a new kind of large-scale and complex but atomized society.

These are only some of the possible glosses on the ordinary bald statement that television has altered our world. Many people hold mixed versions of what are really alternative opinions, and in some cases there is some inevitable overlapping. But we can distinguish between two broad classes of opinion.

In the first – (i) to (iii) – the technology is in effect accidental. Beyond the strictly internal development of the technology there is no reason why any particular invention should have come about. Similarly it then has consequences which are also in the true sense accidental, since they follow directly from the technology itself. If television had not been invented, this argument would run, certain definite social and cultural events would not have occurred.

In the second – (iv) to (vi) – television is again, in effect, a technological accident, but its significance lies in its uses, which are held to be symptomatic of some order of society or some qualities of human nature which are otherwise determined. If television had not been invented, this argument runs, we would still be manipulated or mindlessly entertained, but in some other way and perhaps less powerfully. . . .

It is then necessary to make a further theoretical distinction. The first class of opinion, described above, is that usually known, at least to its opponents, as *techno-logical determinism*. It is an immensely powerful and now largely orthodox view of the nature of social change. New technologies are discovered, by an essentially internal process of research and development, which then sets the conditions for social change and progress. Progress, in particular, is the history of these inventions, which 'created the modern world'. The effects of the technologies, whether direct or indirect, foreseen or unforeseen, are as it were the rest of history. The steam engine, the automobile, television, the atomic bomb, have *made* modern man and the modern condition.

The second class of opinion appears less determinist. Television, like any other technology, becomes available as an element or a medium in a process of change that is in any case occurring or about to occur. By contrast with pure technological determinism, this view emphasizes other causal factors in social change. It then considers particular technologies, or a complex of technologies, as *symptoms* of change of some other kind. Any particular technology is then as it were a by-product of a social process that is otherwise determined. It only acquires effective status when it is used for purposes which are already contained in this known social process.

The debate between these two general positions

occupies the greater part of our thinking about technology and society. It is a real debate, and each side makes
important points. But it is in the end sterile, because each
position, though in different ways, has abstracted technology from society. In *technological determinism*,
research and development have been assumed as self-
generating. The new technologies are invented as it were
in an independent sphere, and then create new societies
or new human conditions. The view of *symptomatic
technology*, similarly, assumes that research and development are self-generating, but in a more marginal way.
What is discovered in the margin is then taken up and
used.

Each view can then be seen to depend on the isolation
of technology. It is either a self-acting force which
creates new ways of life, or it is a self-acting force which
provides materials for new ways of life. These positions
are so deeply established, in modern social thought, that
it is very difficult to think beyond them. . . .

To change these emphases would require prolonged
and co-operative intellectual effort. But in the particular
case of television it may be possible to outline a different
kind of interpretation, which would allow us to see not
only its history but also its uses in a more radical way.
Such an interpretation would differ from technological
determinism in that it would restore *intention* to the
process of research and development. The technology
would be seen, that is to say, as being looked for and
developed with certain purposes and practices already in
mind. At the same time the interpretation would differ
from symptomatic technology in that these purposes and
practices would be seen as *direct*: as known social needs,
purposes and practices to which the technology is not
marginal but central.

The social history of television as a technology

The invention of television was no single event or series
of events. It depended on a complex of inventions and

developments in electricity, telegraphy, photography and motion pictures, and radio. It can be said to have separated out as a specific technological objective in the period 1875–90, and then, after a lag, to have developed as a specific technological enterprise from 1920 through to the first public television systems of the 1930s. Yet in each of these stages it depended for parts of its realization on inventions made with other ends primarily in view. . . .

In photography, the idea of light-writing had been suggested by (among others) Wedgwood and Davy in 1802, and the *camera obscura* had already been developed. It was not the projection but the fixing of images which at first awaited technical solution, and from 1816 (Niepce) and through to 1839 (Daguerre) this was worked on, together with the improvement of camera devices. Professional and then amateur photography spread rapidly, and reproduction and then transmission, in the developing newspaper press, were achieved. By the 1880s the idea of a 'photographed reality' – still more for record than for observation – was familiar.

The idea of moving pictures had been similarly developing. The magic lantern (slide projection) had been known from the seventeenth century, and had acquired simple motion (one slide over another) by 1736. From at latest 1826 there was a development of mechanical motion-picture devices, such as the wheel-of-life, and these came to be linked with the magic lantern. The effect of persistence in human vision – that is to say, our capacity to hold the 'memory' of an image through an interval to the next image, thus allowing the possibility of a sequence built from rapidly succeeding units – had been known since classical times. Series of cameras photographing stages of a sequence were followed (Marey, 1882) by multiple-shot cameras. Friese-Greene and Edison worked on techniques of filming and projection, and celluloid was substituted for paper reels. By the 1890s the first public motion-picture shows were being given in France, America and England.

Television, as an idea, was involved with many of these developments. It is difficult to separate it, in its earliest stages, from photo-telegraphy. Bain proposed a device for transmitting pictures by electric wires in 1842; Bakewell in 1847 showed the copying telegraph; Caselli in 1862 transmitted pictures by wire over a considerable distance. In 1873, while working at a terminal of the Atlantic telegraph cable, May observed the light-sensitive properties of selenium (which had been isolated by Berzelius in 1817 and was in use for resistors). In a host of ways, following an already defined need, the means of transmitting still pictures and moving pictures were actively sought and to a considerable extent discovered. . . . Through this whole period two facts are evident: that a system of television was foreseen, and its means were being actively sought; but also that, by comparison with electrical generation and electrical telegraphy and telephony, there was very little social investment to bring the scattered work together. It is true that there were technical blocks before 1914 – the thermionic valve and the multi-stage amplifier can be seen to have been needed and were not yet invented. But the critical difference between the various spheres of applied technology can be stated in terms of a social dimension: the new systems of production and of business or transport communication were already organized, at an economic level; the new systems of social communication were not. Thus when motion pictures were developed, their application was characteristically in the margin of established social forms – the sideshows – until their success was capitalized in a version of an established form, the motion-picture *theatre*. . . .

What is interesting throughout is that in a number of complex and related fields, these systems of mobility and transfer in production and communication, whether in mechanical and electric transport, or in telegraphy, photography, motion pictures, radio and television, were at once incentives and responses within a phase of general social transformation. Though some of the crucial scientific and technical discoveries were made by isolated and unsupported individuals, there was a crucial community of selected emphasis and intention, in a society characterized at its most general levels by a mobility and extension of the scale of organizations: forms of growth which brought with them immediate and longer-term problems of operative communication. In many different countries, and in apparently unconnected ways, such needs were at once isolated and technically defined. It is especially a characteristic of the communications systems that *all were foreseen – not in utopian but in technical ways – before the crucial components of the developed systems had been discovered and refined*. In no way is this a history of communications systems creating a new society or new social conditions. The decisive and earlier transformation of industrial production, and its new social forms, which had grown out of a long history of capital accumulation and working technical improvements, created new needs but also new possibilities, and the communications systems, down to television, were their intrinsic outcome.

The social history of the uses of television technology

. . . . We have now become used to a situation in which broadcasting is a major social institution, about which there is always controversy but which, in its familiar form, seems to have been predestined by the technology. This predestination, however, when closely examined, proves to be no more than a set of particular social decisions, in particular circumstances, which were then so widely if imperfectly ratified that it is now difficult to see them as decisions rather than as (retrospectively) inevitable results.

Thus, if seen only in hindsight, broadcasting can be diagnosed as a new and powerful form of social integration and control. Many of its main uses can be seen as socially, commercially and at times, politically manipulative. Moreover, this viewpoint is rationalized by its description as 'mass communication', a phrase used by almost all its agents and advisers as well, curiously, as by most of its radical critics. 'Masses' had been the new nineteenth-century term of contempt for what was formerly described as 'the mob'. The physical 'massing' of the urban and industrial revolution underwrote this. A new radical class-consciousness adopted the term to express the material of new social formations: 'mass organizations'. The 'mass meeting' was an observable physical effect. So pervasive was this description that in the twentieth century multiple serial production was called, falsely but significantly, 'mass production': mass now meant large numbers (but within certain assumed social relationships) rather than any physical or social aggregate. Sound radio and television, for reasons we shall look at, were developed for transmission to *individual* homes, though there was nothing in the technology to make this inevitable. But then this new form of social communication – broadcasting – was obscured by its definition as 'mass communication': an abstraction to its most general characteristic, that it went to many people, 'the masses', which obscured the fact that the means chosen was the offer of individual sets, a method much better described by the earlier word 'broadcasting'. It is interesting that the only developed 'mass' use of radio was in Nazi Germany, where under Goebbels's orders the Party organized compulsory public listening groups and the receivers were in the streets. There has been some imitation of this by similar regimes, and Goebbels was deeply interested in television for the same kind of use. What was developed within most capitalist societies, though called 'mass communication', was significantly different.

There was early official intervention in the development of broadcasting, but in form this was only at a technical level. . . . State intervention in broadcasting had some real and some plausible technical grounds: the distribution of wave lengths. But to these were added, though always controversially, more general social directions or attempts at direction. This social history of broadcasting can be discussed on its own, at the levels of practice and principle. Yet it is unrealistic to extract it from another and perhaps more decisive process, through which, in particular economic situations, a set of scattered technical devices became an applied technology and then a social technology.

A Fascist regime might quickly see the use of broadcasting for direct political and social control. But that, in any case, was when the technology had already been developed elsewhere. In capitalist democracies, the thrust for conversion from scattered techniques to a technology was not political but economic. The characteristically isolated inventors, from Nipkow and Rosing to Baird and Jenkins and Zwyorkin, found their point of development, if at all, in the manufacturers and prospective manufacturers of the technical apparatus. The history at one level is of these isolated names, but at another level it is of EMI, RCA and a score of similar companies and corporations. In the history of motion pictures, capitalist development was primarily in production; large-scale capitalist distribution came much later, as a way of controlling and organizing a market for given production. In broadcasting, both in sound radio and later in television, the major investment was in the means of distribution, and was devoted to production only so far as to make the distribution technically possible and then attractive. Unlike all previous communications technologies, radio and television were *systems primarily devised for transmission and reception as abstract processes, with little or no definition of preceding content.* When the question of content was raised, it was resolved, in the main, parasitically. There were state occasions, public sporting events, theatres and so on, which would be communicatively distributed by these new technical means. *It is not only that the supply of broadcasting facilities preceded the demand; it is that the means of communication preceded their content.*

The period of decisive development in sound broadcasting was the 1920s. . . . Crucially, in the mid-1920s, there was a series of investment-guided technical solutions to the problem of building a small and simple domestic receiver, on which the whole qualitative transformation from wireless telegraphy to broadcasting depended. By the mid-1920s – 1923 and 1924 are especially decisive years – this breakthrough had happened in the leading industrial societies: the United States, Britain, Germany and France. By the end of the 1920s the radio industry had become a major sector of industrial production, within a rapid general expansion of the new kinds of machines which were eventually to be called 'consumer durables'. This complex of developments included the motorcycle and motorcar, the box camera and its successors, home electrical appliances and radio sets. Socially, this complex is characterized by the two apparently paradoxical yet deeply connected tendencies of modern urban industrial living: on the one hand mobility, on the other hand the more apparently self-sufficient family home. The early period of public technology, best exemplified by the railways and city lighting, was being replaced by a kind of technology for which no satisfactory name has yet been found: that which served an at once mobile and home-centred way of living: a form of *mobile privatization*. Broadcasting in its applied form was a social product of this distinctive tendency.

The contradictory pressures of this phase of industrial capitalist society were indeed resolved, at a certain level, by the institution of broadcasting. For mobility was only in part the impulse of an independent curiosity: the wish to go out and see new places. It was essentially an impulse formed in the breakdown and dissolution of older and smaller kinds of settlement and productive labour. The new and larger settlements and industrial organizations required major internal mobility, at a primary level, and this was joined by secondary consequences in the dispersal of extended families and in the needs of new kinds of social organization. Social processes long implicit in the revolution of industrial capitalism were then greatly intensified: especially an increasing distance between immediate living areas and the directed places of work and government. No effective kinds of social control over these transformed industrial and political processes had come anywhere near being achieved or even foreseen. Most people were living in the fall-out area of processes determined beyond them. What had been gained, nevertheless, in intense social struggle, had been the improvement of immediate conditions, within the limits and pressures of these decisive large-scale processes. There was some relative improvement in wages and working conditions, and there was a qualitative change in the distribution of the day, the week and the year between work and off-work periods. These two effects combined in a major emphasis on improvement of the small family home. Yet this privatization, which was at once an effective achievement and a defensive response, carried, as a consequence, an imperative need for new kinds of contact. The new homes might appear private and 'self-sufficient' but could be maintained only by regular funding and supply from external sources, and these, over a range from employment and prices to depressions and wars, had a decisive and often a disrupting influence on what was nevertheless seen as a separable 'family' project. This relationship created both the need and the form of a new kind of 'communication': news from 'outside', from otherwise inaccessible sources. . . . The new 'consumer' technology which reached its first decisive stage in the 1920s served this complex of needs within just these limits and pressures. There were immediate improvements of the condition and efficiency of the privatized home; there were new facilities, in private transport, for expeditions from the home; and then, in radio, there was a facility for a new kind of social input – news and entertainment brought into the home. Some people spoke of the new machines as gadgets, but they were always much more than this. They were the applied technology of a set of emphases and responses within the determining limits and pressures of industrial capitalist society. . . .

This theoretical model of the general development of broadcasting is necessary to an understanding of the particular development of television. For there were, in the abstract, several different ways in which television as a technical means might have been developed. After a generation of universal domestic television it is not easy to realize this. But it remains true that, after a great deal of intensive research and development, the domestic television set is in a number of ways an inefficient medium of visual broadcasting. Its visual inefficiency by comparison with the cinema is especially striking, whereas in the case of radio there was by the 1930s a highly efficient sound broadcasting receiver, without any real competitors in its own line. Within the limits of the television home-set emphasis it has so far not been possible to make more than minor qualitative improvements. Higher-definition systems, and colour, have still only brought the domestic television set, as a machine, to the standard of a very inferior kind of cinema. Yet most people have adapted to this inferior visual medium, in an unusual kind of preference for an inferior immediate technology, because of the social complex – and especially that of the privatized home – within which broadcasting, as a system, is operative. The cinema had remained at an earlier level of social definition; it was and remains a special kind of theatre, offering specific and discrete works of one general kind. Broadcasting, by contrast, offered a whole social intake: music, news, entertainment, sport. The advantages of this general intake, within the home, much more than outweighed the technical advantages of visual transmission and reception in the cinema, confined as this was to specific and discrete works. While broadcasting was confined to sound, the powerful visual medium of cinema was an immensely popular alternative. But when broadcasting became visual, the option for its social advantages outweighed the immediate technical deficits.

The transition to television broadcasting would have occurred quite generally in the late 1930s and early 1940s, if the war had not intervened. Public television services had begun in Britain in 1936 and in the United States in 1939, but with still very expensive receivers. The full investment in transmission and reception facilities did not occur until the late 1940s and early 1950s, but the growth was thereafter very rapid. The key social tendencies which had led to the definition of broadcasting were by then even more pronounced. There was significantly higher investment in the privatized home, and the social and physical distances between these homes and the decisive political and productive centres of the society had become much greater. Broadcasting, as it had developed in radio, seemed an inevitable model: the central transmitters and the domestic sets.

2
On screen, in frame:
film and ideology
Stephen Heath

. . . .

Cinema brings historical materialism and psychoanalysis together in such a way that the consideration of film and ideology begins from and constantly returns us to their conjuncture, in such a way that from the analysis of cinema, of film, we may be able to engage with theoretical issues of a more general scope, issues crucial for a materialist analysis of ideological institutions and practices. . . .

In ideology, it is said, is represented the imaginary relation of individuals to the real relations under which they live. It has also to be stressed, however, that this imaginary relation in ideology is itself real, which means not simply that the individuals live it as such (the mode of illusion, the inverted image) but that it is effectively, practically, the reality of their concrete existence, the term of their subject positions, the basis of their activity, in a given social order. The imaginary is not just in ideology (it is in relations) and ideology is not just reducible to the imaginary (it is that real instance in which the imaginary is realized). What is held in ideology, what it forms, is the *unity* of the real relations and the imaginary relations between men and women and the real conditions of their existence. All of which is not to forget the economic instance nor to ideologize reality into the status of an impossible myth; rather, it is to bring out ideology in its reality and to indicate that reality – as against ideology, as its truth – is posed only in process in the specific contradictions of a particular socio-historical moment.

Thus ideology is to be seen as itself productive within a mode of production, taking the latter – Marx's *Produktionsweise* – to refer precisely in historical materialism to the articulation of the economic, political and ideological instances; the ideological instance determines the definition, the reproduction, of individuals as agents/subjects for the mode of production, in the positions it assigns them. To acknowledge this is to recognize the materiality of ideology and to grasp analysis accordingly: ideology is not a kind of cloud of ideas hanging over the economic base and which analysis can 'dispel' to reveal the coherent image of a simple truth but a specific social reality given in a specific set of institutions (or 'ideological state apparatuses'); to analyze an ideology involves its analysis in this existence within the dynamic of a mode of production. . . . At the same time, however, the recognition of the material existence and function of ideology demands – and this will be important for thinking about film – the understanding also of a certain historicity of ideological formations and mechanisms in relation to the processes of the production of subject-meanings (meanings for a subject included as the place of their intention), demands, in other words, the understanding of the *symbolic* as an order that is intersected by but is not merely reducible to the ideological (ideology works *over* the symbolic *on* the subject *for* the imaginary). A history of cinema could be envisaged in this perspective which would be not that of the straight reflection of ideological representations, nor that of the simple autonomy of an ideality of forms, but, as it were, the history of the productions of meaning assumed and established by cinema in specific relations of the individual to subjectivity.

There are one or two remarks which follow immediately from these initial emphases. First, it must be seen that the notion of determination which has proved – or been made to prove – such a stumbling block for ideological analysis cannot be conceived of as a problem in cause-and-effect with its answer an explanation from an absolute point of origin. . . . Analysis will be concerned not with determinations in this mechanistic sense but with contradictions, it being in the movement of these contradictions that can be grasped the *set* of determinations – the 'structural causality' – focused by a particular social fact, institution or work. Second, inevitably, a broad conception is emerging of what might be the *critical* role of art, of a practice of cinema, and in terms precisely of a production of contradictions against the fictions of stasis which contain and mask structuring work, in terms of a fracturing of the vision of representation so as to show, as Brecht puts it, that 'in things, people, processes, there is something that makes them what they are and at the same time something that makes them other'.[1] This last remark, which engages the very *edge* of the present paper, its constant horizon, leads moreover from the more general discussion of ideology to the necessity to consider the vision of cinema, the nature and the area of its intervention. What is the role of cinema in capitalist society as a point of investment and a form of representation and meaning production? What does it sell on? At what levels – how – does analysis need to operate?

The distinction can be made between industry, machine and text. *Industry* refers to the direct economic system of cinema, the organization of the structure of production, distribution and consumption. Studies have shown that such organization has, at least in Britain and America, by and large conformed to typical patterns of capitalist activity. The *text*, the film, is a particular product of that industry. Currency is occasionally given to the idea that the film industry is one of 'prototypes' ('every film a new film'), but it is clear that the optimal exploitation of the production apparatus, which ties up considerable amounts of capital, requires the containment of creative work within established frameworks and that genres, film kinds, even so-called 'studio styles', are crucial factors here. As for the *machine*, this is cinema itself seized exactly between industry and product as the stock of constraints and definitions from which film can be distinguished as *specific signifying practice*. That formulation in turn needs to be opened out a little. *Signifying* indicates the recognition of film as system or series of systems of meaning, film as articulation. *Practice* stresses the process of this articulation, which it thus refuses to hold under the assumption of notions such as 'representation' and 'expression'; it takes film as a work of production of meanings and in so doing brings into the analysis the question of the positionings of the subject within that work. *Specific* is the necessity for the analysis to understand film in the particularity of the work it engages, the difference of its conjuncture with other signifying practices. This last does not entail pulling film as specific signifying practice towards some aesthetic idea of a pure cinematicity (on a line with the idea of 'literarity' derived in literary criticism from Russian Formalism and often become a way of avoiding issues of ideology in its appeal to a technicist 'structuralist poetics'); specificity here is semiotic, and a semiotic analysis of film – of film as signifying practice – is the analysis of a heterogeneity, the range of codes and systems at work in the film-text; specificity, that is, is at once those codes particular to cinema (codes of articulation of sound and image, codes of scale of shot, certain codes of narrative arrangement, etc.) *and* the heterogeneity in its particular effects, its particular inscriptions of subject and ideology, of the subject in ideology.

These effects of inscription are fundamental, the area of the intersection of film in ideology by industry and machine as institution of the subject, as institution of image and position and their shifting regulation *on* the figure of the subject. The hypothesis, in short, is that an important – determining – part of ideological systems in a capitalist mode of production is the achievement of a number of machines (institutions) which move, which *movie*, the individual as subject – shifting and placing desire, the energy of contradiction – in a perpetual retotalization of the imaginary. The individual is always a subject of ideology but is always more than simply the figure of that representation . . . : what the machine involves is the realignment of such excess – desire, contradiction, negativity. As far as analysis is concerned, the hypothesis tends to suggest a kind of returning movement whereby the industry is to be grasped (in terms of 'film and ideology') from the point of the ideological determination of the institution-machine and the latter from the point of its textual effects. In fact, of course, this complexity, this *complex*, may be broken by analysis into its own levels of contradiction: each film is specific in the ideological operation of its text *and* in its operation of the ideological specificity of film. The aim now must be to sketch something of these limits as the necessary focus for critical – creative – resistance.

To focus limits, in other words, is not to declare cinema by nature reactionary but to attempt to exploit understanding dialectically in the interests of a demonstration-transformation of the cinematic institution in its ideological effects. Yet the difficulties should be remembered and they can be seen by considering for a moment the example of Brecht. It is the question of limits that occupies Brecht in his thinking on cinema: the terms of his assessment alter, but in Hollywood he comes to regard cinema as inevitably regressive (identificational) in so far as it cuts off the spectator from production, from performance: 'the public no longer has any opportunity to modify the actor's performance; it is confronted not with a production but with the result of a production, produced in its absence'.[2] This 'fundamental reproach' gains in intensity in the light of the fundamental importance attached by Brecht in his theatrical practice to the *Lehrstück* – and not finally to the epic theatre play – as 'model for the theatre of the future': the purpose of the *Lehrstück*, the 'learning-play' (Brecht's own preferred translation), is 'to show a politically wrong mode of behaviour and hence to teach a correct mode of behaviour', the realization of such a purpose lying 'in the fact that it is acted, not in the fact that it is seen'; 'it completely transforms the role of acting; it suppresses the system actor/spectator, knows only actors who are at the same time apprentices';[3] as model for the future, the *Lehrstück* is thus, in fact, a kind of school of dialectics. Nothing of the sort in film: cinema as art of the product, the public screened from production, fixed in the image. Brecht poses the problem, the difficulties, precisely with regard to subject-position and the implication of cinema in a founding ideology of vision as knowledge, the specularization of reality for the coherence of a subject outside contradiction; the assessment, the reproach, follows from that relation.

What are the terms of this relation of vision? Those of a *memory*, the constant movement of a retention of the individual as subject, framed and narrated.

The screen is the projection of the film frame which it holds and grounds (hence the urgency of the need to fix the position, to forbid the other side). It is not by chance that the word 'frame' – which etymologically means 'to advance', 'to further', 'to gain ground' – should emerge from painting to describe the material unit of the film . . . and that it should then be used to talk about the image in its setting, the delimitation of the image on screen . . . , as well as to provide an expression for the passage of the film in the projector relative to the aperture, 'in frame', and for the camera viewpoint, 'framing' and 'reframing'. . . .

It is the differences in frame between film and painting that are generally emphasized: film is limited to a standard screen ratio (the three to four horizontal rectangle) or, as now, to a number of such ratios . . . ; film

destroys the ordinary laws of pictorial composition
because of its moving human figures which capture
attention against all else. In his essay on 'The work of art
in the age of mechanical reproduction', Walter Benjamin
has a comparison of film and painting which develops
their incompatibility in this way from the position of the
spectator: 'The painting invites the spectator to contem-
plation; before it the spectator can abandon himself to
his associations. Before the movie frame he cannot do
so. No sooner has his eye grasped a scene than it is
already changed. It cannot be arrested. . . . The spectator's process of association in view of these images is
indeed interrupted by their constant sudden change.'[4]
There is much there that would call for comment . . . ;
what needs to be stressed here, however, is the insistence
of the frame which stays in view throughout the comparison, in place, the constant screen. The same con-
stancy (or consistency) carries over the other classic
comparison, that of film and theatre. Where the stage
has 'wings', fixed limits, the screen in this comparison is
said to be lacking in any frame, to know only the implied
continuation of the reality of the image. Thus Bazin will
write: 'The screen is not a frame like that of a picture,
but a mask which allows us to see a part of the event
only. When a person leaves the field of the camera, we
recognize that he or she is out of the field of vision,
though continuing to exist identically in another part of
the screen which is hidden from us. The screen has no
wings. . . . '[5] Once again, however, the frame simply
stays put, transposed as the field of vision of the camera,
and there is no necessity to emphasize the importance of
what Vertov calls 'theatrical cinema'. . . . Moreover, the
illimitation which the theatre comparison seeks to stress
is exactly the confirmation of the force of the frame, its
definition as a 'view' that has ceaselessly to counter
absence by the assertion of the coherence of its presence,
its 'being-in-frame'.

In frame: the place of image and subject, view (in early
French catalogues a film is called a *vue*) and viewer;

frame, framing, is the very basis of disposition – German *Einstellung*: adjustment, centring, framing, moral attitude, the correct position. . . .

The stake of the frame is clear . . . : the frame is the reconstruction of the scene of the signifier, of the symbolic, into that of the signified, the passage through the image from other scene to seen; it ensures distance as correct position, the summit of the eye, *representation*; it redresses (here, paradoxically, is the inversion) reality and meaning, is the point of their match. Analysis must then begin (and much has been done in this field) to examine the history, the techniques, the movements, of the alignment of cinema-eye and human-eye and subject-eye . . ., must trace the windowing identity of subject and camera, the setting of the gaze to accompany the play of 'point of view' between characters in the diegetic space of the film (always the drama of the eye) which organizes the images in the coherence of the fiction.

The fiction, the view, of the characters – the human figures who enter film from the very first, as though of right, spilling out of the train at La Ciotat, leaving the Lyons factory or the photographic congress (is the fascination with people 'arriving' in film simply coincidental?) and who can only be evacuated with great difficulty, in certain modern, 'experimental' films – encloses the film as narrative, establishes that diegetic space. Specifying cinema the machine as mode of communication at the start of *Language et cinéma*, Metz comments that it has 'no particular sector of meaning (no portion of the matter of content in Hjlemslevian terms)'.[6] Yet narrative is there immediately in film, in cinema, to lay out the images, to support the frame against its excess, to suggest laws to hold the movement, to ensure continuity, to *be* 'cinematic form' (thus for Lawson, 'The total rejection of a story, and the accompanying denial of syntax or arrangement, can only lead to the breakdown of cinematic form.'[7]). In the intermittence of its images (Benjamin's 'constant sudden change'), film is a perpetual metonymy over which narrative lays as a model of closure, a kind of conversion of desire (metonymy is the figure of desire in psychoanalytic theory) into the *direction* of the subject through the image-flow (representation, the positioning of the subject, is as much a fact of the organization of the images as of the fact of the image itself).

Narrative, that is, may be seen as a decisive instance of framing in film (the determining links between narrative constraint and conventions of framing have often been stressed); its economy – a relation of transformation between two homogeneities ('beginning' and 'end') in which the second is the replacement of the first, a reinvestment of its elements – *checks* the images, centring and containing, prescribing a reading as correlation of actions and inscribing a subject as, and for, the coherence of that operation, carried through against possible dispersion, the multiple intensities of the text of the film. Frame, narrative placing, subject inscription cut short the interminable movement of the signifier, impose – subject-in-position, on screen, in frame – precisely the continuousness of representation. . . .

Constant narration, different narratives: each text has its particular operation, its particular ideological intersections, its constancies and differences, its terms and their reworking of limits. The analysis in the text of film and system is always imperative, the premise of any consideration of film, of a film, in its specific signifying practice.

The limits sketched out here have done no more than to envisage the ideological place of cinema as an aid to such a consideration and as a response to a Brechtian principle: 'For as long as one does not criticize the social function of cinema, all film criticism is only a criticism of symptoms and has itself a merely symptomatic character.'[8] Is this to come back finally to the 'fundamental reproach'? Yes, perhaps, but displaced a little in its working out, the beginnings of an understanding to be exploited. The problem, the political problem, for film in its intervention can be given as the transformation of the relations of subjectivity and ideology. . . .

Notes

1 Brecht, Bertolt (1967) *Gesammelte Werke*, Frankfurt am Main: Suhrkamp, vol. XVI, pp. 925–6.
2 Brecht, Bertolt (1973) *Arbeitsjournal*, Frankfurt am Main: Suhrkamp, vol. I, p. 400.
3 Brecht, *Gesammelte Werke*, vol. XVII, pp. 1022–34.
4 Benjamin, Walter (1973) 'The work of art in the age of mechanical reproduction', in *Illuminations*, London: Fontana, p. 240.
5 Bazin, André (1959) 'Théâtre et cinéma', in *Qu'est-ce que le cinéma*? Paris: Cerf, vol. II, p. 100.
6 Metz, Christian (1974) *Language and Cinema*, The Hague and Paris: Mouton, p. 38.
7 Lawson, J.H. (1964) *Film: The Creative Process*, New York: Hill & Wang, p. 289.
8 Brecht, *Gesammelte Werke*, vol. XVIII, p. 168.

3

Broadcast TV as cultural form

John Ellis

The very obviousness of the differences between cinema and broadcast TV means that they are often overlooked. Cinema revolves around the purchase of the right to attend a performance of a single film text. The performance is public; the audience is prepared for it by the widespread circulation of the narrative image. Broadcast TV emits a series of signals that are available to anyone who possesses or rents a TV set. Broadcast TV is received overwhelmingly in domestic surroundings. The images involved are different: cinema's is large and projected; broadcast TV's is characteristically small and luminous. This much is obvious. However, the consequences of these differences for each medium are less obvious.

This essay argues that broadcast TV has developed distinctive aesthetic forms to suit the circumstances within which it is used. These forms are distinct to broadcast TV as a phenomenon, rather than to video as a phenomenon. They have as much to do with the fact that broadcasting presents a continuous set of signals that are either received or missed by their potential audience. There is hardly any chance of catching a particular TV programme 'tomorrow' or 'next week sometime' as there is with a cinema film. . . .

Broadcast TV has developed a distinctive aesthetic form. Instead of the single, coherent text that is characteristic of entertainment cinema, broadcast TV offers relatively discrete segments: small sequential unities of images and sounds whose maximum duration seems to be about five minutes. These segments are organized into groups, which are either simply cumulative, like news broadcast items and advertisements, or have some kind of repetitive or sequential connection, like the groups of segments that make up the serial or series. Broadcast TV narration takes place across these segments, characteristically in series or serials which repeat a basic problematic or dilemma rather than resolving it finally. The broadcast images depend upon sound to a rather greater degree than cinema's images. The image is characteristically pared down, and appears as though it is immediate or live. This generates a kind of complicity with the TV viewer, a complicity that tends to produce the events represented as an 'outside world', beyond the broadcast TV institution and the viewer's home alike. The predominant forms in which this 'outside world' is presented tend to be those of the hostile or the bizarre. The viewer tends to delegate his or her look to the TV itself: it is as though the TV institution looks, the viewer passes his or her gaze across the sights in the TV eye. . . .

Broadcast TV is a profoundly domestic phenomenon. The TV set has to be acquired by a person or persons before TV signals can be received, and the manufacture of TV sets has long assumed that its market is the domestic unit. In some countries, a licence to view (which contributes to the costs of producing some broadcasts) has to be purchased as well. This is the case in Britain. Unlike entertainment cinema, which characteristically addresses the couple seeking an evening's entertainment outside the home, broadcast TV is already in the home. The TV set is another domestic object, often the place where family photos are put: the direction of the glance towards the personalities on the TV screen being supplemented by the presence of 'loved ones' immediately above. Broadcast TV is also intimate and everyday, a part of home life rather than any kind of special event.

Broadcast TV institutions respond by conceiving of this domestic and everyday audience in a specific way. Broadcast TV, its institutions and many of its practitioners alike assume that its domestic audience takes the form of families. 'The home' and 'the family' are terms which have become tangled together in the commercial culture of the twentieth century. They both point to a powerful cultural construct, a set of deeply held assumptions about the nature of 'normal' human existence. The family is held to consist of a particular unit of parents and children: broadcast TV assumes that this is the basis and heart of its audience. Broadcast TV's conventional notion of the family is of two parents, the father working, the mother running the home, together with two children of school age. This conception is clearly seen in much advertising material; in the way in which statistics are interpreted on news bulletins ('for the average family, this means . . . '); in 'families' selected for quiz programmes; in 'families' shown in fictional representations of all kinds. The prevalence of this conception of the family is all the more remarkable since only a minority of the population of Britain currently lives like this. Only a third of households currently consist of man, woman and dependent children, according to government statistics. In most of these units, the woman also has a regular job. In some cases, she is the only 'breadwinner'. In all, the supposedly classic nuclear family unit, of working father, housewife mother and dependent school-age children accounts for less than 5 per cent of the population. Yet social policies of all kinds assume this to be the norm, and so does broadcast TV. For many people living in ways that differ from this supposed norm, these ways of living are experienced as exceptions or temporary departures from the norm. The presence of a grandparent, or other relatives, the single-parent family, the childless household, all of these common and by no means 'radical' forms are taken as a passing phase rather than as a real way of living. Such is the power of the conception of the nuclear family in its particular form.

Broadcast TV assumes this norm, as do most of the major institutions of British society. For broadcast TV, it has certain specific effects because TV tends to orient its programmes towards it presumed audience, to try to include the audience's own conception of themselves into the texture of its programmes. Hence broadcast TV gives central place to the series of cultural preoccupations that accompany the nuclear family: to heterosexual romance, to the stability of marriage, to the notions of masculine careers and feminine domesticity, to the conception of the innocence of childhood, to the division of the world in public and private spheres. In addition, this conception of the family-as-audience determines a series of attitudes to what is legitimate material for broadcast TV. Any specialized interests are avoided, especially those which divide across generations. 'Youth' as a specific audience is not catered for by broadcast TV to any appreciable extent; neither, for that matter, are those over sixty. Such categories of audience are normally deployed only as the reasons for prohibitions: no sexually explicit programmes before 9 p.m. because children will be watching; no disturbing programmes about death because old people may be watching on their own. TV programmes are addressed to a generalized audience which is conceived in a very specific way: as isolated nuclear families in their domestic settings.

The particular ideological notion of the nuclear family in its domestic setting provides the overarching conception within which broadcast TV operates. Given this setting, and the multiple distractions that it can offer, broadcast TV cannot assume the same level of attention from its viewers that cinema can from its spectators. So broadcast TV has developed specific forms of narration, and specific forms of organization of its material. The basic organization of material is that of the segment, a coherent group of sounds and images, of relatively short duration, that needs to be accompanied by other similar such segments. The segment as the basic unit according to a short burst of attention is matched by the serial and series form. These provide a particular kind of repetition and novelty that differs markedly from that found in the narrational patterns of classic cinema. In turn, the series and serial imply a third term: scheduling. Scheduling is the means by which a day's broadcasting is arranged so that particular programmes coincide with particular supposed events in the life of the family. Scheduling provides a regular, week by week, slot in which the repetition of particular series formats can take place. . . .

This definition of TV's commodity as a programmed series of meaningful segments used in a domestic context owes much to Raymond Williams's definition of broadcast TV as 'flow'. The notion of 'flow' is a much misused one, and its openness to misuse is the result of the way in which Williams defines the idea. He argues that TV cannot be conceived of as unitary programmes which are 'interrupted' by advertisements and suchlike material. 'Yet it may be even more important to see the true process as flow: the replacement of a programme series of timed sequential units by a flow series of differently related units in which the timing, though real, is undeclared, and in which the real internal organization is something other than the declared organization.'[1] . . . In arguing against two assumptions (that programmes are interrupted; that TV is a series of separate coherent programme items), Williams describes flow as a liquid and even confusing process by which broadcast TV tends to average out the various programme forms that its formal organizations of production claim to keep separate. According to Williams's model of flow, then, everything becomes rather like everything else, units are not organized into coherent single texts like cinema films, but form a kind of montage without overall meaning: 'like having read two plays, three newspapers, three or four magazines, on the same day that one has been to a variety show and a lecture and a football match. And yet it is not like that at all, for though the items may be various the television experience has in some important ways unified them'.[2] Here both the strength and weakness of Williams's argument becomes clear. Flow assembles disparate items, placing them within the same experience, but does not organize them to produce an overall meaning. This is a valuable insight; however, the problem lies in Williams's definition of 'items'. 'Items' are still separate texts, independent works like a cinema film. Finally, for Williams, flow is a feature of TV that severely compromises and alters the separate texts that TV has manufactured. His model is of cinema-style texts which appear in a context that reduces their separation one from another. In doing so, he underestimates the complexity of broadcast TV's particular commodity form, which has very little to do with the single text.

The 'spot' advertisement is in many ways the quint-essence of TV. It is a segment of about thirty seconds, comprising a large number of images and sounds which are tightly organized amongst themselves. This segment is found accompanied by other similar segments: coherent within themselves, they have no particular connection with each other. Meanings are discrete and separate; their interrelation lies in the fact that they belong to a similar class of segments, or, occasionally, in the way that they proudly produce puns upon each other. Watching adver-tisements is often an exhilarating experience because of their short span and their intensity of meaning: they are expensive (more expensive than the programmes they come with) and precisely calculated (often better than TV drama). They are sparklingly diverse, the shiny surface wrapping of a domestically oriented consumerist society. They are also the supremely televisual product: hence another part of their exhilaration, that of seeing a medium used for itself, and not weighed down by cultural presumptions that are not its own.

Yet, being a segment, each advertisement does not stand on its own. The experience of watching adver-tisements is that of seeing segments cluster together, inciting each other. Their specific meanings have relatively little to do with each other; their generalized generic meaning (a domestic consumerist relation to objects) gives them a certain common thematic; but their organization together is something new to western representations. Advertisements on TV cannot be scanned or ignored like the page of a newspaper: they demand short bursts of attention, producing an understanding that rests at the level of the particular segment involved and is not forced to go further, is not made to combine as a montage fragment into a larger organization of meaning. Thirty seconds by thirty seconds, the 'spot' advertisement expands but does not combine: it is the furthest development of broadcast TV's segmental commodity. . . .

In some sense, advertisements, news and current affairs magazine programmes provide the most obvious examples of the segmental aspect of TV. However, this procedure extends very much further across virtually the whole of TV's output. It is not only a characteristic of those TV channels that carry advertisements: it has also become the standard form of TV construction for the BBC as well. First, it can be argued, as Raymond Williams has, that a significant proportion of broadcast TV consists of small segments that fill the gaps between substantial programme units: the announcer sitting in a studio providing a link; the trailer for a programme coming some time in the future; the showcasing extracts of the evening's entertainment, then tomorrow's, the weekend's and so on. The BBC does this just as much as ITV. This segmentation extends to programmes themselves, especially the title sequences. The title sequence is in effect a commercial for the programme itself, and it has all the features of a commercial. It is considerably more expensive per second than the programme it fronts; it is highly organized and synoptic, providing a kind of narrative image for its programme. Every programme has a title sequence, whether a news bulletin or a documentary or chat show or police drama, and their manufacture is a long-established practice. There is a high degree of autonomy for the title sequence, since it is repeated every time the programme format is used and usually provides a highly generalized, gestural conception of the programme it advertises, unlike the material used to showcase individual programmes. A strategy increasingly used with American series is to combine the two forms, so that the standard title sequence integrates shots from the individual programme in a highly enigmatic or incoherent way. This is the closest that TV has come to constructing a narrative image in the cinematic mode. The main difference from cinema's narrative image is that broadcast TV's title sequences invariably come with the programme: there is an immediacy of realization of the narrative image which marks it out from the cinematic practice. . . .

Further, programmes which have a high degree of coherence compared to news, advertisements, promotion material and title sequences can themselves be regarded as being composed of segments. Any fiction series or serial is prone to segmentalization, and the series and serial form the vast bulk of broadcast TV material almost everywhere. This segmentalization takes the form of a rapid alternation between scenes and a frequent return to habitual locations and situations rather than any sustained progression through sequential logic of events. In the series and the serial alike, these segments tend never to coalesce into an overall, totalizing account. The form that tends to be adopted by TV fiction, in this sense, is the same as TV news, with a continuous updating on the latest concatenation of events rather than a final ending or explanation. Even though events are frequently intercut in the series and serial, there is habitually no parallelism implied between the events beyond a simple one of simultaneous occurrence and general connection between the characters.

This segmentalization is TV's own creation, and is not traceable directly to the effects of 'spot' advertisements being scattered at various moments through the TV fiction. One of the classic moments of the development of this process in British TV was the police series *Z-cars* produced by the BBC. *Z-cars* was renowned (among other things) for the fact that it had more scenes than it had minutes, an effect achieved by the intercutting of slightly related events. The segment in this sense is not essentially different from the segment that is found in advertisements. Each scene is coherent in itself, delivering a particular meaning, an event, a relation between characters. Its characteristic effect, however, depends upon its placing in relation to other discrete segments that are also relatively coherent in themselves. This internal coherence in effect prevents the generation of effects of parallelism, contrast or irony between sequences except in special moments. . . .

Any single programme taken as an example of segmentation reveals only the way in which this characteristic procedure has 'invaded' what is characteristically taken to be an independent textual entity: the programme. However, broadcast TV does not consist of programmes in the way that they are listed in programme guides in newspapers or magazines. Here Williams's notion of flow is important: it indicates the way in which TV presents segments in larger or smaller conglomerations. Broadcast TV is characterized by a succession of segments, of internally coherent pieces of dramatic, instructional, exhortatory, fictional or documentary material. The major difference between the BBC TV service without advertising and ITV with advertising lies only in the size of the conglomeration of segments. BBC is capable at certain points of presenting a fairly coherent set of segments, perhaps a whole narrative. But, feature films apart, this is a comparatively rare occurrence, the long documentary or the single play. BBC as much as any other broadcasting institution has adopted the characteristic commodity form of TV, the segment, and its complementary aspect, the series form.

The segment form implies repetition: TV's characteristic form of repetition is the series or the serial, a form of continuity-with-difference that TV has perfected. This form fosters the segmental approach, the generation of large numbers of diverse coherent and relatively self-contained elements. The serial implies a certain narrative progression and a conclusion; the series does not: whether documentary, drama or everlasting soap opera, it has no end in view. The series always envisages its own return. The series itself divides into two types: fictional series that are centred around a particular situation and set of characters, and non-fictional series that are characterized by a recurring format and known set of routines.

The series and serial both provide a means of generating many segments from the basic narrative or expository techniques, and from basic thematic material. The serial aims towards a conclusion which is a number of weeks distant. Like the massive three-decker novels of the nineteenth century, the TV serial multiplies incident along the way. It uses its characters, plays around with the possible permutations of relationships and situations. Its span is often that of generations. It implies a certain knowledge accumulated over the span of its broadcasting, but this itself causes worries within the broadcasting institutions, because it is quite conceivable that a large proportion of the audience will miss one or other episode, or will not be hooked on the expository first episode. Hence a number of techniques: the title sequence that introduces characters (faces connoting a characteristic) and even their relationships; the repetition of material from the end of one episode at the beginning of the next; carefully placed references to events in the conversations of characters. . . .

Serial construction presents problems for broadcast TV, those of ensuring a large enough constant audience. Increasingly, the series form is becoming standard. Here, each episode is more or less self-sufficient, and very little if any narrative progression is implied from episode to episode. *Telford's Change* represents a compromise between serial and series that is becoming increasingly popular. Each episode is coherent enough for the casual viewer, packed with varied and satisfying segments; the serial aspect is provided by the continuing enigmas of whether Telford's change will be a success, and whether his marriage will break up.

The series itself provides a stable situation in which various incidents take place week by week. The incidents usually form a complete group each week (except in the case of soap opera). Such a definition of the series extends over most of TV's output: news programmes, investigatory documentaries, situation comedies, variety shows, chat shows, sports programmes. A fundamental stability and return to zero at the end of each programme or programme section is implied by the series. The news, current affairs, documentary and chat show series provide a stable format in which events from the world beyond TV can appear. The series format ensures that they can appear at all by providing them with a set of known expository procedures. Hence it is expected that the news series will consist of segments that have absolutely no connection between them, whereas the segmentalization of an investigatory programme will tend to construct an overall strategy of relation between segments. . . .

The format series is matched by the fictional series, which operates across all the modalities of fiction from farce to tragedy. It is characterized by the constant repetition of basic narrative situations and characters: a family, a business enterprise, a hospital, etc. Each week the characters encounter a new situation which has no permanent effect upon them: the following week they will be in the same relation one to another. The repetitions are very marked, to the extent of some series (from the USA chiefly) ending their weekly narrative with a kind of coda in which the basic relations between characters are reaffirmed outside of any narrative context. Subordinates joke with boss; children outwit their parents over some domestic chore. The formula, the basic situation, receives a final statement in a segment that tends to echo the title sequence. This has the effect of reaffirming the stasis from which the next episode will depart: a stasis that is more a basic contradiction or power relation than a zero degree. The series, then, relies on repeating a basic problematic which is worked through on each occasion without a final resolution. In a police series, the police catch the criminals in each individual instance of the series, but two things still remain: criminality itself (the episode ends with another call, a trivial assignment, etc.) and the particular relationship between the police involved (*Starsky and Hutch*'s spiky mutual dependency; *The Sweeney*'s blend of antagonism to authority and respect for justice). The series is based upon the notion 'what will happen to them this week?', known elements are repeated with no discernible development from one episode to the next.

The series is very widespread in TV, and complements the construction of TV output into segments. Segments gain their mutual organization and some of their coherence from the complicated series patterns which generate them. The series ensures that each segment will be classified into a particular class of segments because of the repeated elements (character, mode of address, etc.) that play through them. Programming, the art of scheduling, appears in this context as the deliberate policy of TV organizations of ensuring that segmentation does take place. Scheduling determines the way in which an evening's TV will be organized so that one class of segment does not dominate, yet the series will find a permanent 'slot', a place where its particular pattern of repetition can take place. Scheduling effectively provides a supra-segmentation of broadcast TV.

The characteristic broadcast TV experience is a domestic consumption of a succession of segments organized according to the logic of the series. The characteristic entertainment cinema experience is public and collective, an experience of a single text which performs and completes the narrative image circulated for it. Broadcasting has not developed the institution of the narrative image; instead the series provides the necessary expectancy and anticipation, which is distinct from that of the cinema. TV's process of segmentalization of its flow contrasts again with cinema's emphasis on the single unitary film. This also has effects which mean that in their common area of narrative fiction, cinema and TV tend to develop different forms and approaches. . . .

Notes

1 Williams, Raymond (1974) *Television, Technology and Cultural Form*, London: Fontana, p. 89.
2 ibid., p. 95.

4

'While Millicent bucked and writhed . . .'
Stephen Heath

> while Millicent bucked and writhed and chortled
> breathlessly
>
> J.J. Scott, 'The end-away justifies
> the means', a 'fiction' in the magazine
> *Mayfair*, 1980

A characteristic of the kind of society in which we live is the mass production of fictions: stories, romances, novels, photo-novels, radio serials, films, television plays and series – fictions everywhere, all-pervasive, with consumption obligatory by virtue of this omnipresence, a veritable requirement of our social existence. We cannot live today without contact with this fictioning continuum.

This mass production of fictions is the culture of what might be called the 'novelistic', the constant narration of the social relations of individuals, the ordering of meanings for the individual in society. With the development of industrialism and urbanization, what are then seen as traditional forms of community definition and cohesion give way to a social organization, that of capitalism, in which, precisely, society and the individual become the terms of reference, in which the social relations of the individual – 'the individual and society' – become exactly a problem as such. . . . There is then a powerful work of *social* representation of 'the individual', the socially cohesive realization of the latter, people given that sense: stories of life, of lives, patterns of recognition, the ceaseless account of the social as meaning for the individual, experience always in these individual terms. In the nineteenth century this work was the province of the novel and written fiction generally; in the twentieth it has been that also of cinema and television: transmitters of the novelistic, social-for-individual representativity – my, your, our stories, our definitions.

In this 'individual and society' organization, the family has occupied a decisive position, proposed as a kind of mediation between the two: assuming the production of the new individuals needed for the reproduction of the social work-force, it is the first arena of socialization, preceding and then running alongside the systems of formal education, and, equally, it is the given arena of sexual relations, of the social ordering of the sexual. The great subject of the novelistic was thus crucially the family, the family as the bridge between individual and society, private and public, site of their meeting and conflict and resolution in the separate world apart it supposedly offers, the individual's fulfilment as individual in love and affection and the sexual within that love and affection. That so many nineteenth-century novels end in marriage, the union with the perfect mate, is not, of course, by chance or simply some formal convention: the marriage-union ending represents the resolution of 'the individual and society', a firm social unit offered as the privileged mode of the individual, the haven of his or her personal happiness, personal life.

Much of this family feeling and representation is still strong today (switch on your television set or look through the magazines at your newsagent's) but clearly many of the nineteenth-century terms have shifted, and this especially in connection with 'sexual liberation', 'the sexual revolution', leading to various adjustments and rearrangments in the overall representation. For the novelistic is never simply fixed, some static content. On the contrary, its institution in the mass production of fictions is the assurance of a continual *process* of representation, capable of taking up and working over actual social change, responding and redefining, maintaining the social-for-individual intelligibility. When in 1857 divorce laws are passed, there is at once a spate of 'divorce novels' (including the bestselling *East Lynne* by Mrs Henry Wood): the new must be brought into stories, focused in meanings, placed. Today with, for example, the pressure of the women's movement, there is an immediate response in novel after film after television programme, catching up from that pressure, drafting it into an available representation – and then in a way, which is the point, we cannot but deal in that representation, its terms, have difficulty in thinking beyond and grasping the challenge to them that the pressure always was and is and must be. . . . I want now to examine something of the sexological terms – the development of the sexual fix – in today's novelistic, referring particularly to written material – novels, stories, 'fictions'.

The strength of the sexological grasp of the novelistic can be seen straightaway in the appearance of a new and widespread literary genre: the sexual-life testimony. The influence of the Freudian psychoanalytic case-history in which hidden sexual impulses are revealed and laid out as the basis of an individual's character and behaviour is heavy here, as too, subsidiarily, is that of the work of Kinsey, involving as it did the collection of the narratives of thousands of individual lives. People are summoned to bear witness, to report their private worlds, to narrate themselves as sexual experience. Nancy Friday, doing 'research in sexual identity', records, sifts, publishes fantasies: *My Secret Garden: Women's Sexual Fantasies, Forbidden Flowers: More Women's Sexual Fantasies, Men in Love: Men's Sexual Fantasies: The Triumph of Love over Rage*. Bestsellers. Gay Talese researches, fieldworks, interviews, practically experiments (becomes, for instance, client and manager of a massage parlour), publishes *Thy Neighbour's Wife: Sex in the World Today*, an account of his findings in the form of the 'intimate stories' of a number of Americans, a hymn to the dramatic personal awakenings of 'the sexual revolution' with every story a real life, fully authentic ('private papers further authenticated the sexual scenes and attitudes, feelings and fantasies, that appear in the book'). Bestseller.

The idea of the authentic document, of the publication of *research*, is constant and important. Typically, *Mayfair* runs a feature entitled 'Quest: the laboratory of human response', interviews in which the interviewees are asked to testify on some aspect of their 'sex life' ('Receptionist, 30 years old, redhead, town of origin Truro . . . it felt marvellous as he edged into me. I begged him to let it go in all the way, to fill me, but he took it very calmly. . . . '). The point is not that the presentation as research serves as justification or alibi, though no doubt it does for many writers and readers, but that the sexological is fundamental to 'sexuality'. In the same way that Victorian pornography and sexual representation generally are permeated by medical definitions and conceptions, so too, and following on in a basic continuity, our current idea of sexuality is everywhere informed by the terms of that sexology which has indeed been crucial for its very development: 'sexuality' comes quickly and easily as a sexological picture – the clinical picture of the sex life, the laboratory of human response, documentation of that.

Witness, confession, testimony. 'The first time I saw an adult penis, I was very young, perhaps around three', begins a *Playboy* feature article by Lynda Schor ('Some perspectives on the penis'). How to produce a book today? Get a number of personalities, from Dr Spock to Erica Jong, to recount their sexual 'initiation' and publish the results as *For the First Time*. When television and Sunday newspaper performer Clive James offers us his *Unreliable Memoirs* we can reliably expect – and we will not be disappointed – that much of them will be given over to details of his anguishedly exuberant, youthful tonk-pulling. And this is not just a question of public figures. We should all narrate, recount, tell ourselves, fill the testimony columns of *Penthouse* or *Mayfair*, *Playboy* or *Playgirl* ('I had sex with my stylist – it was a sizzling experience'). In the democracy of universal identity, we are all equal, all *the same*. Simply, there are also the experts, those with the knowledge and the experience, those who can report, give us the fruits of research, the lives and fantasies we must buy, consume, match. . . .

As well as the novel, written fictions, there are films and television programmes, not to mention posters, photo magazines, and so many other different modes. Yet the novel occupies what is still in some sense a privileged position, fulfils the crucial role of the work of *saying* sex and sexuality, of giving a solid mesh of meanings, of making available sense. Alongside and informing photo and film, our most powerfully invested modes of sexual imaging, is a constant production of novels, a stream of written fictions: every month, every week, the absolutely 'contemporary' bestseller; every month, every week, 'an entirely new accuracy of fact and of valuation in speaking of sexual experience' (from a blurb-quoted review of a novel by James Jones and by any other bestselling author).

The Victorian novel deals in family romance, in sexual situations (adultery, divorce), in certain of the period's sexual images (the fallen woman), in a certain grotesque comedy of the period's problem and economy and panic of the sexuality newly defined and felt (look at Dickens's *Bleak House* with its young woman narrator simultaneously child and mother to her father-figure guardian who wishes to marry her, surrounded by a host of male characters swelling up out of their skins or else phallicly weak, and in even their very names: Rouncewell, Boythorn, Smallweed, Skimpole; no existence for a woman, only a child or a mother; and no stability of the identity of the man, troubled by the possibility nevertheless of the existence of a woman, castrating and only resolvable by marrying her as child-and-mother). A firm presence of woman writers gives one form of the novel – the first-person woman narrator, perhaps in some governess-type situation – that allows a different expression of sexual affectivity and identity but within confines that can quickly return a conventionally given position of the women (subordination, marriage as resolution, female emotionalism – this being the possibility and the limit of any sexual expression).

What is generally constant in the Victorian novel is a fascination with the image, the figure of 'the woman' – depicted, defined, displayed, diagnosed in a kind of ceaseless concern (the concern for identity, for who I, male, am if she, female, is elsewhere to *my* difference, 'the man'/'the woman', the one *from* the other, like Eve from Adam, *the* difference secured); and this simultaneously with her emergence as a medical problem for society and with her increasing reality as disturbance, engaged even in struggle against her position as 'the woman' and hence against his as 'the man'. . . .

The work of fictional security today – of the novelistic – can be seen in the development and consolidation of terms of representation as strong as those of the nineteenth century with its hypochondria and hysteria which in many ways are continued in this new statement of the sexual concern, in this new picture of 'sexuality'. As would be expected, it is in response to the struggles and movements against established identity and position that the work is most acutely engaged, that statement and picture are most easily grasped in their making up.

Take *Kinflicks* by Lisa Alther ('wildly, ribaldly funny, the dazzling American bestseller'), which at one point describes a commune women's movement meeting ('the Free Farm Women's Weekend'). The heroine wanders from seminar group to seminar group: 'Women and

politics' ('locked in a match of revolutionary oneupmanship'); 'Women and their bodies' ('Laverne was demonstrating to the intrigued gathering how it was possible, if
one possessed the flexibility of an Olympic gymnast, to
view the inside of one's vagina and the mouth of one's
cervix. I stood transfixed, gazing at the moist red hole.
But for the life of me, I couldn't grasp why anyone
would *want* to view the mouth of her cervix as reflected
in a mirror. I felt I couldn't ask Laverne at the risk of
sounding bougie [= bourgeois]'); 'Women and rage'
('where the woman was in the process of hacking her ex-
lover to bits'); 'Women and work' ('I knew that
housework and childbearing were being roundly dumped
on, and that I would feel agonizingly bougie once I felt
compelled to mention what a trip I found cleaning the
shower to be'). In its details, the description mixes
moments of sympathy with a continuing irony; overall, it
gives an incident in the life of the individual heroine, an
aspect of present-day reality that needs to be included
and placed as a stage she must go through – and that
place is quickly tried and limited to the terms of the
contemporary sexual concern. Thus, for example,
Laverne, organizer of the 'Women and their bodies'
group, is earlier portrayed as provoking and revelling in
gang rape: '"Faster! Faster! Don't stop *now*, you
mother fucker! Oh mother of Christ! Don't *stop*!" Her
body was arcing up off the ground and twitching spas-
modically, like a frog's leg hooked into an electric
current. Three men lay in panting heaps next to her, like
bees after stinging' (note the return of the image of the
hysteric: the spasmodic twitching, the *arc-en-cercle*).
Naturally, like all women, the heroine *really* wants that
too: 'My nipples began tingling with excitement. I
realized I wanted to join the fray.' And then for the rest
of her time in the novel, Laverne is shown as perpetually
involved with an electric vibrator with which she finally
blows herself out: 'The doctor held the phallus-shaped
vibrator, turned it over, sniffed it, scratched his head. It
had a big crack all the way up it. Laverne had apparently

achieved her goal of the Ultimate Orgasm.'

Orgasm is everywhere, the very material of the picture, the life. Heroine's name, Virginia Babcock: virgin, baby, cock; married, after the free farm episode, to Ira Bliss IV: I are – or higher? – bliss; preoccupation, orgasm; girlfriend of high-school football star Joe Bob Sparkes, 'this was my first experience with the concept that I have now, after extensive experimentation, formulated into a postulate: It is possible to generate an orgasm at any spot on the human body'; student of Worthley College, A-grade paper on 'Venous congestion and edema as a determining factor in the intensity of human orgasm'; lover of Eddie, a female co-student with whom she experiences 'a breathtaking series of multiple orgasms, triggered by the insertion of greased little fingers into each other's anus'; wife of Ira in a marriage that involves an emotional retreat from orgasm until, deciding she would like to have a baby, she manages 'one that outdid even those with Eddie'; encounter with Hawk, Vietnam deserter, into meditation and mysticism, who, critical of her 'bougie' attitudes ('If you have sex, you want an instant orgasm'), leads her through the ritual preparations for an authentic cosmological sexual experience which fails to come off . . .

This is difficult. *Kinflicks* contains more than this, contains, for instance, a complex presentation of the relationship between the heroine and her dying mother in which terms of experience and understanding are worked out which go far beyond those in which she is constantly cast in the narrative of her life. But then, precisely, that narrative does everywhere run into orgasm and sexual concern as suggested in the brief account given above. But then again, why not? After all, the sexual *is* a fundamental part of a life, of life itself. The assumption of 'life', however, has to be handled with care. A novel is not 'life' but a form of representation and 'life itself' anyway is never simply given outside of forms of representation, of which in our society the novel is one, importantly so (the production of the novelistic). There is a crucial *responsibility* of forms, of representations. Suppose we say that *Kinflicks* reflects aspects of contemporary life; for example, women's groups *do* have sessions devoted to women and their bodies, teaching and developing methods for self-examination and knowledge – *Kinflicks* merely reflects this, shows something that we can easily find in real life. Admitting this reflection idea for the moment, *Kinflicks* is nevertheless a novel, is involved in certain modes of organization and depiction. The linking of the women's group with a character who enjoys gang-bangs and spends all her time with a vibrator is a *certain* way of representing with a *certain* stance, a *certain* position; as too is the narration of the seminars from the heroine's nonparticipatory and ironic point of view, the use of such phrases as 'a match of revolutionary oneupmanship' or 'the flexibility of an Olympic gymnast'.

But more than this, there can be no simple idea of reflection: life is permeated by and – as 'life' – made up of representations, grasping and rendering and ordering all experience. 'Women and their bodies' sessions are not pristine phenomena out there in some untouched world waiting to be described. Like everything else, they exist always within a complex of meanings, of representations in relation to the terms of which they are posed, understood, *apprehended*. No referent – nothing in the world – can be allowed to guarantee a discourse (the suggestion of such a guarantee is itself a discursive strategy, an attempt to naturalize the meaning given, the position constructed): on the contrary, a discourse must be questioned in its own particularity, its specific forms, its characteristic engagement with the complex of meanings, representations, that is the present existence – the cultural-historical reality – of this or that phenomenon, this or that referent. *Kinflicks* does not reflect life like some mirror, it repeats and reworks representations, structures of organization and understanding, falls in with the sexological picture, the sexual concern. It must take responsibility for that repetition, for the meanings and positions its adopts, and that responsibility cannot be avoided by appeals to the rights of comedy, satire, or whatever. There is no reason why, say, the women's movement should be exempt from comedy and satire (and no evidence that internally it is) but comedy and satire are again made up at any time of particular forms which involve choices of meaning and position, of representation. *Kinflicks* refuses, simply, to consider the implications of the forms it adopts; like so many other contemporary novels, it tries to avoid the responsibility of its commitment with the alibi of an engagement in 'the comedy of life itself': so doing, it can only repeat and confirm at so many points the dominant order, make the dominant – and the dominant sexual – sense.

Kinflicks's representation hinges on a basic narrative of the contemporary novelistic, involving orgasm as central and the problem of the woman raised round the themes of her independence and her eventual completion by the discovery of a true femininity. A major emphasis here has become the tracing of the progression from 'feminist' to 'feminine' (remember sexology's advice to women not to be mistaken for 'a badly groomed boy' or 'a second-string halfback').

Take the emphasis and its narrative articulation at their simplest and crudest, as, for instance, in Ian Fleming's *Goldfinger*. Hero James Bond – whose concentration of stereotypes of 'the man' needs no description – confronts two women. First, Tilly Masterson: 'She was beautiful – physically desirable. But there was a cold, hard centre to her that Bond couldn't understand or define.' The woman-enigma, the woman-problem. But, of course, Bond *can* understand and define the cold, hard centre: she is 'one of those girls whose hormones had got mixed up' (the result of 'fifty years of emancipation'), one of a 'herd of unhappy sexual misfits – barren and full of frustrations'. Men are men, women are women (or should be): Tilly is a hysteric, neither one nor the other or both, aggressive and masculine (acts like a *son*, not a daughter); a misfit, she is unhappy and frustrated in her failed femininity (what she really wants and needs is a *master* – Masterson should be master's daughter). Since she cannot place herself correctly to Bond, as woman to man, she gets killed: '"Poor little bitch. She didn't think much of men . . . I could have got her away if she'd only followed me."' Second, Pussy Galore, leader of a lesbian criminal gang, a natural challenge: Bond 'felt the challenge all beautiful lesbians have for men'. Tilly falls for Pussy, Pussy falls for Bond. '"I never met a man before"'. QED. It then only remains to *explain* her lesbianism: she is anti-men (lesbianism is being anti-men) because of a traumatic childhood rape by an uncle (shades exactly of Freud's seduction theory of hysteria); and to prescribe treatment from practising sexologist Bond: '"All you need is a course in TLC . . . Tender Loving Care Treatment" . . . "When's it going to start?" Bond's right hand came slowly up the firm, muscled thighs, over the flat soft plain of the stomach to the right breast. Its point was hard with desire. He said softly, "Now." His mouth came ruthlessly down on hers.' So she fits in the end, finally cured, identity established, his and hers, in her place, name confirmed – pussy galore. . . .

Orgasm is the question of the day, what everything bears on: '"Do you ever have an orgasm?"', Matt Hooper to Ellen Brodie in Peter Benchley's *Jaws*, '"Simon, have you never come? Had an orgasm?"', Ronnie to Simon (short for Simona) in Kingsley Amis's *I Want It Now*; and so on, novel after novel. As marriage is the end and resolution of the nineteenth-century novel, so orgasm – good, proper, authentic, real, successful, total, mind-blowing, truth-revealing, the moment when IT HAPPENS – is that of twentieth-century fictions, the point of representation: 'And then they both began to move again, interlocking, cock and cunt, and nothing else in the world mattering. She came with a shudder that shook her whole body and released another scream from her that scarcely seemed human . . . They lay not moving in the absolute peace after the earthquake . . . ', final moment of Erica Jong's *How To Save Your Own Life*; 'Then suddenly it happened – like a great, glorious, whooshing washing machine – it's the only way I can describe it – leaving me shuddering and shuddering with pleasure at the end, like the last gasps of the spin-dryer. And afterwards I cried some more because I was so happy, and he held me in his arms, telling me how much he loved me until I fell asleep . . . ', last pages of Jilly Cooper's *Octavia*.

In the nineteenth-century novel the concluding marriage was above all the resolution for women; men could cross from the world of feeling to the world of society in which they were accredited active agents, move from private to public and back again for the emotional strength and fulfilment the private is instituted to stand for and provide. The orgasm of the twentieth century binds women and men, the social agency of the latter giving way more and more to an inward-turning engagement on the sole – offered as *the crucial* – terrain of 'personal relations', 'intimate life': 'nothing else in the world mattering'. The use of and investment in lovemaking is in these terms; the representation is that of a general, 'sexuality'-determined psychology which is the very essence of 'life', the basic and deepest reality – I may do this and that in society but I am only really me in bed, confronting my own sexuality, stripped down to a purity of self and experience. John Updike expresses it perfectly in his *Marry Me*: 'Jerry and Sally made love lucidly, like Adam and Eve when the world was of two halves purely'; Adam and Eve, two halves purely, matched in flawless complementarity, 'the original man and woman'. That is where we should be, where we should find ourselves; the novels, their stories, tell of the problems of the achievement of such truth, filled with the sexual concern, written out of the all-pervasive sexological imagination. The contemporary plot is exactly that of the erotic path to the 'Big O', the realization of elemental, original, real being, man and woman, the two halves, cock and cunt; woman brought to reality through man: 'and she thought, feeling that cock slide in and out of her as if it owned her soul, that if she died then, if she died that very minute, it would be all right, she would have known most of it, have lived, have felt it'; man through woman: 'through the strait gate between your legs I had entered this firmament'. . . .

What we have today is a powerful sexual economy of the novel (and of the novelistic, in the production of which the novel plays its – important – part). 'Sexuality' is the stake and the purpose, the constant wager of the representation, over a scale of variations that runs from the elemental Lawrentian, ever present and appealing, to its banalization, its ordinary 'aroundness', the simple and immediate acceptance that *it* is the fundamental topic of interest and preoccupation.

Section 2

Fictioning the nation

Introduction

In his *Prison Notebooks*, Gramsci, observing the vogue for the serialization of nineteenth-century French novels in contemporary Italian newspapers, asks: 'why does the Italian public read foreign literature, popular and non-popular, instead of reading its own?' In addressing this question, Gramsci goes on to pose, and answer, another:

> What is the meaning of the fact that the Italian people prefer to read foreign writers? It means that they *undergo* the moral and intellectual hegemony of foreign intellectuals, that they feel more closely related to foreign intellectuals than to 'domestic' ones, that there is no national intellectual and moral bloc, either hierarchical or, still less, egalitarian. The intellectuals do not come from the people, even if by accident some of them have origins among the people. They do not feel tied to them (rhetoric apart), they do not know and sense their needs, aspirations and feelings. In relation to the people, they are something detached, without foundation, a caste and not an articulation with organic functions of the people themselves.[1]

The issues to which Gramsci points here – the role of popular literature in the formation of national-popular traditions – have become central to the concerns of contemporary Marxist investigations of the mechanisms and functioning of popular fictions, whether literary, filmic or televisual. That this should be so is, in a sense, ironic. For, as Benedict Anderson argues, the phenomenon of nationalism has often 'proved an uncomfortable *anomaly* for Marxist theory and, precisely for that reason, has been largely elided, rather than confronted'.[2] This theoretical elision was related to a political elision as, in the early twentieth century, socialist movements sought to by-pass the nation in their support for forms of internationalism which, in viewing nationalism as an essentially bourgeois phenomenon, would have no truck with nationalist sentiments and traditions, often in spite of their evident deep and widespread popular appeal. The political price of this neglect has been high and long-lasting as, particularly in developed nations – and nowhere more so than in Britain – the ground of the nation, as the dominant form in which communities and peoples are imagined and envisioned, has been ceded to conservative forces. Moreover, its lessons have been underscored by the fact that, where socialist revolutions have been successful, this has largely been where they have been associated with national liberation movements – where, as Anderson puts it, the tasks of 'planning revolution' and 'imagining the nation' have accompanied one another.[3]

The results of more recent Marxist reorientations toward the phenomena of nations and nationalism are nicely summarized by Nicos Poulantzas when he writes that the modern nation is not 'the creation of the bourgeoisie, but the outcome of a *relationship* of forces between the "modern" social classes – one in which the nation is a *stake* for the various classes'.[4] This is to suggest that the struggle for socialism is one that must always be conducted on the pre-given ground of the nation as a set of cultural representations and values, and that such struggle consists, in good part, of an attempt to inflect the meanings of those representations and values such that they come to be associated with the aspirations of socialism in the everyday consciousness and practices of the people. Clearly, a politics which seeks to intervene positively within and reorganize the currency of nationalism in this way requires an understanding as to how nations are organized and constituted. In Benedict Anderson's view, nations are best regarded as particular ways of organizing and representing bonds of solidarity among a people, forging a sense of unity between them by representing them as heirs to a common past and as sharing in the same destiny. As such, Anderson argues, nations are most appropriately distinguished 'by the style in which they are imagined':[5] that is, by the political associations which accrue to the ways in which their imagined pasts and futures are forged.

In thus regarding nations as 'cultural artefacts of a particular kind', Anderson places particular stress on what might be called the 'cultural instruments of nationing': that is, on the interacting network of cultural forms and technologies through which particular ways of imagining the unity, continuity and identity of a nation are instilled in the population of a particular territory. Moreover, Anderson concurs with Gramsci in viewing the popular novel and the newspaper as two of the most important cultural instruments of this kind. In the excerpt from his *Imagined Communities* reprinted here, Anderson thus argues that 'these forms provided the technical means for "re-presenting" the *kind* of imagined community that is the nation' (p.71). The structure of the novel, Anderson argues, is distinguished by its portrayal of acts performed by actors who, though they may be largely unaware of one another, are represented as part of the same imagined world by virtue of the fact that their activities are portrayed as taking place at the same time or in a series of successive identical times. This novelistic effect of a sociological organism bound together by and moving through the same time, Anderson suggests, is 'a precise analogue of the idea of the nation, which also is conceived as a solid community moving steadily down (or up) history' (p.72). More than that, the novel also binds the reader into the imagined community it constructs through the modes of address it uses.

It is important, though, that Anderson does not view this as an effect of the novel in isolation. Turning his attention to the newspaper, he argues that its most striking characteristics consist in its profound fictiveness – that is, in the devices, very similar to those of the novel, it uses to conjure into existence the imagined unity of the nation it addresses. Novels and newspapers, then – and not separately, but in their relations to one another – are assessed as cultural instruments which play a vital role in fictioning the nation into existence as 'fiction seeps quietly and continuously into reality, creating that remarkable confidence of community in anonymity which is the hallmark of modern nations' (p.79).

In his discussion of Rizal's *Noli Me Tangere*, Anderson notes that there developed, alongside the Filipino novel, a nationalist press printed not merely in Spanish but using such 'ethnic' languages as Tagalog too. This raises perhaps one of the most fundamental aspects of nationalism. For how a nation 'thinks' itself is centrally dependent on how it 'speaks' itself and on the relation of its language to other languages. These are the questions Dennis Porter addresses in 'The language of detection'. Leaning on the work of V.N. Voloshinov, Porter argues that 'where for historical reasons new nations develop sharing a common tongue with older nations, the language itself may become an arena for a national cultural struggle' (p.82). American writing, he contends, is a case in point in the sense that a good deal of its history can be read as an attempt to 'stake out an anti-British verbal territory', to forge a distinct American literary idiom as 'an assertion of cultural emancipation and independent national identity' (p.83).

While this is a familiar theme in American literary scholarship, the interest of Porter's analysis lies in his application of this perspective to the school of hard-boiled detective fiction. In the process, he complicates the terms in which such matters are usually discussed by incorporating considerations of class into his analysis. Contrasting the literary styles of Dashiell Hammett and Raymond Chandler with that of Agatha Christie, Porter notes the preference of the former 'for directness over formality, lower-class speech over upper, popular over high culture, American forthrightness over English gentility' (p.88). In thus incorporating the street argot of urban America and the associated working-class values of directness, toughness and plain speech into their literary style, Porter argues that Chandler and Hammett were concerned to promote a particular set of class, linguistic and cultural attributes to the status of cherished national values. Following Stephen Heath in seeing a writer's choice of style as an act of social-historical solidarity, Porter suggests that the pact of solidarity embodied in the language of hard-boiled detective fiction has two dimensions – a pact of solidarity with the sign-community of America against that of Britain and, within the sign-community of America, a pact of solidarity with working-class language and culture against the linguistic and cultural values of American elites.

It's no accident, to return to Anderson for a moment, that he should derive most of his examples from nations which, in order to be 'fictioned into existence', had to overturn and define themselves against the imported nationalisms of foreign imperial powers. For it is in such cases where, as Gramsci puts it, a people undergo the moral and intellectual hegemony of foreign intellectuals, that the issues at stake in the functioning of cultural instruments of nationing are most readily apparent. Working within a broadly Gramscian paradigm, Colin McArthur's essay 'Scotland and cinema: the iniquity of the fathers' offers a telling example of the difficulties involved in organizing a national culture in societies where the very currency of nation-ness is shot through with contradictions owing to the preponderant cultural influence of imperialist powers.

McArthur's starting point is supplied by the representations of Scotland circulated by the international film industry, particularly Hollywood and, in Britain, Ealing Studios. Governed by the conceptions of what he calls 'Tartanry and Kailyard', McArthur shows how filmic representations of Scotland and Scottishness have, in the main, consisted either of kilted Highlanders – a fabrication of English Romanticism – or, where the themes and settings are more contemporary, of a highly idealized and sentimentalized semi-rural folk. Whichever the case, though, the effects are broadly similar, as Scotland is conjured forth as an idealized counterpoint to modernity and industrialism, as the site of either an exoticized feudal past or of 'a range of lovable rural eccentrics and non-conformists' who embody an imaginative resistance to the dehumanizing influence of industrial development.

Ultimately, though, McArthur's concern is with the degree to which these grids through which other cultures construct the Scots have come to supply 'the framework within which Scots largely construct themselves' (p.95). While this is partly a matter of the influence of the American and English film industries on Scottish audiences, it more particularly concerns their influence on film-makers. To the degree that the representations of Scotland and the Scottish people put into circulation through the film industry have come to be influential within Scotland itself, the ability of the Scottish film industry to function as a cultural instrument of nationing has been curtailed. In working with rather than against such representations, McArthur argues, the Scottish film industry has often served to frustrate the development of vibrant and progressive ways of imagining Scotland that would be relevant to the needs of a highly industrialized nation. Just as Joyce regarded Irish art as a 'cracked lookingglass of a servant', so McArthur contends that the Scottish film industry has ill-served Scottish people in reflecting back to them the distorted representations of themselves fashioned to serve English and American audiences as idealized counterpoints to the experience of modernity. That this is so, however, is not due merely to a failure of imagination. The problem, as McArthur

outlines it, has to do with the objective weight of a reper-
toire of cultural representations which continue to frame
and limit the endeavours of even those film-makers who
seek to break with them.

Many of the terms of McArthur's discussion could
well be transposed to an analysis of the Australian film
industry, particularly in its tendency to have recourse to
those images of Australia that have an international
currency in order to sell its products on the world
market. The success of *Crocodile Dundee* perhaps
illustrates these pressures in their starkest form in its
representation of Australia in the romanticized image of
the bushman whose 'unspoilt' roughness, lack of sophistication and raw good humour – as personified in Paul
Hogan – serve not only as an imaginative counterpoint to
the metropolitan centres of western capitalism but, in
Dundee's visit to New York, also imaginarily triumphs
over those centres. Graeme Turner considers the consequences of such processes for Australian audiences.
Tracing the formation of a radical nationalist tradition in
late nineteenth-century Australia – a tradition which
defined the Australian character in terms of qualities
(egalitarianism, mateship, anti-authoritarianism) which
differentiated it from an equally mythical conception of
Englishness – Turner suggests that the reactivation of
this tradition within the contemporary Australian film
industry (in films such as *Breaker Morant* and *Phar Lap*)
has formed a part of its appropriation by conservative
forces. As Turner points out, though, such processes are
rarely without contradictions and he argues that it is
precisely in its excess of populist rhetoric that a film like
The Man from Snowy River exhibits the potential for
challenging the dominant culture.

Notes

1 Gramsci, Antonio (1985) *Selections from Cultural Writings*,
   London: Lawrence & Wishart, p. 209.
2 Anderson, Benedict (1983) *Imagined Communities: Reflections on*

the Origin and Spread of Nationalism, London: Verso, p. 13.
3 ibid., p. 144.
4 Poulantzas, Nicos (1980) *State, Power, Socialism*, London: Verso, p. 115.
5 Anderson, op.cit., p. 15.

5
Apprehensions of time
Benedict Anderson

It would be short-sighted . . . to think of the imagined
communities of nations as simply growing out of and
replacing religious communities and dynastic realms.
Beneath the decline of sacred communities, languages
and lineages, a fundamental change was taking place in
modes of apprehending the world, which, more than
anything else, made it possible to 'think' the nation.

To get a feeling for this change, one can profitably
turn to the visual representations of the sacred
communities, such as the reliefs and stained-glass
windows of medieval churches, or the paintings of early
Italian and Flemish masters. A characteristic feature of
such representations is something misleadingly analogous
to 'modern dress'. The shepherds who have followed the
star to the manger where Christ is born bear the features
of Burgundian peasants. The Virgin Mary is figured as a
Tuscan merchant's daughter. In many paintings the
commissioning patron, in full burgher or noble costume,
appears kneeling in adoration alongside the shepherds.
What seems incongruous today obviously appeared
wholly natural to the eyes of medieval worshippers. We
are faced with a world in which the figuring of imagined
reality was overwhelmingly visual and aural. Christendom assumed its universal form through a myriad of
specificities and particularities: this relief, that window,

this sermon, that tale, this morality play, that relic. While the trans-European Latin-reading clerisy was one essential element in the structuring of the Christian imagination, the mediation of its conceptions to the illiterate masses, by visual and aural creations, always personal and particular, was no less vital. The humble parish priest, whose forebears and frailties everyone who heard his celebrations knew, was still the direct inter-mediary between his parishioners and the divine. This juxtaposition of the cosmic-universal and the mundane-particular meant that however vast Christendom might be, and was sensed to be, it manifested itself *variously* to particular Swabian or Andalusian communities as repli-cations of themselves. Figuring the Virgin Mary with 'Semitic' features or 'first-century' costumes in the restoring spirit of the modern museum was unimaginable because the medieval Christian mind had no conception of history as an end-less chain of cause and effect or of radical separations between past and present. . . .

Auerbach gives an unforgettable sketch of this form of consciousness:

> . . . the here and now is no longer a mere link in an earthly chain of events, it is *simultaneously* something which has always been, and will be fulfilled in the future; and strictly, in the eyes of God, it is something eternal, something omnitemporal, something already consum-mated in the realm of fragmentary earthly event.[1]

He rightly stresses that such an idea of *simultaneity* is wholly alien to our own. It views time as something close to what Benjamin calls Messianic time, a simultaneity of past and future in an instantaneous present.[2] In such a view of things, the word 'meanwhile' cannot be of real significance.

Our own conception of simultaneity has been a long time in the making, and its emergence is certainly connected, in ways that have yet to be well studied, with the development of the secular sciences. But it is a conception of such fundamental importance that, without taking it fully into account, we will find it difficult to probe the obscure genesis of nationalism. What has come to take the place of the medieval conception of simultaneity-along-time is, to borrow again from Benjamin, an idea of 'homogeneous, empty time', in which simultaneity is, as it were, transverse, cross-time, marked not by prefiguring and fulfilment, but by temporal coincidence, and measured by clock and calendar.[3]

Why this transformation should be so important for the birth of the imagined community of the nation can best be so seen if we consider the basic structure of two forms of imagining which first flowered in Europe in the eighteenth century: the novel and the newspaper. For these forms provided the technical means for 're-presenting' the *kind* of imagined community that is the nation.

Consider first the structure of the old-fashioned novel, a structure typical not only of the masterpieces of Balzac but also of any contemporary dollar-dreadful. It is clearly a device for the presentation of simultaneity in 'homogeneous, empty time', or a complex gloss upon the word 'meanwhile'. Take, for illustrative purposes, a segment of a simple novel-plot, in which a man (A) has a wife (B) and a mistress (C), who in turn has a lover (D). We might imagine a sort of time-chart for this segment as follows:

Time:	I	II	III
	A quarrels with B	A telephones C	D gets drunk in a bar
Events:	C and D make love	B shops	A dines at home with B
		D plays pool	C has an ominous dream

Notice that during this sequence A and D never meet, indeed may not even be aware of each other's existence if C has played her cards right. What then actually links A to D? Two complementary conceptions: first, that they are embedded in 'societies' (Wessex, Lübeck, Los

Angeles). These societies are sociological entities of such firm and stable reality that their members (A and D) can even be described as passing each other on the street, without ever becoming acquainted, and still be connected. Second, that A and D are embedded in the minds of the omniscient readers. Only they see the links. Only they, like God, watch A telephoning C, B shopping, and D playing pool all *at once*. That all these acts are performed at the same clocked, calendrical time, but by actors who may be largely unaware of one another, shows the novelty of this imagined world conjured up by the author in his readers' minds.

The idea of a sociological organism moving calendrically through homogeneous, empty time is a precise analogue of the idea of the nation, which also is conceived as a solid community moving steadily down (or up) history. An American will never meet, or even know the names of more than a handful of his 240,000,000-odd fellow-Americans. He has no idea of what they are up to at any one time. But he has complete confidence in their steady, anonymous, simultaneous activity.

The perspective I am suggesting will perhaps seem less abstract if we turn to inspect briefly three fictions from different cultures and different epochs, all but one of which, none the less, are inextricably bound to nationalist movements. In 1887, the 'father of Filipino nationalism', José Rizal, wrote the novel *Noli Me Tangere*, which today is regarded as the greatest achievement of modern Filipino literature. It was also almost the first novel written by an 'Indio'.[4] Here is how it marvellously begins:

> Don Santiago de los Santos was giving a dinner party one evening towards the end of October in the 1880's. Although, contrary to his usual practice, he had let it be known only on the afternoon of the same day, it was soon the topic of conversation in Binondo, where he lived, in other districts of Manila, and even in the Spanish walled city of Intramuros. Don Santiago was better

known as Capitan Tiago – the rank was not military but political, and indicated that he had once been the native mayor of a town. In those days he had a reputation for lavishness. It was well known that his house, like his country, never closed its doors – except, of course, to trade and any idea that was new or daring.

So the news of his dinner party ran like an electric shock through the community of spongers, hangers-on and gate-crashers whom God, in His infinite wisdom, had created and so fondly multiplied in Manila. Some of these set out to hunt polish for their boots; others, collar-buttons and cravats; but one and all gave the gravest thought to the manner in which they might greet their host with the assumed intimacy of long-standing friend-ship, or, if the occasion should arise, make a graceful apology for not having arrived earlier where presumably their presence was so eagerly awaited.

The dinner was being given in a house on Anloague Street which may still be recognized unless it has tumbled down in some earthquake. Certainly it will not have been pulled down by its owner; in the Philippines, that is usually left to God and Nature. In fact, one often thinks that they are under contract to the Government for just that purpose. . . .[5]

Extensive comment is surely unnecessary. It should suffice to note that right from the start of the image (wholly new to Filipino writing) of a dinner party being discussed by hundreds of unnamed people, who do not know each other, in quite different quarters of Manila, in a particular month of a particular decade, immediately conjures up the imagined community. And in the phrase 'a house on Anloague Street which may still be recognized. . . . ' the recognizers are we-the-Filipino-readers. The casual progression of this house from the 'interior' time of the novel to the 'exterior' time of the [Manila] reader's everyday life gives a hypnotic confir-mation of the solidity of a single community, embracing characters, author and readers, moving onward through calendrical time. Notice too the tone. While Rizal has not the faintest idea of his readers' individual identities, he writes to them with an ironical intimacy, as though their relationships with each other are not to the smallest degree problematic. . . .

In 1816, seventy years before the writing of *Noli*, José Joaquín Fernandez de Lizardi wrote a novel called *El Periquillo Sarniento* (The Itching Parrot), evidently the first Latin American work in this genre. In the words of one critic, this text is 'a ferocious indictment of Spanish administration in Mexico: ignorance, superstition and corruption are seen to be its most notable characteristics'.[6] The essential form of this 'nationalist' novel is indicated by the following description of its content:

> From the first, [the hero, the Itching Parrot] is exposed to bad influences – ignorant maids inculcate superstitions, his mother indulges his whims, his teachers either have no vocation or no ability to discipline him. And though his father is an intelligent man who wants his son to practise a useful trade rather than swell the ranks of lawyers and parasites, it is Periquillo's over-fond mother who wins the day, sends her son to university and thus ensures that he will learn only superstitious nonsense . . . Periquillo remains incorrigibly ignorant despite many encounters with good and wise people. He is unwilling to work or take anything seriously and becomes successively a priest, a gambler, a thief, apprentice to an apothecary, a doctor, clerk in a provincial town. . . . These episodes *permit the author to describe hospitals, prisons, remote villages, monasteries*, while at the same time driving home one major point – the Spanish government and the education system encourage parasitism and laziness . . . Periquillo's adventures several times take him among Indians and Negroes.[7]

Here again we see the 'national imagination' at work in the movement of a solitary hero through a sociological landscape of a fixity that fuses the world inside the novel with the world outside. This picaresque *tour d'horizon* – hospital*s*, prison*s*, remote village*s*, monasterie*s*, Indian*s*, Negroe*s* – is none the less not a *tour du monde*. The horizon is clearly bounded: it is that of colonial Mexico. Nothing assures us of this sociological solidity more than the succession of plurals. For they conjure up a social space full of *comparable* prisons, none in itself of any unique importance, but all representative (in their simultaneous, separate existence) of the oppressiveness of *this* colony. (Contrast prisons in the Bible. They are never imagined as *typical* of this or that society. Each, like the one where Salome was bewitched by John the Baptist, is magically alone.)

Finally, to remove the possibility that, since Rizal and Lizardi both wrote in Spanish, the frameworks we have been studying are somehow 'European', here is the opening of *Semarang Hitam* (Black Semarang), a tale by the ill-fated young Indonesian communist-nationalist Mas Marco Kartodikromo, published serially in 1924:

> *It was 7 o'clock, Saturday evening*; young people in Semarang never stayed at home on Saturday night. On this night however nobody was about. Because the heavy day-long rain had made the roads wet and very slippery, all had stayed at home.
>
> For the workers in shops and offices Saturday morning was a time of anticipation – anticipating their leisure and the fun of walking around the city in the evening, but on this night they were to be disappointed – because of lethargy caused by the bad weather and the sticky roads in the kampungs. The main roads usually crammed with all sorts of traffic, the footpaths usually teeming with people, all were deserted. Now and then the crack of a horse-cab's whip could be heard spurring a horse on its way – or the clip-clop of horses' hooves pulling carriages along.
>
> Semarang was deserted. The light from the rows of gas lamps shone straight down on the shining asphalt road. Occasionally the clear light from the gas lamps was dimmed as the wind blew from the east. . . .
>
> A young man was seated on a long rattan lounge reading a newspaper. He was totally engrossed. His occasional anger and at other times smiles were a sure sign of his deep interest in the story. He turned the pages of the newspaper, thinking that perhaps he could find something that would stop him feeling so miserable. All of a sudden

he came upon an article entitled:

PROSPERITY

A destitute vagrant became ill and died on the side of the road from exposure.

> The young man was moved by this brief report. He could just imagine the suffering of the poor soul as he lay dying on the side of the road . . . One moment he felt an explosive anger well up inside. Another moment he felt pity. Yet another moment his anger was directed at the social system which gave rise to such poverty, while making a small group of people wealthy.[8]

Here, as in *El Periquillo Sarniento*, we are in a world of plurals: shops, offices, carriages, kampungs, and gas lamps. As in the case of *Noli*, we-the-Indonesian-readers are plunged immediately into calendrical time and a familiar landscape; some of us may well have walked those 'sticky' Semarang roads. Once again, a solitary hero is juxtaposed to a socioscape described in careful, *general* detail. But there is also something new: a hero who is never named, but who is consistently referred to as '*our* young man'. Precisely the clumsiness and literary naivety of the text confirms the unselfconscious 'sincerity' of this pronominal adjective. Neither Marco nor his readers have any doubts about the reference. If in the jocular-sophisticated fiction of eighteenth- and nineteenth-century Europe the trope 'our hero' merely underlines an authorial play with a(ny) reader; Marco's 'our young man', not least in its novelty, *means* a young man who belongs to the collective body of readers of *Indonesian*, and thus, implicitly, an embryonic Indonesian 'imagined community'. Notice that Marco feels no need to specify this community by name: it is already there. (Even if polylingual Dutch colonial censors could join his readership, they are excluded from this 'ourness', as can be seen from the fact that the young man's anger is directed at 'the', not 'our', social system.) Finally, the imagined community is confirmed by the doubleness of our reading about our young man reading. He does not find the corpse of the destitute vagrant by the side of a sticky Semarang road, but imagines it from the print in a newspaper. Nor does he care the slightest who the dead vagrant individually was: he thinks of the representative body, not the personal life.

It is fitting that in *Semarang Hitam* a newspaper appears embedded in fiction, for, if we now turn to the newspaper as cultural product, we will be struck by its profound fictiveness. What is the essential literary convention of the newspaper? If we were to look at a sample front page of, say, *The New York Times*, we might find there stories about Soviet dissidents, famine in Mali, a gruesome murder, a coup in Iraq, the discovery of a rare fossil in Zimbabwe, and a speech by Mitterrand. Why are these events so juxtaposed? What connects them to each other? Not sheer caprice. Yet obviously most of them happen independently, without the actors being aware of each other or of what the others are up to. The arbitrariness of their inclusion and juxtaposition (a later edition will substitute a baseball triumph for Mitterrand) shows that the linkage between them is imagined.

This imagined linkage derives from two obliquely related sources. The first is simply calendrical coincidence. The date at the top of the newspaper, the single most important emblem on it, provides the essential connection – the steady onward clocking of homogeneous, empty time. Within that time, 'the world' ambles sturdily ahead. The sign for this: if Mali disappears from the pages of *The New York Times* after two days of famine reportage, for months on end, readers do not for a moment imagine that Mali has disappeared or that famine has wiped out all its citizens. The novelistic format of the newspaper assures them that somewhere out there the 'character' Mali moves along quietly, awaiting its next reappearance in the plot.

The second source of imagined linkage lies in the relationship between the newspaper, as a form of book, and the market. It has been estimated that in the forty-odd years between the publication of the Gutenberg Bible and the close of the fifteenth century, more than 20,000,000 printed volumes were produced in Europe.[9] Between 1500 and 1600, the number manufactured had reached between 150,000,000 and 200,000,000.[10]

> From early on . . . the printing shops looked more like modern workshops than the monastic workrooms of the Middle Ages. In 1455, Fust and Schoeffer were already running a business geared to standardized production, and twenty years later large printing concerns were operating everywhere in all [sic] Europe.[11]

In a rather special sense, the book was the first modern-style mass-produced industrial commodity.[12] The sense I have in mind can be shewn if we compare the book to other early industrial products, such as textiles, bricks or sugar. For these commodities are *measured* in mathematical amounts (pounds or loads or pieces). A pound of sugar is simply a quantity, a convenient load, not an object in itself. The book, however – and here it prefigures the durables of our time – is a distinct, self-contained object, exactly reproduced on a large scale. One pound of sugar flows into the next; each book has its own eremitic self-sufficiency. . . .

In this perspective, the newspaper is merely an 'extreme form' of the book, a book sold on a colossal scale, but of ephemeral popularity. Might we say: one-day bestsellers? The obsolescence of the newspaper on the morrow of its printing – curious that one of the earlier mass-produced commodities should so prefigure the inbuilt obsolescence of modern durables – none the less, for just this reason, creates this extraordinary mass ceremony: the almost precisely simultaneous consumption ('imagining') of the newspaper-as-fiction. We know that particular morning and evening editions will overwhelmingly be consumed between this hour and that, only on this day, not that. (Contrast sugar, the use of which proceeds in an unclocked, continuous flow; it may go bad, but it does not go out of date.) The significance of this mass ceremony – Hegel observed that newspapers serve modern man as a substitute for morning prayers – is paradoxical. It is performed in silent privacy, in the lair of the skull. Yet each communicant is well aware that the ceremony he performs is being replicated simultaneously by thousands (or millions) of others of whose existence he is confident, yet of whose identity he has not the slightest notion. Furthermore, this ceremony is incessantly repeated at daily or half-daily intervals throughout the calendar. What more vivid figure for the secular, historically-clocked, imagined community can be envisioned? At the same time, the newspaper reader, observing exact replicas of his own paper being consumed by his subway, barbershop or residential neighbours, is continually reassured that the imagined world is visibly rooted in everyday life. As with *Noli Me Tangere*, fiction seeps quietly and continuously into reality, creating that remarkable confidence of community in anonymity which is the hallmark of modern nations.

Notes

1 Auerbach, Erich (1957) *Mimesis. The Representation of Reality in Western Literature*, Garden City, NY: Doubleday Anchor, p. 86.
2 Benjamin, Walter (1973) *Illuminations*, London: Fontana, p. 265.
3 ibid., p. 263.
4 Rizal wrote this novel in the colonial language (Spanish), which was then the *lingua franca* of the ethnically diverse Eurasian and native elites. Alongside the novel appeared also for the first time a 'nationalist' press, not only in Spanish but in such 'ethnic' languages as Tagalog and Ilocano. See Yabes, Leopoldo Y. (1974) 'The modern literature of the Philippines', in Pierre-Bernard Lafont and Denys Lombard (eds) *Littératures contemporaines de l'Asie du sud-est*, Paris: L'Asiathèque, pp. 287–302.
5 Rizal, José (1961) *The Lost Eden. Noli Me Tangere*, Bloomington, Ind.: Indiana University Press, p. 1.
6 Franco, Jean (1969) *An Introduction to Spanish-American Literature*, Cambridge: Cambridge University Press, p. 34.
7 ibid., pp. 35–6.
8 As translated by Tickel, Paul (1981) in *Three Early Indonesian*

Short Stories by Mas Marco Kartodikromo (c. 1890–1932), Melbourne: Monash University, Centre of South-east Asian Studies, Working Paper No. 23, p. 7. Emphasis added.

9 Febvre, Lucien and Martin, Henri-Jean (1976) *The Coming of the Book. The Impact of Printing, 1450–1800*, London: New Left Books, p. 186.

10 ibid., p. 262.

11 ibid., p. 125.

12 This is one point solidly made amidst the vagaries of McLuhan, Marshall (1962) *The Gutenberg Galaxy: The Making of Typographic Man*, Toronto: University of Toronto Press, p. 125.

6

The language of detection

Dennis Porter

. . . .

It is, of course, a commonplace that like the Italians in a different historical context, American writers have always been preoccupied by the 'questione delle lingua', because the language a people uses raises questions of national identity at the deepest level. The story of the Americans' relation to their language is familiar. In literature especially, the search for a native American idiom is among other things an expression of the traditional American ambivalence felt for British life, culture and institutions. It was originally rooted in the historical circumstance of having inherited a mother tongue from a rejected fatherland, a circumstance that seemed to require the undertaking of a cultural and linguistic rebellion similar to the one that had already been completed in the political sphere.

If consciousness functions only by means of the material medium of language, as Marx already implied,[1] the difficulty of developing a different form of consciousness begins with the obstacle of an alien idiom. If we are to believe Voloshinov, in fact, as far as the individual is concerned the task is impossible to the extent that the existence of communal language always precedes the coming to consciousness. Language is a semiotic system without which there is no inner speech any more than there is outer speech:

> consciousness can arise and become a viable fact only in
> the material embodiment of signs. . . . Consciousness
> takes shape and being in the interest of signs created by
> an organized group in the process of social interaction.
> The individual consciousness is nurtured on signs: it
> derives its growth from them: it reflects their logic and
> laws.[2]

Moreover, given further that 'the domain of ideology
coincides with the domain of signs', the problem for the
individual of escaping from the ideology of a given
language system seems insoluble. Yet Voloshinov also
provides the concept which suggests that for self-
conscious groups within a wider language community, at
least, there is a way out. The concept involved is that of
'the social multiaccentuality of the ideological sign'.
What Voloshinov means by the term 'multiaccentuality'
is that in practice all the natural languages of complex
societies are likely to possess a variety of more or less
conflicting speech levels. New modes of consciousness
may therefore be fabricated on the contrastive systems
within the broad system:

> Class does not coincide with the sign community, i.e.,
> with the community that is the totality of users of the set
> of signs for ideological communication. Thus various
> different classes will use one and the same language. As
> a result, differently oriented accents intersect in every
> ideological sign. Sign becomes an arena of the class
> struggle.[3]

Further, where for historical reasons new nations develop
sharing a common tongue with older nations, the
language itself may become an arena for a national
cultural struggle. In the case of the rival claims made on
English by the British and the Americans, it is clear that
the national struggle has from the beginning been
combined with a class struggle.

The task of inventing a new American man, undertaken during the revolutionary and early republican eras,
therefore, had to begin with a language that, if it could

not itself be new, should at least be perceptibly different from the original British model. The reason why American authors from Mark Twain on were peculiarly preoccupied with the task of fashioning an American vernacular adapted to serious literary ends was consciously ideological. They were responding to the widely felt need to make the language of a class-conscious monarchy suitable for the use of a democratic people living under a republic. Within the British verbal Empire, they sought to stake out an anti-British verbal territory. The creation of a recognizably American form of literary English was, therefore, tantamount to an assertion of cultural emancipation and independent national identity. Thus it is not surprising that in the Anglo-American fictional tradition the Americans are the ones more consistently preoccupied with the problem of 'style', because what is involved is not simply the inscription of individuality but an *écriture*, that is to say a national style that is at the same time a class style. And what is true for the history of the American novel in general is confirmed by the detective novel.

The self-consciousness of the pursuit of an appropriate American idiom has been explored by, among others, Richard Bridgman, and his study confirms Chandler's own awareness that the represented speech of fiction is always different from actual spoken language.[4] Chandler makes clear . . . how for Hammett as for everyone else a vernacular literary style is always a question of art:

> He had style, but his audience didn't know it, because it was in a language not supposed to be capable of such refinements. They thought they were getting a good meaty melodrama written in the kind of lingo they imagined they wrote themselves. It was, in a sense, but it was much more. All language begins with speech, and the speech of common men at that, but when it develops to the point of becoming a literary medium it only looks like speech. Hammett's style at its worst was as formalized as a page of *Marius the Epicurean*: at its best it could say almost anything.[5]

Chandler's point is that it is nonsense to assume that adult American males have ever actually talked like Sam Spade or Philip Marlowe any more than American country boys once sounded like Huckleberry Finn. In both cases the languages employed were created by their authors for literary purposes. In a Twain or Chandler novel the reader is faced with a fabricated vernacular that is a form of idealized speech. The voices of Philip Marlowe and Huckleberry Finn are more American than American life itself. The stylistic level chosen to represent their speech is important for its connotative power apart from anything it might denote. Its real significance is mythic because it was invented to express by itself class and regional values that aspire to the status of cherished national values. As Stephen Heath has put it, 'The choice of an *écriture* is the choice of a set of values, a way of seeing, an act of socio-historical solidarity'.[6] Thus Mark Twain's *écriture* is the class style of middle-class, small-town, midwestern America, the literary idiom of the heartland. It is a class style that Hammett and Chandler were to update as something more urban and fast-paced.

A comparison of the opening passages of three first novels by Agatha Christie, Dashiell Hammett and Raymond Chandler respectively suggest the gap consciously opened up by the American writers:

> The intense interest aroused in the public by what was known at the time as 'The Styles Case' has now somewhat subsided. Nevertheless, in view of the world-wide notoriety which attended it, I have been asked, both by my friend Poirot and the family themselves, to write an account of the whole story. This, we trust, will effectually silence the sensational rumours which still persist.
>
> I will therefore briefly set down the circumstances which led to my being connected with the affair.[7]

> I first heard Personville called Poisonville by a red-haired mucker named Hickey Dewey in the Big Ship at Butte. He also called a shirt a shoit. I didn't think anything of what he had done to the city's name. Later I heard men who could manage their r's give it the same pronunciation.

I still didn't see anything in it but the meaningless sort of humour that used to make richardsnary the thieves' word for dictionary. A few years later I went to Personville and learned better.[8]

It was about eleven o'clock in the morning, mid-October, with the sun not shining and a look of hard wet rain in the clearness of the foothills. I was wearing my powder-blue suit, with dark blue shirt, tie and display handker-chief, black brogues, black wool socks with dark blue clocks on them. I was neat, clean, shaved and sober, and I didn't care who knew it. I was everything the well-dressed private detective ought to be. I was calling on four million dollars.[9]

The style chosen by Agatha Christie as the idiom of her narrator is that of a formal written prose characterized by its roundness and a fondness for the parenthetical phrase. The cumbersome but well-constructed sentences with their predictable adjectives – 'intense interest', 'world-wide notoriety', 'sensational rumours' – and their British adverbs – 'somewhat subsided', 'effectively silenced' – connote social confor-mity, circumspection and sobriety. They also suggest the self-confidence of a class that took its own vernacular for the norm of correct English speech and that therefore found it necessary to put the speech of farm labourers, shopkeepers and cockneys into quotation marks. . . .

Agatha Christie's choice of the polished version of polite middle-class English speech for the ideolect of her narrator was obviously made in full consciousness of the audience she was writing for. Moreover, it is characteristic of the formal detective genre that it does not incorporate any other level of speech into itself apart, occasionally, from the country or cockney speech of odd lower-class characters. Unlike that literary tradi-tion which from Villon to Fielding, Dickens and Victor Hugo admitted an element of underworld speech into its representation of criminal milieus for the sake of its inventiveness and irreverent energy, the formal detective story insists on good taste to the point of suppressing the threat of the underworld down to its slang. . . .

Further, the opening paragraph of Agatha Christie's first novel is also typical because it is deliberately constructed on the irony of claiming to deny the sensational in order to excite an interest in it. As such, it serves as a reminder that the formal detective novel is founded on the central irony of the surprise of crime, which expresses itself in three characteristic forms soon to become a predictable formula. To the endlessly repeated irony of the most unlikely suspect, the formal detective novel added those of the most unlikely detective and the most unlikely place. A foppish lord, a vain and overweight Belgian, and an elderly gentlewoman are only the most familiar of twentieth-century English examples of eccentric detectives. There is a similar eccentricity in siting crime in circumstances of order and beauty, from rural communities in Oxford colleges and gentlemen's clubs, rather than in the chaotic cities. The force of such ironies is to establish an ambience of play.

In this connection, the purpose of the circumlocutionary beginning here is to establish distance. Agatha Christie is still working in the tradition of Poe, Collins and Doyle to the extent that she writes not a novel of spoken action in the mode of Hammett and Chandler but a form of memoir novel supposedly set down by a narrator/witness after the fact. The Holmes stories typically take the form of casebooks, written in tranquillity by Dr Watson. This strategy explains in part the cooler temperature of the formal detective novel when compared with the thriller.

In spite of the wit in the opening paragraph of *Red Harvest*, on the other hand, there is nothing playful about Hammett's novel. If a sentence were needed to introduce the tone of the new wave in detective fiction, it would be hard to improve on Hammett's first two lines: 'I first heard Personville called Poisonville by a red-haired mucker named Hickey Dewey in the Big Ship at Butte.' The paragraph is a typically strong opening characterized by richness of verbal texture in the vein of the antipicturesque. It not only identifies memorably a place and points ahead to a dilemma, it introduces an unforgettable voice. Yet the reason it attracts immediate attention is rhetorical. The fact that Hammett forces the reader to pay attention to his medium suggests immediately that we are in the presence of a *texte de plaisir*. That first sentence is remarkable because of its staccato rhythms, its alliterative energy and its internal rhymes as well as by the way in which it plays suggestively with evocative, no-nonsense American names. The whole paragraph recalls a direct, conversational American speech that is both funny and tough. Finally, with a movement characteristic of the hard-boiled tradition, it moves toward a climax which is understated but sinister. In other words, although Hammett makes references to contemporary American speech in this passage, the stylistic subtlety is of a kind associated with written prose.

In *The Big Sleep* Chandler follows the example of Hammett's first novel in closing the gap between narrator and detective common in the British tradition. His private eye reports directly, telling it both 'like it is' and how it happens, combining the highly rated American skills of the newspaper reporter and the sports commentator. In the tradition of the hard-boiled detective story the technique of the first-person detective narrator is valuable because it permits a perfect match between language and behaviour, speech and ethics.

In the first paragraph of his first novel, Chandler provides a flashier example of the antipicturesque than does Hammett. The passage introduces the characteristic note of toughness with its opening negative – 'with the sun not shining'. But in this particular passage the toughness is suggested largely through speech characterized by casualness and elliptical colloquialisms – 'about eleven o'clock', 'mid-October'.

As with Hammett, however, the apparent casualness of represented speech hides a mastery of tone and rhythm. The four sentences following the opening evocation of a scene are typical of the rhetorical complexity to be found in Chandler's prose. All four are characterized by a structural similarity with rhythmic variation. They all open with the same 'I was' and are followed by descriptions. As a result, at the same time that they communicate the information which defines a place, a task and a point of view, because of a parallelism in structure the four sentences also prepare a surprise for the reader. Whereas the first three sentences are longer and involve a progression in describing details of personal appearance, the last sentence is short and describes an occurrence. It is the swift and unexpected climax of a slow buildup. The effect obtained is that of the punch line.

The whole passage is typical of the way in which Chandler's rhetorical control is designed to serve a functional end. The structure of the opening paragraph not only enables him to deliver the attention-grabbing last line – a lesser writer like Spillane would have to throw in a corpse – it also permits him to introduce an ethos and a type. If the 'I's' are all up front here, it is in order to establish 'the character' who will go by the name of Philip Marlowe. Chandler invents the speech in order to create the brash assurance of a self-advertising type with a sense of irony and an unapologetic city-bred, West Coast taste in manner and clothes. If in life speech is the most profoundly revelatory of all kinds of human behaviour, in literature it creates such behaviour. In a novel, speech makes the man who is offered up for the reader's evaluation.

What we find in the language of the two American writers is, then, the implied preference for directness over formality, lower-class speech over upper, popular over high culture, American forthrightness over English gentility. The language chosen is a mode of address, a style of self-presentation, and an affirmation of American manliness. Through the medium of written speech both Hammett and Chandler provide clear examples of what Voloshinov has called 'behavioral ideology', that is to say, ideology not as systematized in 'art, ethics, law' but as perceptible in 'the whole aggregate of life experiences and the outward expressions directly connected with it'.[10] . . .

At the same time the refashioning of American literary language was also crucial in the production of a new kind of action writing, an action writing that attempted to go as far as verbally possible in making the reader experience the pace and violence of the events narrated. As I noted earlier, however, the hard-boiled story strains verisimilitude by representing such events as the first-person commentary of a character who is simultaneously involved in the violent action. The reason the hard-boiled writers accepted such a risk was that it was a way of bringing the reader closer to the action as well as of justifying in print the colloquial American voice. The illusion created is of a point of view so close to the action that it is not so much from the ringside as from within the ring itself. A shoot-out scene in a dark apartment from Hammett's 'The Whosis Kid' is typical.

> The Kid, whatever he was up to, made no sound.
> The dark woman began to sob beside me. Throat noises that could guide bullets.
> I lumped her with my eyes and cursed the lot – not aloud, but from the heart.
> My eyes smarted. Moisture filmed them. I blinked it away, losing sight of the watch for precious instants. The butt of my gun was slimy with my hand's sweat. I was thoroughly uncomfortable, inside and out.
> Gunpowder burned at my face.
> A screaming maniac of a woman was crawling all over me.
> My bullet hit nothing lower than the ceiling.
> I flung, maybe kicked, the woman off, and snaked backward. She moaned somewhere to one side. I couldn't see the Kid – couldn't hear him. The watch was visible further away. A rustling.
> The watch vanished.
> I fired at it.
> Two points of light near the door gave out fire and thunder.

> My gun-barrel as close to the floor as I could hold it.
> I fired between those points. Twice.
> Twin flames struck at me again.[11]

Perhaps the most striking feature of the passage is its graphic disposition on the page. It is made up of short sentences that are either isolated as if they were paragraphs or combined in twos and threes to make paragraphs that themselves never exceed roughly three lines. In defiance of the traditional norms of prose fiction, the spaces around words are exploited for the purpose of emphasis. A similar purpose is also served by a syntactical simplicity that takes the form of short declarative sentences, verbless sentences and sentences of isolated words, all of which contribute to suggest the idea of speed and tension. A comparable technique of ellipsis also operates on the semantic level, where the action sequence is narrated as a series of sharp perceptions experienced in the body of a participant observer. A sensation of burning is noted without the report of a gunshot, the destination of the bullet from the Continental Op's gun is recorded, but there is no reference to his having fired it. Finally, there is the characteristic fondness for verbs that connote conflict ('flung', 'kicked', 'snaked backward'), tough colloquialisms ('lumped her', 'maybe kicked') and a reaching for neologisms or metaphors that make sensation new ('filmed' for cover with a film, 'burned at' for burned and 'snaked backward'). . . .

In *The Colloquial Style in America* Richard Bridgman estimates that what he calls 'the process of establishing a literary imitation of colloquial speech and then polishing it' took until the 1920s to complete.[12] Hemingway's first published book, *Three Stories and Poems*, appeared in 1923, six years before Dashiell Hammett's, and in Bridgman's view it was only with Hemingway that a satisfactory synthesis was finally achieved. In deference to American democratic principles, the effect was, in any case, not simply to remove the quotation marks in the texts from non-standard speech. It was also to confer the dignity of print on what sounded like the language of ordinary people.

Richard Bridgman also asserts that 'the motor force of a native style in the United States' was the triple one of 'romantic individualism, nationalistic pride, and practical necessity'.[13] Whether or not these three contributing causes were equally valid in the nineteenth century, it seems certain that in the twentieth a further force was the spirit of populist anti-elitism.

The point to note here is that in order to fulfill such drives, the literary language invented does not have to be American; it has only to sound, or better still, to read like American. And it could achieve this by reading differently from standard British English. In general, as the above passage from Hammett suggests, for a written language to read like American meant choosing concrete words rather than abstract, and colloquial ones rather than their learned equivalents. It also meant preferring the simpler declarative sentences and repetitive rhetorical devices of conversation over the syntactically complex sentences and formal ornament of traditional literary prose. The style alone should suffice to remind the reader that 'the abstract watchwords of a yeoman republic were . . . honesty, manliness, simplicity'.[14] The goal was a written word responsive to the belief still expressed in the 1920s by Sherwood Anderson that the truth lay among 'farmers, working men, business men, painters'.[15] It is on comparable ideological grounds that both Hammett and Chandler find in the tough talk of their private eyes the last refuge of truth in America. . . .

The examples of Hammett and Chandler are a reminder of the bridge that exists in all fiction between style as verbal choice and style as behaviour. As far as the American authors are concerned, the precedent for such first-person narrators, who were both Western loud-mouths and heroic men of action, extends far back into the nineteenth century. In 'Big Bear of Arkansas' Thomas B. Thorpe's backwoodsman, Jim Doggett, is part clown, part hero, whose 'class and condition are reflected in dress, boisterous manners and dialect'.[16] Similarly, in Chandler's novels the texture and tone of the written words create the character of the private eye and not vice versa. Philip Marlowe's spirit of independence is in the language Chandler chooses to express him before it is made explicit through commentary and incident. Chandler's fondness for stylish prose makes his stylish hero. Conversely, what Chandler's novels also reveal is that to equip a sympathetic and popular American hero with a colloquial style was to end up with the quintessentially American stylistic feature of the wisecrack and its figurative equivalent, the ostentatious simile.

Chandler not only constructs fictions that contain a great many arresting one-liners, therefore, he is also influenced by the form of the wisecrack in the construction of paragraphs and chapters as well as in the evocation of character, decor and attitudes. What animates Chandler's narrative at all levels is the stylist's impulse to shape everything he writes in preparation for the delivery of the punch line. Such, for instance, is the case with the opening paragraph of *The Big Sleep* already quoted and with the denouement of the same work. That the arch-criminal turns out in the end to be the perverted baby doll who falls into Marlowe's arms on the fourth page of the novel has about it the swift and unanswerable finality of the best punch lines and, in the context, warrants the sustained darkness of the mood with which the novel ends. Apart from anything else, Chandler's fondness for the form of the detective novel could be explained by a characteristic plot structure which ends with the shock of revelation.

In its own right, the wisecrack is the maxim of the American working classes. As with the maxim of the European aristocratic tradition, the wisecrack combines at its level the quintessence of style with the body of wisdom. Like the maxim it is pointed and elliptical, but unlike the maxim, since its point of view is from the bottom up, it relies for its power on a cynical irreverence often made memorable by the shock of the vernacular. And it was above all Chandler who first realized the expressive possibilities of that most American of oral folk forms and allowed it to influence the structure, style and choice of hero of a novel.

Notes

1 Marx, Karl and Engels, Friedrich (1965) *The German Ideology*, London: Lawrence & Wishart, p. 42.
2 Voloshinov, V.N. (1973) *Marxism and the Philosophy of Language*, New York and London: Seminar Press, pp. 10–14.
3 ibid., p. 23.
4 Bridgman, Richard (1966) *The Colloquial Style in America*, New York: Oxford University Press. See also Poirier, Richard (1966) *A World Elsewhere: The Place of Style in American Literature*, New York: Oxford University Press.
5 Chandler, Raymond (1968) 'The simple art of murder', in James Nelson (ed.) *The Simple Art of Murder*, New York: W.W. Norton, p. 530.
6 Heath, Stephen (1971) *The Nouveau Roman*, London: Elek, p. 208.
7 Christie, Agatha (1961) *The Mysterious Affair at Styles*, New York: Bantam Books, p. 1. Originally published 1926.
8 Hammett, Dashiell (1965) *Red Harvest. The Novels of Dashiell Hammett*, New York: Knopf, p. 3. Originally published 1929.
9 Chandler, Raymond (1971) *The Big Sleep*, New York: Ballantine Books, p. 1. Originally published 1939.
10 Voloshinov, op. cit., p. 91.
11 Marcus, Steven (ed.) (1975) *The Continental Op*, New York: Vintage, pp. 234–5.
12 Bridgman, op. cit., p. 9.
13 ibid., p. 41.
14 ibid., p. 42.
15 Cited in ibid., p. 154.
16 *Regeneration through Violence*, p. 479.

7

Scotland and cinema: the iniquity of the fathers

Colin McArthur

> . . . visiting the iniquity of the fathers upon the children and upon the children's children unto the third and to the fourth generation.
>
> (*Exodus* 34: 7)

The place, Texas; the time, that indeterminate period between the ending of the Civil War and the closing of the frontier which all moviegoers recognize as the span of the Western. The characteristic iconography and narrative form of that genre begin to unfold: dusty terrain and isolated homestead; an attack by Mexican bandits with sombreros slung round their necks; the ride to the rescue by the seven sons of the homestead. But perhaps there is something out of the way about this family; something rarely seen in the Western. One of the retreating bandits says 'I'd rather fight a tribe of Apaches'; the sons of the family are querulous and argue about whisky; one of them is excessively religious; the womenfolk are hospitable to a fault. The homestead's walls are hung with tartan, eighteenth-century pistols and claymores. The older menfolk wear kilts and bonnets and there is even a running gag about thriftiness. The family is, indeed, constructed within an armature of what are popularly, but misleadingly, called *stereotypes* of the Scots but which ought more accurately to be called discursive positions relating to Scotland.

What is most startling of all, however, is that the film is called *Sette pistole per i MacGregor* (Seven Guns for the MacGregors) (1965): it is one of the so-called Spaghetti Westerns cycle of the 1960s and 1970s. An Italo-Spanish co-production, it was written by four Italians, was directed by another and has a cast made up primarily of Italians and Spaniards.

These facts are noted not to sneer at Italian Westerns nor to impugn the legitimacy of one society representing another in its art, but to demonstrate that the mélange of images, characters and motifs constituting Tartanry and Kailyard is not only the framework within which Scots largely construct themselves but is also the grid within which other cultures construct the Scots.

The reasons why Italian cinematic culture in the mid-1960s comes to construct Scotland and the Scots within the categories evident in *Seven Guns for the MacGregors* are complex and, historically, far-reaching. The generative cause was, of course, that massive act of 'symbolic appropriation' in the eighteenth century whereby rationalist, scientific Europe defined its own identity by fashioning the identity of the peoples on its periphery (and those it encountered in colonial conquest) in terms of a set of binary oppositions to the qualities it most celebrated in itself.[1] In true dialectical style, this had the effect of hatching, within Europe, the complex set of identifications with its own constructed alter ego retrospectively described as Romanticism. Within this process, Scotland was ripe, geographically and historically, to become the Romantic domain *par excellence*, which, with the advent of MacPherson's *Ossian* and Sir Walter Scott, duly happened. Thereafter, the causes relate to the appropriation, within Italian Romanticism, of Scott's novels and their widespread adaptation into plays and operas in the nineteenth century; the popular perception of Scotland through travel books and, later, through photographic and fashion magazines; and, not least, Italian access to filmic representations of Scotland and the Scots produced inside the United Kingdom itself and in other cultures. In most of these, the dominant discourses were Tartanry, Kailyard or hybrids of the two. This hybridization of the two discourses is very important. Axiomatically it could be asserted that representations of Scotland and the Scots offer tartan exteriors and Kailyard mores.

From the silent cinema onwards there have been representations of Scotland and the Scots on the screen. . . . With regard only to the narrative fiction film, it is significant that one of the earliest such films was *Bonnie Prince Charlie* (1923), the well-known story of which sounds again the elegiac note of the Ossian cycle. *The Young Lochinvar* (1923) was already articulating for the cinema the discourse which can usefully be called *baronialism* whereby much of the Tartanry dimension of cinema is carried. As well as offering the pictorialism of Scottish scenery, *baronialism* offers a site, the dark Scottish castle, within which certain kinds of specifically 'Scottish' stories – principally hinging on treachery and the betrayal of hospitality – can be played out.

The Kailyard dimension in cinema is carried in the early days by adaptations of the most popular Kailyard novels such as *Beside the Bonnie Brier Bush* (1921) and *The Lilac Sunbonnet* (1922). A concern to define the essential 'Scottishness' of Kailyard should not obscure the extent to which it forms part of the corpus of popular sentimental literature of the late nineteenth and early twentieth century. It is this literature, and the more hard-boiled literature which succeeded it in popular taste in the post-First World War period, which the cinema has consistently fed on and, in return, has nourished. A concern therefore with popular sentimental forms is evident right from the beginnings of cinema (the films of D.W. Griffith provide the best-known examples). The immense popular success of the Kailyard novels in the United Kingdom and the USA ensured that they would rapidly become cinema fodder. This joined with other internationally important sentimental Scottish material of the time (most notably the songs and stage routines of

Harry Lauder) to ensure that 'Scottishness' was signified from very early on in the cinema. Like the novels themselves, the films based on them are primarily machines for producing tears and, to a certain extent, wry laughter. The decline of sentimental forms in popular taste (or their sophistication and toughening in such cinematic genres as the woman's picture) has meant that later versions of cinematic Kailyard have increasingly foregrounded the comic aspects.

The operation of 'classical' Kailyard in the cinema is best exemplified by *The Little Minister* (1934), the last of three film adaptations of Barrie's novel. To emphasize its relatedness to other popular sentimental impulses in early cinema, its tear-producing mechanisms are primarily centred on elderly mothers and children, the two elderly mothers being played by actresses (Mary Gordon and Beryl Mercer) who fulfilled similar roles in other forms – the latter was James Cagney's mother in *The Public Enemy* (1931). Some indication of the emotional register in which *The Little Minister* functions can be got from the playing and the dialogue of Mary Gordon on her imminent removal to the poor house: 'Oh mither, mither, you little thocht when you bore me that I would come to this . . . ' The signifying of 'Scottishness' in *The Little Minister* is conveyed in the marked 'Stage Scots' of most of the players, in the fey quality of the playing, in the dress and decor (baronial in Lord Rintoul's castle, rustic elsewhere) and, very centrally, in the music involving at various times 'Loch Lomond', 'The Campbells are Coming', 'Comin' Thro the Rye', 'The Bluebells of Scotland' and a pastiche Scottish air specially written for the film, 'Scotch Love'. As in the original novel, potentially disruptive elements in the film – the weavers' riot against increased charges for materials, the sending in of the military to quell them, and the ostracizing of the local constable – are either heavily recuperated or rendered comic. To have dealt adequately with these elements the film would have had to crack itself apart, to pull back into history a community that the very form of

The Kailyard tear-machine in *The Little Minister*

Kailyard had rendered history-less.

Pre-war films like *Bonnie Prince Charlie, The Young Lochinvar, Beside the Bonnie Brier Bush* and *The Little Minister* articulated into cinema the discourses of Tartanry and Kailyard, the roots of the former going back to the eighteenth century and those of the latter to the nineteenth century. From these roots the discourses entered various forms and artefacts: poems, novels, operas, paintings, prints, photographs, postcards, short-bread tins and soft furnishings as well as films and, later, television programmes. Since there were simply no alter-native traditions of representation with comparable power, the tendency was for any film dealing with Scotland, or having a Scot as a character, to be pulled strongly towards the armature of images, characters and stories making up Tartanry and Kailyard. Thus it was exploited in several films of the 1930s, both British and American, dealing with Scottish soldiers on the Northwest Frontier of India: *The Drum* (1937), *Gunga Din* (1939), *Wee Willie Winkie* (1937), *Bonnie Scotland* (1935). The armature was flexible enough to include anti-Kailyard elements (much as the novel *The House With the Green Shutters* was written in opposition to, and therefore defined itself within, Kailyard). In this respect the predominantly baronial construction of Scotland in *The 39 Steps* (1935) could include the darkly Calvinist figure of John Laurie's cotter and a post-war film like *The Hasty Heart* (1950), although set in the Far East, could construct its whole *raison d'être* round the archetypal querulousness of the Scot.

In the decade and a half following the Second World War, however, there emerged the remarkable series of representations of Scotland which constitute the definitive modern statements of Tartanry and Kailyard in the cinema. Since the days of Alexander Korda in the 1930s, the Holy Grail which the British film industry had sought (and had failed to find) was penetration of the American market. Its consistent strategy for achieving this was the making of costly costume dramas such as

Katharine Hepburn's fey Scottishness in *The Little Minister*

The Private Life of Henry VIII (1933), *Rembrandt* (1936) and, abortively, *I, Claudius* (1937), under Korda in the 1930s, and the Gainsborough pictures such as *The Wicked Lady* (1945) and *The Man in Grey* (1948) in the 1940s. It was within this strategy that the first of the two major Romantic constructions of Scotland was produced – *Bonnie Prince Charlie* (1948). The second, *Rob Roy: The Highland Rogue* (1953), was a production of the Disney Company, whose sentimental conception of cinema on several occasions found expression in Scottish whimsy (e.g. *Kidnapped* (1960), *Greyfriars Bobby* (1961) and *The Three Lives of Thomasina* (1964)), which, needless to say, allowed free passage to Tartanry and Kailyard. Every frame of these two films recapitulates the visual style of easel-painting representations of the Scotland constructed in the European imagination in the late eighteenth and early nineteenth centuries and the characters and actions relate to the same Ossianic

Tartanry and the picturesque: Richard Todd in *Rob Roy: The Highland Rogue*

tradition: warlike heroes; wan maidens; wise, white-haired patriarchs; blind seers and treacherous enemies. The cinematic apotheosis of this tradition is both articulated and deconstructed in the American film *Brigadoon* (1954). At one level it takes the Romantic representation of Scotland as a given, but at another level – that of the working through of the personal obsession of its director, Vincente Minnelli, with the question of illusion and reality – this representation is revealed as the dream *par excellence*, as a fiction created to escape from the urban horrors of the twentieth century. No British feature film has the progressive force of *Brigadoon* in this regard.

Like *Bonnie Prince Charlie* and *Rob Roy*, the cluster of comedy films which emerged in the late 1940s and in the 1950s, for example *Whisky Galore* (1949), *Laxdale Hall* (1952), *The Maggie* (1953) and *Rockets Galore* (1958), while offering a representation of Scotland and the Scots, were meaningful along another axis, this time a British social axis. Not all of these films emerged from the Ealing studio, but all had about them the 'feel' of the Ealing ethos discernible across a wide range of that studio's films. Central to this was a detestation of modernity as it related to the city and to the power of capital (though the films are by no stretch of the imagination pro-socialist; they are rather pro-feudal) and particularly to the power of central government bureaucracy. Set against these ills, the films construct a set of contrary humane values invested in a range of lovable rural eccentrics and non-conformists.

Their narratives are constructed in terms of the modern world (represented by English soldiers, an American tycoon, English MPs and Glasgow poachers) getting its come-uppance at the hands of the shrewd and canny highland Scots. *The Maggie*, directed by a Scot, Alexander Mackendrick, represents Scotland at its most self-lacerative. Precisely at the moment, the early 1950s, when the massive penetration of American capital into Scotland was gathering pace, *The Maggie* actually sets the two halves of the contradiction – American entrepreneur and Scottish workers – in opposition to each other, but with almost wilful perversity the film has the Scots win hands down. In true Kailyard style, what is not achievable at the level of political struggle is attainable in the delirious Scots imagination. Having given the powerful Americans their come-uppance, there was no stopping the breast-beating Scots. In 1955, with *Geordie*, they showed the world – by having the kilted figure of the title win the hammer event at the 1956 Melbourne Olympics – that, whatever historical processes might be doing to Scotland, it was still (in a phrase

American enterprise and English aspirations outfoxed by canny Scots: *The Maggie* . . .

attributed to Ally Macleod) 'the best wee nation ever God put breath in'.

The objective function of popular cinema is very often to paper over the cracks in the society, to mask contradictions. This has been a particularly urgent task for British cinema in its representations of Scotland as the clear benefits to Scotland of being a junior partner in imperial exploitation give way to the disabilities of being tied to a post-imperial geriatric with undiminished ambition for maintaining great-power status. The ideological manoeuvre whereby this contradiction is masked is most

. . . and *Rockets Galore*

clearly evident in *Rockets Galore* (1958) which, characteristically, reserves its most carefully-mounted scenes for images of the Scots lamenting the putative loss of their island with dignity, and – unlike the actuality of these things – draws back from the brink of evicting the people by giving them the canny ruse of painting some seagulls pink and having the island declared a bird sanctuary. With a nod, a wink and a dram the Scots once more triumph at the level of the imagination while in the real world their country gets pulled out from under them. . . .

There have been a limited number of attempts to make feature-length fiction films representing Scotland and the Scots from a standpoint more appropriate to the twentieth century. . . . It is appropriate that one of these attempts to construct Scotland within a discourse other than Tartanry/Kailyard, *Floodtide* (1949), should have

Looking at the Clyde: Gordon Jackson and Rona Anderson in *Floodtide*

been based on a novel, and co-written, by the harshest Scottish critic of Kailyard, George Blake. In his book, *Barrie and the Kailyard School* (1951) he writes:

> . . . Most people know that modern, workaday Scotland is far from being a paradise for clansmen in kilts, with heather trimmings and stags at eve, as it is from being a pantomime land of comedians, in which haggis, haddocks, bagpipes, whisky and an ill-tempered God affect in their various ways the souls of its pawky inhabitants. The daily newspaper reading of the most self-centred Cockney should have convinced him by now that Scotland is, in its most urgent aspect, a highly industrialized country, a sort of British Ruhr, with a great productivity of 'heavy' goods – coal, ships, steel – square mile upon square mile of slum, 'a passionate public interest in professional football and in the hazards of distant English racecourses, a lot of dog-racing tracks,

and a rapidly decreasing respect for the authority of the
Parish minister. . . .

Almost inevitably, therefore, *Floodtide* seeks to define
the meaning of Scotland in relation to the Clyde. The
impulse behind this was extremely progressive – *Floodtide* opens with a dedication to Clydeside workers – and
it must always be recalled how ordinary Glaswegians
were thrilled at the time of the film's release to see their
own milieu up there on the screen (Imagine! *Barrowland*!), to see aspects of their own lives depicted and to
hear for the first time the cadences of Glasgow speech
coming from the sound system of a public cinema. This
dimension of the film – and it is perhaps the aspect
which wears best – is carried primarily in the figure of
Tim Brogan, played by Jimmy Logan, a popular
Glasgow music hall comic. This image of the Clyde as
the bustling nerve-centre of a modern nation was to
beckon successive generations of Scottish film-makers
with progressive instincts. The problem consistently has
been the ideological framework within which the Clyde
has been perceived – the celebration of its people rather
than the analysis of their situation – and the formal
means of representation, in later decades Griersonian
documentary and in the case of *Floodtide* classical realist
narrative. . . .

Following through the ideological dimension first, the
film opens with an attempt to appropriate the meaning
of the Clyde from one discourse to another, from country to city, from farming to shipbuilding. The opening
frames of the narrative might indeed have come from a
Tartanry/Kailyard film with a cart rolling towards a
rustic cottage set in the hills on the Firth of Clyde. But
very quickly oppositions are set up: the central figure,
David Shields (Gordon Jackson), encouraged by his
uncle who is a foreman in the shipyard, wants to build
ships while his father wants him to remain and farm the
land. The father is associated with all the regressive
discourses George Blake traduces: 'There's been a Shields

in Glentoran since the time of Bonnie Prince Charlie'
and '[the city is] a Sodom and Gomorrah, all noise and
hammers and temptation.' However, the uncle (being a
freemason and therefore adept at ideological manoeuvre)
manages to conflate the apparently incompatible discourses ('The sea's as old as the hills and a good ship's
as wonderful a work of God as a blackface ewe . . . ')
and secure David's move to the Glasgow shipyard.
Although the film does, of course, show shipbuilding as
a socio-economic process, its celebratory tone seeks to
raise Clyde shipbuilding to a mystical level as evidence of
the worth of the men who make the ships. This is done
mainly by the central device by which classical narrative
cinema signifies mystical possession: the look.
Throughout the film there are scenes in which David
stands with a faraway look in his eyes and contemplates
the Clyde, a half-built hull, or a model ship in a glass
case in the Kelvingrove Museum. From time to time also
the shipyard workers are presented in ways reminiscent
of the stakhanovite art of the Soviet Union, primarily
through the framing of the figures. This is particularly
marked in the scene of the final launching.

Progressive though *Floodtide*'s impulses are, its
perspective on the process of shipbuilding is consensualist
– everyone from the Chairman of the company to the
workers on the shopfloor is pulling together for the
greater glory of shipbuilding and the Clyde. The
shallowness of this dimension of the film has been
bitterly exposed by history. In order to function
mystically and consensually, two discourses prevalent in
the actuality of the Clyde had to be evacuated from the
text of the film – the class discourse and the sectarian
discourse. The latter surfaces very briefly in the
disclosure that David's uncle is going to a 'lodge
meeting'. But for the film to have pursued this further
into the structure of power conferred in the yard –
particularly at foreman level – by organized sectarian
allegiance, would have opened fissures which would have
cracked the mystical consensuality apart.

Signalling David's change of class: Gordon Jackson and
Jimmy Logan in *Floodtide*

The discourse of class – and specifically its being set in
motion then being repressed and evacuated – is more
interesting in *Floodtide* and is perhaps best discussed in
the context of the other problematic aspect of the film:
its seeking to be progressive within the framework of
classical realist narrative. The master structure of this
narrative form – stability, disruption, restoration of new
stability – and the attendant features of conflict,
apparent resolution, reversal and final resolution, are
carried both in David's progress from the shopfloor to
the drawing office and in his progress from the girl he
meets at Barrowland to his union with the shipyard
boss's daughter. Both of these movements fit easily
within the form of classical realist narrative as practised
up till that time. However, these developments are so
nakedly class-based that they seriously trouble this ostensibly progressive film, which then has to find ways of

masking their implications. . . . It is in order to clear the decks for David to marry the boss's daughter that the film has to do the greatest violence to the psychological realism of the classical narrative form. In order to re-activate the drama and the reversals demanded by that form, the working-class girl, Judy, having vanished from the action, is reintroduced in order to trouble David's relationship with the boss's daughter. Earlier in the film she had been constructed as a warm-hearted girl who makes the running in the relationship with David but later in the film, to mask the class basis of David's rejection of her, she is constructed as a slatternly virago who goes for the boss's daughter with a broken bottle, in Tim Brogan's phrase 'a right bad yin'. The final ideological leap of *Floodtide* is to contrive a separation between David and the boss's daughter so that they can be reunited, on the day of the launching of the first ship he has designed, on a hill overlooking the Firth. In this final scene the Clyde is made to function in two discourses simultaneously: the Scotland of beautiful hills and lochs and the Scotland of dynamic industrial activity. *Floodtide*, with the best of intentions, deploys inadequate ideological and formal strategies for dealing with the material reality of Scottish industrial life. This is a failure which will be recapitulated when indigenous Scots filmmakers come to grapple with the same problem. . . .

Elsewhere . . . Forsyth Hardy argues spiritedly and lucidly on behalf of the achievement of Films of Scotland, for two decades after its formation in 1955 the almost exclusive channel through which indigenous Scottish film production flowed and the determining structure on the practice of several generations of Scottish filmmakers.[2] The conjuncture within which Films of Scotland emerged is spelled out by Forsyth Hardy: the key elements being the withdrawal of government money for civil service-based film production in Scotland; the presence of a well-connected and energetic ex-civil servant (Hardy himself) whose own cultural formation was strongly determined by Griersonian documentary;

Boss's daughter confronts Barrowland girl in *Floodtide*: Elizabeth Sellars, Jimmy Logan and Rona Anderson

and the entrée to commercial cinema screens facilitated by Sir Alexander King, the Chairman of Films of Scotland. There is no reason whatsoever to dissent from Forsyth Hardy's conclusion that Films of Scotland's remit 'to project the life and achievement of Scotland' was reasonably carried out over the twenty years and one hundred and fifty films of his tenure as Director, and indeed in the years succeeding. However, if the argument proceeds from different premises Films of Scotland can be shown to have given, in many of its films, new and monstrous life to the regressive discourses of Tartanry and Kailyard; to have encouraged alternatives to these discourses which were politically inappropriate; and, by its hegemony in Scottish film production, to have pre-empted the emergence of alternative production structures which might have dealt more adequately with Scottish history, politics and contemporary life. . . .

The evidence on which judgements can be made (virtually the total output of Films of Scotland) is to be found in the Scottish Central Film Library in Glasgow. . . . Given the awesome power and international omnipresence of Tartanry and Kailyard, it is scarcely surprising that much of the output of Films of Scotland should be deeply marked by them. Put another way, the hegemonic discourses about Scotland within which Scots, including Scottish film-makers, are interpellated, are set in place as social actors, provide a severely limited set of representations of the country and its people. It is not an issue of the talent or lack of it of Scottish film-makers; pound for pound they are no better or worse than those of any other country. But they have two particular disabilities: the dominant filmic representations of their country have been articulated elsewhere, and the indigenous Scottish institutions which exist to foster film culture have never articulated as a priority the helping of Scottish film-makers towards the discourses which would effectively counter the dominant ones. . . .

It comes as no surprise, therefore, to find the Tartan Monster (the phrase is Tom Nairn's) stalking the pages of the Films of Scotland catalogue. Some of the very titles chill the spine: *A Song for Prince Charlie* (1958); *By Lochaber I Will Go* (1960); *Edinburgh Tattoo* (1972); *The Black Watch* (1971); *Come Away In* (1974); *The Tartans of Scotland* (1966); *Cock O' The North* (1972); *A Touch of Scotland* (1964). These and many more give free passage to, take absolutely no critical distance from, Tartanry and Kailyard.

From among these films it would be possible to construct, Frankenstein monster-like, the Ur-Tartan Documentary. It would open, accompanied by a clarsach or plaintive Scottish violin tune, on a panorama of lochs and bens, preferably in autumn since the lament is the dominant tone of the form. Against this Landseerian background (the more gross versions actually include a kilted and claymored highlander) the commentary begins to unfold. The choice of narrator is crucial: the voice must call up the cluster of motifs characteristic of the genre: beauty, sadness, dignity, loss. Such a voice is that of Duncan Macintyre, a frequent narrator of Films of Scotland productions, with a voice reminiscent of the late Duncan Macrae in one of his highland roles. The visual, verbal and musical rhetorics are sustained throughout with a frequent closure on a loch at sunset (one notorious film closes with clinking glasses of a Scottish liqueur held, in be-laced hands, against the sky). The following extracts from the actual commentaries of such films indicate both the subject matter and tone of the genre: 'in the dance Scottish soldiers find a way of expressing their joy and pride in their calling and their country'; 'in Skye the past has a habit of coming alive now'; '[the battlefield of Culloden] moves the Scottish heart today as much as it did Rabbie Burns'; 'Honour the name of it: drink to the fame of it – the tartan!'; 'the honour, the glory, and the romance of the Scots'; 'love of his native land and its romantic tradition'; 'with a kind of inward joy he looked on the Eildon Hills. He had indeed come home'; '[on] that battleground of dreadful memory . . . the sorrow of defeat is here recorded'; '[the statue of Flora Macdonald] searching in vain for the lost Jacobite cause'; 'here, on the edge of the Atlantic, everything seems to stand still'; 'Soon more clansmen came; a trickle, a tumble, a cataract'; 'Scottish hearts were high as the young prince marched through the Lowlands'; 'the River Esk ran with blood and the English soldiers scattered like sheep'.

Dire as this dimension of its output is, Films of Scotland is not monolithic. Other discourses about Scotland are evident. Indeed, as Forsyth Hardy makes clear, both he and Grierson were extremely critical of Tartanry/Kailyard and throughout their careers sought to create representations of Scotland and the Scots more in keeping with the contemporary world. The discourse which emerged from this impulse constructed Scotland as a bustling, thrusting, modern industrial nation and its people, rural as well as urban, not as hopeless dreamers crying into their whisky over the failure of the '45, but as strong, practical souls drawing strength from the land and from the past, but more than able to cope with the affairs of the modern world. . . .

This 'Scotland on the Move' discourse first emerged in the brief Films of Scotland venture of 1938 which Forsyth Hardy describes. It can be illustrated with reference to *They Made the Land* (1938). Although the film is about Scotland, its stylistic points of reference are the British documentary films of the 1930s and the Soviet cinema of the 1920s. It is frankly instructional, concerned with the details of processes such as draining peat bogs; but in common with British documentary films of the time, it displays its interest in 'poetry' in the rhetoric of its images and its commentary. When the narration refers to the 'strong, handsome women' who helped work the land, the camera frames them from below and against the sky in the manner of Soviet cinema. Similarly, the clipped, Anglicized commentary – there were no Scottish production units operating in this form of cinema in the 1930s – refers to Scottish trees having 'strong roots defying the tempest' and frequently deploys the rhetorical trope of repetition which sets it apart from the more literal forms of documentary: 'the wind blew over the crops in the new-laid fields . . . the wind blew over the crops and knocked them down. . . . ' With the re-emergence of Films of Scotland in 1955, this 'Scotland on the Move' discourse loomed very large indeed and is to be found in many of the titles in the Films of Scotland catalogue: e.g. *The Tay Road Bridge* (1967); *From Glasgow Green to Bendigo* (1958) – about Templeton's carpets; *Livingston: A Town for the Lothians* (1970); *County on the Move* (1960); *Cumbernauld: Town for Tomorrow* (1971); and *Seawards The Great Ships* (1959).

It was this discourse which received Grierson's personal imprimatur (he wrote the treatments for several of the films constructed within it) and which attracted some of the most talented of the indigenous Scottish film-makers.

It is convenient to discuss the modern version of this discourse in relation to the work of two such film-makers, Laurence Henson and Eddie McConnell, because their work demonstrates both its possibilities and also its limitations. . . . In many respects the work of Henson and McConnell is the apotheosis of Griersonianism with its bringing 'beauty' to bear on socio-economic processes. Introducing one of their films on television, Grierson said: 'documentary suggests public reports and social problems. I see it as a visual art which can convey a sense of beauty above the ordinary world.' *Heart of Scotland* moves across the Carse of Stirling and seeks to weld together elements as disparate as the battlefield of Bannockburn and the oil refinery at Grangemouth. It achieves this through a rhetoric of poeticization and abstraction which is carried in the rich visual style, the 'literary' commentary and the modern, abstract music. The continuity it seeks to make between the past and the present is essentially a mystical one of strength passing from the land to the people and to modern, industrial processes. The achievements of this discourse – particularly in the hands of Henson and McConnell – are evident enough: great pictorial beauty and a sense of social continuity and unity. Its principal limitation is equally evident: a failure to accommodate analysis and contradiction. . . .

Tartanry/Kailyard and 'Scotland on the Move' in Films of Scotland films operate relatively independently of each other with occasional transitions from one to another in particular films – 'We are a people with traditions, but . . . ' While most Scots can see right through the empty posturings of Tartanry and Kailyard, the absence of a tough, popularly-based and analytic cinematic tradition has meant that the 'Scotland on the Move' discourse has largely filled the vacuum, especially for the left. However, at its most pernicious . . . it simply replaces the older discourses as the cue which sets the tartan snake uncoiling in the stomach.

This essay has argued that the discourses within which Scotland and the Scots have been represented in films have been wholly inadequate for dealing with the historical and contemporary reality of Scotland. Some of these filmic discourses – for example the Tartanry of *Bonnie Prince Charlie* or *Rob Roy: The Highland Rogue* and the Kailyardry of *The Little Minister* or *Whisky Galore* – Scots film-makers have been powerless to oppose, since they were deployed within production structures fashioned outside Scotland. Nevertheless, they had a pernicious two-fold effect. On the one hand, they defined the cinematic terrain within which several generations of Scots actors could function, setting a limited range of roles and foregrounding particular modes of acting. This has had a cruelly stunting effect on Scots actors which, in terms of the growth of individual talents, could only be remedied by working outside Scotland and within different, non-Scottish discourses. The second pernicious effect of the dominance of Tartanry/Kailyard is that, when indigenous Scots film-makers came to make their own films, these powerful existing traditions of representation beckoned them Circe-like and lured more than a few onto the rocks. However, even when indigenous Scots film-makers were able to produce a discourse which sloughed off Tartanry/Kailyard and attempted to come to grips with the reality of contemporary Scotland – as was the case with the adaptation of the Griersonian impulse, the 'Scotland on the Move' discourse, it allowed talents to develop and produced formally attractive works, but proved hopelessly inadequate for dealing both with the meaning of Scottish history and the complex socio-political condition of contemporary Scotland. . . .

Notes

1 See Chapman, M. (1978) *The Gaelic Vision in Scottish Culture*, London.
2 'An interview with Forsyth Hardy', in Colin McArthur (ed.) (1982) *Scotch Reels. Scotland in Cinema and Television*, London: British Film Institute.

8

Representing the nation

Graeme Turner

. . . In contemporary theory nationalism is most often seen critically. Its consensual function enables it to obscure differences and divisions that may well need to be recognized and addressed, and its power to establish the overriding priorities for the culture has extensive possibilities. As Patrick Wright points out, the 'nation' acts within the culture as a 'ground for the proliferation of other definitions of what is normal, appropriate or possible'.[1] If the maintenance of hegemony depends upon the winning of assent and upon the regular mobilization of consensus, then the idea of the nation is an important medium though which this consensus can be drafted. The idea of the nation is thus a target of Marxist critiques of culture which emphasize the political nature and effects of the construction of national identity.[2] Within such constructions, it is argued, minorities are marginalized; and divisions or conflicts within society are minimized in deference to the overriding, accepted priorities of the nation which unite the people. As the national character is valorized, the discourses of nationalism therefore tend to become areas occupied by those interests seeking to centre themselves within the culture. . . .

In Australia, the discourses of nationalism are drawn almost exclusively from the mythologized past, specifically the radical past – the time when Australia was represented as the 'social laboratory of the world', its commitment to democracy manifest in the secret ballot and in votes for women, and its essential character being seen to reside in the organic, egalitarian society of the bush communities.[3] That the myth of Australia's radicalism and egalitarianism can survive the contradictions of one's everyday experience reveals how effectively it has been mythologized. The representations of the past in film, fiction, fine art and television tend to propose a continuity between nineteenth-century Australia and the present that is unquestioned despite its inconsistency with aspects of contemporary life. The relationship is narrativized as a story which reaches its end in the present. The typical depiction of the authentic Australian in the past is that of the common man of authentic values, who is constantly oppressed and victimized by British imperialism or by authority generally. Both the romanticizing of the figure of the bushranger or the mythologizing of the democratic spirit of Eureka are examples of this. And the net effect of such a representation of the national character in the past is to declare that the struggles depicted as necessary for that character need not be continued into the present; that, for us, the struggle is over; and that the battles fought for Australia in the past have borne fruit in the conditions which we now enjoy. . . . The representation of Australia's radical and formative past, then, is not only available to the left-wing radicals who might see themselves as the inheritors of the tradition, but also to more conservative elements within the culture who would see this version of the past as justifying the present. Indeed, representations of the past seem, in film for instance, especially acceptable to the establishment critics and other guardians of culture – and certainly the eulogizing of the past is for them preferable to the treatment of the present.

The key issue in talking about the role and nature of the presence of nationalism in Australian narrative is thus not so much the range of meanings made available but the fact of the dominance of one set of terms, one body of myth or discourse, as the accepted mode of *representation* of the meaning of the nation. . . .

Australian cinema is no exception to the rule. John Tulloch has more than adequately charted the treatment of the bush legend in the early film industry in Australia, and he has also indicated the ways in which this cinematic treatment drew on the literary sources and put the myth to hegemonic use.[4] . . .

In more recent times, we have seen a spate of nationalistic films emerging from the industry. The nationalism is now more sophisticated than the kind involved in the films identified with Chips Rafferty, or in those films which attempt to make populist tales of country life in the 1950s (films which were formally different, but equally naive) such as Cecil Holmes's *Three in One* (1957) and Anthony Kimmins's *Smiley* (1956). Nevertheless, the construction of Australian-ness through reference to these earlier representations is no less common. Russell Boyd has talked of using Tom Roberts as a guide to getting 'the light of the Australian countryside' in *Picnic at Hanging Rock*, and sees the achievement of this as a 'coming of age'; Gill Armstrong used Roberts and McCubbin in the design of *My Brilliant Career*, and the influence of Roberts's shearing paintings is clear in both *The Chant of Jimmie Blacksmith* and *Sunday Too Far Away*.[5] These may not be seen as nationalist films; but such works as *Breaker Morant, Gallipoli, The Man From Snowy River*, or *Phar Lap* certainly demand to be seen as nationalist texts, the mode of their nationalism – again – that of the 1890s. This has been recognized: one reviewer describes *Breaker Morant* as nationalist to the point of 'jingoism'; *Gallipoli* advertised itself as the film which will make you 'proud to be Australian'; and Banjo Paterson's powerful celebration of the Australian virtues, the poem of 'The Man From Snowy River' becomes, in Max Harris's phrase, the 'logo' of the film.[6] In particular, the Lawson-Furphy brand of nationalism in fiction includes not only a set of definitions of Australian cultural identity, but also a major strategy for measuring that identity against the English, and valorizing those aspects of our national character which depart from English values and loyalties.[7] And the two 'war' films, *Breaker Morant* and *Gallipoli*, make direct use of this strategy.

In *Breaker Morant* the execution of Morant and Handcock is seen as a racist act; the features which define the characters as Australian (Morant is seen as Australian, despite his birthplace, and the three central characters encapsulate the various positive formations of the Australian – the larrikin, the worldly misfit from Europe, and the innocent) are precisely those which incite the British to destroy them. They are represented to us as individualist, independent, resistant to authority and determinedly iconoclastic. British and Australian values are directly contrasted through the most unequivocal of structures – the courtroom drama. The conventional roles of the innocent and the guilty, the gaoler and the convict, are neatly and characteristically inverted so that the Australian convicts are seen, yet again, as honest and courageous while their English persecutors are treacherous and cowardly. The simplicity of the equation sits awkwardly with the film's considerable moral ambiguity, but, true to the tradition of the battler, the audience's identification with the Australians develops in proportion to the film's establishment of their position as underdogs, outmanoeuvred by the system.

The English in *Gallipoli*, while contained within a less unequivocally nationalist narrative context, are equally stereotyped – monocled and parading on camels when they are not sending our boys into the battle zones to provide cover for their own troops. Peter Weir represents the English in Egypt with the crude nationalism of an 1890s *Bulletin* cartoon, and while this is not central to the film's purpose it is an important moment for the film's relationship with its audience because it proffers an invitation for them to indulge their preference for the

Australians by finding the English ridiculous. The anti-English attitude modulates easily, as it does in our history, into a general suspicion of authority. In both films, the paradigm of authority – bureaucratic force aligned against human vulnerability – is English. The Australian versions of authority tend to tacitly condone the larrikin, independent and undisciplined behaviour of the troops; the Breaker allows his subordinates to address him as Harry and is the 'acceptable' version of authority who participates in his troops 'unmilitary' but understandable revenge on the Boers, while in *Gallipoli* Australian officers incite the riot that disrupts the mock battle in training. The avuncular Major Barton . . . actually renounces his authority in the suicidal last attack; and declaring that he will not ask his men to do anything he would not do himself, he dies with them. So that the only recommended authority is, paradoxically, an egalitarian one.

The basis for the social structure assumed under this egalitarian principle is mateship. The bond between Morant and Handcock is an obvious example of the automatic 'me, too' mateship. As they are marched off to their execution Morant and Handcock are asked if they have a religion. Morant replies that he is a 'pagan'; Handcock asks him what that is, and the answer – that a pagan is someone who does not believe in a Divine being who controls all – satisfies him. 'I'm a pagan, too', then says Handcock; and it is the separation of their values from the civilized and effete values of the English (not their paganism) that is once more celebrated. *Breaker Morant*, however, unlike *Gallipoli*, is capable of at least intimating the existence of a more radical and political bond between men than that of nationality or mateship. Despite Stephen Crofts's claim to the contrary, the film does suggest that the Australian soldiers are lackeys to an imperialist power whose interests are intrinsically opposed to theirs.[8] Morant's suggestion that they are fighting on the wrong side – against 'farmers' like themselves – is a critique of the system itself. To see a greater brotherhood between the Boers and the Australians than between the Australians and the English is to go beyond nationalism to a more political understanding of the social structure, and it is a perception that *Gallipoli*, in contrast, is unable to reproduce in its depiction of the classless Australians and their upper-class English officers.

In both *Gallipoli* and *Breaker Morant* the nationalism is sufficiently woven into the narrative to make it a good point for reviewers to retrieve and display. In *The Man From Snowy River* the nationalism is so pronounced that it produces a backlash. Probably the most nationalistic film that has been produced since the beginning of the 1970s revival, *Snowy River* was, ironically, attacked for selling out to American values. Unlike *Gallipoli* and *Breaker Morant*, it is unashamedly populist; it selected an American star to play not one but two Australians; and, stylistically, it flies in the face of the critical preferences current in the Australian film culture. *The Man From Snowy River* is all plot, it seems, developing at a breakneck pace and with ruthless economy in a style more reminiscent of the golden years of Hollywood than the Australian 'renaissance'. It is enthusiastically romantic – and since the romantic fiction of the nineteenth century, and the ballads of Paterson and Gordon, romance does tend to have disappeared from Australian narrative traditions. Despite its debts to Hollywood, the film is constructed, as Tom O'Regan has pointed out,[9] in order to appeal to as wide a section of the Australian population as possible; and it deliberately uses the specific terms of Australian nationalist myths in order to set up an alternative tradition of frontier romance, an Australian genre that is different in meaning to the American Western. This particular meaning of the film has been approached from a number of positions: Jack Clancy has described it as an allegory of cultural independence from the twin threats of English and American imperialism,[10] but since it is still so frequently seen as a 'sellout' of Australian values, it is worth outlining why in my view *Snowy River* is such a vividly nationalist film.

Unlike the two films discussed so far, the version of Australian identity articulated in *Snowy River* is not dependent upon a comparison with England; apparently the makers were confident enough of their idea to concentrate on the Australian's relationship with his own land. That confidence is clearly evident in the visuals; the camera is exuberantly active, swooping and soaring among the mountain scenery in a celebration of the landscape that is brash and naive. The harshness and indomitability of the landscape, so clearly caught by Russell Boyd's blinding vistas of reflected light in *Gallipoli*, is here presented simply by its scale – the screen is packed with busy horizons, shot from cranes and helicopters. The result is a vision of a land that is awesome but not unimaginable, inspiring affection and a qualified optimism as befits the romantic form.

Although the film carries the same keynotes of mateship, of egalitarianism and of the bush ethos which we find in Paterson's poem, it is in the depiction of the relationship with the land that it is most faithful to the poem and the most nationalistic. The land is tough, dangerous and beautiful. Jessica sees this when she is trapped on the cliff in the storm: 'It changes so fast,' she says; 'one minute it's Paradise, the next it's trying to kill you.' Accommodation within this murderous Paradise is the goal which the hero, Jim Craig, pursues. His acceptance of the challenge that the landscape presents differentiates him from the squatters in the valley below, while his affinity with the bush horses invests his quest with hope by connecting him with the film's strongest metaphor for the spirit of the land. Jim and Jessica meet through a staged demonstration of his familiarity with horses (he teaches her a rope trick that the villainous station horse breaker, Curly, spends the rest of the film trying to master) and he reaches what the film defines as manhood by matching the bush horses on their own terrain. His respect for the 'colt from Old Regret' is the clearest example of his harmony with the Australian version of nature, and it is important that he trains the horse by 'gentling it' rather than by dominating it.

This is the thematic substance of the film and it is central to the nationalist myth and the ideology of the invented Australian; ours is not, like the American, a myth of the imposition of the individual on the land – of the politics of conquest; ours is a myth of accommodation and acceptance which admits the impossibility of conquering the land and merely recommends a manner of survival by learning to live in partnership with it. In what it means to be a 'man' in *Snowy River*, we have an Australian transformation of the individualistic ethic of the American Western; in this country the 'man' is not the toughest one, but the one who can accept and live with the priorities of the land. Jim's success is rewarded with the love of Jessica, whose family background typifies the range of alternatives that Jim rejects – the values and ways of the city and an exploitative attitude to the land. Jessica, too, rejects these – as the daughter of 'Matilda' she is anything but the archetypal civilizing female. Through their union the film offers us a conventional romantic resolution, but also a paradigm of existence in harmony with the land justifying the nostalgic sense of acceptance which also underlies Paterson's poem.

Admittedly, *The Man From Snowy River* is atypical of nationalist films for a number of reasons. First, its camp, even witty, awareness of its own myth-making activity separates it off from the myth itself. This enables the representation of Clancy of the Overflow, for example, to be perceived as a work of romantic invention in which the audience is asked to collaborate. Importantly, *Snowy River* is received as fiction as well as history. Second, the film also uses its romantic form to present an optimistic and positive image of Australian existence. It is not necessary to 'win' as much as Jim Craig does in order to produce a satisfying articulation of Australian-ness. Indeed, in the follow-up film, *Phar Lap*, the doomed horse with the oversized heart becomes the type of the

Aussie battler whose very talent results in his death. The film begins with that death, so that it eliminates expectations of transcendence immediately; and only afterwards do Phar Lap's battles against the predictably upperclass, Anglocentric and clubbish racing officials follow. Again, the process of definition is one of establishing differences between Australian and foreign values. *Phar Lap* represents its 'hero' as the victim of the struggle between, on the one hand, the Australian turf officials with their need to protect their privileged structure from infiltration and, on the other, the commercial imperatives of the American owner. Like Australia, Phar Lap is the subject of colonization by European civilized values and American capitalism. Phar Lap is the champion of the working man in the film (although the 'class struggle' is implicitly depicted as free enterprise versus monopoly rather than labour against capital) but his death is not a triumphant one. Despite his defiant victory in the Melbourne Cup, his death is made, by the very structure of the narrative, inevitable.

As *Phar Lap* reveals, the nationalist discourse can be much more than just egalitarian; it can also naturalize certain proletarian values, whereby the authenticity of a working-class, unsophisticated way of life is preferred to those civilized values which are seen to be both the regrettable objectives of the Australian ruling class and the hallmarks of foreign (particularly British) domination. . . .

If nationalist constructions do support existing social and economic conditions – by naturalizing and romanticizing the battler, for instance, in order to disconnect the figure from a class position – this is not necessarily *all* that they do. Indeed, the case of *Snowy River* suggests that genuinely populist films – even nationalist ones – seem to have subversive potential. The notion of 'popularity' is open to several constructions; one can see it simply in terms of large-scale commercial success, while another can see it as a resistant, subversive expression of the needs of a subordinated class.[11] Popular art, in this second formulation, is a rejection of the dominant bourgeois ideology, and such a view of the popular could explain some of the critical response to *Snowy River*. Certainly there seems to be a class motivation behind the critical reaction in the press, since its box-office success is in inverse proportion to its critical evaluation. . . . Like the ocker comedies, *Snowy River* attacks the dominant notions underlying the 'Australian film' (what Susan Dermody calls the AFI genre, typified by *Picnic* and *My Brilliant Career*).[12] Thus it is culturally important in that it establishes a connection between commercial success and a successful rejection of those pretensions towards high art which enclose most depictions of the Australian type. . . .

Thus the meanings carried by nationalist discourse are not simple or self-evident. Certainly, the function of nationalism in a 'quality' film and the exploitation of it in a 'soap opera' is affected by the form: in the quality film, the high art, universalizing codes effectively cloak the political dimension of nationalism, by enabling the essentially egalitarian or proletarian myths to be connected with their opposite, the universalizing and civilizing notions of value. And so the discourses of nationalism are made acceptable. But this does not apply where the populist form articulates the mythic content in a different fashion. Even if one does not see populist art in Brechtian ways – as ultimately revolutionary – but (as Stuart Hall does) as a site of constant struggle between the dominant trying to contain the subordinate, and the subordinate attempting to resist this containment,[13] *Snowy River* does seem to resist containment sufficiently to alarm part of our film culture. One is tempted to examine *Snowy River* for oppositional content, for the ways in which it subverts hegemonic constructions of property or progress, in order to account for the response. But even without doing this, the conservative reaction to the film suggests that although nationalism does normally serve an hegemonic function, its articulation through popular representational forms provides it with the potential for recovering class divisions and for challenging the dominant points of view of the culture. . . .

Notes

1 Wright, Patrick (1984) 'A blue plaque for the Labour Movement? Some political meanings of the national past', in *Formations of Nation and People*, London: Routledge & Kegan Paul.
2 Exemplary would be the account of ideology and hegemony given in Hall, Stuart (1982) 'The rediscovery of ideology: the return of the repressed in media studies', in Michael Gurevitch *et al.* (eds) *Culture, Society and the Media*, London: Methuen, pp. 56–90.
3 The central example of this approach is Phillips, A.A. (1958) *The Australian Tradition*, Melbourne: Longman Cheshire.
4 Tulloch, John (1981) *Legends on the Screen: The Narrative Film in Australia 1919–29*, Sydney: Currency Press.
5 See *Cinema Papers* 10; centrefold; *Cinema Papers* 15: 249; Matthews, Sue, *35 MM Dreams*, p. 141.
6 Clancy, Jack (1981) *'Breaker Morant'*, *Cinema Papers* 28 (August–September): 283; Harris, Max (1982) 'Banjo would have hated it', *Weekend Australian Magazine* 27 March: 7.
7 Wilkes, G.A. (1981) *The Stockyard and the Croquet Lawn: Literary Evidence for Australia's Cultural Development*, Melbourne: Edward Arnold.
8 Crofts, Stephen (1980–1) *'Breaker Morant* rethought: eighty years on the culture still cringes', *Cinema Papers* 30 (December–January): 420–1.
9 O'Regan, Tom (1982) 'Ride the high country: in and around *The Man From Snowy River*', *Filmnews* (September).
10 Clancy, Jack (1983) 'Parents and orphans', *Cinema Papers* 42 (March): 50–2.
11 See O'Sullivan, Tim, *et al.* (1983) *Key Concepts in Communication*, London: Methuen, pp. 174–6.
12 With Elizabeth Jacka in *Screening Australia* (forthcoming).
13 Hall, Stuart (1981) 'Notes on deconstructing the popular' in Raphael Samuel (ed.) *People's History and Socialist Theory*, London: Routledge & Kegan Paul.

Section 3

Pleasure, gender, sexuality: feminist reappraisals

Introduction

Toward the end of *Loving with a Vengeance* Tania Modleski takes issue with accounts which attribute the popularity of such genres as romance and soap opera to 'the successful conspiracy of a group of patriarchal capitalists plotting to keep women so happy at home that they remain unwilling to make demands which would greatly restructure the workplace and the family'.[1] Her purpose in doing so, however, is not to establish a canon of 'feminine genres' which, in appealing primarily to women, might also be regarded as affording their readers pleasures which, from a feminist perspective, should be unambiguously and positively valued. Rather, it is to insist that analysis must come to terms with the nature of those pleasures, which, in turn, entails taking account of their often complex and contradictory properties. This means, on the one hand, recognizing that to categorize and deplore a text as patriarchal does not displace the pleasures it produces, and sometimes goes on producing – even for women – after it has been so named. But it also means recognizing that the effects of patriarchy are not limitless and that, even within texts whose governing properties are properly described as patriarchal, there are contradictory tendencies at work so that, in the 'rub' between these, conflicting pleasures may be produced as the reader's inscription in the text oscillates – caught in a dialectic of collusion with and subversion of patriarchal conceptions of the feminine. And even where this is not the case, Modleski argues, the uses to which romance and soap operas are put and the parts they play in, and in relation to, women's daily lives may well mean that pleasures are invested in their consumption which a feminist criticism, if it is not to be politically misdirected, should excavate and analyse.

In these respects, *Loving with a Vengeance* represents what has become, since the late 1970s, a recognizably distinct and increasingly significant tendency in feminist criticism. Alert to contradictions within both the textual mechanisms which organize reading practices as well as the cultural technologies which regulate how texts are deployed and used within social relations of specific kinds, this tendency is perhaps most distinctively characterized by its distrust of generalizing theoretical formulations which have the effect of placing specific regions of cultural production and consumption beyond the reach – because viewed entirely negatively – of effective political intervention. Teresa de Lauretis succinctly summarizes this orientation when she argues the need, in relation to the concerns of feminist film theory:

> to oppose the simply totalizing closure of final statements (cinema is pornographic, cinema is voyeuristic, cinema is the imaginary, the dream-machine in Plato's cave, and so on); to seek out contradictions, heterogeneity, ruptures in the fabric of representation so thinly stretched – if powerful – to contain excess, division, difference, resistance; to open up critical spaces in the seamless narrative space constructed by dominant cinema *and* by dominant discourse (psychoanalysis, certainly, but also the discourse on technology as autonomous instance, or the notion of a total manipulation of the public sphere, the exploitation of cinema, by purely economic interests); finally, to displace those discourses that obliterate the claim of other social instances and erase the agency of practice in history.[2]

Clearly there are similarities between this shift of

emphasis in feminist studies of popular fiction and the tendency, over the same period, for Marxist critics to move away from the view of popular fiction as simply a vehicle for the imposition of dominant ideologies on the members of subordinate classes and to insist, rather, on a more complex intrication of the relations between pleasure and ideology within both the internal organization of popular fictional texts and the circumstances of their consumption. Indeed, these two tendencies have both fed off and informed one another and, in the case of socialist feminist criticism, have been combined in studies concerned to examine the complexly interacting ways in which popular fictions function in relation to both class and gender relations. None the less, the tendency has been more pronounced in feminist criticism where the forms of reappraisal to which it has led have often been quite radical in their implications.

While this has been true across the full range of popular fictions, it is within the study of cinema that earlier positions have been most thoroughgoingly re-examined. In the early 1970s, feminist film theory, strongly influenced by the mixture of linguistics and psychoanalysis associated with the work of Christian Metz, had been prone to the 'totalizing closure of final statements' de Lauretis refers to above in its tendency to view the cinema as such, and therefore all the pleasures produced within it, as male-centred. Laura Mulvey provided one of the more influential statements of this position in her article 'Visual pleasure and narrative cinema'. Examining the articulation of looks within the classic narrative film of Hollywood, Mulvey argued that the relations between these – that is, the look of the camera, the look of the spectator and the looks of the characters – operated so as to inscribe the spectator in a position of voyeuristic dominance in relation to woman as the primary, and sexualized, object of the cinematic gaze. Thus, no matter what the content of any individual film, the subordination of women is ensured by the very organization of the primary cinematic spectacle: the reduction of woman to connoting the quality of 'to-be-looked-atness' in relation to the male-centred look of the camera and, thereby, of the spectator also. 'Women, whose image has continually been stolen and used for this end,' Mulvey thus concluded, 'cannot view the decline of the traditional film form with anything much more than sentimental regret.'[3]

In 'Afterthoughts on "Visual pleasure and narrative cinema" inspired by *Duel in the Sun*', the first essay collected here, Mulvey reconsiders her earlier arguments. However, she seeks less to jettison than to qualify them by considering whether the patterning of the spectator's desire and pleasure may be more complex and ambiguous – especially for the female spectator – in films where a female character occupies the centre of the narrative. Thus, in the case of King Vidor's *Duel in the Sun* (1946), she argues that the central character, Pearl, caught between her conflicting desire for two male characters – one of whom beckons her into a life of social respectability and to an appropriately passive form of female sexuality and femininity, while the other calls her to a life outside the law and, related to this, a tomboyish, but active and independent sexuality – reactivates in the female spectator 'a phantasy of "action" that correct femininity demands should be repressed' (p. 150). While this phantasy of action is indeed ultimately repressed through the film's narrative resolution (Pearl's death), Mulvey's analysis suggests that, on the way, dormant patterns of female desire, ones resistant to the powers of patriarchy, are '"pleasured" in stories of this kind' (p. 150).

While this reading is suggestive in itself, the more significant aspect of Mulvey's article consists in her treatment of Pearl's position as a metaphor for the position of the female spectator in the cinema, whose pleasure, she argues, may be more complex and deeply rooted than her earlier article had allowed to the degree that identification with the active and controlling male gaze of the camera confers illusions of power and activity reminiscent of a repressed phase of desire. The masculinization of the pleasures of looking within the cinema may thus, Mulvey concludes, offer the female spectator a specific kind of pleasure, albeit one that 'is always to some extent at cross purposes with itself, restless in its transvestite clothes' (p. 151).

Clearly, Mulvey is not concerned to redeem mainstream Hollywood cinema by identifying 'positive' attributes which might offset its 'negative' ones. Her analysis goes beyond any such simple additive approach to the relations between pleasure and ideology in its concern, rather, to identify the contradictory spaces for pleasure which patriarchal texts must put into play in order to police the boundaries of gender and sexuality. Jane Placey has a similar purpose in view in her reappraisal of *film noir*, a genre which, at the level of its narrative formula, is deeply misogynist as, in common with many other genres of popular fiction but more explicitly than most, the narrative works to remove the threat – through death or immolation – of the dominant, sexually aggressive woman. As does Mulvey, however, Placey insists on the need for methods of analysis which do not reduce films, or their pleasures, to the moments of their narrative resolution. Focusing, instead, on the distinctive visual style of *film noir* she argues that it often overwhelms the narrative with consequences which sometimes contradict its central tendencies:

> Visually, *film noir* is fluid, sensual, extraordinarily expressive, making the sexually expressive woman, which is its dominant image of woman, extremely powerful. It is not their inevitable demise we remember but rather their strong, dangerous, and above all, exciting sexuality. (p. 153)

Annette Kuhn's work has always exhibited a strong sense of the need to locate the study of cinema within a broader cultural context, paying attention both to the more widely distributed cultural meanings which film texts play on and activate as well as to the differing social contexts in which film texts are viewed.[4] It is thus characteristic that her essay 'Sexual disguise and cinema', an investigation of the significance of crossdressing films – those which, 'as a central element of the plot, involve at least one character who assumes the conventional clothing of the opposite sex' (p. 174), should begin with an inquiry into the cultural meanings associated with crossdressing as a performance code capable of being used on the stage and in everyday life as well as on the screen. In posing the possibility of a distance between body and clothing, between the fixed gender attributes implied by the ideological ordering of sexual difference and the persona that is assumed by means of sexual disguise, crossdressing, Kuhn suggests, subverts the view that gender identity is biologically ordained. It calls 'attention to the artifice of gender identity', revealing it as the effect of the systems of signs through which sexual difference is conventionally signified and constructed.

Turning her attention to the cinema, Kuhn then considers the functioning of codes of crossdressing viewed in the light of their articulation with both the narrative conventions of different genres and the more specifically cinematic conventions governing the organization of looks in mainstream film. While the narratives of comedy films and thrillers, the two genres in which codes of crossdressing most frequently occur, often work to close down the gap between apparent and 'real' gender identity which such codes open up – by restoring a correct distribution of character and clothing at the end of the film, for example – this is not always the case. And even where it is, Kuhn argues, such endings do not entirely undo the moments of *jouissance*, the pleasure which erupts in the fracturing and overturning of sexual difference, which are produced along the way. Moreover, Kuhn suggests, the phenomenon of crossdressing sometimes permits the development of a heightened degree of self-referentiality in the cinema, enabling attention to be called to the operation of cinematic codes and conventions which, as a condition of their effectivity, usually remain invisible.

In the final reading selected here, our attention turns from the cinema to television. While feminist reappraisals in the area of film theory have been centrally concerned with qualifying earlier arguments to the effect that the very language of mainstream film and the institution of cinema were systematically anti-feminine, there is no equivalent tradition within television studies. This is, in part, because no convincing case has yet been made for the view that television has a specific language which effects a gendered structure of looking across the full range of its output. Debate has, in consequence, tended to be more genre specific and, for feminists, few genres have compelled more attention than soap opera, in view of its far greater popularity with female than with male viewers. As Tania Modleski makes clear in the opening paragraphs of 'The search for tomorrow in today's soap operas', few genres have been viewed with greater condescension than soap opera – and often just as much so by feminists as by male scholars. Arguing against the tendency for feminists to accept and reproduce a male-biased hierarchy of genres (detective fiction is worth taking seriously, soap opera isn't), Modleski seeks to take both soap operas and their viewers seriously. She is not alone in doing so as recent years have seen a number of attempts to reappraise soap opera more sympathetically.[5] Modleski's discussion, however, is unusual in seeking to account for the popularity of soap operas – especially day-time soap operas – in terms not only of the often contradictory and ambivalent narrative pleasures they afford but in also assessing those pleasures in relation to the rhythms of many women's daily lives in the home. More than that, Modleski also sees in soap opera a number of formal and thematic innovations which, she argues, may justify its being regarded as 'in the vanguard not just of TV art but of all popular narrative art' (p. 190).

Notes

1 Modleski, Tania (1982) *Loving with a Vengeance: Mass Produced Fantasies for Women*, New York and London: Methuen, p. 113.
2 De Lauretis, Teresa (1984) *Alice Doesn't: Feminism, Semiotics, Cinema*, London: Macmillan, pp. 29–30.
3 Mulvey, Laura (1975) 'Visual pleasure and narrative cinema', in Tony Bennett *et al.* (eds) (1981) *Popular Television and Film*, London: British Film Institute, p. 215.
4 See Kuhn, Annette (1982) *Women's Pictures: Feminism and Cinema*, London: Routledge & Kegan Paul.
5 See, for example, Hobson, Dorothy (1982) *Crossroads: The Drama of a Soap Opera*, London: Methuen; Brunsdon, Charlotte (1982) '*Crossroads*: Notes on Soap Opera', *Screen* 22 (4); and Lovell, Terry (1981) 'Ideology and *Coronation Street*', in Richard Dyer *et al.*, *Coronation Street*, London: British Film Institute.

9

Afterthoughts on 'Visual pleasure and narrative cinema' inspired by *Duel in the Sun*

Laura Mulvey

So many times over the years since my 'Visual pleasure and narrative cinema' article was published in *Screen*, I have been asked why I only used the *male* third person singular to stand in for the spectator. At the time, I was interested in the relationship between the image of woman on the screen and the 'masculinization' of the spectator position, regardless of the actual sex (or possible deviance) of any real live movie-goer. The in-built patterns of pleasure and identification seemed to impose masculinity as 'point of view'; a point of view which is also manifest in the general use of the masculine third person. However, the persistent question 'what about the women in the audience?' and my own love of Hollywood melodrama (equally shelved as an issue in 'Visual pleasure') combined to convince me that, however ironically it had been intended originally, the male third person closed off avenues of inquiry that should be followed up. Finally, *Duel in the Sun* and its heroine's crisis of sexual identity brought both areas together. I still stand by my 'Visual pleasure' argument, but would now like to pursue the other two lines of thought. First (the 'women in the audience' issue), whether the female spectator is carried along, as it were by the scruff of the text, or whether the pleasure is more deep rooted and complex. Second (the 'melodrama' issue), how the text and its attendant identifications are affected by a *female* character occupying the centre of the narrative arena. So far as the first issue is concerned, it is always possible that the female spectator may find herself so out of key with the pleasure on offer, with its 'masculinization', that the spell of fascination is broken. On the other hand she may not. She may find herself secretly, unconsciously almost, enjoying the freedom of action and control over the diegetic world that identification with a hero provides. It is this female spectator that I want to consider here. So far as the second issue is concerned, I want to limit the area under consideration in a similar manner. Rather than discussing melodrama in general, I am concentrating on films in which a woman central protagonist is shown to be unable to achieve a stable sexual identity, torn between the deep blue sea of passive femininity and the devil of regressive masculinity.

There is an overlap between the two areas, between the unacknowledged dilemma faced in the auditorium and the drama double-bind up there on the screen. Generally it is dangerous to elide the two separate worlds. In this case, the emotions of the women accepting 'masculinization', while watching action movies with a male hero, are illuminated by the emotions of a heroine of a melodrama whose resistance to a 'correct' feminine position is the crucial issue at stake. This oscillation, this inability to achieve stable sexual identity, is reminiscent of the woman spectator's masculine 'point of view' mentioned earlier. Both generate a consciousness of sexual difference in the cinema that is given depth and thrown into relief by Freud's position on femininity.

The female spectator's pleasure

Freud and femininity

For Freud, femininity is complicated by the fact that it emerges out of a crucial period of parallel development between the sexes; a period he sees as masculine, or phallic, for both boys and girls. The terms he uses to conceive of femininity are the same as those he has mapped out for the male, causing certain problems of language and boundaries to expression. These problems reflect, very accurately, the actual position of women in patriarchal society (suppressed, for instance, under the generalized male third person singular). One term gives rise to a second as its complementary opposite, the male to the female, in that order. Some quotations:

> I will only emphasize here that the development of femininity remains exposed to disturbances by the residual phenomena of the early masculine period. Regressions to the pre-Oedipus phase very frequently occur; in the course of some women's lives there is a repeated alternation between periods in which femininity or masculinity gain the upper hand.
>
> (*On Femininity*)

> In females, too, the striving to be masculine is ego-syntonic at a certain period – namely in the phallic phase, before the development of femininity sets in. But it then succumbs to the momentous process of repression, as so often has been shown, that determines the fortunes of a woman's femininity.
>
> (*Analysis Terminable and Interminable*)

. . . To continue the quotation from *On Femininity*:

> We have called the motive force of sexual life 'the libido'. Sexual life is dominated by the polarity of masculine–feminine; thus the notion suggests itself of considering the relation of the libido to this anthisesis. It would not be surprising if it were to turn out that each sexuality had its own special libido appropriated to it, so that one sort of libido would pursue the aims of a masculine sexual life and another sort those of a feminine one. But nothing of the kind is true. There is only one libido which serves both the masculine and the feminine functions. To it itself we cannot assign any sex; if, following the conventional equation of activity and masculinity, we are inclined to describe it as masculine, we must not forget that it also covers trends with a passive aim. Nevertheless, the

juxtaposition 'feminine libido' is without any justification. Furthermore it is our impression that more constraint has been applied to the libido when it is pressed into the service of the feminine function, and that – to speak teleologically – Nature takes less care and account of its (that function's) demands than in the case of masculinity. And the reason for this may lie – thinking once again teleologically – in the fact that the accomplishment of the aims of biology has been entrusted to the aggressiveness of men and has been made to some extent independent of women's consent.

One particular point of interest in this passage is Freud's shift from the use of active/masculine as *metaphor* for the function of the libido to an invocation of Nature and biology that appears to leave the metaphoric usage behind. There are two problems here: Freud introduces the use of the word *masculine* as 'conventional', apparently simply following an established social-linguistic practice (but which, once again, confirms the masculine 'point of view'); however, secondly, and constituting a greater intellectual stumbling block, the feminine cannot be conceptualized as different, but rather only as *opposition* (passivity) in an antinomic sense, or as *similarity* (the phallic phase). This is not to suggest, on my part, that a hidden, as yet undiscovered femininity exists (as is perhaps implied by Freud's use of the word 'Nature') but that its structural relationship to masculinity under patriarchy cannot be defined or determined within the terms offered. This shifting process, this definition in terms of opposition or similarity, leaves women also shifting between the metaphoric opposition 'active' and 'passive'. The correct road femininity leads to increasing repression of 'the active' (the 'phallic phase' in Freud's terms). In this sense Hollywood genre films structured around masculine pleasure, offering an identification with the *active* point of view, allow a woman spectator to rediscover that lost aspect of her sexual identity, the never fully repressed bed-rock of feminine neurosis.

Narrative grammar and trans-sex identification

The 'convention' cited by Freud (active/masculine) structures most popular narratives whether film, folk-tale, or myth (as I argued in 'Visual pleasure'), where Freud's metaphoric usage is acted out literally in the story. Andromeda stays tied to the rock, a victim, in danger, until Perseus slays the monster and saves her. It is not my aim, here, to debate on the rights and wrongs of this narrative division of labour or to demand positive heroines, but rather to point out that the 'grammar' of the story places the reader, listener or spectator *with* the hero and that the woman spectator in the cinema not only has her own memories but an age-old cultural tradition adapting her to this convention, which eases a transition out of her own sex into another. In 'Visual pleasure' my argument was axed around a desire to identify a pleasure that was specific to cinema, that is the eroticism and cultural conventions surrounding the look. Now, on the contrary, I would rather emphasize the way that popular cinema inherited traditions of storytelling that are common to other forms of folk and mass culture, with attendant fascinations other than those of the look.

Freud points out that 'masculinity' is, at one stage, ego-syntonic for a woman. Leaving aside, for the moment, problems posed by his use of words, his general remarks on stories and day-dreams provide another angle of approach, this time giving a cultural rather than psychoanalytic insight into the dilemma.

He emphasizes the relationship between the ego and the narrative concept of the hero:

> It is the true heroic feeling, which one of our best writers has expressed in the inimitable phrase, 'Nothing can happen to me!' It seems, however, that through this revealing characteristic of invulnerability we can immediately recognize His Majesty the Ego, the hero of every day-dream and every story.
>
> (*Creative Writers and Day-Dreaming*)

Although a boy might know quite well that it is most *unlikely* that he will go out into the world, make his fortune through prowess or the assistance of helpers, and marry a princess, the stories describe the male phantasy of ambition, as Freud describes it, reflecting perhaps, something of an experience and expectation of dominance (the active). For a girl, on the other hand, the cultural and social overlap is more confusing. Freud's argument that a young girl's day-dreams concentrate on the erotic ignores his own position on her early masculinity and the active day-dreams necessarily associated with this phase. In fact, all too often, the erotic function of the woman is represented by the passive, the waiting, (Andromeda again) acting above all as a formal closure to the narrative structure. Three elements can thus be drawn together: Freud's concept of 'masculinity' in women, the identification triggered by the logic of narrative grammar, and the ego's desire to phantasize itself in a certain, active, manner. All these suggest that, as desire is given cultural materiality in a text, for women (from childhood onwards) trans-sex identification is a *habit* that very easily becomes *second Nature*. However, this Nature does not sit easily and shifts restlessly in its borrowed transvestite clothes.

A heroine causes a generic shift

The Western and Oedipal personifications

Using a concept of character function based on Vladimir Propp's *The Morphology of the Folk-Tale* (1968), I want to argue through a chain of links and shifts in narrative pattern, showing up the changing function of 'woman'. The Western (allowing, of course, for as many deviances as one cares to enumerate) bears a residual imprint of the primitive narrative structure analysed by Vladimir Propp in folk-tales. Also, in the hero's traditional invulnerability, the Western ties in closely with Freud's remarks on day-dreaming. As I am interested primarily in character function and narrative pattern, not in genre definition, many issues about the Western as such are being summarily side-stepped. For present purposes, the Western genre provides a crucial node in a series of transformations that *comment* on the function of 'woman' (as opposed to 'man') as a narrative signifier of sexual difference, as personifications of 'active' or 'passive' elements in a story.

In the Proppian tale, an important aspect of narrative closure is 'marriage', a function characterized by 'princess' or equivalent. This is the only function that is sex specific, and thus essentially relates to the sex of the hero and his marriageability. This function is very commonly reproduced in the Western, where, once again, 'marriage' makes a crucial contribution to narrative closure. However, in the Western the function's presence has also come to allow a complication in the form of its complementary opposite, 'not marriage'. Thus, while the social integration represented by marriage is an essential aspect of the folk-tale, in the Western it can be accepted . . . or not. A hero can gain in stature by refusing the princess and remaining alone (Randolph Scott in the Ranown series of movies). As the resolution of the Proppian tale can be seen to represent the resolution of the Oedipus complex (integration into the symbolic), the rejection of marriage personifies a nostalgic celebration of phallic, narcissistic omnipotence. . . .

The tension between two points of attraction, the symbolic (social integration and marriage) and nostalgic narcissim, generates a common splitting of the Western hero into two, something unknown in the Proppian tale. Here two functions emerge, one celebrating integration into society through marriage, the *other* celebrating resistance to social demands and responsibilities, above all those of marriage and the family, the sphere represented by woman. A story such as *The Man Who Shot Liberty Valance* juxtaposes these two points of attraction, and spectator phantasy can have its cake and eat it too. This particular tension between the doubled hero also brings out the underlying significance of the drama, its relation to the symbolic, with unusual clarity. A folk-tale story revolves around conflict between hero and villain. The flash-back narration in *Liberty Valance* seems to follow these lines at first. The narrative is generated by an act of villainy (Liberty rampages, dragon-like, around the countryside). However, the development of the story acquires a complication. The issue at stake is no longer how the villain will be defeated, but how the villain's defeat will be inscribed into history, whether (Ranse) the *upholder* of *the* law as a symbolic system will be seen to be victorious, or (Tom) the *personification* of law in a more primitive manifestation, closer to the good or the right. *Liberty Valance*, as it uses a flash-back structure, also brings out the poignancy of this tension. The 'present tense' story is precipitated by a funeral, so that the story is shot through with nostalgia and sense of loss. Ranse Stoddart mourns Tom Doniphon.

This narrative structure is based on an opposition between two irreconcilables. The two paths cannot cross. On one side there is an encapsulation of power, and phallic attributes, in an individual who has to bow himself out of the way of history. On the other, an individual impotence rewarded by political and financial power, which, *in the long run*, in fact, becomes history. Here the function 'marriage' is as crucial as it is in the folk-tale. It plays the same part in creating narrative resolution, but is even more important in that 'marriage' is an integral attribute of the upholder of the law. In this sense Hallie's choice between the two men is pre-determined. Hallie equals princess equals Oedipal resolution rewarded, equals repression of narcissistic sexuality in marriage.

Woman as signifier of sexuality

In a Western working within these conventions, the

function 'marriage' sublimates the erotic into a final, closing, social ritual. This ritual is, of course, sex specific, and the main rationale for any female presence in this strand of the genre. This neat *narrative* function restates the propensity for 'woman' to signify 'the erotic' already familiar from *visual* representations (as, for instance, argued in 'Visual pleasure').

Now I want to discuss the way in which introducing a woman as central to a story shifts its meanings, producing another kind of narrative discourse. *Duel in the Sun* provides the opportunity for this. While the film remains visibly a 'Western', the generic space seems to shift. The landscape of action, although present, is not the dramatic core of the film's story, rather it is the interior drama of a girl caught between two conflicting desires. The conflicting desires, first of all, correspond closely with Freud's argument about female sexuality quoted above, that is: an oscillation between 'passive' femininity and regressive 'masculinity'. Thus, the symbolic equation woman = sexuality still persists, but now rather than being an image or a narrative function, the equation opens out a narrative area previously suppressed or repressed. She is no longer the signifier of sexuality (function 'marriage') in the 'Western' type of story. Now the female presence as centre allows the story to be actually, *overtly*, about sexuality: it becomes a melodrama. It is as though the narrational lens had zoomed in and opened up the neat function 'marriage' ('and they lived happily . . . ') to ask 'what next?' or onto the figure of the princess, waiting in the wings for her one moment of importance to ask 'what does *she* want?'. Here we find the generic terrain for melodrama, in its woman-oriented strand. The second question ('what does *she* want?') takes on a greater significance when the hero function is split, as described above in the case of *Liberty Valance*, where the heroine's choice puts the seal of married grace on the upholder of the Law. *Duel in the Sun* opens up this question.

In *Duel in the Sun* the iconographical attributes of the

two male (oppositional) characters, Lewt and Jesse, conform very closely to those of Ranse and Tom in *Liberty Valance*. But now the opposition between Ranse and Tom, (who represent an abstract and allegorical conflict over Law and history), is given a completely different twist of meaning. As Pearl is at the centre of the story, caught between the two men, their alternative attributes acquire meaning *from* her, and represent different sides of her desire and aspiration. They personify the split in *Pearl*, not a split in the concept of *hero*, as argued previously for *Liberty Valance*.

However, from a psychoanalytic point of view, a strikingly similar pattern emerges. Jesse (attributes: book, dark suit, legal skills, love of learning and culture, destined to be Governor of the State, money and so on) sign-posts the 'correct' path for Pearl, towards learning a passive sexuality, learning to 'be a lady', above all sublimation into a concept of the feminine that is socially viable. Lewt (attributes: guns, horses, skill with horses, Western get-up, contempt for culture, destined to die an outlaw, personal strength and personal power) offers sexual passion, not based on maturity but on a regressive, boy/girl type mixture of rivalry and play. With Lewt, Pearl can be a tomboy (riding, swimming, shooting). Thus the Oedipal dimension persists, but now illuminates the sexual ambivalence it represents for femininity.

In the last resort, there is no more room for Pearl in Lewt's world of misogynist machismo, than there is room for her desires as Jesse's potential fiancée. The film consists of a series of oscillations in her sexual identity, between alternative paths of development, between different desperations. Whereas the regressive, phallic male hero (Tom in *Liberty Valance*) had a place (albeit a doomed one) that was stable and meaningful, Pearl is unable to settle or find a 'femininity' in which she and the male world can meet. In this sense, although the male characters personify Pearl's dilemma, it is their terms that make and, finally, break her. Once again, however, the narrative drama dooms the phallic, regressive, resistant to the symbolic. Lewt, Pearl's masculine side, drops out of the social order. Pearl's masculinity gives her the 'wherewithal' to achieve heroism and death. The lovers shoot each other and die in each other's arms. Perhaps in *Duel* the erotic relationship between Pearl and Lewt also exposes a dyadic interdependence between hero and villain in the primitive tale, now threatened by the splitting of the hero with the coming of the Law.

In *Duel in the Sun*, Pearl's inability to become a 'lady' is highlighted by the fact that the perfect lady appears, like a phantasmagoria of Pearl's failed aspiration, as Jesse's perfect future wife. Pearl recognizes her and her rights over Jesse, and that she represents the 'correct' road. In an earlier film by King Vidor, *Stella Dallas* (1937), narrative and iconographic structures similar to those outlined above make the dramatic meaning of the film *although it is not a Western*. Stella, as central character, is flanked on each side by a male personification of her instability, her inability to accept correct, married 'femininity' on the one hand, or find a place in a macho world on the other. Her husband, Stephen, demonstrates all the attributes associated with Jesse, with no problems of generic shift. Ed Munn, representing Stella's regressive 'masculine' side, is considerably emasculated by the loss of Western accoutrements and possibility for action (it should also be said that the fact that Stella is a mother, and that her relationship to her child constitutes the central drama, undermines a possible sexual relationship with Ed). He does, interestingly, retain residual traces of Western iconography. His attributes are mapped through associations with horses and betting, the racing scene. However, more importantly, his relationship with Stella is regressive, based on 'having fun', most explicitly in the episode in which they spread itching powder among the respectable occupants of a train carriage. In *Stella Dallas*, too, a perfect wife appears for Stephen, representing the 'correct' femininity that Stella rejects (very similar to Helen, Jesse's fiancée in *Duel in the Sun*).

I have been trying to suggest a series of transform-ations in narrative pattern that illuminate, but also show shifts in, Oedipal nostalgia. The 'personifications' and their iconographical attributes do not relate to parental figures or reactivate an actual Oedipal moment. On the contrary, they represent an internal oscillation of desire, which lies dormant, waiting to be 'pleasured' in stories of this kind. Perhaps the fascination of the classic Western, in particular, lies in its rather raw touching on this nerve. However, for the female spectator the situation is more complicated and goes beyond simple mourning for a lost phantasy of omnipotence. The masculine identification, in its phallic aspect, reactivates for her a phantasy of 'action' that correct femininity demands should be repressed. The phantasy 'action' finds expression though a metaphor of masculinity. Both in the language used by Freud and in the male personifications of desire flanking the female protagonist in the melodrama, this metaphor acts as a straitjacket, becoming itself an indicator, a litmus paper, of the problems inevitably activated by any attempt to represent the feminine in patriarchal society. The memory of the 'masculine' phase has its own roman-tic attraction, a last ditch resistance, in which the power of masculinity can be used as postponement against the power of patriarchy. Thus Freud's comments illuminate both the position of the female spectator and the image of oscillation represented by Pearl and Stella:

> . . . in the course of some women's lives there is a repeated alternation between periods in which femininity and masculinity gain the upper hand.

> . . . the phallic phase . . . but it then succumbs to the momentous process of repression as has so often been shown, that determines the fortunes of women's femininity.

I have argued that Pearl's position in *Duel in the Sun* is similar to that of the female spectator as she temporarily accepts 'masculinization' in memory of her 'active' phase. Rather than dramatizing the success of masculine identification, Pearl brings out its sadness. Her 'tomboy' pleasures, her sexuality, are not accepted by Lewt, except in death. So, too, the female spectator's phantasy of masculinization is always to some extent at cross purposes with itself, restless in its transvestite clothes.

10
Women in *film noir*

Janey Place

The dark lady, the spider woman, the evil seductress who tempts man and brings about his destruction is among the oldest themes of art, literature, mythology and religion in western culture. She is as old as Eve, and as current as today's movies, comic books and dime novels. She and her sister (or *alter ego*), the virgin, the mother, the innocent, the redeemer, form the two poles of female archetypes.

Film noir is a male fantasy, as is most of our art. Thus woman here as elsewhere is defined by her sexuality: the dark lady has access to it and the virgin does not. That men are not so deterministically delineated in their cultural and artistic portrayal is indicative of the phallocentric cultural viewpoint: women are defined *in relation to* men, and the centrality of sexuality in this definition is a key to understanding the position of women in our culture. The primary crime the 'liberated' woman is guilty of is refusing to be defined in such a way, and this refusal can be perversely seen (in art, or in life) as an attack on men's very existence. *Film noir* is hardly 'progressive' in these terms – it does not present us with role models who defy their fate and triumph over it. But it does give us one of the few periods of film in which women are active, not static symbols, are intelligent and powerful, if destructively so, and derive power, not weakness, from their sexuality. . . .

Two aspects of the portrayal of women in *film noir* are remarkable: first, the particular mix and versions of the more general archetypes that recur in *film noirs*; and second the style of that expression. Visually, *film noir* is fluid, sensual, extraordinarily expressive, making the sexually expressive woman, which is its dominant image of woman, extremely powerful. It is not their inevitable demise we remember but rather their strong, dangerous, and above all, exciting sexuality. In *film noir* we observe both the social action of myth which damns the sexual woman and all who become enmeshed by her, and a particularly potent stylistic presentation of the sexual strength of women which man fears. This operation of myth is so highly stylised and conventionalized that the final 'lesson' of the myth often fades into the background and we retain the image of the erotic, strong, unrepressed (if destructive) woman. The style of these films thus overwhelms their conventional narrative content, or interacts with it to produce a remarkably potent image of woman.

This expression of the myth of man's 'right' or need to control women sexually is in contrast to the dominant version of it in 'A' films of the 1930s, 1940s and 1950s, which held that women are so weak and incapable they need men's 'protection' to survive. In these films, it is the woman who is portrayed benefiting from her dependence on men; in *film noir*, it is clear that men need to control women's sexuality in order not to be destroyed by it. The dark woman of *film noir* had something her innocent sister lacked: access to her own sexuality (and thus to men's) and the power that this access unlocked. . . .

The spider woman

The meaning of any film image is a complex function of its visual qualities (composition, angle, lighting, screen size, camera movement, etc.), the content of the image

'It is not their inevitable demise we remember but rather their strong, dangerous, and above all, exciting sexuality.' Barbara Stanwyck in *Double Indemnity*

'. . . the image of the erotic, strong, unrepressed (if destructive) woman.' Claire Trevor in *Farewell, My Lovely*.

'. . . a particularly potent stylistic presentation of the sexual strength of women which man fears.' Jane Greer in *Out of the Past*.

(acting, stars, iconography, etc.), its juxtaposition to surrounding images and the context of the narrative. Even more broadly, meaning is affected by ever-enlarging contexts, such as the conventions of a particular genre, of film generally, and of the time in which the film is made and in which it is viewed. It would be presumptuous and an impossible undertaking to attempt to establish a 'dictionary' of meanings within a system which is so bound for specific meaning to such complex elements and their interaction. Nevertheless, *film noir* is a movement, and as such is remarkably stylistically consistent. It thus becomes possible to identify recurrent visual motifs and their general range of meanings. Within these recurrent patterns, some drawn from conventions not specifically filmic, others specific to film generally, and still others to *film noir* or the detective film genre, the source and operation of

Sunset Boulevard: Gloria Swanson as Norma Desmond emphasizes the perverse, decaying side of *film noir* sexuality, with her claw-like hands, dark glasses and bizarre cigarette holder.

the sexual woman's dangerous power is expressed visually. . . .

The source and the operation of the sexual woman's dangerous power and its danger to the male character is expressed visually both in the iconography of the image and in the visual style. The iconography is explicitly sexual, and often explicitly violent as well: long hair (blond or dark), makeup, and jewellery. Cigarettes with their wispy trails of smoke can become cues of dark and immoral sensuality, and the iconography of violence (primarily guns) is a specific symbol (as is perhaps the cigarette) of her 'unnatural' phallic power. The *femme fatale* is characterized by her long lovely legs: our first view of the elusive Velma in *Murder My Sweet (Farewell My Lovely)* and of Cora in *The Postman Always Rings Twice* is a significant, appreciative shot of their bare legs,

a *directed* glance (so directed in the latter film that the shot begins on her calves, cuts to a shot of her whole body, cuts back to the man looking, then finally back to Lana Turner's turban-wrapped, angelic face) from the viewpoint of the male character who is to be seduced. In *Double Indemnity* Phyllis's legs (with a gold anklet significantly bearing her name) dominate Walter's and our own memory of her as the camera follows her descent down the stairs, framing only her spike heels and silk-stockinged calves. Dress – or lack of it – further defines the woman: Phyllis first is viewed in *Double Indemnity* wrapped in a towel, and the sequinned, tight, black gown of the fantasy woman in *Woman in the Window* and the nameless 'dames' of *film noir* instantly convey the important information about them and their role in the film.

The strength of these women is expressed in the visual style by their dominance in composition, angle, camera movement and lighting. They are overwhelmingly the

'The moral and physical chaos is easily expressed in crime.'
John Garfield and Lana Turner in *The Postman Always Rings Twice*.

compositional focus, generally centre frame and/or in the foreground, or pulling focus to them in the background. They control camera movement, seeming to direct the camera (and the hero's gaze, with our own) irresistibly with them as they move. (In contrast, the 'good' women of *film noir* and many of the seduced, passive men are predominantly static, both within the frame and in their ability to motivate camera movement and composition.) The *femme fatale* ultimately loses physical movement, influence over camera movement, and is often actually or symbolically imprisoned by composition as control over her is exerted and expressed visually: sometimes behind visual bars (*The Maltese Falcon*), sometimes happy in the protection of a lover (*The Big Sleep*), often dead (*Murder My Sweet, Out of the Past, Gun Crazy, Kiss Me Deadly, Double Indemnity*), sometimes symbolically rendered impotent (*Sunset*

Boulevard). The ideological operation of the myth (the absolute necessity of controlling the strong, sexual woman) is thus achieved by first demonstrating her dangerous power and its frightening results, then destroying it.

Often the original transgression of the dangerous lady of *film noir* (unlike the vamp seductress of the 1920s) is ambition expressed metaphorically in her freedom of movement and visual dominance. This ambition is inappropriate to her status as a woman, and must be confined. She wants to be the owner of her own nightclub, not the owner's wife (*Night and the City*). She wants to be a star, not a recluse (*Sunset Boulevard*). She wants her husband's insurance money, not her comfortable, middle-class life (*Double Indemnity*). She wants the 'great whatsit', and ends up destroying the world (*Kiss Me Deadly*). She wants independence, and sets off a chain of murders (*Laura*). She wants to win an uninterested lover, and ends up killing him, herself and two other people (*Angel Face*). She wants money, and succeeds only in destroying herself and the man who loves her (*Gun Crazy, The Killers*). She wants freedom from an oppressive relationship, and initiates events that lead to murder (*The Big Combo, The Postman Always Rings Twice*). Whether evil (*Double Indemnity, Gun Crazy, Kiss Me Deadly, Night and the City, The Maltese Falcon, The Postman Always Rings Twice*) or innocent (*Laura, The Big Combo*), her desire for freedom, wealth or independence ignites the forces which threaten the hero.

Independence is her goal, but her nature is fundamentally and irredeemably sexual in *film noir*. The insistence on combining the two (aggressiveness and sensuality) in a consequently dangerous woman is the central obsession of *film noir*, and the visual movement which indicates unacceptable activity in *film noir* women represents the man's own sexuality, which must be repressed and controlled if it is not to destroy him.

The independence which *film noir* women seek is often visually presented as self-absorbed narcissism: the

'. . . self-absorbed narcissism: the woman gazes at her own reflection in the mirror.' Rita Hayworth in *Gilda*.

woman gazes at her own reflection in the mirror, ignoring the man she will use to achieve her goals. This attention to herself instead of the man is the obvious narrative transgression of Norma Desmond whose images – both reflected and pictures – dominate her mansion in *Sunset Boulevard*. She hires Joe Gillis to work on her script for her comeback, and she continues to insist he participate in her life rather than being interested in his. He dreams he is her pet chimp, and he actually becomes victim of her Salome. Joe finds an acceptable lover in Betty, the young woman who types while he dictates, smells like soap instead of perfume, dreams of *his* career, and is content to be behind the camera instead of in front. Self-interest over devotion to a man is often the original sin of the *film noir* woman and metaphor for the threat her sexuality represents to him.

Another possible meaning of the many mirror shots in *film noir* is to indicate women's duplicitous nature. They

'This attention to herself instead of the man is the obvious narrative transgression of Norma Desmond . . .' *Sunset Boulevard*.

are visually split, thus not to be trusted. Further, this motif contributes to the murkey confusion of *film noir*: nothing and no one is what it seems. Compositions in which reflections are stronger than the actual woman, or in which mirror images are seen in odd, uncomfortable angles, help to create the mood of threat and fear.

In some films the 'spider women' prove not to be so and are thus redeemed. Gilda and Laura are validated as individuals (Gilda was simply acting out the paranoid fantasies of her true love, Johnny, and Laura was an innocent catalyst for men's idealizations), but the images of sexual power they exhibit are more powerful than the narrative 'explanation'. The image of Gilda we remember is the close-up introduction to her, with long hair tossed back over her head to reveal her beautiful face. Her song, 'Put the Blame on Mame, Boys' (for every natural and economic disaster to hit the world) is ironic, but

'Mirror images . . . seen in odd, uncomfortable angles help to create the mood of threat and fear.' *The Big Heat*.

stripping as she performs, the power she possesses as a sexually alive woman seems almost up to the task. Laura's beautiful, dominating portrait that haunts the characters and determines the action of the film when she is believed dead is the strongest visual image even when she reappears alive.

The framed portrait of a woman is a common motif in *film noir*. Sometimes it is contrasted with the living woman: in *Night and the City* Helen is a nagging, ambitious, destructive bitch, but her husband gazes longingly at her 'safe' incarnation in the framed portrait – under control, static, and powerless. Laura's portrait is compositionally dominating, inciting Mark's fantasies and giving visual expression to Waldo's idealized vision of her, but only when she unexpectedly turns up alive does further trouble ensue as she refuses to conform to the fantasies inspired by the portrait. In *Woman in the Window*, an elderly, respectable professor puts his wife

(top): 'The image of Gilda we remember is the close-up introduction to her . . .' (bottom) 'Laura's beautiful, dominating portrait that haunts the characters . . .'

Out of the Past: (top) 'one woman (Ann) is firmly rooted in the pastoral environment.' (bottom) '. . . the other (Kathie) is exciting, criminal, very active and sexy.'

and children on a train, and longing for adventure, dreams a beautiful portrait comes to life and involves him in murder. He is about to take his own life when he wakes up, cured of his longing for adventure. The lesson is obvious: only in a controlled, impotent powerless form, powerless to move or act, is the sexual woman no threat to the *film noir* man.

On the rare occasions that the normal world of families, children, homes and domesticity appears in *film noir* it is either so fragile and ideal that we anxiously anticipate its destruction (*The Big Heat*), or, like the 'good' but boring women who contrast with the exciting, sexy *femme fatales*, it is so dull and constricting that it offers no compelling alternative to the dangerous but exciting life on the fringe.

The nurturing woman

The opposite female archetype is also found in *film noir*: woman as redeemer. She offers the possibility of integration for the alienated, lost man into the stable world of secure values, roles and identities. She gives love, understanding (or at least forgiveness), asks very little in return (just that he come back to her) and is generally visually passive and static. Often, in order to offer this alternative to the nightmare landscape of *film noir*, she herself must not be a part of it. She is then linked to the pastoral environment of open spaces, light, and safety characterized by even, flat, high-key lighting. Often this is an idealized dream of the past and she exists only in memory, but sometimes this idealization exists as a real alternative.

Out of the Past is one of the best of the latter type: one woman (Ann) is firmly rooted in the pastoral environment, static, undemanding and rather dull, while the other (Kathie) is exciting, criminal, very active and sexy. In this film the lack of excitement offered by the safe woman is so clearly contrasted with the sensual, passionate appeal of the other that the detective's

(top): *They Live By Night*: Bowie and Keetchie are visually confined by lighting and composition as the outside world makes their love impossible. (bottom): 'Mary (*On Dangerous Ground*) is . . . cut off from the corruption of greed, money and power of the urban environment by living in a rural setting.'

destruction is inevitable. Kathie appears out of the misty haze of late afternoon in a little Mexican town, walking towards the detective hero as he sits in a bar, waiting for this woman whose image has already been set up for him by the man she shot and ran away from, who wants her back at any cost. They later embrace against the tumultuous sea, a sudden rainstorm, and the dark rich textures created by low-key lighting.

The redemptive woman often represents or is part of a primal connection with nature and/or with the past, which are safe, static states rather than active, exciting ones, but she can sometimes offer the only transcendence possible in *film noir. They Live By Night* and *On Dangerous Ground* (both directed by Nicholas Ray, 1949 and 1950) are characterized by the darkly romantic element that can exist with the cynical. In the former film, the young lovers are doomed, but the possibility of their love transcends and redeems them both, and its failure criticizes the urbanized world that will not let them live. Their happiest moments are outdoors in the sunlight, with 'normalcy' an ideal they can never realize because there is no place in the corrupt world for them. Mary (*On Dangerous Ground*) is not only cut off from the corruption of greed, money and power of the urban environment by living in a rural setting, she is further isolated (and purified) by her blindness. She teaches the badly disturbed and violent Jim to feel, and her reliance on him releases him from his emotional prison. Both characters are crippled – he emotionally and she physically – and need each other to achieve the wholeness of health. This interdependence keeps both characters and their relationship exciting, while other 'innocents' of *film noir* who exist only to contrast with the dangerous woman simply fade into forgetfulness.

Film noir contains versions of both extremes of the female archetypes, the deadly seductress and the rejuvenating redeemer. Its special significance lies in the combination of sensuality with activity and ambition which characterizes the *femme fatale*, and in the mode of control that must be exerted to dominate her. She is not often won over and pacified by love for the hero, as is the strong heroine of the 1940s who is significantly less sexual than the *film noir* woman. Indeed, her strength is emphasized by the general passivity and impotence which characterizes the *film noir* male, making her a threat to him far greater than the career woman of the 1940s was, and thus only actual or symbolic destruction is an effective control. Even more significant is the form in which the 'spider woman's' strength and power is expressed: the visual style gives her such freedom of movement and dominance that it is her strength and sensual visual texture that is inevitably printed in our memory, not her ultimate destruction.

The tendency of popular culture to create narratives in which male fears are concretized in sexually aggressive women who must be destroyed is not specific to the 1940s to mid-1950s in the United States, but is seen today to a degree that might help to account for the sudden popularity of these films on college campuses, television and film retrospectives. But despite their regressive ideological function on a strictly narrative level, a fuller explanation for the current surge of interest in *film noir* must acknowledge its uniquely sensual visual style which often overwhelms (or at least acts upon) the narrative so compellingly that it stands as the only period in American film in which women are deadly but sexy, exciting and strong.

11

Sexual disguise and cinema

Annette Kuhn

. . . In dominant cinema, stories are told through the medium of the moving picture according to a circumscribed set of conventions. Films consequently produce meanings in ways different from, say, still photographs. In films of sexual disguise, cinematic conventions – notably codes of narrativity, genre and spectacle – intersect cultural meanings surrounding practices of crossdressing. This essay attempts to trace the operation of various textual and cultural codes in specific crossdressing films.

Analysing films in this way, unpacking the various layers of meaning at work in them, demands in this instance attention to the particular ways in which sexual difference is constructed. In films of the kind considered here, stories pivot around mistaken identifications of gender. The narrativization of such themes may provoke questions about the ways in which gender is socially constructed: it may even subject to certain interrogation the culturally taken-for-granted dualities of male/female and masculine/feminine. Just how transgressive such a strategy can finally be when deployed through the conventions of dominant cinema is arguable. But perhaps the pleasure of the most popular films of sexual disguise does nevertheless lie in their capacity to offer, at least momentarily, a vision of fluidity of gender options; to provide a glimpse of 'a world outside the order normally seen or thought about' – a utopian prospect of release from the ties of sexual difference that bind us into meaning, discourse, culture.

How many films have been made in which characters take on the conventional clothing of the opposite sex? Even restricting the list to mainstream film, there appears to be quite a lot of cinematic crossdressing about: *Queen Christina, Some Like It Hot, Psycho, Tootsie, Privates on Parade, Sylvia Scarlett, Thunderbolt and Lightfoot, Dressed to Kill, Calamity Jane, Victor/Victoria.* . . .

But why crossdressing? How does it work in these very different films? A move away from listing titles towards analysing film texts provokes interesting questions, not all of them to do directly with cinema. What cultural meanings are drawn on and constructed in representations of crossdressing? How are such meanings worked over, transformed and recirculated as they intersect pre-existing forms, discourses, genres and modes of representation? Looked at in this light, the subject of crossdressing and cinema assumes its place within the wider arena of cultural production. And yet, of course, cinema has its own specificity as a mode of representation, its own apparatus of institutional contexts, genres and modes of address, within which meanings of any sort – including meanings surrounding crossdressing – are produced in particular ways. This localized work of meaning-making does nevertheless take place within the wider social/cultural contexts in which crossdressing assumes and organizes certain meanings: and approaching the question of how cinema activates these meanings in its own way calls for a negotiation of broader issues. . . .

Crossdressing, performance and sexual difference

As a set of cultural meanings, crossdressing intersects two discourses. It draws on meanings centring on the one hand on performance, and on the other on constructs of gender identity and sexual difference. Understood in its everyday sense, performance is allied with acting, and acting is regarded as an activity that involves pretence, dissimulation, an intent to seem to be something or someone one is, in reality, not. An actor's role is assumed like a mask, the mask concealing the performer's 'true self'. The disguise is a cover, and in many schools of acting the more the audience is taken in by the performance, the better that performance is judged to be. In effecting a distance between assumed persona and real self, the practice of performance constructs a subject which is both fixed in the distinction between role and self and at the same time, paradoxically, called into question in the very act of performance. For over against the 'real self', performance poses the possibility of a mutable self, of a fluidity of subjectivity.

Discourses on gender identity and sexual difference hold together a range of notions centring on biological sex, social gender, sexual identification and sexual object choice. The incorporation of these in constructs of gender identity is a historically-grounded ideological project whose effect, it has been argued, has been to set up a heterogeneous and determinate set of biological, physical, social, psychological and psychic constructs as a unitary, fixed and unproblematic attribute of human subjectivity. Within this ideological project, subjectivity is always gendered and every human being is, and remains, either male or female. . . . Moreover, in ideology gender identity is not merely absolute: it also lies at the very heart of human subjectivity. Gender is what crucially defines us, so that an ungendered subject cannot, in this view, be human. The human being, in other words, is a gendered subject. And so a fixed subjectivity and a gendered subjectivity are, in ideology, one and the same.

Together, performance and gender identity incorporate a range of meanings which are activated and reconstituted in a particular way in the instance of crossdressing. . . . Crossdressing, by definition, involves clothing: and in itself clothing signifies. It carries a range of meanings, the most culturally prominent of which pivot on gender. In many societies, our own included, dress is gender specific. Clothing is associated with gender, serving as an outward mark of difference, of a fundamental attribute of the wearer's identity. But so to identify dress with gender identity, and gender identity with selfhood, is to step into a minefield of contradiction. What are the implications for a subjectivity which is held to be fixed and absolute of a mark of such a subjectivity that is conventional and in consequence changeable? Far from being a fixed signifier of a fixed gender identity, clothing has the potential to disguise, to alter, even to reconstruct, the wearer's self. Clothing can dissemble – it may be costume, mask, masquerade. Put another way, clothing can embody performance. As a means to, even the substance of, a commutable persona, clothing as performance threatens to undercut the ideological fixity of the human subject.

If clothing can be costume, capable of being modified at the wearer's will, it follows that the gender identity conventionally signified by dress may be just as easily changeable. Change your clothes and you change your self. Change your clothes and you change your sex. The potential threat to fixed subjectivity and gender identity represented by clothing goes a long way towards explaining the social prohibitions on some kinds of crossdressing, and the containment of others within traditionally acceptable forms and practices.

In its performance aspect, clothing sets up a play between visible outward appearance – in this case, gender as signified by dress – and an essence which may not be visible but is none the less held to be more 'real' than appearance – here the gender of the person whose true nature may be concealed, both literally and metaphorically, beneath the clothes. What is at stake in this expression of the dualism of appearance and essence is a fundamentalism of the body, an appeal to bodily attributes as final arbiter of a basic truth. The truth lies under the clothing, and although it might well be expected that in ordinary circumstances it will not and should not do so, clothing can obscure rather than reveal the truth. Dress constantly poses the possibility of distance between body and clothing, between 'true' self, the fixed gender of ideology, and assumed persona. Crossdressing as a realization of such a potential turns this distance to account, constructing sexual disguise as a play upon the fixity and the fluidity of gender identity. . . .

In its specificity crossdressing, with its play on the distance between a gendered body and gendered clothing, also opens up a space of self-referentiality. In this sense, crossdressing comments, with irony, on the conflation in ideology of body, gender, gender identity and subjectivity. If clothing as performance threatens to undercut the subject fixed in ideology, crossdressing as a particular expression of it goes one step further. It highlights the centrality of gender constructs in processes of subjectivity and comments upon a culturally salient means by which a would-be fixed gender identity is marked and constructed. It subverts the construct, offering at the same time ironic comment on its status as convention. By calling attention to the artifice of gender identity, crossdressing effects a 'wilful alienation' from the fixity of that identity: it has the potential, in consequence, to denaturalize it, to 'make it strange'. Crossdressing, then, may denaturalize that phenomenon held in our culture to be most evidently and pre-eminently natural: sexual difference. . . .

Crossdressing and narrativity

Fictional narratives involving crossdressing, it may be argued, problematize the ideological construction of sexual difference as natural and absolute. . . . But this is not to suggest that in such texts the ideological fixity of sexual difference is necessarily subject to challenge, for this depends on a variety of textual and contextual considerations, including the structure, trajectory and viewpoint of the narrative itself and the social and historical contexts of its production, distribution and reception. . . .

Narratives involving crossdressing – representations concerned in one way or another with gender identity and its mutability – always, in offering the promise of a 'visionary multiplicity' of gender relations, open up a space for *jouissance*. But many of them . . . go no further than to hint at a possibility that is ultimately closed off in the revelation of the body beneath the clothes. A quest to uncover the truth of the concealed body may be precisely the desire that activates a narrative of sexual disguise. When the body is confirmed as the location of an absolute difference, this desire is gratified in the pleasure offered in the resolution. If crossdressing narratives always in some measure problematize gender identity and sexual difference, then, many do so only to confirm finally the absoluteness of both, to reassert a 'natural' order of fixed gender and unitary subjectivity. Nevertheless, the denaturalizing potential of sexual disguise may be carried through, in texts which construct openness throughout, which pose from beginning to end fluidity of gender, androgyny, multiplicity of identifications and subjectivity in process.

In fictions of sexual disguise, openness and closure are articulated in the first instance in the organization of their narratives, which involve at least one character who assumes the conventional clothes of the opposite sex, or who might be suspected of not, in terms of gender, being what his or her clothing would signify. Such characters are positioned in a variety of ways in relation to events in the fiction. Their positioning varies according to the structure of the narrative – what sets the story in motion and how its resolution is brought about; the trajectory of the narrative – how events between beginning and end are constructed in relation to one another; and the point of view of the narrative – how the reader is placed in relation to the telling of the story and the knowledge the reader possesses, *vis-à-vis* characters in the fiction, about events.

In crossdressing narratives, sexual disguise must usually be accounted for, given some sort of explanation within the story. Where a character assumes sexual disguise during the course of the narrative, this move typically constitutes a disruption that sets the story in motion: in this case, the reader is usually aware from the outset of the character's 'true' gender. There exists in fact a set of stock narrative situations which motivate, or explain, a character's assumption of sexual disguise. In the light of some of the arguments advanced above, it is interesting to note that in a number of narrative films involving crossdressing, performance constitutes a central theme, and characters assuming sexual disguise are often (in the story) performers by profession. In such a situation, sexual disguise is explained plausibly in terms of the character's job and its requirements. When, as is often the case, crossdressing narratives go to great lengths outwardly to disavow any suggestion of perversion attaching to such characters (and to the actors playing them), sexual perversion still often works as a subtext. Indeed, a play of acknowledgement and disavowal around sexuality and sexual perversion can be a fertile source of comedy. In conjunction with the performance motif, this is what identifies a certain type of crossdressing film with the genre of musical comedy.

In films of this type, the story typically opens with the plight of an unemployed or otherwise desperate performer who resorts to sexual disguise in order to get work. Beginnings of this kind characterize some of the most celebrated crossdressing films – *Some Like It Hot* (Wilder, 1959), *Victor/Victoria* (Edwards, 1982) and *Tootsie* (Pollack, 1982) for example. Each of these has performers of some sort – musicians, singer, actor – as central characters. . . .

While films in which sexual disguise is explained as performance may downplay outward connotations of sexual perversion, other crossdressing films bring such associations to the centre of the story. When perversity substitutes for performance, sexual disguise becomes transvestism – a practice constituted, in the clinical discourse which names it, as pathological. The sexually disguised character is constructed as sick, or criminal, or both: and crossdressing, far from being comic, becomes threatening. In crossdressing films of this type, narratives are rarely activated by a character's assumption of sexual disguise. A more typical opening move is a 'villainy' such as a disappearance, a theft, or – likeliest of all – a murder.[1] If the villain at some point in the story adopts sexual disguise, the crossdressing is constructed narratively as either a symptom of his psychopathy or an outward sign of his wickedness and depravity. Crossdressing, in other words, explains why the villain does what he does: for in the world of this sort of story, personal pathology is plausible and a sufficient explanation of criminal acts. Such inflections identify films of this kind with the genre of thriller. . . .

Within the classic narrative, intradiegetic explanations for crossdressing seem to operate both at a general level – facing outward, as it were, to the social/cultural context in which meanings attaching to crossdressing are produced, and also, more specifically, such explanations look inward to the conventions of the classic narrative and of certain film genres. In the musical comedy, sexual disguise acquires cultural plausibility by reference to such values as the work ethic and the necessity for economic survival, while in the thriller it is naturalized through discourses on sexual deviance, psychopathology and criminality. In either case, cultural references work within the respective generic conventions of the musical comedy and the thriller, at the same time reproducing and reconstructing those conventions. Intratextual reference to cultural and generic convention operates effectively to contain the denaturalizing potential of crossdressing narrative. In this sense, such reference marks a pervasive closure which operates in addition to the more commonly-acknowledged form of narrative closure – the resolution at the end of the story of narrative enigmas.

Enigmas are questions set up, gaps opened up, in narratives which construct a readerly desire for plenitude and resolution. . . . In the classic narrative the resolution of a story typically involves some restoration of equilibrium to the world of the fiction, a world disrupted by whatever event or situation sets the story in motion in the first place. Even classic narratives, though, vary in the degree to which closure is implied in their conclusions. If, for example, a story opens with a character assuming sexual disguise, the ultimate restoration of 'correct' dress to that character would suggest a considerable degree of closure in its resolution.

Thus, the film *Victor/Victoria* (in the final scene of which the Julie Andrews character appears wearing a dress and escorted by her boyfriend) might be regarded as more closed in its resolution than *Some Like It Hot*, in which the questions both of dress and of gender identity, certainly in relation to the Jack Lemmon character, 'Daphne', are in some respects left rather unresolved in the speedboat scene which ends the film. Nevertheless, in neither film is there ever any question of doubt on the spectator's part about the 'true' gender of sexually disguised characters. . . .

In all narratives, beginnings and endings are separated by a process, a trajectory through which each story traces its own particular path. Fictions of sexual disguise generate certain kinds of questions, specific desires that keep the story moving along its track. Dominant among these is the desire, however expressed, to fathom the appearance/essence conundrum, to lay bare the reality beneath the clothing and to settle the crucial question of who is male and who is female. Although this may be only one of several respects in which crossdressing narratives are centrally *about* gender and sexual difference, it is perhaps the most important if only because through this particular desire sexual difference is constructed in the same moment both as a question of import in a particular narrative and also as a cultural and ideological problem.

In crossdressing narratives, desire to resolve the problem of sexual difference may be embodied in certain characters in the fiction, characters set up as deceived or uncertain about the gender of another character. For example, a pivotal sequence in the film *Victor/Victoria* is constructed around the premiss that King Marchand (James Garner) is desperately keen to know whether or not Victor (Julie Andrews) is actually a boy. It is interesting, in view of the ideological conflation of subjectivity, gender and body discussed above, that Marchand's desire can apparently be gratified only by his contriving to see Victor naked. A desire to resolve the matter of sexual difference is not necessarily confined to characters within the fiction, however. The reader may be positioned in exactly this way, too, especially if the narrative solicits identification with a character who is on a quest for some sort of truth about gender identity. While in *Victor/Victoria* the spectator, unlike Marchand, knows all along that Victor is really Victoria,[2] it is nevertheless possible still to identify with Marchand's desire: to want to know whether, how, and with what consequences this character discovers the truth. Although what Marchand finally sees is not actually revealed (the reverse shot that would show his point of view on the crucial part of Victor/Victoria's naked body is withheld), 'how' is detailed at some length, and in this respect the narrative finally yields to all the various components of the spectator's, as well as of Marchand's, desire.

This example highlights a property of narrativity which is of particular importance to fictions of sexual disguise: narrative point of view, through which readers are positioned as knowing or otherwise in relation to events in the fiction. Stories differ in the degree to which their telling, their narration, lets readers in on what is going on. In the classic narrative, the reader tends to be placed in a position of superior knowledge *vis-à-vis* characters in the story: Marchand, for example, does not know whether Victor is male or female, while the spectator does. Such an all-embracing narrative point of view has been termed the 'view behind', its operation contrasting with a narration through which the reader is placed in a position of knowledge more-or-less equivalent to that enjoyed by characters in the fiction: the 'view with'.[3] . . . Narrative point of view constitutes another co-ordinate of openness or closure, the 'view behind' being associated with narrative closure.

In crossdressing films which, like *Victor/Victoria*, have a performance theme, the assumption of sexual disguise is usually what activates the narrative, and the narration straightaway puts spectators in a privileged position: they already know the 'truth' about the gender of disguised characters while other characters in the fiction do not. Such an advantage (never enjoyed in quite the same way by spectators of film thrillers with a crossdressing theme) must be regarded as a condition of comedy. Thus in *Some Like It Hot*, the bedtime scene on the train, for example, could work as comedy only with a narrative 'view behind'. The spectator has to know that 'Daphne' is not really a girl, and that Sugar (Marilyn Monroe) is deceived in her belief to the contrary, in order to be able to draw on the range of cultural references around court-ship and sexuality that makes this particular case of mistaken identity so funny. It is funny not only because of the disparity in knowledge between Sugar and the spectator, but also because throughout the sequence the spectator is constantly being reminded of that disparity. To this extent, a measure of sadism on the spectator's part is necessary to the comic effect. Crossdressing films that are regarded as comedies are characterized by a narration which ensures that the spectator is never for an instant in doubt as to which of the characters is 'really' male and which 'really' female. The unchallenged spec-tator is free, from a secure vantage point, to laugh at the travesty, the comedy of errors attending the ignorance and confusion of the fiction's characters. Comedy, in this sense, does not denaturalize sexual difference.

If a 'view behind' characterizes the narration of the comedy of sexual disguise, in other types of crossdressing film – notably the thriller – the spectator, far from being sure from the outset about the gender of particular characters, may at times be just as uncertain as characters within the fiction itself. A 'view with', apart from enhancing the mystery which the narrative sets out to solve, may temporarily shake the spectator's conviction that gender distinctions are absolute, and so generate anxiety and a compensating desire for a return to certainty about these matters. Despite the fact that this desire is usually in the final instance gratified, the moment of uncertainty is of some consequence.

In *Psycho*, for example, the spectator is at first not simply uncertain, but in fact deceived, as to the gender of Marion's murderer. The shadow – of what appears to be a female figure – on the shower curtain turns out to be a false clue. In this case, the narration 'knows' more than the spectator, and much of the subsequent story plays on the spectator's apparent knowledge and effective deception. . . . In narratives which seem to offer little knowledge about what is 'really going on', the reader tends to be 'integrated into the world of the characters'.[4] When characters in the fiction are unsure about what is happening in their world, the reader is in an equally ambiguous position and must remain suspended in uncertainty or try to solve the riddle with what little information is offered. A narrative viewpoint as potentially unsettling as this typically characterizes moments at least of film thrillers. . . .

Crossdressing, cinema and sexual difference

An examination of narrative organization and narrative viewpoint usefully highlights the ways in which cinema draws on narrativity as a set of codes which cut across different forms and modes of representation. It cannot, however, address the question of the operation of cinema precisely as *cinema*, as a specific mode of representation. . . .

As spectacle, cinema does not only claim a peculiar

credibility on behalf of the visible, however: in doing this, it appeals also to certain forms of pleasure. In privileging in its own ways the instance of looking, classic narrative cinema offers visual pleasure of specific kinds: through engagement of desire for pleasurable looking, the spectator is caught up with the image on the screen. The act of watching a film, it has been suggested, involves relations of looking which evoke the very processes in which the human subject is psychically constructed as fixed and gendered. If looking and visual pleasure in general construct sexual difference, then so do spectator-text relations in cinema. Laura Mulvey has offered an explanation of how this process operates concretely in cinema – for example in the constitution of women characters in films as spectacle, constructed in the image as 'to-be-looked-at' and confirmed as such not only by the spectator's gaze, but also by that of male protagonists of the fiction.[5]

Consideration of sexual difference and the look as central moments in spectator–text relations in cinema acquires a special significance with regard to crossdressing films. . . . More importantly, perhaps, it also brings into focus an issue of some import for representations of crossdressing which has not yet been examined in the present context: the direction of crossdressing. Given the arguments about the specificity of the construction of woman as spectacle in classic narrative cinema, the question of whether a narrative film involving sexual disguise is about male–female or female–male crossdressing acquires some significance.

Where crossdressing in films is, as seems most frequently the case, male–female, sexually disguised characters are subject to being constructed as spectacle: so that, for instance, cinematic codes through which 'real' female characters in films are routinely set up in this way – lingering close-ups, soft-focus, point-of-view shots – may be activated. But when the spectator knows that these characters in women's dress are 'really' men, this courting of the spectator's look draws attention to certain conventions of cinematic representation, and so involves the text in a degree of self-referentiality as well. Through the construction of sexually disguised male characters as objects of pleasurable looking, attention may be drawn to conventions of cinematic representation which are in ordinary circumstances so much taken-for-granted as to be invisible. Where the spectator is aware that the characters are, clothes notwithstanding, not really women, such self-referentiality heightens the comedy.

This reflexivity is nowhere more evident than in the sequence in *Some Like It Hot* in which the musicians Joe and Gerry appear for the first time in their disguise as women. Hurrying along a station platform to catch the train that will take them with Sweet Sue's band to Florida, they get a first look at their glamorous colleague-to-be, Sugar.

1
MLS rear view two pairs   *Music starts*
of legs below waist. Track
forward.

2
Medium 2-shot 'Josephine'   LOUDSPEAKER: Florida
and 'Daphne' walk along   One leaving on track one for
platform. Track back.   Washington,

3
MCU 'Josephine'.
Track back.

... Charleston, Jackson and Miami. All aboard!

4
MCU 'Daphne'.
Track back.

... All aboard!

5
MLS rear view as 1 to LS.
D stumbles and looks back.

D: Ow! *Music stops*

6
Medium 2-shot J and D as 2. They stop.

J: What's the matter now?
D: How do they walk in these things? How do they keep their balance?
J: Must be the way the weight's distributed.

They start walking.

Now come on!

Track back.

They stop.

They stop and look.

D: It's so draughty. They must be catching cold all the time, huh?
J: Will you quit stalling? We're gonna miss the train.
D: I feel naked. I feel like everybody's staring at me.
J: With those legs? Are you crazy? Now come on!
D: Uh-oh!

7
LS girls in the band line up to board train.

Female chatter

8
Medium 2-shot J and D as 6.

D: It's no use, we're not gonna get away with it, Joe.
J: The name is Josephine, and this was your idea in the first place.

9a
MCU Sugar. Track back. S walks past J and D who turn and stare after her, offscreen right.

9b
Music starts

10
MCU rear view S's legs
from below waist to LS.
Steam shoots from train,
S stumbles and looks
back. Runs to join band.   *Music ends*

11
Medium 2-shot J and D as
9b, staring offscreen right.

D: Look at that! Look how
she moves! It's just like Jello
on springs. Must have some
sort of built-in motor or
something. I tell ya, it's a
whole different sex!
J: What are you afraid of?
Nobody's asking you to have
a baby. This is just to get us
out of town. Once we get to
Florida, we'll blow this
whole setup.
D: Joe, this time I am not
going to let you talk me into
something that . . .

Looking, in fact, is precisely what is at stake here. This short sequence of less than two minutes, in introducing Sugar, 'Josephine' and 'Daphne' as, in a sense, 'new' characters, marks a major move forward in the film's narrative and sets up a series of significant analogies and distinctions. On one level, the visual treatment of both Sugar and the Josephine/Daphne duo evokes some of the conventions by which classic narrative cinema constructs female characters as objects of the spectator's look. The first shot, for example, offers a voyeuristic view of legs and behinds which in cultural terms would suggest that the objects of the camera's gaze are female. At the same time, a rear view of this kind obviously withholds the identity of the owners of the legs (though the stumble would perhaps offer a retrospective clue). But any suspense is in any case shortlived, because the problem of identity is solved in the next three shots: the legs belong to Joe and Gerry, now in drag. In these shots, too, the signification of the conventionally female clothes and make-up worn by the characters is underscored by the fact that, in cinematic terms, they are effectively 'feminized', notably in the lingering individual close-ups of shots 3 and 4.

These first shots of Josephine and Daphne are formally similar to shot 10 and the opening of shot 9, in which Sugar makes her first appearance. But there is nevertheless one highly significant difference between these rhyming sets of shots. In the Josephine/Daphne series, the point-of-view is that of the camera. The camera, in other words, is the enunciator: it tells the story. Both shots of Sugar, by contrast, are point-of-view shots, motivated by the looks of Josephine and Daphne. Shot 8, for example, which precedes the first view of Sugar, ends on the two disguised musicians gazing offscreen left, so that shot 9 – our first sight of Sugar – clearly at least begins as a point-of-view shot (although this shot is interesting in that point-of-view shifts within it away from the characters and back to the camera). When, as here, the spectator's look coincides with that of characters in the fiction, the source of enunciation is both camera and characters.

This coincidence of point-of-view also occurs in shot 10, a rear view of Sugar whose composition is similar to that of the first shot of the sequence: this time, however, the view is motivated by the goggle-eyed stares of Josephine and Daphne which end shot 9. This pair of shots is confirmed as a point-of-view sequence when bracketed by shot 11, which repeats the end of shot 9 and underscores the centrality of the look in the dialogue:

Daphne: Look at that! Look how she moves! . . . I tell ya, its a whole different sex!

Daphne's exclamation serves also as a reminder of how looking functions in the construction of sexual difference. For in this sequence is neatly condensed a complex interplay of cinematic codes which construct difference through cinematic enunciation and spectacle. On the one hand, Josephine and Daphne, pretending to be women, seem to receive the same sort of visual treatment as the 'real' woman, Sugar. At the same time, however, the shifts of point-of-view between the camera on one side and Josephine/Daphne on the other mark these characters as masculine. For if it is true that in classic cinema looks within the diegesis tend to originate with male characters, an identity of character and camera in a point-of-view shot is readable as a masculine identification.

Here the rhyming of shots, and the simultaneous undercutting of the rhyme by shifts of point-of-view, call attention to the cinematic conventions, through which women are constructed as 'to-be-looked-at', while at the same time affirming the difference between the 'real' woman and the counterfeits. Moreover, in appealing to their prior knowledge of both narrative viewpoint and conventions of cinematic representation, this sequence constructs spectators precisely as *knowing*: knowing about the artifice not only of cinema but also of conventional signs of gender identity. For the knowing spectator – and in this case all spectators are addressed as knowing – irony and comedy are interpolated in layers of self-referentiality. . . .

Notes

1 This argument is informed by a structural approach to narrative. See especially Propp, Vladimir (1968) *Morphology of the Folk-Tale*, Austin: University of Texas Press.
2 William Luhr and Peter Lehman also make this point in (1983) ' "Crazy world full of crazy contradictions": Blake Edwards's *Victor/Victoria*', *Wide Angle* 5 (4): 4–13.
3 Todorov, Tzvetan (1970) 'Categories of the literary narrative', *Film Reader* 2: 19–37.
4 Todorov, Tzvetan (1970) 'The fantastic in fiction', *Twentieth Century Studies* 3: 76–92.
5 Mulvey, Laura (1975) 'Visual pleasure and narrative cinema', *Screen* 16 (3): 6–18.

12

The search for tomorrow in today's soap operas

Tania Modleski

I

. . . If television is considered by some to be a vast
wasteland, soap operas are thought to be the least
nourishing spot in the desert. The surest way to damn a
film, a television program, or even a situation in real life,
is to invoke an analogy to soap operas. In the same way
that men are often concerned to show that what they are,
above all, is not women, not 'feminine', so television
programs and movies will, surprisingly often, tell us that
they are not soap operas. . . . An afternoon 'Money
Movie', *Middle of the Night*, an interminable Paddy
Chayevsky affair starring Frederick March, dealt with
one man's life-crisis as, on the brink of old age, he falls
in love with a very young Kim Novak and struggles
against the petty and destructive jealousy of his sister and
daughter. 'This is *not* a soap opera,' he reprimands the
sister at one point. Since to me it had all the ingredients
of one, I could only conclude that men's soap operas are
not to be thought of as soap operas only because they are
for men (or about men).

It is refreshing, therefore, to read Horace Newcomb's
book, *TV: The Most Popular Art*, in which he suggests
that far from being the nadir of art forms, as most
people take them to be, soap operas represent in some

ways the furthest advance of TV art. In other words, for all their stereotypical qualities, they combine to the highest degree two of the most important elements of the television aesthetic: 'intimacy' and 'continuity'. Television, says Newcomb, is uniquely suited to deal with character and interpersonal relations rather than with action and setting. Soap operas, of course, play exclusively on the intimate properties of the medium. Newcomb also points out that because of the serial nature of the programs television can offer us depictions of people in situations which grow and change over time, allowing for a greater 'audience involvement, a sense of becoming a part of the lives and actions of the characters they see'.[1] Thus far it is mainly soap opera which has taken advantage of these possibilities for continuity, nighttime programs, by and large, tending to 'forget' from week to week all of the conflicts and lessons which have gone before.

Newcomb's book is important in that, by refusing to indulge in an anti-feminine bias against soap operas, it reveals a new way of seeing these programs which allows them to be placed in the vanguard of TV aesthetics (dubious as this distinction may seem to many people). My approach is different from, though in no sense opposed to, Newcomb's. I propose not to ignore what is 'feminine' about soap operas but to focus on it, to show how they provide a unique narrative pleasure which, while it has become thoroughly adapted to the rhythms of women's lives in the home, provides an alternative to the dominant 'pleasures of the text' analyzed by Roland Barthes and others. Soap operas may be in the vanguard not just of TV art but of all popular narrative art.

II

Whereas the meaning of Harlequin Romances depends almost entirely on the sense of an ending, soap operas are important to their viewers in part because they never end. Whereas Harlequins encourage our identification with one character, soap operas invite identification with numerous personalities. And whereas Harlequins are structured around two basic enigmas, in soap operas, the enigmas proliferate: 'Will Bill find out that his wife's sister's baby is really his by artificial insemination? Will his wife submit to her sister's blackmail attempts, or will she finally let Bill know the truth? If he discovers the truth, will this lead to another nervous breakdown, causing him to go back to Springfield General where his ex-wife and his illegitimate daughter are both doctors and sworn enemies?' Tune in tomorrow, not in order to find out the answers, but to see what further complications will defer the resolutions and introduce new questions. Thus the narrative, by placing ever more complex obstacles between desire and fulfillment, makes anticipation of an end an end in itself. Soap operas invest exquisite pleasure in the central condition of a woman's life: waiting – whether for her phone to ring, for the baby to take its nap, or for the family to be reunited shortly after the day's final soap opera has left *its* family still struggling against dissolution.

According to Roland Barthes, the hermeneutic code, which propounds the enigmas, functions by making 'expectation . . . the basic condition for truth: truth, these narratives tell us, is what is *at the end* of expectation. This design implies a return to order, for expectation is a disorder.'[2] But, of course, soap operas do not end. Consequently, truth for women is seen to lie not 'at the end of expectation', but *in* expectation, not in the 'return to order', but in (familial) disorder. . . .

One critic of soap opera remarks, 'If . . . as Aristotle so reasonably claimed, drama is the imitation of a human action that has a beginning, a middle, and an end, soap opera belongs to a separate genus that is entirely composed of an indefinitely expandable middle.'[3] It is not only that successful soap operas do not end, it is also that they cannot end. In *The Complete Soap Opera Book*, an interesting and lively work on the subject, the authors show how a radio serial forced off the air by television tried to wrap up its story.[4] It was an impossible task. Most of the storyline had to be discarded and only one element could be followed through to its end – an important example of a situation in which what Barthes calls the 'discourse's instinct for preservation' has virtually triumphed over authorial control.[5] Furthermore, it is not simply that the story's completion would have taken too long for the amount of time allotted by the producers. More importantly, I believe it would have been impossible to resolve the contradiction between the imperatives of melodrama – the good must be rewarded and the wicked punished – and the latent message of soap operas – everyone cannot be happy at the same time, no matter how deserving they are. The claims of any two people, especially in love matters, are often mutually exclusive.

John Cawelti defines melodrama as having

> at its center the moral fantasy of showing forth the essential 'rightness' of the world order. . . . Because of this, melodramas are usually rather complicated in plot and character; instead of identifying with a single protagonist through his line of action, the melodrama typically makes us intersect imaginatively with many lives. Subplots multiply, and the point of view continually shifts in order to involve us in a complex of destinies. Through this complex of characters and plots we see not so much the working of individual fates but the underlying moral process of the world.[6]

It is scarcely an accident that this essentially nineteenth-century form continues to appeal strongly to women, whereas the classic (male) narrative film is, as Laura Mulvey points out, structured 'around a main controlling figure with whom the spectator can identify'.[7] Soap operas continually insist on the insignificance of the individual life. A viewer might at one moment be asked to identify with a woman finally united with her lover, only to have that identification broken in a moment of intensity and attention focussed on the sufferings of the woman's rival.

If, as Mulvey claims, the identification of the spectator

with 'a main male protagonist' results in the spectator's becoming 'the representative of power',[8] the multiple identification which occurs in soap opera results in the spectator's being divested of power. For the spectator is never permitted to identify with a character completing an entire action. Instead of giving us one 'powerful ideal ego . . . who can make things happen and control events better than the subject/spectator can',[9] soap operas present us with numerous limited egos, each in conflict with the others, and continually thwarted in its attempts to control events because of inadequate knowledge of other people's plans, motivations and schemes. . . .

The subject/spectator of soap operas, it could be said, is constituted as a sort of ideal mother: a person who possesses greater wisdom than all her children, whose sympathy is large enough to encompass the conflicting claims of her family (she identifies with them all), and who has no demands or claims of her own (she identifies with no one character exclusively). The connection between melodrama and mothers is an old one. Harriet Beecher Stowe, of course, made it explicit in *Uncle Tom's Cabin*, believing that if her book could bring its female readers to see the world as one extended family, the world would be vastly improved. But in Stowe's novel, the frequent shifting of perspective identifies the reader with a variety of characters in order ultimately to ally her with the mother/author and with God who, in their higher wisdom and understanding, can make all the hurts of the world go away, thus insuring the 'essential "rightness" of the world order'. Soap opera, however, denies the 'mother' this extremely flattering illusion of her power. On the one hand, it plays upon the spectator's expectations of the melodramatic form, continually stimulating (by means of the hermeneutic code) the desire for a just conclusion to the story, and, on the other hand, it constantly presents the desire as unrealizable, by showing that conclusions only lead to further tension and suffering. Thus soap operas convince women that their highest goal is to see their families united and happy, while consoling them for their inability to realize this ideal and bring about familial harmony.

This is reinforced by the character of the good mother on soap operas. In contrast to the manipulating mother who tries to interfere with her children's lives, the good mother must sit helplessly by as her children's lives disintegrate; her advice, which she gives only when asked, is temporarily soothing, but usually ineffectual. Her primary function is to be sympathetic, to tolerate the foibles and errors of others. Maeve Ryan, the mother on *Ryan's Hope*, is a perfect example. *Ryan's Hope*, a soap opera centered around an Irish-Catholic, bar-owning family which, unlike the majority of soap families, lives in a large city, was originally intended to be more 'realistic', more socially oriented than the majority of soap operas.[10] Nevertheless, the function of the mother is unchanged: she is there to console her children and try to understand them as they have illegitimate babies, separate from their spouses (miraculously obtaining annulments instead of divorces), and dispense birth control information in the poor neighbourhoods.

It is important to recognize that soap operas serve to affirm the primacy of the family not by presenting an ideal family, but by portraying a family in constant turmoil and appealing to the spectator to be understanding and tolerant of the many evils which go on within that family. The spectator/mother, identifying with each character in turn, is made to see 'the larger picture' and extend her sympathy to both the sinner and the victim. She is thus in a position to forgive all. As a rule, only those issues which can be tolerated and ultimately pardoned are introduced on soap operas. The list includes careers for women, abortions, premarital and extra-marital sex, alcoholism, divorce, mental and even physical cruelty. An issue like homosexuality, which could explode the family structure rather than temporarily disrupt it, is simply ignored. Soap operas, contrary to many people's conception of them, are not conservative but liberal, and the mother is the liberal par excellence. By constantly presenting her with the many-sidedness of any question, by never reaching a permanent conclusion, soap operas undermine her capacity to form unambiguous judgments. . . .

These remarks must be qualified. If soap operas keep us caring about everyone; if they refuse to allow us to condemn most characters and actions until all the evidence is in (and, of course, it never is), there is one character whom we are allowed to hate unreservedly: the villainess, the negative image of the spectator's ideal self. Although much of the suffering on soap opera is presented as unavoidable, the surplus suffering is often the fault of the villainess who tries to 'make things happen and control events better than the subject/spectator can'. The villainess might very possibly be a mother trying to manipulate her children's lives or ruin their marriages. Or perhaps she is a woman avenging herself on her husband's family because it has never fully accepted her.

This character cannot be dismissed as easily as many critics seem to think. The extreme delight viewers apparently take in despising the villainess testifies to the enormous amount of energy involved in the spectator's repression and to her (albeit unconscious) resentment at being constituted as an egoless receptacle for the suffering of others. The villainess embodies the 'split-off fury' which, in the words of Dorothy Dinnerstein, is 'the underside of the "truly feminine" woman's monstrously overdeveloped talent for unreciprocated empathy'.[11] This aspect of melodrama can be traced back to the middle of the nineteenth century when *Lady Audley's Secret*, a drama based on Mary Elizabeth Braddon's novel about a governess turned bigamist and murderess, became one of the most popular stage melodramas of all time. In her discussion of the novel, Elaine Showalter shows how the author, while paying lipservice to conventional notions about the feminine role, managed to appeal to 'thwarted female energy':

> The brilliance of *Lady Audley's Secret* is that Braddon
> makes her would-be murderess the fragile blond angel of
> domestic realism. . . . The dangerous woman is not the
> rebel or the bluestocking, but the 'pretty little girl'
> whose indoctrination in the female role has taught her
> secrecy and deceitfulness, almost as secondary sex
> characteristics.[12]

Thus the villainess is able to transform traditional
feminine weaknesses into the sources of her strength.

Similarly, on soap operas, the villainess seizes those
aspects of a woman's life which normally render her
most helpless and tries to turn them into weapons for
manipulating other characters. She is, for instance,
especially good at manipulating pregnancy, unlike most
women, who, as Mary Ellman wittily points out, tend to
feel manipulated by it:

> At the same time, women cannot help observing that
> conception (their highest virtue, by all reports) simply
> happens or doesn't. It lacks the style of enterprise. It can
> be prevented by foresight and device (though success here,
> as abortion rates show, is exaggerated), but it is
> accomplished by luck (good or bad). Purpose often
> seems, if anything, a deterrent. A devious business
> benefitting by indirection, by pretending not to care, as
> though the self must trick the body. In the regrettable
> conception, the body instead tricks the self – much as it
> does in illness or death.[13]

In contrast to the numerous women on soap operas who
are either trying unsuccessfully to become pregnant or
who have become pregnant as a consequence of a single
unguarded moment in their lives, the villainess manages,
for a time at least, to make pregnancy work for her. She
gives it the 'style of enterprise'. If she decides she wants
to marry a man, she will take advantage of him one night
when he is feeling especially vulnerable and seduce him.
And if she doesn't achieve the hoped-for pregnancy,
undaunted, she simply lies to her lover about being pregnant. The villainess thus reverses male/female roles:
anxiety about conception is transferred to the male. He

is the one who had better watch his step and curb his promiscuous desires or he will find himself burdened with an unwanted child. . . .

Furthermore, the villainess, far from allowing her children to rule her life, often uses them in order to further her own selfish ambitions. One of her typical ploys is to threaten the father or the woman possessing custody of the child with the deprivation of that child. She is the opposite of the woman at home, who at first is forced to have her children constantly with her, and later is forced to let them go – for a time on a daily recurring basis and then permanently. The villainess enacts for the spectator a kind of reverse *fort-da* game, in which the mother is the one who attempts to send the child away and bring it back at will, striving to overcome feminine passivity in the process of the child's appearance and loss. Into the bargain, she also tries to manipulate the man's disappearance and return by keeping the fate of his child always hanging in the balance. And again, male and female roles tend to get reversed: the male suffers the typically feminine anxiety over the threatened absence of his children. On *Ryan's Hope*, for example, Delia continually uses her son to control her husband and his family. At one point she clashes with another villainess, Raye Woodward, over the child and the child's father, Frank Ryan, from whom Delia is divorced. Raye realizes that the best way to get Frank interested in her is by taking a maternal interest in his child. When Delia uncovers Raye's scheme, she becomes determined to foil it by regaining custody of the boy. . . .

The villainess thus continually works to make the most out of events which render other characters totally helpless. Literal paralysis turns out, for one villainess, to be an active blessing, since it prevents her husband from carrying out his plans to leave her; when she gets back the use of her legs, therefore, she doesn't tell anyone. And even death doesn't stop another villainess from wreaking havoc; she returns to haunt her husband and convince him to try to kill his new wife. . . .

Soap operas, then, while constituting the spectator as a 'good mother', provide in the person of the villainess an outlet for feminine anger: in particular, as we have seen, the spectator has the satisfaction of seeing men suffer the same anxieties and guilt that women usually experience and seeing them receive similar kinds of punishment for their transgressions. But that anger is neutralized at every moment in that it is the special object of the spectator's hatred. The spectator, encouraged to sympathize with almost everyone, can vent her frustration on the one character who refuses to accept her own powerlessness, who is unashamedly self-seeking. Woman's anger is directed at woman's anger, and an eternal cycle is created.

And yet, if the villainess never succeeds, if, in accordance with the spectator's conflicting desires, she is doomed to eternal repetition, then she obviously never permanently fails either. When, as occasionally happens, a villainess reforms, a new one immediately supplants her. Generally, however, a popular villainess will remain true to her character for most or all of the soap opera's duration. And if the villainess constantly suffers because she is always foiled, we should remember that she suffers no more than the good characters, who don't even try to interfere with their fates. Again, this may be contrasted to the usual imperatives of melodrama, which demand an ending to justify the suffering of the good and punish the wicked. While soap operas thrive they present a continual reminder that women's anger is alive, if not exactly well.

III

Critics have speculated before now about why the narrative form of soap opera seems to have special appeal to women. Marcia Kinder, reviewing Ingmar Bergman's *Scenes from a Marriage*, suggests that the 'open-ended, slow paced, multi-climaxed' structure of soap opera is 'in tune with patterns of female sexuality'.[14] While this is certainly a plausible explanation, it should be clear by now that soap opera as a narrative form also reflects and cultivates the 'proper' psychological disposition of the woman in the home. Nancy Chodorow provides us with a nice description of women's work in the home and usefully contrasts it to work performed in the labor force:

> Women's activities in the home involve continuous connection to and concern about children and attunement to adult masculine needs, both of which require connection to, rather than separateness from, others. The work of maintenance and reproduction is characterized by its repetitive and routine continuity, and does not involve specified sequence or progression. By contrast, work in the labor force – 'men's work' – is likely to be contractual, to be more specifically delimited, and to contain a notion of defined progression and product.[15]

. . . Chodorow stresses the 'connectedness' of women's work in the home, but this is only half the picture. The wife's job is further complicated by the fact that she must often deal with several people with different, perhaps conflicting moods; and further she must be prepared to drop what she is doing in order to cope with various conflicts and problems the moment they arise. Unlike most workers in the labor force, the housewife must beware of concentrating her energies exclusively on any one task – otherwise, the dinner could burn or the baby could crack its skull (as happened once on *Ryan's Hope* when the villainess became so absorbed in a love encounter that she forgot to keep an eye on her child). The housewife functions, as many creative women have sadly realized, by distraction. Tillie Olsen writes in *Silences*, 'More than in any other human relationship, overwhelmingly more, motherhood means being instantly interruptable, responsive, responsible. . . . It is distraction, not meditation, that becomes habitual: interruption, not continuity; spasmodic, not constant toil.'[16] Daytime television plays a part in habituating women to distraction, interruption and spasmodic toil.

These observations have crucial implications for current television theory. In his book *Television: Technology and Cultural Form* Raymond Williams suggests that the shifts in television programming from one type of show to another and from part of a show to a commercial should not be seen as 'interruptions' – of a mood, of a story – but parts of a whole. What at first appear to be discrete programming units in fact interrelate in profound and complex ways. Williams uses the term 'flow' to describe this interaction of various programs with each other and with commercials. 'The fact of flow,' he says, defines the 'central television experience.'[17] Against Williams I would argue that the flow within soap operas as well as between soap operas and other programming units reinforces the very principle of interruptability crucial to the proper functioning of women in the home. In other words, what Williams calls 'the central television experience' is a profoundly decentering experience.

'The art of being off center,' wrote Walter Benjamin in an essay on Baudelaire, 'in which the little man could acquire training in places like the Fun Fair, flourished concomitantly with unemployment.'[18] Soap operas also provide training in the 'art of being off center'. . . . The housewife, of course, is in one sense, like the little man at the Fun Fair, unemployed, but in another sense she is perpetually employed – her work, like a soap opera, is never done. Moreover, as I have said, her duties are split among a variety of domestic and familial tasks, and her television programs keep her from desiring a focused existence by involving her in the pleasures of a fragmented life.

Interruptions may be, as Benjamin thought, one of the fundamental devices of all art, but surely soap opera relies on them to a far greater extent than any other art.[19] Revelations, confrontations and reunions are constantly being interrupted and postponed by telephone calls, unexpected visitors, counterrevelations, catastrophes, and switches from one plot to another.

These interruptions are both annoying and pleasurable: if we are torn away from one exciting story, we at least have the relief of picking up the thread of an unfinished one. Like the (ideal) mother in the home, we are kept interested in a number of events at once and are denied the luxury of a total and prolonged absorption. Commercials constitute another kind of interruption, in this case from *outside* the diegesis. Commercials present the housewife with mini-problems and their resolutions, so after witnessing all the agonizingly hopeless dilemmas on soap operas, the spectator has the satisfaction of seeing something cleaned up, if only a stained shirt or a dirty floor.

Although daytime commercials and soap operas are both set overwhelmingly within the home, the two views of the home seem antithetical, for the chief concerns of commercials are precisely the ones soap operas censor out. The saggy diapers, yellow wax build-up and carpet smells making up the world of daytime television ads are rejected by soap operas in favor of *Another World*, as the very title of one soap opera announces, a world in which characters deal only with the 'large' problems of human existence: crime, love, death and dying. But this antithesis embodies a deep truth about the way women function in (or, more accurately, around) culture: as both moral and spiritual guides and household drudges: now one, now the other, moving back and forth between the extremes, but obviously finding them difficult to reconcile.[20]

Similarly, the violent mood swings the spectator undergoes in switching from quiz shows, the other popular daytime television fare, to soap operas also constitutes a kind of interruption, just as the housewife is required to endure monotonous, repetitive work but to be able to switch instantly and on demand from her role as a kind of bedmaking, dishwashing automaton to a large sympathizing consciousness. . . .

The formal properties of daytime television thus accord closely with the rhythms of women's work in the home. Individual soap operas as well as the flow of various programs and commercials tend to make repetition, interruption and distraction pleasurable. But we can go even further and note that for women viewers reception itself often takes place in a state of distraction. According to Benjamin, 'reception in a state of distraction . . . finds in the film its true means of exercise.'[21] But now that we have television we can see that it goes beyond film in this respect, or at least the daytime programs do. For the consumption of most films as well as of nighttime programs in some ways recapitulates the work situation in the factory or office: the viewer is physically passive, immobilized, and all his attention is focused on the object before him. Even the most allegedly 'mindless' program requires a fairly strong degree of concentration if its plot is to make sense. But since the housewife's 'leisure' time is not so strongly demarcated, her entertainment must often be consumed on the job. As the authors of *The Complete Soap Opera Book* tell us:

> The typical fan was assumed to be trotting about her daily chores with her mop in one hand, duster in the other, cooking, tending babies, answering telephones. Thus occupied, she might not be able to bring her full powers of concentration to bear on *Backstage Wife*.[22]

This accounts, in part, for the 'realistic' feel of soap operas. The script writers, anticipating the housewife's distracted state, are careful to repeat important elements of the story several times. Thus, if two characters are involved in a confrontation which is supposed to mark a final break in their relationship, that same confrontation must be repeated, with minor variations, a few times in order to make sure the viewer gets the point. 'Clean breaks' – surely a supreme fiction – are impossible on soap operas. . . .

Ironically, critics of television untiringly accuse its viewers of indulging in escapism. In other words, both high art critics and politically oriented critics, though motivated by different concerns, unite in condemning daytime television for *distracting* the housewife from her real situation. My point has been that a distracted or distractable frame of mind is crucial to the housewife's efficient functioning *in* her real situation, and at this level television and its so-called distractions, along with the particular forms they take, are intimately bound up with women's work.

IV

Given the differences in the ways men and women experience their lives, it is not surprising to find that 'narrative pleasure' can sometimes mean very different things to men and women. This is an important point. Too often feminist criticism implies that there is only one kind of pleasure to be derived from narrative and that it is an essentially masculine one. Hence, it is further implied, feminist artists must first of all challenge this pleasure and then out of nothing begin to construct a feminist aesthetics and feminist form. This is a mistaken position, in my view, for it keeps us constantly in an adversary role, always on the defensive, always, as it were, complaining about the family but never leaving home. Feminist artists don't have to start from nothing; rather, they can look for clues to women's pleasure which are already present in existing forms, even if this pleasure is currently placed at the service of patriarchy. . . . Clearly, women find soap operas eminently entertaining, and an analysis of the pleasure these programs afford can provide feminists with ways not only to challenge this pleasure but to incorporate it into their own artistic practices.

   The fact that soap operas never reach a full conclusion has usually been viewed in an entirely negative light. Here are the words of Dennis Porter, who, working from Roland Barthes's theories of narrative structures and ideology, completely condemns soap operas for their failure to resolve all problems:

Unlike all traditionally end-oriented fiction and drama, soap opera offers process without progression, not a climax and a resolution, but mini-climaxes and provisional denouements that must never be presented in such a way as to eclipse the suspense experienced for associated plot lines. Thus soap opera is the drama of perepetia without anagnorisis. It deals forever in reversals but never portrays the irreversible change which traditionally marks the passage out of ignorance into true knowledge. For actors and audience alike, no action ever stands revealed in the terrible light of its consequences.[23]

These are strange words indeed, coming from one who purports to be analyzing the ideology of narrative form. They are a perfect illustration of how a high art bias, an eagerness to demonstrate the worthlessness of 'low' art, can lead us to make claims for high art which we would ordinarily be wary of professing. Terms like 'progression', 'climax', 'resolution', 'irreversible change', 'true knowledge' and 'consequences' are certainly tied to an ideology; they are 'linked to classical metaphysics', as Barthes observes. '[The] hermeneutic narrative in which truth predicts an incomplete subject, based on expectation and desire for its imminent closure, is . . . linked to the kerygmatic civilization of meaning and truth, appeal and fulfillment.'[24] To criticize classical narrative because, for example, it is based on a suspect notion of progress and then criticize soap opera because it *isn't* will never get us anywhere – certainly not 'out of ignorance into true knowledge'. A different approach is needed.

Luce Irigaray, describing woman's 'rediscovery' of herself, writes, 'It is a sort of universe in expansion for which no limits could be fixed and which, for all that, would not be incoherence.'[25] The similarities between this description and soap opera as a form are striking. They suggest the possibility that soap operas may not be an entirely negative influence on the viewer; they may also have the force of a *negation*, a negation of the typical (and masculine) modes of pleasure in our society. This challenge, is, moreover, very like the one being mounted in current literary and film theory. Theorists have recently been pointing out the pleasures of the kind of text which breaks the illusion of unity and totality provided the reader or spectator by the 'classic text'. Hence the emphasis since the structuralists has been on 'decentering the subject'. But, as we have seen, women are, in their lives, their work, and in certain forms of their pleasure, already decentered – 'off center'. As Mark Poster remarks in his *Critical Theory of the Family*, 'the feeling of being the center of creation is typical of the ego-structure of the bourgeois male'.[26] This fact seems to me to be of crucial importance to anyone interested in formulating a feminist aesthetic. Indeed, I would like to argue that soap operas are not altogether at odds with an already developing, though still embryonic, feminist aesthetics.

'Deep in the very nature of soaps is the implied promise that they will last forever.'[27] This being the case, a great deal of interest necessarily becomes focused upon those events which retard or impede the flow of the narrative. If, on the one hand, these constant interruptions provide consolation for the housewife's sense of missed opportunities, by illustrating for her the enormous difficulty of getting from desire to fulfillment, on the other hand, the notion of what Porter contemptuously calls 'process without progression' is one endorsed by many innovative women artists. In praising Nathalie Sarraute, for example, Mary Ellmann observes that she is not

> interested in the explicit speed of which the novel is capable, only in the nuances which must tend to delay it. In her own discussions of the novel, Nathalie Sarraute is entirely anti-progressive. In criticizing ordinary dialogue, she dislikes its haste: there not being 'time' for the person to consider a remark's ramifications, his having to speak and to listen frugally, his having to rush ahead toward his object – which is of course 'to order his own conduct'.[28]

Soap opera is similarly anti-progressive. Just as Sarraute's work is opposed to the traditional novel form, soap opera is opposed to the classic (male) film narrative, which, with maximum action and minimum, always pertinent dialogue, speeds its way to the restoration of order. . . .

Notes

1 Newcomb, Horace (1974) *TV: The Most Popular Art*, New York: Anchor Books, p. 253.
2 Barthes, Roland (1974) *S/Z*, New York: Hill & Wang, p. 76.
3 Porter, Dennis (1977) 'Soap time: thoughts on a commodity art form', *College English* 38: 783.
4 Edmondson, Madelaine and Rounds, David (1976) *From Mary Noble to Mary Hartman: The Complete Soap Opera Book*, New York: Stein & Day, pp. 104–10.
5 Barthes, op. cit., p. 135.
6 Cawelti, John G. (1976) *Mystery and Romance*, Chicago: University of Chicago Press, pp. 45–6.
7 Mulvey, Laura (1975) 'Visual pleasure and narrative cinema', in Karyn Kay and Gerald Peary (eds) (1977) *Women and the Cinema*, New York: E.P. Dutton, p. 420.
8 ibid., p. 420.
9 ibid., p. 420.
10 Mayer, Paul (1977) 'Creating *Ryan's Hope*', in Judy Fireman (ed.) *TV Book*, New York: Workman Publishing Co.
11 Dinnerstein, Dorothy (1976) *The Mermaid and the Minotaur: Sexual Arrangements and Human Malaise*, New York: Harper & Row, p. 236.
12 Showalter, Elaine (1977) *A Literature of Their Own*, Princeton, N.J.: Princeton University Press, p. 204.
13 Ellmann, Mary (1968) *Thinking about Women*, New York: Harvest Books, p. 181. Molly Haskell makes a similar point in her discussion of 'The women's film' in M. Haskell (1974) *From Reverence to Rape: The Treatment of Women in the Movies*, New York: Penguin, pp. 172–3.
14 Kinder, Marsha (1974–5) 'Review of *Scenes from a Marriage*, by Ingmar Bergman', *Film Quarterly* 28 (2): 51.
15 Chodorow, Nancy (1978) *The Reproduction of Mothering: Psychoanalysis and the Sociology of Gender*, Berkeley: University of California Press, p. 179.
16 Olsen, Tillie (1979) *Silences*, New York: Dell Publishing Co., pp. 18–19.
17 Williams, Raymond (1975) *Television: Technology and Cultural Form*, New York: Schocken Books, p. 95.
18 Benjamin, Walter (1969) 'On some motifs in Baudelaire', in

Illuminations, New York: Schocken Books, p. 176.

19 Benjamin, Walter (1969) 'What is epic theatre?', in *Illuminations*, p. 151.

20 See Sherry B. Ortner's brilliant discussion of women's position in culture, 'Is female to male as nature is to culture?', in Michelle Rosaldo Zimbalist and Louise Lamphere (eds) (1974) *Women, Culture and Society*, Stanford, Ca: Stanford University Press.

21 Benjamin, Walter (1969) 'The work of art in the age of mechanical reproduction', in *Illuminations*, p. 240.

22 Edmondson and Rounds, op. cit., pp. 46–7.

23 Porter, op. cit., 783–4.

24 Barthes, op. cit., p. 45.

25 Irigaray, Luce 'Ce sexe qui n'en est pas un', in Elaine Marks and Isabelle Courtivron (eds) (1980) *New French Feminisms*, Amherst, Mass.: University of Massachusetts Press, p. 104.

26 Poster, Mark (1978) *Critical Theory of the Family*, New York: Continuum Books, p. 9.

27 Edmondson and Rounds, op. cit., p. 112.

28 Ellmann, op. cit., pp. 222–3.

Section 4

Knowledge, power, ideology: detective fiction

Introduction

Few questions have been quite so radically unsettled in recent years as those concerning the relations between literary forms and ideology. For some time prior to the 1960s the prevailing consensus in Marxist thought had been a sociologized version of conventional theories of authorship: the literary work gave form and coherence, not to the views of the exceptional individual, but to the world-view or ideology of a particular social group or class. Under the influence of structuralism, this view was called into question within Marxism, where the formulations of Louis Althusser and Pierre Macherey provided an alternative conception of the literature/ideology relationship.[1] According to this view, ideology furnishes the literary work with its raw materials which are then reworked as the distinctive formal devices of literature are brought to bear upon them. The literary work which results from this process, it is argued, is not an expression of ideology but a specifically literary production of ideology which makes visible its fault-lines and contradictions.

While this reformulation of Marxist concerns has proved richly productive in the new critical work it has enabled, more severe difficulties have been raised from within contending bodies of theory – more severe because they call into question the utility of the category of ideology and, thereby, the validity, or indeed purpose, of seeking to analyse literary works in terms of their relations to ideology. Perhaps the most influential criticisms of this sort have been those advanced by Michel Foucault for whom one of the main weaknesses with the category of ideology is that 'it always stands in virtual opposition to something else which is supposed to count as truth.'[2] Rather than drawing rigid boundary lines between truth or science on the one hand and ideology on the other, Foucault suggests that inquiry should instead concern itself with 'seeing historically how effects of truth are produced within discourses which in themselves are neither true nor false.'[3] Literary theorists influenced by Foucault's epistemological agnosticism have thus tended to consider literary works in their relations to social knowledges – that is, to bodies of thought which function as the truth for particular societies or periods – and to be particularly concerned with their deployment within the power relations of which such knowledges form a part.

The repercussions of these debates, while affecting many areas in the study of popular fiction, have been especially marked in relation to the study of detective fiction, particularly its classical forms. Detective fiction has, in any case, always been one of the more fully studied popular genres, partly because its beginnings can be fixed with relative certainty and some precision. Of course, the genre has its precursors, Voltaire's *Zadig* and William Godwin's *Caleb Williams* being among those most frequently cited. None the less, it is generally agreed that Edgar Allan Poe's 'The Murders in the Rue Morgue' (1841) and 'The Purloined Letter' (1845) constituted a distinct innovation in organizing the narrative around the intellectual virtuosity of a detective hero who reconstructs the scene of a crime and apprehends the guilty party through the traces left behind – an innovation Sir Arthur Conan Doyle was to translate into a commercially successful formula in his Sherlock Holmes stories, the first of which appeared in 1887. The genre has thus been of particular interest to sociologically inclined theorists concerned to account for its rise and development in terms of its social articulations.

There is, moreover, a fair degree of agreement concerning which of the genre's social articulations should be looked to in this respect. Ideologies of individualism, of science and of rationality; the development of the city; the development of police forces and related forms of surveillance – these are the kinds of considerations invoked in virtually all accounts of the genre's development. However, there has and continues to be a marked divergence of opinion regarding the precise ways in which these social articulations of the genre should be theorized and related to one another in accounting for both its development and its effects. The readings assembled here have been selected with a view to illustrating some of these differences as well as to showing how they are shaped by differing conceptions of the relations between literature, ideology, knowledge and power.

Dana Brand's account, which focuses on Poe's stories, takes its bearings from Walter Benjamin's now classic discussion of the relations between the literary figures of the detective and the *flâneur*.[4] Although Benjamin's perspectives on detective fiction are developed as a series of asides to his main purpose – a discussion of Baudelaire's *Fleurs du Mal* – they have proved significantly influential in virtually all subsequent writings on the genre. Nor is it difficult to see why. In effect, Benjamin reversed the emphasis of earlier accounts of the genre which had seen it as both expressing and celebrating the values of individualism as personified in the detective hero.[5] To the contrary, Benjamin argues, the impetus of detective fiction is orientated toward the *erasure* of individuality. Relating the origins of the genre to the massification and impersonality of social life associated with the development of the city, Benjamin argues that the form offered an antidote to the situation in which 'the masses appear as the asylum that shields an asocial person from his persecutors'.[6] If, as Benjamin goes on to argue, the 'original social content of the detective story was the obliteration of the individual's traces in the big-city crowd,'[7] the genre lifts the veil of anonymity the urban crowd affords the criminal in rendering him imaginatively knowable through his traces: fingerprints, cigar ash, etc. Although detective fiction thus subjects the city to a controlling and individualizing gaze (that of the detective) in which there is 'no hiding place' for the criminal, that gaze at the same time effects a reduction in the value of individuality, which, in the tell-tale clues through which it is revealed, is defined as a statistical effect rather than as the product of a unique psyche.

The immediate literary context against which Benjamin sets his discussion of Poe's detective stories is provided by the nineteenth-century physiologies through which the opacity of city life was penetrated and rendered knowable in being portrayed as inhabited by a series of predictable types revealed to, and ordered by, the gaze of the *flâneur* or city stroller. In extending the terms of Benjamin's discussion, Brand argues that the figure of the *flâneur* and, subsequently, that of the detective offered imaginative defences against the overwhelming multiplicity of appearances and experiences provided by daily life in Europe's capital cities:

> This defense may be broadly defined as the fantasy of a spectatorial subjectivity capable of establishing epistemological and aesthetic control over an environment commonly perceived to be threatening and opaque. By reducing the city to a legible model or emblem of itself, and by demonstrating his control over his reduction, such a subjectivity assumes a paternalistic or heroic role in relation to an urban literary audience. He comforts city-dwellers by suggesting that the city can be read and mastered, despite all appearances to the contrary.[8]

Detective fiction, on this analysis, thus occupies a distinctive phase in a broader literary problematic, and one with a longer history: that of the legibility of the city. Poe's achievement, seen in this perspective, was two-fold: first, to 'demonize the gap in the urban text' by linking urban unintelligibility with crime so that 'the opacity of the urban crowd ceases to be merely confusing' and 'becomes actively threatening' (p. 224); second, to provide, in the figure of Dupin, an elevated standpoint from which legibility could be restored to the city and that threat averted. The special interest of Brand's account consists in its detailed demonstration of the respects in which this imaginative dominance over the city was produced by means of a critique and transcendence of the forms of reading the city associated with the earlier figure of the *flâneur*.

It was not merely in the realm of fiction, however, that the threat of urban illegibility presented itself; nor were the responses to it merely imaginative. As Benjamin points out at some length, the development of a position of imaginative spectatorial dominance afforded by detective fiction was accompanied by, and corresponded to, the development of new mechanisms of surveillance which – precisely through their bureaucratic reduction of individuality to a set of knowable traces – rendered the city legible to the gaze of power. This aspect of Benjamin's discussion bears a marked resemblance to Foucault's analysis of the principles of panopticism within what he regards as the distinctive modern economy of power developed in the course of the nineteenth century – a similarity which Franco Moretti exploits in elaborating an account of detective fiction, and of the Sherlock Holmes stories in particular, which works between and seeks to reconcile Marxist and Foucauldian perspectives.

In absolutist regimes, Foucault argues in *Discipline and Punish*, the power of the king is dependent on its being made manifest in the form of public rituals – such as executions or floggings – as part of a public dramaturgy in which the naked fact of power is written as a message on the body of the condemned for society to read. Viewed in this light, the popular literature of crime – the confessions of the condemned circulated in broadsheets – was complicit with, indeed formed a part of, this apparatus of power, one of the means by which power was broadcast and dramatized although not, Foucault notes, without being contested in the process.[9] In the course of the nineteenth century, by contrast, incarceration – in prisons and mental asylums – increasingly became the major form of punishment, the way in which power over the body was exercised. Power was no longer dependent on public display for its exercise.

Why? The reason, Foucault suggests, is that new forms of surveillance formed a capillary network through which power was distributed throughout society, rendering all its domains constantly visible to the gaze of government. Sight, in this context, became the key metaphor for power and – through the development of institutionalized systems of looking – the main means by which it was organized. The carceral institutions of this period developed this system of looking to perfection in rendering everything visible, subordinate to a central and controlling gaze of power. This was the principle of Jeremy Bentham's Panopticon – a model prison in which the surveillance of the inmates was to have been complete and total. The principle of panopticism, however, was of a more general importance. Embodying the dream of a society rendered totally transparent to the gaze of power, panopticism, claims Foucault, became the regulative principle of a wide range of new forms of social discipline and surveillance – a gaze which, in its capacity to penetrate even the murkiest depths of society, to generate a file for, and therefore to know, the beggar, the vagrant, the orphan, transfixed individuality so that it could be classified and catalogued and, thereby, transformed into an object of social administration.

The 'private eye' of detective fiction, it has been argued, provided a complement to this public eye of power, realizing, in the realm of the imagination, the dream of rendering society totally visible to the gaze of power. By the time of the Sherlock Holmes stories, as

Dennis Porter puts it, 'the Great Detective of fiction had himself the essential qualities of the unseen seer, who stands at the centre of the social panopticon and employs his "science" to make all things visible on behalf of the forces of order.'[10] It is this vein of argument that Moretti draws on in his contention that the classical detective story embodies the 'totalitarian aspiration towards a *transparent* society' (p. 240). However, Moretti also adds a more specific social content to his analysis of the anti-individualizing impetus of the form in suggesting that it represents the transition from the phase of liberal capitalism to that of monopoly capitalism. Noting that the criminal in the Holmes stories is always either a noble or an upstart, Moretti argues that both of these embody a threat to the achieved property relations of monopoly capitalism. The noble seeks to reverse the historical process of bourgeois capital accumulation by increasing his own wealth through 'a revival of feudal arbitrary will' (p. 244). The upstart reverts to the earlier stage of what Marx called primitive accumulation in seeking to acquire property through violence and theft. In its opposition to the individuality of both noble and upstart – disruptive individualities which the narration works to efface – Moretti suggests that the classical detective story promoted an adjustment to the requirements of mono- poly capitalism in separating 'individuality and bourgeoisie' by representing the latter as 'no longer the champion of risk, novelty and imbalance, but of prudence, conservation and stasis' (p. 243).

In 'Morelli, Freud and Sherlock Holmes: clues and scientific method', Carlo Ginzburg focuses on an aspect of detective fiction which, although remarked upon by both Benjamin and Moretti, does not lead them in the same direction: the fact that it is through close attention to the apparently inconsequential aspects of character and behaviour that the hero is able to detect the wayward individuality whose crime disturbs the social order. This aspect of the genre, first announced by Poe, was developed into a cliché in the Sherlock Holmes stories where Holmes, in contrast to Watson's befuddled focus on the obvious aspects of the case in hand, solves the mystery though his attention to apparently 'insignificant trifles'. Ginzburg compares the role accorded such details in the Holmes stories with the similar importance attributed to 'inadvertent little gestures' as the key to character in Freud's psychoanalysis and the art criticism of Giovanni Morelli – both contemporaries of Conan Doyle. In doing so he offers a reading of the Holmesian method which calls into question Moretti's contention that the detective story served to restore faith in a positivist model of science in positing a single and necessary connection between cause and effect which the detective hero infallibly discovers. Rather, Ginzburg suggests, the writings of Freud, Morelli and Conan Doyle embodied a model of knowledge – he calls it 'the conjectural paradigm' – which, in contradistinction to positivism, concedes to all knowledge an inescapably semiotic character. Knowledge, in this view, always involves the interpretation of signs – Holmes's clues, symptoms in the case of medicine, slips of the tongue for Freud – in which the leap from signs to the reality they are said to represent is always conjectural, a hunch founded on probabilities rather than a cast-iron certainty.

Catherine Belsey is also sceptical of the view that the Holmes stories embody an ideology of scientific rationalism and, in querying this, incorporates a feminist perspective into her discussion. Viewing the Holmes stories as texts organized on two levels, Belsey locates their ideological significance in the interplay between these. At one level, the texts espouse the view that the use of logical deduction and scientific method may render all mysteries clear and accountable to reason. At another level, however, they deny this in their silence and evasiveness over the nature of women's sexuality. In expressing the values of science, the text also simultaneously calls those values into question as, in a formulation indebted to Althusser's and Macherey's conception of the literature/ideology relationship, Belsey argues that 'the presentation of so many women . . . as shadowy, mysterious and magical figures precisely contradicts the project of explicitness, transgresses the values of the texts, and in doing so throws into relief the poverty of the contemporary concept of science' (p. 283).

Notes

1 See Althusser, Louis (1971) 'A letter on art in reply to Andre Daspre', in *Lenin and Philosophy, and Other Essays*, London: New Left Books, and Macherey, Pierre (1978) *A Theory of Literary Production*, London: Routledge & Kegan Paul.
2 Foucault, Michel (1980) 'Truth and power', in *Power/Knowledge: Selected Interviews and Other Writings, 1972–1977*, New York: Pantheon Books, p. 118.
3 ibid., p. 118.
4 See Benjamin, Walter (1973) *Charles Baudelaire: A Lyric Poet in the Era of High Capitalism*, London: New Left Books.
5 Such views are most clearly restated – but then qualified and developed into a more complex argument – in Knight, Stephen (1980) *Form and Ideology in Detective Fiction*, London: Macmillan.
6 Benjamin, op. cit., p. 40.
7 ibid., p. 43.
8 Brand, Dana Aron (1986) *The Spectator and the City: Fantasies of Urban Legibility in Nineteenth-Century England and America*, Ann Arbor, Mich.: University Microfilms International, pp. iv–v.
9 See Foucault, Michel (1977) *Discipline and Punish: The Birth of the Prison*, London: Allen Lane, pp. 65–9.
10 Porter, Dennis (1981) *The Pursuit of Crime: Art and Ideology in Detective Fiction*, New Haven, Conn. and London: Yale University Press, p. 125.

13

From the *flâneur* to the detective: interpreting the city of Poe
Dana Brand

Edgar Allan Poe's story 'The Man of the Crowd' begins with the representation of a figure strikingly similar to [Dickens's] Boz. The narrator of this story, in a special mood he attributed to a sense of renewed strength after an illness, feels 'a calm but inquisitive interest in everything' (507).[1] He is sitting at the 'large bow window' of a coffee-house in London, observing a passing crowd with a detachment figuratively represented by the mediating window itself. Unnoticed by the crowd, the narrator begins to read it as if it were a text. He claims that his special mood has given him extraordinary interpretive powers, enabling him to determine the professions and characters of passers-by simply by observing their 'varieties of figure, dress, air, gait, visage, and expression of countenance' (507). . . . The crowd is divided into discrete types, each of which is signified by a specific set of external characteristics. 'Upper clerks of staunch firms,' the reader is told, all dress the same way, they all have 'slightly bald heads', and right ears that 'stand off on end' (508). However much this reductive uniformity contradicts the reader's empirical experience of urban crowds, it still has a strong appeal as a fantasy. The *flâneur* 'demonstrates' what the reader would like to believe but does not, that the urban crowd can be epistemologically and imaginatively mastered. . . .

In his special mood, the city becomes as legible to Poe's *flâneur* as the newspaper he lays aside at the moment he begins to read the crowd. This flow of legible physiognomy however, is suddenly interrupted by the old man, whose face 'like a certain German book . . . does not permit itself to be read' (506). The narrator leaves his seat and pursues the man through the London streets, trying to fill this gap in the urban text, and trying to resolve the anxiety it has caused. Representing this pursuit, Poe offers a complex analysis and critique of the subjectivity I have described as that of the *flâneur*. His analysis and critique is preliminary to Poe's transformation of the *flâneur* into the detective in the Auguste Dupin stories written shortly after 'The Man of the Crowd'. . . .

The first indication that the narrator's language is inadequate comes when he encounters a face that cannot be reduced to a reading. The old man is a gap in the urban text, a gap that threatens to unravel the narrator's sense of imaginative control over that which he has reduced to a text. The narrator pursues the old man in an effort to close this gap, in an effort to restore the totality of his interpretive control. This effort appears to be obsessive. It is improbable that a convalescent with any actual control over his actions would pursue an old man through cold and rainy London streets for twenty-four hours. . . . This implausibility, however, far from weakening the story, highlights the extraordinary intensity of the narrator's need to fill this gap in his reading of the city. . . . The narrator says, in reference to the old man, that he was 'firmly resolved that we should not part until I had satisfied myself in some measure respecting him' (513). . . .

In order to understand the nature of the narrator's extraordinary curiosity, it is first of all necessary to consider its object. . . .

The individual pursued by the narrator of 'The Man of the Crowd' . . . resembles the metropolitan man described by Wordsworth in his 'Preface' to the *Lyrical Ballads*.

'The encreasing accumulation of men in cities,' according to Wordsworth, has contributed to the production of a type of individual who is incapable of mental excitement 'without the application of gross and violent stimulants'.[2] Such an individual becomes a slave to his own 'craving for extraordinary incident' and is in this way reduced 'to a state of almost savage torpor'. Wordsworth described this type of individual in Book VII of the *Prelude*. He asserted that city-dwellers 'even' the 'highest minds' among them, cannot escape the reduction of consciousness to a 'perpetual flow/ Of trivial objects'.[3] For a consciousness reduced to a pure spontaneous rush of objects, the greatest fear is of the arrest of the flow since there is no interior resource from which new objects for consciousness can come. This is the dilemma of 'the man of the crowd'. 'He refuses to be alone' (515), because his mind has lost the ability to synthetically produce experience. His imagination has been destroyed, overwhelmed by stimuli. In this state of 'savage torpor', he has become dependent upon 'the application of gross and violent stimulants'. If this external stimulation were to cease, if the old man were to find himself truly alone, he would experience a pure emptiness, a terrifying and intolerable ennui.

It is the terror of the prospect of this emptiness that drives the old man through the London streets. It is the source of his anxiety when he perceives that a group of people he has been following through an increasingly empty city has begun to disperse. It is the reason he emits 'a half shriek of joy' (515) when he finds an open gin-shop in the early morning hours. The fear of this emptiness is also a crucial part of what distinguishes the old man from the narrator. The narrator describes his mood of 'interest' as 'precisely the converse of ennui'. He is able, apparently, to experience interest and ennui alternately. The old man, on the other hand, experiences these mental states simultaneously. He is driven, in his search for stimuli, by an ennui that perpetually recurs in the gaps between successive stimuli.

The differing nature of the gaps in their respective fields of experience can serve as the key to the differences between these two modes of consciousness. The 'gap' that drives the old man through the streets of London is an absence of stimuli. The 'gap' that sends the narrator in pursuit is an absence of a reading. The narrator, as a *flâneur*, defines himself by his ability to read the city as a text. The old man simply wishes to experience the city as a flood of unconnected stimuli. He is therefore the *badaud* who . . . is defined by Victor Fournel as one whose

> individuality is absorbed by the outside world . . . which intoxicates him to the point where he forgets himself. Under the influence of the spectacle which presents itself to him, the *badaud* becomes an impersonal creature; he is no longer a human being, he is part of the public, of the crowd. . . . The *flâneur*, [by contrast] is always in full possession of his individuality.[4]

The *flâneur* and the *badaud*, the reader and the gaper, are therefore opposites of a sort. Yet the *flâneur*, when confronted with a 'gap' in his desired field of experience, responds by embarking on an obsessive quest to fill the gap which is very much like the quest of the *badaud*. . . .

One of the most important of these resemblances is suggested by what the narrator believes to be his resolution of the problem of 'the man of the crowd'. The narrator, at the end of the story, extricates himself from the old man with the pronouncement that 'This old man is the type and the genius of deep crime' (515). On the face of it, it does not appear that the reader has been adequately prepared for this interpretation. Although it is true that the narrator thinks he sees a diamond and a dagger under the old man's coat, these are not certain signs that any crime has been committed and we do not see the old man commit any crimes in this story. Among the profuse and conflicting readings the narrator originally attaches to the old man are some qualities, such as 'avarice', 'coolness', 'malice', and 'blood-thirstiness', which are conventionally associated with crime but none of these readings are borne out by the events of the story. What happens in the story does, however, suggest several possible explanations for the narrator's interpretations of the old man as 'the type and genius of deep crime'.

The identity of 'the man of the crowd' disintegrates into the city itself. The urban criminal also wishes to lose himself in the city. Although the two forms of identity loss referred to here are quite different, their effects can be similar. By immersing themselves in the crowd, both the criminal and the *badaud* simultaneously become outsiders in terms of it. For the criminal, the crowd becomes nothing more than a concealing environment. For the *badaud*, it becomes nothing more than a source of stimuli. For the *flâneur*, who sees the criminal in the *badaud* but who can see neither in himself, the crowd becomes a text. . . .

The narrator's association of the old man with 'deep crime' appears to rest upon the fact that he does not permit himself to be read. 'The Man of the Crowd' begins and ends with the narrator associating 'deep crime' with illegibility. One implication of this reiterated association is that illegibility is itself a form of crime. It is a transgression against the interpretive laws imposed by the *flâneur* upon the city. Superficial crimes, as we see in the opening paragraphs of this story, are not guilty of this transgression. The narrator easily identifies pickpockets, gamblers, conmen and prostitutes. Finding them transparent, he views them with a detached amusement. They cause him no anxiety. Given the *flâneur*'s nearly exclusive concern with interpretive mastery, only that which he cannot read can cause him anxiety. When the narrator encounters a face that 'does not permit itself to be read', he associates it with that which is unintelligible in moral behaviour. In this way, he demonizes the gap in the urban text. By linking urban unintelligibility with 'deep crime' the narrator fuses the chief source of epistemological anxiety in the city with the chief source of physical anxiety. In this way, the opacity of the urban crowd ceases to be merely confusing. It becomes actively threatening. The narrator's association of the 'type and genius of deep crime' with the abstract 'man of the crowd' indicates that his conception of the source of this malevolence is neither localized nor defined. Rather, the old man's unintelligibility has opened up the possibility that no man or woman of the crowd can be read as the narrator has presumed to read them. The entire crowd, according to this formulation, threatens the physical and epistemological well-being of the narrator.

Concluding in this manner, 'The Man of the Crowd' completes its project of deconstructing the interpretive strategies of the *flâneur*. By this, I simply mean that Poe unravels the interpretations of the *flâneur* by interpreting their significant gaps and omissions. The *flâneur*'s system of superficial interpretation fares no better than analogous systems in other Poe stories. A limited narrator once again stands in the ruins of his system, unsure of what has happened. In this particular story the narrator is able to recognize that there is a gap in his interpretive control of reality. He does not, however, interpret this gap. Instead, he leaves the old man with the observation that 'perhaps it is but one of the great mercies of God' that 'the worst heart of the world' (515) cannot be read. The *flâneur*, the domesticator of reality, aspiring to reduce it to a comfortable transparency, remains unable to read the unlocalized malevolence he has uncovered. . . .

As a critique of the interpretive strategies of the *flâneur*, 'The Man of the Crowd' lays the groundwork for their transcendence. It implies that an urban observer is needed who can read and in some sense master what the *flâneur* cannot. It may also imply that a literary approach to the city is needed that will not deny the phenomenological qualities of urban life and will therefore be able to exploit the fascination of terrifying and illegible cities. Walter Benjamin has called 'The Man of the Crowd' an 'X-ray of the detective story. In it the drapery represented by crime has disappeared. The mere armature has remained: the pursuer, the crowd and an unknown man.'[5] Benjamin appears to be unaware here of the American publication dates of Poe's stories. It would be more accurate to call 'The Man of the Crowd' an embryo of the detective story. 'The Murders in the Rue Morgue', conventionally considered the first detective story, was written by Poe immediately after the publication of 'The Man of the Crowd'. In 'The Murders in the Rue Morgue' and in 'The Mystery of Marie Roget', written a few years later, we see Poe trying to come to terms with some of the issues he raised in 'The Man of the Crowd'.

In 'The Murders in the Rue Morgue' and 'The Mystery of Marie Roget', that which the *flâneur* leaves out of his city is given special prominence. 'Deep crime' and illegibility, two concepts the *flâneur* uncomprehendingly joins at the end of 'The Man of the Crowd', are powerfully combined in images of brutalized corpses whose murders cannot be understood. From shortly after the beginning of either of these stories, the reader knows that he or she is not in the safe, legible, and predictable city of the *flâneur*. Poe, in fact, does everything he can to increase the reader's anxiety. The corpses are graphically described. Each appears to have had no expectation of her murder and each appears to have been particularly helpless at the hands of her murderer. Mme and Mlle L'Espanaye were preparing for bed in a locked room in an upper storey of a building. Marie Roget disappears into a crowd, on her way to visit an aunt, or perhaps to meet a lover, and is discovered dead in a suburban grove a few days later. The nature of these murders is such as to imply that, in the metropolis virtually anything can happen to anyone at any time. This impression is confirmed by Dupin's reference, in 'The Mystery of Marie Roget', to 'the great frequency, in large cities, of such atrocities as the one described.'

In addition to representing the unpredictable and violent nature of urban life, the murdered corpses figuratively represent what Benjamin refers to as 'the obliteration of the individual's traces in the big-city crowd'.[6] Benjamin identified such obliteration as the 'original social content of the detective story'.[7] Living in almost complete seclusion, Mme and Mlle L'Espanaye were, in life, virtually unknown to the crowd which takes such interest in them as corpses. Marie Roget has a much wider circle of acquaintances, but her anonymity in a city as large as Paris is hardly less extreme. Refuting the comforting suggestion of a newspaper reporter that 'It is impossible that a person so well known to thousands as this young woman was, should have passed three blocks without someone having seen her' (749), Dupin observes:

> For my part, I should hold it not only as possible but as very more than probable, that Marie might have proceeded, at any given period, by any one of the many routes between her residence and that of her aunt, without meeting a single individual whom she knew, or by whom she was known. In viewing this question in its full and proper light, we must hold steadily in mind the great disproportion between the personal acquaintance of even the most noted individual in Paris and the entire population of Paris itself. (749–50)

. . . The anonymous individuals in Poe's Paris are opaque to one another. They are all monads. Mme L'Espanaye and her daughter are recluses. Like Dupin and the narrator, they shut themselves off from social interaction and from the scrutiny of others. The motivations and activities of Marie Roget are also mysterious. Her case is complicated by the fact that no one is sure who has the correct 'reading' of her. The sense of the opacity of urban individuals to each other is heightened by the fact that Paris, in each of the stories, is represented as a sort of Babel. Most of those who hear the voices of the alleged murderers of Mme L'Espanaye and her daughter are foreigners. Each speaks a different language and each interprets the shrill voice of the ape differently. In 'The Mystery of Marie Roget', we find a similar though figurative profusion of languages. Each newspaper has a different interpretation of the case and each vies with the others to establish the superior credibility of its theory. The interpretation of each newspaper becomes a language, the general conclusions of each theory determining the way in which each detail of the case is read. The city of Poe's detective stories contains a profusion of interpretive languages as well as a profusion of opaque texts. It differs markedly from the *flâneur*'s city in which there is only the *flâneur*'s language and in which every face and object can be easily read.

The illegible corpses at the center of Poe's detective stories suggest the general illegibility of urban individuals to each other. A face in a crowd, Poe implies, is as opaque as a murdered corpse. Without the possibility of access to their consciousness, each appears to be an empty representation of a human being. 'Clues' as to their identity can be observed but they can be read in a variety of different ways, according to a variety of available interpretive systems. They can never be read as easily as the *flâneur* would have us believe. The corpse of Marie Roget in particular is made to serve as a representation of general urban anonymity. It is decomposed to the point that identification poses some difficulty. One newspaper even develops the theory that the corpse is not that of Marie Roget. When M. Beauvais suggests to the editor of that newspaper that the corpse is in fact hers, he is criticized in the columns of the paper for being unable to offer any convincing reasons for his identification. Dupin says, in relation to this: 'Nothing is more vague than impressions of individual identity. Each man recognizes his neighbor, yet there are few instances in which any one is prepared to give a reason for his recognition' (748). The brutalization and decomposition of the corpse suggest here the mangling and obliteration of human identity in the metropolis.

By beginning the development of the stories with graphic journalistic descriptions of the murdered corpses, Poe produces an experience in his reader that can best be described as shock. The reader is confronted with an image that condenses a range of urban anxieties. In this way, Poe's detective story differs markedly from the *flâneur*'s sketch. Although the strategies of the *flâneur* develop in response to urban anxiety and dislocation, these experiences are not represented in the *flâneur*'s text itself. In the literature of the *flâneur*, the reader is shielded from all potential sources of anxiety at the moment he encounters them. When, for example, the *flâneur* acknowledges the ability of a rapidly changing city to obliterate the traces of the individual, he will do so in the act of recovering the traces. Although Poe's detective stories introduce the detective before they introduce the corpses, the resolution of the murders is achieved only after some effort and some time. By representing the original traumatic experience prior to (rather than simultaneously with) its resolution, Poe postpones, or defers, the action of the defenses which, in the form of a 'reading' of the corpses, will protect consciousness from the shock they produce. In this way, he exploits the aesthetic appeal of the shock. The structure of the detective story permits the reader to experience both the thrill of epistemological and physical anxiety in the city and the pleasure of its resolution. . . .

In order to allow this controlled exposure to urban anxiety, Poe invents a figure [the detective] capable of mastering the urban environment *without* inhibiting its capacity to produce anxiety and terror. . . .

Walter Benjamin, in his essay 'The *flâneur*', proposed a link between the *flâneur* and the detective. He observes that the detective story develops out of the intensifying perception of 'the disquieting and threatening aspects of urban life' in the early nineteenth century. Chief among these aspects in terms of creating the detective story was the way in which 'the masses appear as the asylum that shields an asocial person from his persecutors'.[8] The *flâneur*, whose sole activity was to observe the crowd, was particularly well-placed to assume the responsibility of solving crimes and finding criminals. His much vaunted interpretive skills would certainly have been useful for these tasks. According to Benjamin, 'in times of terror', like the period of rapid urban expansion in the nineteenth century, the *flâneur* 'is . . . turned into an unwitting detective . . . This does him a lot of good socially, for it accredits his idleness. He only seems to be indolent for behind this indolence there is the watchfulness of an observer who does not take his eyes off a miscreant.'[9] . . .

The derivation of Poe's detective from the *flâneur* is evident, first of all, in the fact that C. Auguste Dupin has several habits and personal qualities conventionally associated with the *flâneur*. Secluding himself by day in a mansion with closed shutters, Dupin explores the Paris streets by night, associating with no one except a narrator with no distinctive character traits of his own. He is therefore, like the *flâneur*, distanced from and invisible to the inhabitants of the city through which he moves. Like the *flâneur*, also, Dupin has an appetite for urban observation. Every evening, the narrator relates, he and Dupin 'sallied forth into the streets. . . . roaming far and wide until a late hour, seeking amid the wild lights and shadows of the populous city, that infinity of mental excitement which quiet observation can afford' (533). Like that of the *flâneur* in 'The Man of the Crowd', Dupin's appetite for urban observation has become an absorbing obsession. As Dupin says at one point in 'The Murders in the Rue Morgue', 'observation has become with me, of late, a species of necessity' (535). Dupin's preference for gaslight over daylight recalls the *flâneur*'s fascination with the city evening in 'The Man of the Crowd'. . . . Dupin and the narrator prefer darkness when engaged in any of the forms of contemplative activity with which they occupy themselves. Their days in the artificially darkened mansion are spent 'in dreams – reading, writing, or conversing' (533). Their evening activity seems interchangeable with those of the daytime. Urban observation, for them as for the *flâneur*, is a kind of escapist reading in solitude, demanding darkness for concentration.

Dupin's social position and economic status also suggest some traditional characteristics of the *flâneur*. He comes from an 'illustrious family' that has 'been reduced to poverty' (531). He has, however, been able to retain enough of his patrimony to remain financially independent. Like the traditional *flâneur*, Dupin is a sort of aristocrat whose nobility manifests itself in his mental and interpretive powers, not in his possession of 'worldly' power or goods. Like a true Cynic philosopher, Dupin has enough physical support to remain idle but not enough to surround himself with superfluities. The narrator observes that the 'energy of Dupin's character' had succumbed to this decline in the family's fortunes. Accordingly 'he ceased to bestir himself in the world or to care for the retrieval of his fortunes' (531). His social and economic situation has bred in Dupin a detached passivity ideal for a *flâneur*. An aspect of Dupin's detached and aristocratic passivity which further identifies him with the *flâneur* is his perpetual openness to a refined, and morally callous, form of pleasure. Boz, as we saw in the *Sketches*, was always in search of 'amusement', even when he was observing the misery of others. Dupin, after reading of the murders in the Rue Morgue, says to the narrator: 'As for these murders, let us enter into some examination for ourselves, before we make up an opinion respecting them. An inquiry will afford us some amusement.' The narrator, writing what the reader may be thinking after this statement, adds, in parentheses, '(I thought this an odd term, so applied, but said nothing.)' (546) . . .

In some crucial ways, Dupin's techniques of reading resemble those of the *flâneur*. Like the *flâneur*, he claims that reality may be read simply by looking at its commonly accessible surface in the proper way. Dupin says to the narrator, in 'The Murders in the Rue Morgue', that 'as regards the more important knowledge, I do believe that she is invariably superficial' (545). In order to be able to read reality: 'The necessary knowledge is that of *what* to observe' (530). In his lengthy discussion of the game of whist, at the opening of 'The Murders in the Rue Morgue', Dupin stresses the particular importance of physiognomical reading. The crucial things a proficient whist player must observe are very close to what the narrator of 'The Man of the Crowd' observes. The whist player notices the 'countenance', the 'air', and the changes in facial expressions of his opponents. Simply by reading these external signs, he will be 'in full possession of the contents of each hand', after 'the first two or three rounds have been played' (530).

Soon after this illustration, Dupin demonstrates his own proficiency at this sort of reading when, during one of his nocturnal rambles, he astonishes the narrator by correctly deriving an entire chain of thought from the latter's facial expressions and gestures. Dupin's improbable proficiency at superficial interpretation is reminiscent of the narrator of 'The Man of the Crowd' and the latter's putative ability to read the professions, motivations and histories of people in a crowd by observing their external traits. Dupin, however, is able to suggest a specific mechanism for such readings. Someone possessed of particularly acute 'analytic' faculties of mind is able to 'throw himself into' a person he wishes to read, and 'identify[ing] himself' with him, may understand and even predict his behaviour' (529). This is how Dupin traces the narrator's chain of thought. He 'throws himself' into the narrator and follows an 'inevitable' progression from street stone to stereotomy to Epicurus, to recent theories of cosmogony to Orion, to an actor named Chantilly. Such an analysis is perfectly convincing unless one assumes that other minds work in different ways from one's own. The genre invented here depends however on the assumption that the detective is capable of throwing himself into every other consciousness in the story. The detective in the Dupin tradition is the epitome of Baudelaire's 'active and fertile poet', immersing himself in the crowd, 'like those wandering souls who go looking for a body, he enters as he likes into each man's personality'.[10] . . . The interpretive mastery of the *flâneur* also depended upon an uncanny ability to throw himself into others. Nothing in the *flâneur*'s sketch or in the detective story is permitted to break this illusion. . . . In the detective story, as in the *flâneur*'s sketch, the 'external world' corresponds perfectly to the projections of the central reader. Both genres are fantasies of control over the otherness of the urban multitude. . . .

Living, however, in a generally malevolent and opaque urban environment, the detective must develop different interpretive techniques than those of the *flâneur*. It will no longer do to 'read the history of long years in a single glance'. The detective's interpretive techniques may be understood as a response to the inadequacy and incompleteness of those of the *flâneur*, as demonstrated in 'The Man of the Crowd'. A central principle is evident in each. Every aspect of the detective's method seeks to impose an interpretive order upon experience only after its originally chaotic nature has been demonstrated. Unlike the *flâneur*, the detective never attempts to create the illusion within it. In order to assemble his reading of the city, the detective chooses as his text those elements of urban experience which appear as gaps in the reading of the *flâneur*.

The *flâneur*, seeking to reduce the city to a set of manageable and predictable types, is always looking for what he has already seen and defined. The unprecedented and undefined produces within him, as we saw in the 'The Man of the Crowd', a state of epistemological anxiety. Dupin, on the other hand, asserts that truth can only be discovered by reading the unprecedented and undefined. In both 'The Murders in the Rue Morgue' and 'The Mystery of Marie Roget', he makes exactly the same remark to the narrator:

> I have observed that it is by deviations from the plane of the ordinary, that reason feels her way, if at all, in her search for the true. In investigations such as we are now pursuing, it should not be so much asked 'what has occurred?' as 'what has occurred that has never occurred before?' (548)[11]

In 'The Murders in the Rue Morgue', Dupin puts this principle into practice. In order to solve the case, Dupin finds it necessary to interpret the ways in which it differs from an ordinary robbery and murder. The normal examination of acquaintances, possible motives, etc., would not have led to a solution. The solution can only be found by reading such 'deviations from the plane of the ordinary' as the fact that a drawer of linens was rifled while several valuable objects were in plain view. Such 'deviations' as the unnecessary brutality of the murders and the preternatural agility required of the escaping murderer also contribute to the solution of the case. Dupin's method, we are led to believe, is effective because it assumes what the nature of these murders illustrates about urban experience. Life in a giant city is filled with encounters with the unprecedented and undefined. It is a perpetual exposure to the breaking of social and epistemological laws. The murder of the two women is a deviation from human law. The character of these murders is itself a deviation from what is conventionally expected of murders. The method of the *flâneur*, which organizes urban experience by codifying expectations into law, is entirely inadequate to interpret an environment in which deviation from all forms of law is the norm. If Poe is willing to go much further than previous authors in developing an aesthetic of urban shock, he also develops here a 'technique' for reading the shocks. The gaps and ruptures in the *flâneur*'s framework are no longer a source of anxiety. They are, for the detective, the means by which 'reason feels her way . . . in her search for the true.'

In his 'search for the true', Dupin accepts yet another aspect of urban life which the *flâneur* implicitly denies. For the *flâneur*, his is the only language in the city. Every object or person appropriated as a sign has no life or meaning other than that which the *flâneur* attributes to him, her, or it. No other interpretations are apparent within the *flâneur*'s text. The city of Dupin, on the other hand, is filled not only with different interpretations but also with different languages for interpretation. In these two stories, the detective accepts the multiplicity of languages and develops a way of reading reality by reading the interaction between the languages. Once again the detective takes what the *flâneur* represses and uses it to discover a truth far more complex than any the *flâneur* could have found.

The simplest example of this technique is, of course, Dupin's determination that the shrill voice heard by those who climbed the stairs to the apartment of Mme L'Espanaye and her daughter was not that of a human being. Dupin comes to this conclusion by integrating the different interpretations of the voice by speakers of different languages. Among those who testify is a Frenchman who thinks that the voice is that of a Spaniard. Another Frenchman thinks that it was the voice of an Italian. A German believes the shrill voice to be French and an Englishman and an Italian hear it as a Russian. None of these individual readers can correctly interpret the voice. Each is imprisoned within his own language. Dupin, on the other hand, by comparing their testimony, is able to function as a meta-reader. His perspective, which enables him to interpret the differing interpretations, permits him to construct an interpretation which is beyond the scope of any of the respective languages.

Dupin's role as a meta-reader of urban languages is more complex in 'The Mystery of Marie Roget'. In this later story, he derives crucial facts about the case by analysing the different interpretations of it in the different newspapers. The bulk of this long story is devoted to Dupin's demonstrations of the way in which each newspaper uses a different and, in each case, limited language to interpret the murder of Marie Roget. A paper entitled *L'Etoile*, for example, attempts to prove that the discovered corpse is not that of Marie Roget and that she herself has run off with a lover. Dupin observes that 'it is the mingled epigram and melodrame of the idea . . . rather than any true plausibility' that prompts the newspaper to promote it (738). Once it has decided on this hypothesis, Dupin goes on to show, the newspaper interprets every detail of the case in such a way as to support it. First it tries to support its assertion by alleging apathy on the part of Marie's relatives. When this allegation is shown to be false, it asserts that Beauvais is a party to the scheme, possibly the lover himself, and it throws suspicion on his supposed attempts to prevent other acquaintances and relatives from examining the corpse. Later, in reference to another article in *L'Etoile*, Dupin observes that:

> The first aim of the writer is to show, from the brevity of the interval between Marie's disappearance and the finding of the floating corpse, that this corpse cannot be that of Marie. The reduction of this interval to its smallest possible dimension, becomes thus, at once, an object with the reasoner. In the rash pursuit of this object, he rushes into mere assumption at the outset. (738)

The writer of the article assumes that if Marie left her mother's house at nine on Sunday morning, her corpse could not possibly have been thrown into the river before midnight that evening. As Dupin rather easily demonstrates, this is an unfounded assumption and constitutes a blind spot in *L'Etoile*'s theory. He goes on to show that this assumption of *L'Etoile* implies yet another assumption: that the murder was committed at some distance from the river and the corpse had to be carried to it. This assumption creates another blind spot in *L'Etoile*'s interpretation. . . .

Throughout this story, Dupin's technique remains the same. He solves a murder, solely on the basis of newspaper accounts, not by combining their insights and interpretations, but by analysing their omissions. Though it is far more complex, and though it is so drawn out as to have bored many readers of this story, his method is essentially the same as that used to determine that 'the shrill voice' in 'The Murders in the Rue Morgue' was not that of a human being. In each case, a correct interpretation is assembled by exploring the gaps and blind spots in the interpretations offered by several limited languages.

The viewpoint of the detective is, like that of the *flâneur*, panoramic. His powers allegedly derive from an ability to grasp more at any one time than any of the more limited individuals he observes. Like the *flâneur*, he removes and distances himself from what he observes in order to achieve his panoramic perspective. . . . The control established by the detective over the urban text is, however, quite different from that of the traditional *flâneur*. Rather than achieving a personal sense of mastery by reducing the city to a harmless and legible model of itself, the detective resolves a mystery that is emblematic of urban experience itself. By resolving his emblematic mystery, the detective implies that he has the power to solve virtually all of the city's mysteries. Like the *flâneur* the detective masters the city by mastering a synechdoche. The nature of his synechdochic replacement, however, is quite different. It focuses, rather than denies, the city's power to produce shock and dislocation. . . .

Notes

1 All page numbers in parenthesis are references to 'Tales and sketches', in Thomas Ollive Mabbott (ed.) (1978) *Collected Works of Edgar Allan Poe*, Cambridge, Mass.: Harvard University Press.

2 Wordsworth, William, 'Preface to the *Lyrical Ballads*', in W.J.B. Owen and Jane Worthington (eds) (1974) *The Prose Works of William Wordsworth*, Oxford: Oxford University Press, p. 128.

3 Wordsworth, William, *The Prelude or Growth of a Poet's Mind*, ed. E. de Selincourt, revised by Helen Darbishire.

4 Cited in Benjamin, Walter (1973) *Charles Baudelaire: A Lyric poet in the Era of High Capitalism*, London: New Left Books, p. 69.

5 ibid., p. 48.

6 ibid., p. 43.

7 ibid., p. 43.

8 ibid., p. 40.

9 ibid., p. 41.

10 Baudelaire, Charles (1970) 'Crowds', in *Paris Spleen*, trans. Louise Varese, New York: New Directions, p. 20.

11 See also pp. 736–7.

14
Clues

Franco Moretti

. . . .

Baker Street and surroundings

The criminal

A good rule in detective fiction is to have only one
criminal. This is not because guilt isolates, but, on the
contrary, because isolation breeds guilt. The criminal
adheres to others only instrumentally: for him association is merely the expedient that allows him to attain his
own interests. The metaphysics of the 'social pact'
becomes his own and he takes it for what it is: pure
form, a continuous pretence, which is not difficult to
enact, because the world of detective fiction is crowded
with stereotypes. The difference between innocence and
guilt returns as the opposition between stereotype and
individual. Innocence is conformity; individuality, guilt.
It is, in fact, something irreducibly personal that betrays
the individual: traces, signs that only he could have left
behind. The perfect crime – the nightmare of detective
fiction – is the featureless, deindividualized crime that
anyone could have committed because at this point
everyone is the same.[1] Such is the case of Robbe-
Grillet's *Erasers*, where everyone has the same pistol, the

same clothes, the same words: at the end, it is the detective who commits the crime. Detective fiction, however, exists expressly to dispel the doubt that guilt might be impersonal, and therefore collective and social. 'A typewriter', says Holmes, 'has really quite as much individuality as a man's handwriting' ('A Case of Identity'). As if to say: a guilty party can always be found.[2] *A* guilty party: crime is always presented as an exception, which by now the individual must be. His defeat is the victory and the purge of a society no longer conceived of as a 'contract' between *independent entities*, but rather as an organism or social *body*. The best known detective's assistant – Watson – is a doctor. And, as we shall see, so is Sherlock Holmes.

Holmes: 'Man, or at least criminal man, has lost all enterprise and originality' ('The Adventures of the Copper Beeches'). Spirit of initiative (enterprise, in particular, economic enterprise) and individuality: this is what Holmes wants to eliminate. He is not moved by pity for the victim, by moral or material horror at the crime, but by its *cultural quality*: by its *uniqueness* and its *mystery*. In detective fiction everything that is *repeatable* and *obvious* ceases to be criminal and is, therefore, unworthy of 'investigation': Agatha Christie's first book is set at the same time as the massacres of the Great War, yet the only murder of interest occurs on the second floor of Styles Court. Uniqueness and mystery: detective fiction treats every element of individual behaviour that desires secrecy as an offence, even if there is no trace of crime (for example, 'The Man with the Twisted Lip', 'The Yellow Face', 'A Scandal in Bohemia').[3] The idea that anything the individual desires to protect from the interference of society – the liberal 'freedom from' – favours or even coincides with crime is gradually insinuated, and is the source of the fascination with 'locked room mysteries'. The murderer and the victim are inside, society – innocent and weak – outside. The victim seeks refuge in a private sphere, and precisely there, he encounters death, which would not have struck him

down in the crowd. The door was invented by the bourgeoisie to protect the individual; now it becomes a threat;
one is advised never to turn the key. . . . This is the
totalitarian aspiration towards a *transparent* society: 'My
dear fellow', says Holmes to Watson, 'if we could fly out
that great window hand in hand, hover over this great
city, gently remove the roofs, and peep in at the queer
things which are going on . . . ' ('A Case of Identity').
Holmes exists because Peter Pan does not: it is not yet
possible to fly through keyholes.

Murderer and victim meet in the locked room because
fundamentally they are similar. In at least a third of
Conan Doyle's stories, the criminal has been the victim
of a preceding offence and vice versa. The victim, that is,
has *asked for it*: because of his shady past and because
he wanted to keep secrets, thus fending off society's
'assistance'; and finally because, exactly like the
criminal, he is still devoted to the idea of *individual
property*. Detective fiction originates at the same time as
the trusts, the big banks, and monopolies: mechanisms
that make wealth impersonal and separate capital and
capitalist. The victim, on the other hand, is still attached
to his small capital, like the criminal who covets it. They
are betrayed by economic independence. Detective fiction
enacts the antithesis between life and property and
between life and individuality: to have one, it is necessary
to give up the other. Kafka's inexorable law is already at
work, but detective fiction cannot see the Castle that
promulgates it.

The percentage of homicides in Conan Doyle's stories
increases over the years. After him, they become the
norm. Detective fiction *needs* death, on which it confers
archaic features.[4] It is never a natural and universal
event. On the contrary: it is always *voluntary*, always
individualized. It is always a struggle (agony,
antagonism). It is always the *punishment* of one who,
wilfully or not, trespassed the boundaries of normality.
He who distinguishes himself has his destiny marked out.
To avoid death (and who wouldn't want to?) it is

suggested that one conform to a stereotype: in this way, one will never be a victim or a criminal. . . . And detective fiction's characters are inert indeed: they do not grow. In this way, detective fiction is radically anti-novelistic: the aim of the narration is no longer the character's development into autonomy, or a change from the initial situation, or the presentation of plot as a conflict and an evolutionary spiral, image of a developing world that it is difficult to draw to a close. On the contrary: detective fiction's object is to *return to the beginning*. The individual initiates the narration not because he lives – but because he *dies*. Detective fiction is rooted in a sacrificial rite. For the stereotypes to live, the individual must die, and then die a second time in the guise of the criminal. For the story to begin and the stereotypes to come alive, a victim is necessary: otherwise there would be *nothing to say*. 'Innocent' characters must, in fact, demonstrate only that they really are, were, and will be the stereotypes they seem to be: that is, that they *know no history*. . . . Reinstate a preceding situation, return to the beginning, prove an alibi; declare oneself *elsewhere*, extraneous to the place where the disturbing forces broke loose; demonstrate, again, that one has always been the same: detective fiction's syntactic regression (from *sjuzet* to *fabula*, from crime to prelude) duplicates the 'good-guys' compulsion to repeat. So it is too with the reader who, attracted *precisely* by the obsessively repetitive scheme, is 'unable' to stop until the cycle has closed and he has returned to the starting point. *Bildung*, expelled from within the narrative, is then evaporated by its relationship with the reader. One reads only with the purpose of remaining as one already is: innocent. Detective fiction owes its success to the fact that it teaches nothing.

The criminal who simply sets absolute store by self-preservation in reality has the weaker personality; the habitual criminal is an inadequate individual. . . . The ability to stand apart from the environment as an individual, and at the same time to enter into contact with that environment – and gain a foothold in it – through the approved forms of communication, was eroded in the criminal. He represented a trend which is deep-rooted in living beings, and whose elimination is a sign of all development: the trend to lose oneself in the environment instead of playing an active role in it; the tendency to let oneself go and sink back into nature. Freud called it the death instinct. . . . There is negation in the criminal which does not contain resistance.[5]

Detective fiction turns this image on its head. It is the innocent, not the criminal, who is defenceless and yielding. The criminal is the opposite of Raskolnikov, who *must* confess to his action, bare himself to the world, and demolish his individual shield *by himself*: whence the irrelevance of detection in *Crime and Punishment*. On the contrary, detective fiction always presents the criminal as a self-sufficient watertight consciousness wholly bent on an aim. For the sacrifice of the individual to be effective and 'educational', he must be endowed with all attributes. This reflects a new relationship with legal punishment: in the middle of the nineteenth century, the focus of attention shifts from *execution* to the *trial*. While the former underlines the individual's *weakness* by destroying his body, trials *exalt* individuality: they condemn it precisely because they have demonstrated its deadly greatness. The criminal is the person who always acts *consciously*. On this premiss, detective fiction detaches prose narration from historiography and relates it to the world of Law:

> Modern law is directed against the agent, not against the action . . . [and] enquires into subjective 'guilt' whereas history, as long as it seeks to remain an empirical science, inquires into the 'objective' grounds of concrete events and the consequence of concrete 'actions'; it does not seek to pass judgement on the agent.[6]

In detective fiction, as in law, history assumes importance only as *violation* and as such, must be ultimately repressed. Again, the ideal is for nothing to happen. But it is a *negative* ideal, based on a *lack* (as with the stereotypes and innocence), and in order to seem real, it has an obsessive need of its opposite.

I have insisted upon the individualistic ethic that detective fiction ascribes to the criminal. Reading Conan Doyle, however, one discovers that the criminals are *never* members of the bourgeoisie. Detective fiction separates individuality and bourgeoisie. The bourgeoisie is no longer the champion of risk, novelty and imbalance, but of prudence, conservation and stasis. The economic ideology of detective fiction rests entirely upon the idea that supply and demand tend quite naturally towards a perfect balance. Suspicion often originates from a violation of the law of exchange between equivalent values: anyone who pays more than a market price or accepts a low salary can only be spurred by criminal motives.[7] These 'excessive' expenses – which distinctly recall risky investments – underline and disconcert a world which maintains that the distribution of incomes has occurred once and for all, and the possibilities of social climbing have vanished (England at the end of the nineteenth century, which begins its parasitical decline on the dividends of the Empire). What, indeed, is theft if not a violent redistribution of social wealth? And is it truly an accident that it becomes a great cultural symbol in the first country to experience a strong trade union movement? But theft is crucial for yet another reason. Money is always the motive of crime in detective fiction, yet the genre is wholly silent about *production*: that unequal exchange between labour-power and wages which is the true source of social wealth. Like popular economics, detective fiction incites people to seek the secret of profit in the sphere of circulation, where it cannot be found – but in compensation, one finds thefts, con-jobs, frauds, false pretences and so on. The indignation against what is rotten and immoral in the economy must concentrate on these phenomena. As for the factory – it is innocent, and thus free to carry on.

Let us return to the criminal who generally belongs to

one of two major sociological types: the *noble* and the *upstart*. In the first case, he attempts to react to the thinning out of his wealth, to oppose the *natural* course of history. The detective's intervention aims precisely at assuring that the economy will follow its own logic, and will not be violated by what appears to be a revival of feudal arbitrary will. The upstart, on the other hand, aspires to a sudden social jump. The spectre of primitive accumulation materializes through him: capital as theft, and even as murder. By catching him, the detective annihilates a memory painful to his philistine audience: the original sin of nineteenth-century 'legality'. Just as this world will have no future, so its infected roots in the past must be eradicated.

There is also a third tenured criminal: the stepfather, the adoptive father who steps in to seize the inheritance. This is perhaps the greatest obsession of detective fiction, as is to be expected in an economic imagination interested only in *perpetuating* the existing order, which is also a *legitimate* state of affairs, founded on the authority of the real father and sanctioned by the family tie, which moderates and spiritualizes individual egoism. The stepfather barges into this Victorian idyll, to break and degrade all ties for his exclusive gain. The stepfather is there to illustrate the difference between a 'father' (motivated by his children's well-being) and a 'private citizen' (who wants to rob them). Observing his wickedness, one is led to say: 'a father would never have done that'. Instead, this poor man does precisely what the real father did in more elegant forms. He wants to suppress those children – of whom there are too many – that the real fathers of the English middle bourgeoisie of the time (according to demographic studies) tried at all costs not to bring into the world. This particular economy was won through sexual abstention and coitus interruptus – at the price, presumably, of profound erotic frustration and lacerating emotional tensions, which were then projected on to the relationships with the children and, in particular, the *daughters*. Conan

Doyle's adoptive fathers hide their stepdaughters from the eyes of the world, imprison them, or even seduce them under false pretences: all transparent manifestations of sexual jealousy. That is, the poor stepfather is a bit like the well-known 'uncle' evoked by early psychoanalysis: a mask for the father. Needless to say, Conan Doyle, unlike Freud, was not trying to make a sticky subject 'acceptable': had he suspected this, his pen would have frozen in his hand. . . .

The detective

Holmes: 'If I claim full justice for my art, it is because it is an impersonal thing – a thing beyond myself' ('The Adventure of the Copper Beeches'). Holmes lives to serve this impersonal thing, detection. He does not use it for personal gain: 'As to reward, my profession is its own reward' ('The Adventure of the Speckled Band'). He sacrifices his individuality to his work: his endless series of disguises, sleepless nights, and inability to eat during an investigation are all metaphors for this. Thus Holmes prefigures and legitimates the sacrifices of the other individuality – the criminal's. The detective abandons the individualistic ethic voluntarily, but still retains the memory of it. For this reason he can 'understand' the criminal (and, when necessary, enact criminal deeds): potentially, he too was a criminal. In the figures of detective and criminal, a single renunciation, a sole sacrifice, is enacted, in different ways. This is seen in 'The Final Problem' when Holmes and Moriarty, 'locked in each other's arms', plunge into Reichenbach Falls.

This voluntary repression of the self is at one with Holmes's (and every other classic detective's) dilettantism. Dilettantism is not superficiality, but work done for the pleasure of work: 'To the man who loves art for its own sake . . . it is frequently in its least important and lowliest manifestations that the keenest pleasure is to be derived' ('The Adventure of the Copper Beeches'). Thus, Holmes is not a policeman, but a decadent intellectual (as is blatantly obvious from his escapes into music and cocaine). He is the intellectual who is no longer a person but a product: '[This case] saved me from ennui. . . . "L'homme c'est rien – l'oeuvre c'est tout", as Gustave Flaubert wrote to George Sands' ('The Red-Headed League'). He is the intellectual Max Weber and T.S. Eliot discuss:

> In the field of science only he who is devoted *solely* to the work at hand has 'personality'. And this holds not only for the field of science; we know of no great artist who has ever done anything but serve his work and only his work.[8] . . .

To return to Holmes. He is not a policeman but a private detective: in him, detection is disengaged from the purposes of the law. His is a *purely cultural* aim. It is preferable for a criminal to escape (as, in fact, happens) and the detection to be complete – rather than for him to be captured and the logical reconstruction be pre-empted. But the corollary of this is that the cultural universe is the most effective means of policing. Detective fiction is a hymn to culture's coercive abilities: which prove more effective than pure and simple institutional repression. Holmes's culture – just like mass culture, which detective fiction helped found – will reach you anywhere. This culture knows, orders and defines all the significant data of individual existence as part of social existence. Every story reiterates Bentham's Panopticon ideal: the model prison that signals the metamorphosis of liberalism into total scrutability.[9] Moreover, Holmes's culture resolves the deep anxiety of an expanding society: the fear that development might liberate centrifugal energies and thus make effective social control impossible. This problem emerges fully in the *metropolis*, where anonymity – that is, impunity – potentially reigns and which is rapidly becoming a tangled and inaccessible hiding place. We have seen detective fiction's answer to the first problem: the guilty party can never hide in the crowd. His tracks betray him as an individual, and therefore a vulnerable, being. But detective fiction also offers reassurance on the second point. All Holmes's investigations are accompanied and supported by the new and perfect mechanisms of transportation and communication. Carriages, trains, letters, telegrams, in Conan Doyle's world, are all crucial and *always* live up to expectations. They are the tacit and indispensable support of the arrest. Society expands and becomes more complicated: but it creates a framework of control, a network of relationships, that holds it more firmly together than ever before.

Let us, however, look more closely into the image of culture that detective fiction transmits. Since Poe, the detective has incarnated a *scientific* ideal: the detective discovers the causal links between events: to unravel the mystery is to trace them back to a *law*. The point is that – at the turn of the century – high bourgeois culture wavers in its conviction that it is possible to set the functioning of society into the framework of scientific – that is, objective – laws. Max Weber:

> We ask . . . how in general is the attribution of a concrete effect to an individual 'cause' possible and realizable in principle in view of the fact that in truth an *infinity* of causal factors have conditioned the occurrence of the individual 'event' and that indeed absolutely all of those individual causal factors were indispensable for the occurrence of the effect in its concrete form. The possibility of selecting from among the infinity of determinants is conditioned, first, by the mode of our historical *interest*.[10]

According to Weber, then, social science can no longer produce *general agreement*. Just as there is no 'general interest' in economic and political life, so a common value system cannot exist. There are only values in the plural, each perennially in struggle with other ideals which are 'just as sacred to others as ours are to us'.[11] This picture is not completely convincing: there is a complex and surprising relationship between the conflictual partiality of the modern value system and its levelling and integrative potential. But we must return to detective fiction, which aims to keep the relationship between science and society *unproblematic*. What, indeed, does detective fiction do? It creates a problem, a 'concrete effect' – the crime – and declares a sole cause relevant: the criminal. It slights other causes (why is the criminal such?) and dispels the doubt that every choice is partial and subjective. But, then, discovering that unique cause means reunifying causality and objectivity and reinstating the idea of a general interest in society, which consists in solving *that* mystery and arresting *that* individual – and no one else. In finding one solution that is valid for all – detective fiction does not permit alternative readings – society posits its unity, and, again, declares itself innocent. . . . Because the crime is presented in the form of a mystery, society is absolved from the start: the solution of the mystery proves its innocence.

As we have seen with stereotypes, innocence, in the world of detective fiction, is lack of experience: stasis. Holmes's 'science' is also static. Its most striking features – the gratuitous 'revelations' for clients and friends ('You have been in Afghanistan, I perceive' ('A Study in Scarlet') are his first words to poor Watson) – owes its existence to the fact that Holmes knows all the possible causes of every single event. Thus the relevant causes are always a *finite* set. They are also fixed: they always produce the same effect.[12] Holmes cannot go wrong, because he possesses the stable code, at the root of every mysterious message – mysterious, that is, for the reader, who is kept in the dark with regard to the code, while Holmes takes in the only possible meaning of the various clues in a glance. Perhaps 'symptoms' is better than 'clues', for they are effects which are systematically and absolutely correlated to univocal and stable causes, whereas Eco writes, 'As a matter of fact clues are seldom coded, and their interpretation is frequently a matter of complex inference rather than of sign-function recognition, which makes criminal novels more interesting than the detection of pneumonia'.[13] This is not true of the archetypal detective. Yet it detracts nothing from his fascination: for someone who feels ill, the doctor's diagnosis will always be spectacular, especially if reassuring. And Holmes is just that: the great *doctor* of the late Victorians, who convinces them that society is still a great *organism*: a unitary and knowable body. His 'science' is none other than the ideology of this organism: it celebrates its triumph by instantaneously connecting *work* and *exterior appearances* (body, clothing): in reinstating an idea of *status society* that is externalized, traditionalist, and easily controllable. In effect, Holmes embodies science as ideological common sense, 'common sense systematized'. He degrades science: just as it had been humiliated by both the English productive structure and the education system at the turn of the century. But, at the same time, he exalts it. The need for a myth of science was felt precisely by the world that produced *less* of it. England did not attain the second industrial revolution: but it invented science fiction.

Clues, whether defined as such or as 'symptoms' or 'traces', are not facts, but verbal procedures – more exactly, *rhetorical figures*. Thus, the famous 'band' in a Holmes story, an excellent metaphor, is gradually deciphered as 'band', 'scarf' and finally 'snake'. As is to be expected, clues are more often metonymies: associations by contiguity (related to the past), for which the detective must furnish the missing term. The clue is, therefore, that particular element of the story in which the link between signifier and signified is altered. It is a signifier that always has several signifieds and thus produces *numerous* suspicions. 'This is significant', Poirot never tires of repeating: meaning that he finds himself before something that transcends the usual, literal meaning. This is also part of the criminal's guilt: he has created a situation of semantic ambiguity, thus questioning the usual forms of human communication and human interaction. In this way, he has composed an audacious *poetic work*. The detective, on the other hand, must dispel the entropy, the cultural equiprobability that is produced by and is a relevant aspect of the crime: he will have to reinstate the univocal links between signifiers and signifieds.

Notes

1   'It seems, from what I gather, to be one of those simple cases which are so extremely difficult.'
     'That sounds a little paradoxical.'
     'But it is profoundly true. Singularity is almost invariably a clew. The more featureless and commonplace a crime is, the more difficult it is to bring it home. . . . '   ('The Boscombe Valley Mystery')

2 The mass success of detective fiction became irreversible in 1891 with Conan Doyle's first short stories in *Strand Magazine*. 'A Study in Scarlet', which came out four years earlier and was absolutely identical to the later stories, was almost a fiasco. Between these two dates there fell the year of Jack the Ripper, 1889, and a series of unsolved crimes, that is, crimes *without a subject*. Detective fiction must quell the fear that the criminal may remain unknown and therefore continue to circulate in society.

3   'You have heard me remark that the strangest and most unique things are very often connected not with the larger but with the smaller crimes, and occasionally, indeed, where there is room for doubt whether any positive crime has been committed.'   ('The Red-Headed League')

4 Fuchs, Werner (1969) *Todesbilder in der modernen Gesellschaft*, Frankfurt am Main.

5 Horkheimer, Max and Adorno, Theodor W. (1973) *Dialectic of Enlightenment*, London: Allen Lane, pp. 226–8.

6 Weber, Max (1949) *The Methodology of the Social Sciences*, New York, p. 169.

7 In the same way, every *superfluous* object – an ornamental bell-pull, a kite – proves to be an instrument of death. For this reason there is no room for love in detective fiction. Love – the overrating of the object ('she/he is not like the others') and the refusal to exchange it ('him/her or no one') – could indeed be indicted for gross contempt of the principle of equivalence. It is no wonder that true passion always ends by playing into the hands of the criminal.

8 Weber, Max, 'Science as a vocation' in H.H. Gerth and C. Wright Mills (eds) (1970) *From Max Weber: Essays in Sociology*, London: Routledge & Kegan Paul, p. 137.

9 On this, see Polanyi, Karl (1945) *Origins of Our Time: The Great Transformation*, London: Gollancz; and Foucault, Michel (1977) *Discipline and Punish: The Birth of the Prison*, London, Allen Lane.

10 Weber, *The Methodology of the Social Sciences*, p. 169.
11 ibid., p. 57.
12 The only problem can consist in an unusual *combination* of causes, which Poe very early saw as the only possible form of novelty. The same idea will crop up in numerous twentieth-century handbooks addressed to would-be mystery writers, where detective fiction is often compared to chess ('The Purloined Letter' opens with a discussion of games), which allows an infinite number of situations with a finite set of rules and pieces.
13 Eco, Umberto (1977) *A Theory of Semiotics*, London: Macmillan, p. 224. To touch on a parallel currently in vogue: the true investigator, who has to *build* a previously *non-existent* code to explain the clues, is not Holmes but Freud.

15

Morelli, Freud and Sherlock Holmes: clues and scientific method

Carlo Ginzburg

God is hidden in details – G. Flaubert and A. Warburg

In the following pages I will try to show how, in the late nineteenth century, an epistemological model (or, if you like, a paradigm) quietly emerged in the sphere of the social sciences. Examining this paradigm, which has still not received the attention it deserves, and which came into use without ever being spelled out as a theory, can perhaps help us to go beyond the sterile contrasting of 'rationalism' and 'irrationalism'.

Clues

Clues: the art historian

Between 1874 and 1876 a series of articles on Italian painting was published in the German art history journal *Zeitschrift für bildende Kunst*. They bore the signature of an unknown Russian scholar, Ivan Lermolieff, and the German translator was also unknown, one Johannes Schwarze. The articles proposed a new method for the correct attribution of old masters, which provoked much discussion and controversy among art historians. Several years later the author revealed himself as Giovanni

Morelli, an Italian (both pseudonyms were adapted from his own name). The 'Morelli method' is still referred to by art historians.[1]

Let us take a look at the method itself. Museums, Morelli said, are full of wrongly-attributed paintings – indeed assigning them correctly is often very difficult, since often they are unsigned, or painted over, or in poor repair. So distinguishing copies from originals (though essential) is very hard. To do it, said Morelli, one should refrain from the usual concentration on the most obvious characteristics of the paintings, for these could most easily be imitated – Perugino's central figures with eyes characteristically raised to heaven, or the smile of Leonardo's women, to take a couple of examples. Instead one should concentrate on minor details, especially those least significant in the style typical of the painter's own school: earlobes, fingernails, shapes of fingers and toes. So Morelli identified the ear (or whatever) peculiar to such masters as Botticelli and Cosmé Tura, such as would be found in originals but not in copies. Then, using this method, he made dozens of new attributions in some of the principal galleries of Europe. Some of them were sensational: the gallery in Dresden held a painting of a recumbent Venus believed to be a copy by Sassoferrato of a lost work by Titian, but Morelli identified it as one of the very few works definitely attributable to Giorgione.

Despite these achievements – and perhaps because of his almost arrogant assurance when presenting them – Morelli's method was very much criticized. It was called mechanical, or crudely positivistic, and fell into disfavour. . . . We owe the recent revival of interest in his work to the art historian Edgar Wind, who suggests it is an example of a more modern approach to works of art, tending towards an appreciation of detail more than of the whole. Wind relates this attitude to the cult of the spontaneity of genius, so current in romantic circles.[2] But this is unconvincing. Morelli was not tackling problems at the level of aesthetics (indeed this was held against him), but at a more basic level, closer to philology. The implications of his method lay elsewhere, and were much richer, though Wind did, as we shall see, come close to perceiving them.

Clues: the detective

> Morelli's books look different from those of any other writer on art. They are sprinkled with illustrations of fingers and ears, careful records of the characteristic trifles by which an artist gives himself away, as a criminal might be spotted by a fingerprint . . . any art gallery studied by Morelli begins to resemble a rogue's gallery. . . .[3]

This comparison was brilliantly developed by an Italian art historian, Enrico Castelnuovo, who drew a parallel between Morelli's methods of classification and those attributed by Arthur Conan Doyle only a few years later to his fictional creation, Sherlock Holmes.[4] The art connoisseur and the detective may well be compared, each discovering, from clues unnoticed by others, the author in one case of a crime, in the other of a painting. Examples of Sherlock Holmes's skill at interpreting footprints, cigarette ash, and so on are countless and well-known. But let us look at 'The Cardboard Box' (1892) for an illustration of Castelnuovo's point: here Holmes is as it were 'morellising'. The case starts with the arrival of two severed ears in a parcel sent to an innocent old lady. Here is the expert at work:

> [Holmes] was staring with singular intentness at the lady's profile. Surprise and satisfaction were both for an instant to be read upon his eager face, though when she glanced round to find out the cause of his silence he had become as demure as ever. I [Watson] stared hard myself at her flat grizzled hair, her trim cap, her little gilt earrings, her placid features, but I could see nothing which would account for my companion's evident excitement.

Later on Holmes explains to Watson (and to the reader) the lightning course of his thoughts:

> As a medical man, you are aware, Watson, that there is no part of the human body which varies so much as the human ear. Each ear is as a rule quite distinctive, and differs from all other ones. In last year's *Anthropological Journal* you will find two short monographs from my pen upon the subject. I had, therefore, examined the ears in the box with the eyes of an expert, and had carefully noted their anatomical peculiarities. Imagine my surprise then, when, on looking at Miss Cushing, I perceived that her ear corresponded exactly with the female ear which I had just inspected. The matter was entirely beyond coincidence. There was the same shortening of the pinna, the same broad curve of the upper lobe, the same convolution of the inner cartilage. In all essentials it was the same ear.
>
> Of course, I at once saw the enormous importance of the observation. It was evident that the victim was a blood relation, and probably a very close one . . .[5]

Clues: the psychoanalyst

We shall shortly see the implications of this parallel.[6] Meanwhile, we may profit from another of Wind's helpful observations.

> To some of Morelli's critics it has seemed odd 'that personality should be found where personal effort is weakest'. But on this point modern psychology would certainly support Morelli: our inadvertent little gestures reveal our character far more authentically than any formal posture that we may carefully prepare.[7]

'Our inadvertent little gestures' – we can here without hesitation replace the general term 'modern psychology' with the name of Sigmund Freud. Wind's comments on Morelli have indeed drawn the attention of scholars to a neglected passage in Freud's famous essay, 'The Moses of Michelangelo' (1914). At the beginning of the second section Freud writes:

Long before I had any opportunity of hearing about psychoanalysis, I learned that a Russian art-connoisseur, Ivan Lermolieff, had caused a revolution in the art galleries of Europe by questioning the authorship of many pictures, showing how to distinguish copies from originals with certainty, and constructing hypothetical artists for those works of art whose former authorship had been discredited. He achieved this by insisting that attention should be diverted from the general impression and main features of a picture, and by laying stress on the significance of minor details, of things like the drawing of the fingernails, of the lobe of an ear, of halos and such unconsidered trifles which the copyist neglects to imitate and yet which every artist executes in his own character-istic way. I was then greatly interested to learn that the Russian pseudonym concealed the identity of an Italian physician called Morelli, who died in 1891. It seems to me that his method of inquiry is closely related to the techni-que of psychoanalysis. It, too, is accustomed to divine secret and concealed things from despised or unnoticed features, from the rubbish-heap, as it were, of our obser-vations. . . .[8]

Freud and Morelli

. . . But what significance did Morelli's essays have for Freud, still a young man, still far from psychoanalysis? Freud himself tells us: the proposal of an interpretative method based on taking marginal and irrelevant details as revealing clues. Here details generally considered trivial and unimportant, 'beneath notice', furnish the key to the highest achievements of human genius. The irony in this passage from Morelli must have delighted Freud:

> My adversaries are pleased to call me someone who has no understanding of the spiritual content of a work of art, and who therefore gives particular importance to external details such as the form of the hands, the ear, and even, *horrible dictu* [how shocking], to such rude things as fingernails.[9]

. . . Furthermore, these marginal details were revealing,

in Morelli's view, because in them the artist's subordination to cultural traditions gave way to a purely individual streak, details being repeated in a certain way 'by force of habit, almost unconsciously'. Even more than the reference to the unconscious – not exceptional in this period – what is striking here is the way that the innermost core of the artist's individuality is linked with elements beyond conscious control.

The triple analogy: diagnosis through clues

We have outlined an analogy between the methods of Morelli, of Holmes, and of Freud. We have mentioned the connection between Morelli and Holmes, and that between Morelli and Freud. The peculiar similarities between the activities of Holmes and Freud have been discussed by Stephen Marcus.[10] . . . In all three cases tiny details provide the key to a deeper reality, inaccessible by other methods. These details may be symptoms, for Freud, or clues, for Holmes, or features of paintings, for Morelli.[11]

How do we explain the triple analogy? There is an obvious answer. Freud was a doctor; Morelli had a degree in medicine; Conan Doyle had been a doctor before settling down to write. In all three cases we can invoke the model of medical semiotics, or symptomatology – the discipline which permits diagnosis, though the disease cannot be directly observed, on the basis of superficial symptoms or signs, often irrelevant to the eye of the layman, or even of Dr Watson. . . . But it is not simply a matter of biographical coincidences. Toward the end of the nineteenth century (more precisely, in the decade 1870–80), this 'semiotic' approach, a paradigm or model based on the interpretation of clues, had become increasingly influential in the field of human sciences. Its roots, however, were far more ancient.

Roots of the conjectural model

Hunters and diviners

For thousands of years mankind lived by hunting. In the course of endless pursuits, hunters learned to reconstruct the appearance and movements of an unseen quarry through its tracks – prints in soft ground, snapped twigs, droppings, snagged hairs or feathers, smells, puddles, threads of saliva. They learnt to sniff, to observe, to give meaning and context to the slightest trace. They learned to make complex calculations in an instant, in shadowy wood or treacherous clearing.

Successive generations of hunters enriched and passed on this inheritance of knowledge. We have no verbal evidence to set beside their rock paintings and artefacts, but we can turn perhaps to the folk tale, which sometimes carries an echo – faint and distorted – of what those far-off hunters knew. Three brothers (runs a story from the Middle East told among Kirgiz, Tartars, Jews, Turks, and so on) meet a man who has lost a camel (or sometimes it is a horse).[12] At once they describe it to him: it's white, and blind in one eye; under the saddle it carries two skins, one full of oil, the other of wine. They must have seen it? No, they haven't seen it. So they're accused of theft and brought to be judged. The triumph of the brothers follows: they immediately show how from the barest traces they were able to reconstruct the appearance of an animal they'd never set eyes on.

The three brothers, even if they are not described as hunters, are clearly carriers of the hunters' kind of knowledge. Its characteristic feature was that it permitted the leap from apparently insignificant facts, which could be observed, to a complex reality which – directly at least – could not. And these facts would be ordered by the observer in such a way as to provide a narrative sequence – at its simplest, 'someone passed this way'. Perhaps indeed the idea of a narrative, as opposed to spell or exorcism or invocation, originated in a hunting society, from the experience of interpreting tracks. Obviously this is speculation, but it might be reinforced by the way that even now the language of deciphering tracks is based on figures of speech – the part for the whole, the cause for the effect – relating to the narrative pole of metonymy (as defined in a well-known essay by Jakobson),[13] strictly excluding the alternative pole of metaphor. The hunter could have been the first 'to tell a story' because only hunters knew how to read a coherent sequence of events from the silent (even imperceptible) signs left by their prey.

This 'deciphering' and 'reading' of the animals' tracks is metaphorical. But it is worth trying to understand it literally, as the verbal distillation of a historical process leading, though across a very long time-span, toward the invention of writing. The same connection is suggested in a Chinese tradition explaining the origins of writing, according to which it was invented by a high official who had remarked the footprints of a bird in a sandy riverbank. Or abandoning the realms of myth and hypothesis for that of documented history, there are undoubtedly striking analogies between the hunters' model we have been developing for hunters, and the model implicit in the texts of Mesopotamian divination, which date from at least 3000 years BC.[14] Both require minute examination of the real, however trivial, to uncover the traces of events which the observer cannot directly experience. Droppings, footprints, hairs, feathers, in the one case; animals' innards, drops of oil in water, stars, involuntary movements, in the other. It is true that the second group, unlike the first, could be extended indefinitely, since the Mesopotamian diviners read signs of the future in more or less anything. But to our eyes another difference matters more: the fact that divination pointed toward the future, while the hunters' deciphering pointed toward the actual past – albeit occurring a few instants before. Yet in terms of under-standing, the approach in each case was much alike; the intellectual stages – analysis, comparison, classification – identical, at least in theory. . . .

So after a long detour we come back to medical semiotics. We find it in a whole constellation of disciplines (and anachronistic terms of course) with a common character. It might be tempting to distinguish between 'pseudo-sciences' like divination and physiognomy, and 'sciences' like law and medicine, and to explain this bizarre contiguity by the great distance in space and time from the society that we have been discussing. But it would be a superficial explanation. There was a real common ground among these Mesopotamian forms of knowledge (if we omit divination through inspiration, which was based on ecstatic possession): an approach involving analysis of particular cases, constructed only through traces, symptoms, hints. Again, the Mesopotamian legal texts do not just list laws and ordinances, but discuss a body of actual cases. In short, we can speak about a symptomatic or divinatory paradigm which could be oriented towards past or present or future, depending on the form of knowledge called upon. Toward future – that was divination proper; toward past, present and future – that was the medical science of symptoms, with its double character, diagnostic, explaining past and present, and prognostic, suggesting the likely future; and toward past – that was jurisprudence, or legal knowledge. But lurking behind this symptomatic or divinatory model one glimpses the gesture which is the oldest, perhaps, of the intellectual history of the human race: the hunter crouched in the mud, examining a quarry's tracks.

The growth of disciplines based on reading the evidence

What we have said so far should explain why a Mesopotamian divination text might include how to diagnose an earlier head wound from a bilateral squint; or more generally, the way in which there emerged historically a group of disciplines which all depended on the deciphering of various kinds of signs, from symptoms to writing.

Passing on to the civilizations of ancient Greece, we find this group of disciplines changes considerably, with new lines of study developing, like history and philology, and with the newly acquired independence (in terms both of social context and of theoretical approach) of older disciplines like medicine. The body, speech and history were all for the first time subjected to dispassionate investigation which from the start excluded the possibility of divine intervention. This decisive change characterized the culture of the Greek city-states, of which we of course are the heirs. It is less obvious that an important part of this change was played by a model which may be seen as based on symptoms or clues. This is clearest in the case of Hippocratic medicine, which clarified its methods by analysing the central concept of symptom (*semeion*). Followers of Hippocrates argued that just by carefully observing and registering every symptom it was possible to establish precise 'histories' of each disease, even though the disease as an entity would remain unattainable. This insistence on the evidential nature of medicine almost certainly stemmed from the distinction (expounded by the Pythagorean doctor, Alcmaeon) between the immediacy and certainty of divine knowledge, and the provisional, conjectural nature of human knowledge. If reality was not directly knowable, then by implication the conjectural paradigm which we have been describing was legitimate. In fact, according to the Greeks, various spheres of activity were based on it. Physicians, historians, politicians, potters, joiners, mariners, hunters, fishermen and women in general were held, among others, to be adept in the vast areas of conjectural knowledge. . . . But this semiotic paradigm continued to be merely implicit; it was completely overshadowed by Plato's theory of knowledge, which held sway in more influential circles and had more prestige.[15]

Galileo and the new scientific writing

. . . Here of course the decisive shift is the emergence of a new scientific paradigm, based on (but outliving) Galileian physics. Even if modern physics finds it hard to define itself as Galileian (while not rejecting Galileo), the significance of Galileo for science in general, from both an epistemological and a symbolical point of view, remains undiminished.[16]

Now it is clear that none – not even medicine – of the disciplines which we have been describing as conjectural would meet the criteria of scientific inference essential to the Galileian approach. They were above all concerned with the qualitative, the individual case or situation or document *as individual*, which meant there was always an element of chance in their results: one need only think of the importance of conjecture (a word whose Latin origin lies in divination)[17] in medicine or philology, let alone in divination. Galileian science was altogether different; it could have taken over the scholastic saying 'individuum est ineffabile' ('we can say nothing about the individual'). Using mathematics and the experimental method involved the need to measure and to repeat phenomena, whereas an individualizing approach made the latter impossible and allowed the former only in part. . . .

Galileo here set the natural sciences firmly on a path they never left, which tended to lead away from anthropocentrism and anthropomorphism. In the map of knowledge a gap emerged, which was bound to widen more and more. Certainly there could be no greater contrast than between the Galileian physicist, professionally deaf to sounds and forbidden to taste or smell, and the physician of the same period, who ventured his diagnosis after listening to a wheezy chest, or sniffing faeces, or tasting urine. . . .

The human sciences – anchored in the qualitative

. . . Still, the group of human sciences remained firmly anchored in the qualitative, though not without uneasiness, especially in the case of medicine. Although progress had been made, its methods still seemed uncertain, its results unpredictable. Such a text as *An Essay on the Certainty of Medicine* by the French ideologue Cabanis, which appeared at the end of the eighteenth century,[18] admitted this lack of rigour, while at the same time insisting that medicine was nevertheless scientific in its own way. There seem to be two basic reasons for medicine's lack of certainty. First, descriptions of particular diseases that were adequate for their theoretical classification were not necessarily adequate in practice, since a disease could present itself differently in each patient. Second, knowledge of a disease always remained indirect and conjectural; the secrets of the living body were always, by definition, out of reach. Once dead, of course, it could be dissected, but how did one make the leap from the corpse, irreversibly changed by death, to the characteristics of the living individual?[19] . . . The discussions on the 'uncertainty' of medicine provided early formulations of what were to be the central epistemological problems in the human sciences.

The expropriation of common knowledge

Between the lines of Cabanis's book there shines through an impatience which is not hard to understand. In spite of the more or less justified objections to its methods which could be made, medicine remained a science which received full social recognition. But not all the conjectural disciplines fared so well in this period. Some, like connoisseurship, of fairly recent origin, held an ambiguous position on the borders of the acknowledged disciplines. Others, more embedded in daily practice, were kept well outside. The ability to tell an unhealthy horse from the state of its hooves, a storm coming up from a shift in the wind, or unfriendly intentions from the shadow in someone's expression would certainly not be learned from treatises on the care of horses, or on weather, or on psychology. In each case these kinds of knowledge were richer than any written authority on the subject; they had been learned not from books but from listening, from doing, from watching; their subtleties could scarcely be given formal expression and they might not even be reducible to words; they were the heritage – partly common and partly split – of men and women of any class. A fine common thread connected them; they were all born of experience, of the concrete and individual. That concrete quality was both the strength of this kind of knowledge and its limit; it could not make use of the powerful and terrible tool of abstraction.[20]

From time to time attempts would be made to write down some part of this lore, locally rooted but without known origin or record or history, to fit it into a straitjacket of terminological precision. This usually constricted and impoverished it. . . . It was perhaps only with medicine that the codifying and recording of conjectural lore produced a real enrichment; but the story of the relation between official and popular medicine has still to be written. In the course of the eighteenth century things changed. In a real cultural offensive the bourgeoisie appropriated more and more of the traditional lore of artisans and peasants, some of it conjectural, some not; they organized and recorded it, and at the same time intensified the massive process of cultural invasion which had already begun, though taking different forms and with different content, during the counter-reformation. . . .

The systematic collecting of such 'little insights', as Winckelmann called them elsewhere,[21] was the basis of fresh formulations of ancient knowledge during the eighteenth and nineteenth centuries, from cookery to hydrology to veterinary science. To a growing number of readers, access to specific experience was increasingly had through the pages of books. The novel provided the bourgeoisie with a substitute, on a different level, for initiation rites, that is, for access to real experience altogether. And indeed it was thanks to works of fiction that the conjectural paradigm in this period had a new and unexpected success.

Hunter to detective

In connection with the hypothetical origin of the conjectural model among long-ago hunters, we have already told the story of the three brothers who, by interpreting a series of tracks, reconstruct the appearance of an animal they have never seen. This story made its European debut in a collection by Sercambi.[22] It subsequently reappeared as the opening to a much larger collection of stories, presented as translations into Italian from Persian by an Armenian called Christopher, which came out in Venice in the mid-sixteenth century under the title *Peregrinaggio di tre giovani figliuoli del re di Serendippo* (Travels of the three young sons of the king of Serendippo). This book went through a number of editions and translations – first into German, then, during the eighteenth-century fashion for things oriental, into the main European languages. The success of this story of the sons of the king of Serendippo led Horace Walpole in 1745 to coin the word 'serendipity', for the making of happy and unexpected discoveries 'by accidents and sagacity'. Some years before, Voltaire, in the third chapter of *Zadig*, reworked the first volume of *Travels*, which he had read in the French translation. In his version the camel of the original becomes a bitch and a horse, which Zadig is able to describe in detail by deciphering their tracks. Accused of theft and taken at once before the judges, Zadig proves his innocence by recounting the mental process which had enabled him to describe the animals he had never seen:

I saw in the sand the tracks of an animal, and I judged

without difficulty that it was a small dog. Long shallow furrows across mounds in the sand, between the paw-prints, told me that it was a female with sagging teats, who had therefore recently given birth . . .[23]

In these lines and in those which follow lies the embryo of the detective story. They inspired Poe and Gaboriau directly, and perhaps indirectly Conan Doyle.

The extraordinary success of the detective story is well-known; we shall return to some of the reasons for it. But for the moment it is worth remarking that it is based on a cognitive model which is at once very ancient and very new. We have already discussed its ancient roots. For its modern elements we shall quote Cuvier's praise in 1834 for the methods and successes of the new science of palaeontology:

> Today, someone who sees the print of a cloven hoof can conclude that the animal which left the print was a ruminant one, and this conclusion is as certain as any that can be made in physics or moral philosophy. This single track therefore tells the observer about the kind of teeth, the kind of jaws, the haunches, the shoulder, and the pelvis of the animal which has passed: it is more certain evidence than all Zadig's clues.[24]

More certain perhaps, but of a very comparable kind. The name of Zadig came to stand for so much that in 1880 Thomas Huxley, in a series of lectures aimed at publicizing the discoveries of Darwin, defined as 'Zadig's method' the procedure common to history, archaeology, geology, physical astronomy, and palaeontology: that is, the making of retrospective predictions. These disciplines, being deeply concerned with historical development, could scarcely avoid falling back on the conjectural or divinatory model (Huxley indeed made explicit reference to divination directed toward the past),[25] and putting aside the Galileian paradigm. When causes cannot be repeated, there is no alternative but to infer them from their effects.

Uses of the conjectural model

Its complex character

This inquiry may be compared to following the threads in a piece of weaving. We have now reached the point where they can be seen to make a composite whole, a homogeneous and closely woven cloth. . . .

The cloth is the paradigm which we have summoned up from way back, out of various contexts – hunting, divining, conjectural, or semiotic. These are obviously not synonyms, but alternative descriptions which nevertheless refer back to a common epistemological model, worked out for a number of disciplines, themselves often linked by borrowed methods or key words. Now between the eighteenth and the nineteenth century, with the emergence of the 'human sciences', the constellation of conjectural disciplines changed profoundly: new stars were born, which (like phrenology) were soon to fall, or which (like palaeontology) would achieve great things, but above all it was medicine which confirmed its high social and scientific status. It became the reference point, explicit or by implication, of all the human sciences. But what area of medicine? Around the middle of the eighteenth century two alternatives became visible: the anatomical model, and the semiotic. The metaphor of 'the anatomy of the civil society', used in a critical passage by Marx,[26] expresses the aspiration for a system of knowledge, at a time when the last great system of philosophy – Hegelianism – was already crumbling. But in spite of the great success of Marxism, the human sciences ended up by accepting more and more (with an important exception which we shall come to) the conjectural paradigm of semiotics. And here we return to the Morelli–Freud–Conan Doyle triad where we began.

From nature to culture

So far we have been using the term conjectural paradigm

(and its variants) broadly. It is time to take it to pieces.
It is one thing to analyse footprints, stars, faeces (animal
or human), catarrhs, corneas, pulses, snow-covered fields
or dropped cigarette ash, and another to analyse writing
or painting or speech. The distinction between nature
(inanimate or living) and culture is fundamental,
certainly much more important than the far more superficial and changeable distinctions between disciplines.
Morelli's idea was to trace out within a culturally determined sign-system the conventions of painting, signs
which, like symptoms (and like most clues), were
produced involuntarily. Not just that: in these involuntary signs, in the 'tiny details – a calligrapher would call
them flourishes' such as the 'favourite words and
phrases' which 'most people, whether talking or writing,
make use of without meaning to and without noticing
that they do so' – Morelli located the most certain clue
to artistic identity.[27] . . . The time when these principles
finally came to fruition was perhaps not altogether at
random. It coincided with the emergence of an increasingly clear tendency for state power to impose a close-
meshed net of control on society, and once again the
method that was used involved attributing identity
through characteristics which were trivial and beyond
conscious control.

Identification of the individual in society

Every society needs to distinguish its members, and the
ways of meeting this need vary with place and time.
There is, first of all, the name, but the more complex the
society, the less satisfactorily a name can represent the
individual's identity without confusion. In Egypt during
the Graeco-Roman period, for instance, a man who came
to a notary wanting to get married or to carry out some
financial transaction would have to set down not only his
name but also brief details of his appearance, including
any scars or other particular marks. But even so the
chances of mistake or of fraudulent impersonation

remained high. By comparison, a signature at the bottom of a contract was much better: at the end of the eighteenth century the abbot Lanzi, in a passage of his *Storia pittorica* (History of Painting), which discussed the methods of the connoisseur, maintained that the impossibility of imitating handwriting was intended by nature for the 'security' of 'civil society' (that is, bourgeois society). Of course, even signatures could be faked; and above all, they provided no check on the illiterate. In spite of these shortcomings, European societies over centuries felt no need for more reliable or practical means of identification – not even when large-scale industrial development, the social and geographical mobility which it produced, and the rapid growth of vast urban concentrations had completely changed the fundamentals of the problem. In this kind of society it was child's play to cover one's tracks and reappear with a new identity – and not only in London or Paris. It was only in the last decades of the nineteenth century that new systems of identification – competing with each other – began to be put forward. This followed contemporary developments in class struggle: the setting up of an international workers' association, the repression of working-class opposition after the Paris Commune, and the changing pattern of crime.

In England from about 1720 onwards,[28] in the rest of Europe (with the Napoleonic code) a century or so later, the emergence of capitalist relations of production led to a transformation of the law, bringing it into line with new bourgeois concepts of property, and introducing a greater number of punishable offences and punishment of more severity. Class struggle was increasingly brought within the range of criminality, and at the same time a new prison system was built up, based on longer sentences of imprisonment.[29] But prison produces criminals. In France the number of recidivists was rising steadily after 1870, and toward the end of the century was about half of all cases brought to trial.[30] The problem of identifying old offenders, which developed in these years, was the bridgehead of a more or less conscious project to keep a complete and general check on the whole of society.

For this identification of old offenders it was necessary to show (i) that a person had previously been convicted, and (ii) that the person in question was the same as the one previously convicted. The first problem was resolved by the setting up of police files. The second was more difficult. The ancient punishments which had involved marking or mutilating an offender for life had been abolished. In Dumas's *The Three Musketeers*, the lily branded on Milady's shoulder had allowed D'Artagnan to recognize her as a poisoner already punished in the past for her misdeeds, whereas in his *The Count of Montecristo*, or in Hugo's *Les Misérables*, the escaped prisoners Edmond Dantes and Jean Valjean were able to reappear on the social scene with false identities. These examples should convey the hold which the old offender had on the nineteenth-century imagination.[31] The bourgeoisie required some identifying sign which would be as indelible as those imposed under the Ancien Régime, but less bloodthirsty and humiliating.

The idea of an immense photographic archive was at first rejected because it posed such huge difficulties of classification: how could discrete elements be isolated in the continuum of images? The path of quantification seemed easier and more rigorous. From 1879 onward an employee at the prefecture of Paris, Alphonse Bertillon, developed an anthropometric method – which he set out in various writings – based on careful measuring of physical details which were then combined on each person's card.[32] Obviously a miscarriage of justice could result (theoretically) from a mistake of a few millimetres; but there was a still more serious defect in Bertillon's anthropometric system, the fact that it was purely negative. It permitted the elimination of those whose details on examination did not match up, but it could not prove that two sets of identical details referred to the same person. The elusive quality of individuality could not be shut out; chased out through the door by quantification, it came back through the window. So Bertillon proposed combining the anthropometric method with what he called a 'word-portrait', that is, a verbal description analysing discrete entities (nose, eyes, ears and so on) which taken together were supposed to reconstitute the image of the whole person, and so to allow identification. . . .

A method of identification which made both the collection and the classification of data much easier was put forward in 1888 by Galton, in a memoir which was later revised and expanded.[33] This, of course, was based on fingerprints. As Galton himself quite properly admitted, he was not the first to suggest it.

The scientific analysis of fingerprints began in 1823 with a work by Purkyné, the founder of histology, called *Commentatio de examine physiologico organi visus et systematis cutanei* (Commentary on the physiological examination of the organs of sight and the skin system).[34] He distinguished and described nine basic types of line in the skin, but argued that no two individuals ever had identical combinations in their fingerprints. The practical implications of this were ignored, though not the philosophical, which were taken up in a chapter called 'De cognitione organismi individualis in genere' (On the general recognition of individual organisms). . . .

Let us leave Europe for the moment and look at Asia. Unlike their European counterparts, and quite independently, Chinese and Japanese diviners had taken an interest in these scarcely visible lines which criss-cross the skin of the hand. And in Bengal, as well as in China, there was a custom of imprinting letters and documents with a fingertip dipped in ink or tar: this was probably a consequence of knowledge derived from divinatory practice. Anyone who was used to deciphering mysterious messages in the veins of stone or wood, in the traces left by birds, or in the shell of a tortoise, would find it easy to see a kind of message in the print of a dirty finger. In 1860 Sir William Herschel, District Commissioner of Hooghly in Bengal, came across this usage, common among local people, saw its usefulness, and thought to profit by it to improve the functioning of the British administration. . . . But really, as Galton was to observe, there was a great need for some such means of identification: in India as in other British colonies the natives were illiterate, disputatious, wily, deceitful, and to the eyes of a European, all looked the same. In 1880 Herschel announced in *Nature* that after 17 years of tests, fingerprints had been officially introduced in the district of Hooghly, and since then had been used for three years with the best possible results. The imperial administrators had taken over the Bengalis' conjectural knowledge, and turned it against them.

Herschel's article served Galton as starting-point for a systematic reorganization of his thought on the whole subject. His research had been made possible by the convergence of three separate elements: the discoveries of a pure scientist, Purkyné; the concrete knowledge, tied in with everyday practice, of the Bengali populace; and the political and administrative acumen of Sir William Herschel, faithful servant of Her Britannic Majesty. . . .

Galton not only made a crucial contribution to the analysis of fingerprints, he also, as we have said, saw the practical implications. In a very short time the new method was introduced in England, and thence gradually to the rest of the world (one of the last countries to give in to it was France). Thus every human being – as Galton boastfully observed, taking for himself the praise which had been bestowed on his rival, Bertillon, by a colleague in the French Ministry of the Interior – acquired an identity, was once and for all and beyond all doubt constituted an individual.[35]

In this way what to the British administrators had seemed an indistinguishable mass of Bengali faces (or 'snouts', to recall Filarete's contemptuous words) now became a series of individuals each one marked by a biological specificity. This extraordinary extension of the notion of individuality happened because of the relationship of the state and its administrative and police forces. Every last inhabitant of the meanest hamlet of Europe or Asia thus became, thanks to fingerprints, possible to identify and check.

Understanding society through clues

The same conjectural paradigm, in this case used to develop still more sophisticated controls over the individual in society, also holds the potential for understanding society. In a social structure of ever-increasing complexity like that of advanced capitalism, befogged by ideological murk, any claim to systematic knowledge appears as a flight of foolish fancy. To acknowledge this is not to abandon the idea of totality. On the contrary; the existence of a deep connection which explains superficial phenomena can be confirmed when it is acknowledged that direct knowledge of such a connection is impossible. Reality is opaque; but there are certain points – clues, symptoms – which allow us to decipher it. . . .

Notes

1 On Morelli, see Wind, Edgar (1963) *Art and Anarchy*. For a re-examination of Morelli's method, see Wollheim, R. (1973) 'Giovanni Morelli and the origins of scientific connoisseurship', in *On Art and the Mind: Essays and Lectures*.

2 Wind, op. cit., pp. 42–4.

3 ibid., pp. 40–1.

4 Castelnuovo, E. (1968) 'Attribution', in *Encyclopaedia Universalis*, p. 782. A more general comparison is made between Freud's 'detective' methods and Morelli's in Hauser, Arnold (1959) *The Philosophy of Art History*.

5 Doyle, Arthur Conan, 'The Cardboard Box' in *The Complete Sherlock Holmes*, pp. 932 and 937 (and for another striking example 'The Boscombe Valley Mystery', pp. 92–5). 'The Cardboard Box' first appeared in *The Strand Magazine*, V, January–June 1893. From Baring-Gould, W.S. (ed.) (1968) *The Annotated Sherlock Holmes* we learn (p. 208) that *The Strand Magazine*

several months later published an unsigned article on the varieties of the human ear. Baring-Gould thinks the author likely to have been Conan Doyle, publishing Holmes's anthropological treatise on ears. But 'Ears' followed an earlier article on 'Hands', which was signed Beckles Wilson, and was presumably by the same writer. Nevertheless, the page illustrating possible shapes of ears does irresistibly recall illustrations to Morelli's work, which at least confirms that the notion was in common circulation during these years.

6 It is just possible that the parallel was more than a coincidence. An uncle of Conan Doyle's, Henry Doyle, painter and art critic, was made Director of the Dublin Art Gallery in 1869 (see Nordon, P. (1964) *Sir Arthur Conan Doyle, The Man and His Work*, Paris). In 1887 Morelli met Henry Doyle, and wrote about him to Sir Henry Layard. . . . Doyle's acquaintance with the Morelli method is proved (though it could have been assumed in an art historian) by the 1890 *Catalogue of the Works of Art in the National Gallery of Ireland*, which he edited, and which made use of Kugler's manual, which was thoroughly reworked by Layard in 1887 under the guidance of Morelli. The first English translation of Morelli appeared in 1883. . . . The first Holmes story ('A Study in Scarlet') was published in 1887. This does allow the possibility that Conan Doyle was, through his uncle, familiar with the Morelli method. But in any case such a supposition is not essential, since Morelli's writings were certainly not the only vehicle for these ideas.

7 Wind, op. cit., p. 40.

8 Freud, Sigmund, 'The Moses of Michelangelo', in *Collected Works*, Standard Edition, vol. XIII, p. 222.

9 Morelli, G. *Della Pittura Italiana*, p. 4.

10 See his introduction to Doyle, Arthur Conan (1976) *The Adventures of Sherlock Holmes. A facsimile of the stories as they were first published in the Strand Magazine*, New York, pp. x–xi.

11 For distinctions between symptoms and signs or clues, see Segre, C. (1975) 'La Gerarchia dei Segni', in A. Verdiglione (ed.) *Psicanalisi e semiotica*, Milan: p. 33; Sebeok, T.A. (1976) *Contributions to the Doctrine of Signs*, Bloomington, Ind.: Indiana University Press.

12 Wesselofsky, A. (1886) 'Eine Märchengruppe', *Archiv für slavische Philologie* 9: 308–9.

13 Jakobson, R. and Halle, M. (1956) *Fundamentals of Language*, The Hague, pp. 55–87.

14 Here I am making use of the excellent essay by I. Bottéro, 'Symptômes, signes, écritures', in J.P. Vernant *et al.* (eds) (1974) *Divination et Rationalité*, Paris.

15 On all this see the rich study by Detienne, M. and Vernant, J.P.

(1974) *Les ruses de l'intelligence. La Metis des grecs*, Paris.

16 Feyerabend, P.K. (1971) *I problemi dell'empirismo*, Milan, pp. 105ff. and (1975) *Against Method*, London, throughout; and also the controversial remarks of Rossi, P. (1977) *Immagini della scienza*, Rome, pp. 149–50.

17 The *coniector* was a priestly soothsayer or diviner. Here and elsewhere I draw on Timpanaro, S. (1976) *The Freudian Slip*, London, though so to speak turning it inside out. Very briefly, Timpanaro thinks psychoanalysis is too close to magic to be acceptable, while I am suggesting that not only psychoanalysis but most of the so-called human or social sciences are rooted in a divinatory approach to the construction of knowledge. . . .

18 Cabanis, P.J.G. (1974) *La certezza nella Medicina*, ed. S. Moravia, Bari.

19 On this point see Foucault, M. (1973) *Birth of the Clinic*, London, and (1977) *Microfiscia del potere. Interventi politici*, Turin.

20 See Ginzburg, Carlo (1980) *The Cheese and the Worms. The Cosmos of a Sixteenth-Century Miller*, London: Routledge & Kegan Paul.

21 See Winckelmann (1954) *Briefe*, Berlin, vol. II, p. 316 and note on p. 498.

22 Cerulli, E. (1975) 'Una raccolta persiana di novelle tradotte a Venezia nel 1557', in *Atti dell'Academia Nazionale dei Lincei* CCCLXXII.

23 Voltaire, 'Zadig ou la destinée', in R. Pomeau (ed.) (1966) *Romans et Contes*, Paris, p. 36.

24 Cited in Messac, R. (1929) *Le 'Detective Novel' et l'influence de la pensée scientifique*, Paris, pp. 34–5.

25 See Huxley, T. (1881) 'On the method of *Zadig*: retrospective prophecy as a function of science', in *Science and Culture*, London, pp. 128–48.

26 'My research has reached the conclusion. . . . that the anatomy of civil society must be sought in political economy.' Karl Marx, Preface (1859) to *A Contribution to the Critique of Political Economy*.

27 Morelli, op. cit., p. 71.

28 Thompson, E.P. (1975) *Whigs and Hunters. The Origin of the Black Act*, London.

29 Foucault, Michel (1977) *Discipline and Punish. The Birth of the Prison*, London.

30 Perrot, M. (1975) 'Délinquance et système pénitentiaire en France au XIXe siècle', *Annales ESC* 30: 67–91 (esp. 68).

31 Branding was abolished in France in 1832. *The Count of Montecristo* dates from 1844, like *The Three Musketeers* (both by Alexandre Dumas); Victor Hugo's *Les Misérables* from 1869. The list of literary convicts for this period could be extended both for

France (Vautrin, etc.), and from English novels, especially Dickens.

32 See Bertillon, A. (1883) *L'Identité des récidivistes et la loi de relegation*, Paris.
33 Galton, F. (1892) *Finger Prints*.
34 Purkyné, J.E. (1948) *Opera Selecta*, Prague, pp. 29–56.
35 Galton, op. cit., p. 169.

16

Deconstructing the text: Sherlock Holmes

Catherine Belsey

. . . . In 'Charles Augustus Milverton', one of the short stories from *The Return of Sherlock Holmes*, Conan Doyle presents the reader with an ethical problem.[1] Milverton is a blackmailer; blackmail is a crime not easily brought to justice since the victims are inevitably unwilling to make the matter public; the text therefore proposes for the reader's consideration that in such a case illegal action may be ethical. Holmes plans to burgle Milverton's house to recover the letters which are at stake, and both Watson and the text appear to conclude, after due consideration, that the action is morally justifiable. The structure of the narrative is symmetrical: one victim initiates the plot, another concludes it. While Holmes and Watson hide in Milverton's study a woman shoots him, protesting that he has ruined her life. Inspector Lestrade asks Holmes to help catch the murderer. Holmes replies that certain crimes justify private revenge, that his sympathies are with the criminal and that he will not handle the case. The reader is left to ponder the ethical implications of his position.

Meanwhile, on the fringes of the text, another narrative is sketched. It too contains problems but these are not foregrounded. Holmes's client is the Lady Eva Blackwell, a beautiful debutante who is to be married to the Earl of Dovercourt. Milverton has secured letters she has written 'to an impecunious young squire in the country'. Lady Eva does not appear in the narrative in person. The content of the letters is not specified, but they are 'imprudent, Watson, nothing worse'. Milverton describes them as 'sprightly'. Holmes's sympathies, and ours, are with the Lady Eva. None the less we, and Holmes, accept without question on the one hand that the marriage with the Earl of Dovercourt is a desirable one and on the other that were he to see the letters he would certainly break off the match. The text's elusiveness on the content of the letters, and the absence of the Lady Eva herself, deflects the reader's attention from the potentially contradictory ideology of marriage which the narrative takes for granted.

This second narrative is also symmetrical. The murderer too is a woman with a past. She is not identified. Milverton has sent her letters to her husband who in consequence 'broke his gallant heart and died'. Again the text is unable to be precise about the content of the letters since to do so would be to risk losing the sympathy of the reader for either the woman or her husband.

In the meantime Holmes has become engaged. By offering to marry Milverton's housemaid he has secured information about the lay-out of the house he is to burgle. Watson remonstrates about the subsequent fate of the girl, but Holmes replies:

> You can't help it, my dear Watson. You must play your cards as best you can when such a stake is on the table. However, I rejoice to say that I have a hated rival who will certainly cut me out the instant that my back is turned. What a splendid night it is.

The housemaid is not further discussed in the story.

The sexuality of these three shadowy women motivates the narrative and yet is barely present in it. The disclosure which ends the story is thus scarcely a disclosure at all. Symbolically Holmes has burnt the letters, records of women's sexuality. Watson's opening paragraph constitutes an apology for the 'reticence' of the narrative: ' . . . with *due suppression* the story may be told. . . . '; 'The reader will excuse me if I conceal the date *or any other fact. . . .* ' (my italics).

The project of the Sherlock Holmes stories is to dispel magic and mystery, to make everything explicit, accountable, subject to scientific analysis. The phrase most familiar to all readers – 'Elementary, my dear Watson' – is in fact a misquotation, but its familiarity is no accident since it precisely captures the central concern of the stories. Holmes and Watson are both men of science. Holmes, the 'genius', is a scientific conjurer who insists on disclosing how the trick is done. The stories begin in enigma, mystery, the impossible and conclude with an explanation which makes it clear that logical deduction and scientific method render all mysteries accountable to reason:

> I am afraid that my explanation may disillusionize you, but it has always been my habit to hide none of my methods, either from my friend Watson or from anyone who might take an intelligent interest in them.
>
> ('The Reigate Squires', *The Memoirs of Sherlock Holmes*)[2]

The stories are a plea for science not only in the spheres conventionally associated with detection (footprints, traces of hair or cloth, cigarette ends), where they have been deservedly influential on forensic practice, but in all areas. They reflect the widespread optimism characteristic of their period concerning the comprehensive power of positivist science. Holmes's ability to deduce Watson's train of thought, for instance, is repeatedly displayed, and it owes nothing to the supernatural. Once explained, the reasoning process always appears 'absurdly simple', open to the commonest of common sense.

The project of the stories themselves, enigma followed by disclosure, echoes precisely the structure of the classic realist text. The narrator himself draws attention to the parallel between them:

> 'Excellent!' I cried.
>
> 'Elementary,' said he. 'It is one of those instances where the reasoner can produce an effect which seems remarkable to his neighbour because the latter has missed the one little point which is the basis of the deduction. The same may be said, my dear fellow, for the effect of some of these little sketches of yours, which is entirely meretricious, depending as it does upon your retaining in your own hands some factors in the problem which are never imparted to the reader. Now, at present I am in the position of these same readers, for I hold in this hand several threads of one of the strangest cases which ever perplexed a man's brain, and yet I lack the one or two which are needful to complete my theory. But I'll have them, Watson, I'll have them!'
>
> ('The Crooked Man', *Memoirs*)

. . . The project also requires the maximum degree of 'realism' – verisimilitude, plausibility. In the interest of science no hint of the fantastic or the implausible is permitted to remain once the disclosure is complete. This is why even their own existence as writing is so frequently discussed within the texts. The stories are alluded to as Watson's 'little sketches', his 'memoirs'. They resemble fictions because of Watson's unscientific weakness for story-telling:

> I must admit, Watson, that you have some power of selection which atones for much which I deplore in your narratives. Your fatal habit of looking at everything from the point of view of a story instead of as a scientific exercise has ruined what might have been an instructive and even classical series of demonstrations.
>
> ('The Abbey Grange', *Return*)

In other words, the fiction itself accounts even for its own fictionality, and the text thus appears wholly transparent. The success with which the Sherlock Holmes stories achieve an illusion of reality is repeatedly demonstrated. In their foreword to *The Sherlock Holmes Companion* Michael and Mollie Hardwick comment on their own recurrent illusion 'that we were dealing with a figure of real life rather than of fiction. How vital Holmes appears, compared with many people of one's own acquaintance.'[3]

De Waal's bibliography of Sherlock Holmes lists twenty-five 'Sherlockian' periodicals apparently largely devoted to conjectures, based on the 'evidence' of the stories, concerning matters only hinted at in the texts – Holmes's education, his income and his romantic and sexual adventures.[4] According to *The Times* in December 1967, letters to Sherlock Holmes were then still commonly addressed to 221B Baker Street, many of them asking for the detective's help.

None the less these stories, whose overt project is total explicitness, total verisimilitude in the interests of a plea for scientificity, are haunted by shadowy, mysterious and often silent women. Their silence repeatedly conceals their sexuality, investing it with a dark and magical quality which is beyond the reach of scientific knowledge. In 'The Greek Interpreter' (*Memoirs*) Sophie Kratides has run away with a man. Though she is the pivot of the plot she appears only briefly: 'I could not see her clearly enough to know more than that she was tall and graceful, with black hair, and clad in some sort of loose white gown.' Connotatively the white gown marks her as still virginal and her flight as the result of romance rather than desire. At the same time the dim light surrounds her with shadow, the unknown. 'The Crooked Man' concerns Mrs Barclay, whose husband is found dead on the day of her meeting with her lover of many years before. Mrs Barclay is now insensible, 'temporarily insane' since the night of the murder and therefore unable to speak. In 'The Dancing Men' (*Return*) Mrs Elsie Cubitt, once engaged to a criminal, longs to speak but cannot bring herself to break her silence. By the time Holmes arrives she is unconscious, and she remains so for the rest of the story. Ironically the narrative concerns the breaking of the code which enables her former lover to communicate with her.

Elsie's only contribution to the correspondence is the word, 'Never'. The precise nature of their relationship is left mysterious, constructed of contrary suggestions. Holmes says she feared and hated him; the lover claims, 'She had been engaged to me, and she would have married me, I believe, if I had taken over another profession.' When her husband moves to shoot the man whose coded messages are the source of a 'terror' which is 'wearing her away', Elsie restrains him with compulsive strength. On the question of her motives the text is characteristically elusive. Her husband recounts the story:

> I was angry with my wife that night for having held me back when I might have caught the skulking rascal. She said that she feared that I might come to harm. For an instant it had crossed my mind that what she really feared was that *he* might come to harm, for I could not doubt that she knew who this man was and what he meant by those strange signals. But there is a tone in my wife's voice, Mr Holmes, and a look in her eyes which forbid doubt, and I am sure that it was indeed my own safety that was in her mind.

After her husband's death Elsie remains a widow, faithful to his memory and devoting her life to the care of the poor, apparently expiating something unspecified, perhaps an act or a state of feeling, remote or recent.

'The Dancing Men' is 'about' Holmes's method of breaking the cipher. Its project is to dispel any magic from the deciphering process. Elsie's silence is in the interest of the story since she knows the code. But she also 'knows' her feelings towards her former lover. Contained in the completed and fully disclosed story of the decipherment is another uncompleted and undisclosed narrative which is more than merely peripheral to the text as a whole. Elsie's past is central and causal. As a result, the text with its project of dispelling mystery is haunted by the mysterious state of mind of a woman who is unable to speak.

The classic realist text had not yet developed a way of

signifying women's sexuality except in a metaphoric or symbolic mode whose presence disrupts the realist surface. Joyce and Lawrence were beginning to experiment at this time with modes of sexual signification but in order to do so they largely abandoned the codes of realism. So much is readily apparent. What is more significant, however, is that the presentation of so many women in the Sherlock Holmes stories as shadowy, mysterious and magical figures precisely contradicts the project of explicitness, transgresses the values of the texts, and in doing so throws into relief the poverty of the contemporary concept of science. These stories, pleas for a total explicitness about the world, are unable to explain an area which nonetheless they cannot ignore. The version of science which the texts present would constitute a clear challenge to ideology: the interpretation of all areas of life, physical, social and psychological, is to be subject to rational scrutiny and the requirements of coherent theorization. Confronted, however, by an area in which ideology itself is uncertain, the Sherlock Holmes stories display the limits of their own project and are compelled to manifest the inadequacy of a bourgeois scientificity which, working within the constraints of ideology, is thus unable to challenge it.

Perhaps the most interesting case, since it introduces an additional area of shadow, is 'The Second Stain' (*Return*), which concerns two letters. Lady Hilda Trelawney Hope does speak. She has written before her marriage 'an indiscreet letter . . . a foolish letter, a letter of an impulsive, loving girl.' Had her husband read the letter his confidence in her would have been for ever destroyed. Her husband is nonetheless presented as entirely sympathetic, and here again we encounter the familiar contradiction between a husband's supposed reaction, accepted as just, and the reaction offered to the reader by the text. In return for her original letter Lady Hilda gives her blackmailer a letter from 'a certain foreign potentate' stolen from the dispatch box of her husband, the European Secretary of State. This political letter is symbolically parallel to the first sexual one. Its contents are equally elusive but it too is 'indiscreet', 'hotheaded'; certain phrases in it are 'provocative'. Its publication would produce 'a most dangerous state of feeling' in the nation. Lady Hilda's innocent folly is the cause of the theft: she knows nothing of politics and was not in a position to understand the consequences of her action. Holmes ensures the restoration of the political letter and both secrets are preserved.

Here the text is symmetrically elusive concerning both sexuality and politics. Watson, as is so often the case where these areas are concerned, begins the story by apologizing for his own reticence and vagueness. In the political instance what becomes clear as a result of the uncertainty of the text is the contradictory nature of the requirements of verisimilitude in fiction. The potentate's identity and the nature of his indiscretion cannot be named without involving on the part of the reader either disbelief (the introduction of a patently fictional country would be dangerous to the project of verisimilitude) or belief (dangerous to the text's status as fiction, entertainment; also quite possibly politically dangerous). The scientific project of the texts requires that they deal in 'facts', but their nature as fiction forbids the introduction of facts.

The classic realist text installs itself in the space between fact and illusion through the presentation of a simulated reality which is plausible but *not real*. In this lies its power as myth. It is because fiction does not normally deal with 'politics' directly, except in the form of history or satire, that it is ostensibly innocent and therefore ideologically effective. But in its evasion of the real also lies its weakness as 'realism'. Through their transgression of their own values of explicitness and verisimilitude, the Sherlock Holmes stories contain within themselves an implicit critique of their limited nature as characteristic examples of classic realism. They thus offer the reader through the process of deconstruction a form of knowledge, not about 'life' or 'the world', but about the nature of fiction itself.

Thus, in adopting the form of classic realism, the only appropriate literary mode, positivism is compelled to display its own limitations. Offered as a science, it reveals itself to a deconstructive reading as ideology at the very moment that classic realism, offered as verisimilitude, reveals itself as fiction. In claiming to make explicit and *understandable* what appears mysterious, these texts offer evidence of the tendency of positivism to push to the margins of experience whatever it cannot explain or understand. In the Sherlock Holmes stories classic realism ironically tells a truth, though not the truth about the world which is the project of classic realism. The truth the stories tell is the truth about ideology, the truth which ideology represses, its own existence as ideology itself.

Notes

1 Doyle, Arthur Conan (1976) *The Return of Sherlock Holmes*, London: Pan Books.
2 Doyle, Arthur Conan (1950) *The Memoirs of Sherlock Holmes*, Harmondsworth: Penguin Books.
3 Hardwick, Michael and Mollie (1962) *The Sherlock Holmes Companion*, London: John Murray.
4 De Waal, Ronald (1972) *The World Bibliography of Sherlock Holmes*, Greenwich, Conn.: New York Graphic Society.

Section 5

Production

Introduction

It is now generally agreed that the base/superstructure metaphor proposed by Marx as a way of 'thinking' the relations between the economic aspects of social life and its cultural and ideological aspects has proved more of a hindrance than a help to research. The suggestion, in Marx's original formulation, that culture and ideology should be regarded as the mere secondary manifestations of economic determinations – the 'real foundations' of social life upon which all other aspects of society are erected and to which they 'correspond' – has proved inoperable. Attempts to apply it literally have resulted in a yawning chasm between, on the one hand, a proliferation of information regarding the economic relations of cultural production in specific contexts and, on the other, the cultural texts those relations are supposed to illuminate. In study after study it has had to be affirmed, and affirmed again, that cultural forms do have their own properties which analysis must attend to and which cannot sensibly – or usefully – be regarded as a mere by-product of economic relations, not even in the last instance.

One early response to these difficulties, as noted in the introduction to Section 1, was to argue that economic determinations impinged upon the sphere of culture not directly but via a series of mediations – specific conventions, institutions and traditions – regarded as so many staging-posts between the imperatives of the economy and the realm of cultural texts, passing those imperatives on but at the same time filtering and modifying their influence. The chief difficulty with such approaches was that the main mediating role in this process was typically assigned to the author who, having been shown out of the front door, re-entered through the back door as a privileged point in the relay of determinations from the sphere of economic relations to the texts bearing his or her name.

For all these difficulties, though, the more general spirit of Marx's suggestion that the processes of cultural production should be regarded as material processes grounded in and affected by economic relationships and pressures – rather than as free-floating and spiritual affairs – remains one of the great milestones in social and cultural theory. Recent attempts to hold on to this aspect of Marxist thought while avoiding the difficulties outlined above have tended to do so – and here the influence of Althusser has been decisive – by rethinking the concept of production as not merely the locus of a set of economic imperatives but as a complex process in which economic, technological, political and ideological determinations interpenetrate and condition one another. When so viewed, the concept of production context – for a film or a television series, for example – ceases to be thought of as an external backdrop to the text and becomes, instead, the place of a more lively and dynamic (and often contradictory) set of processes and relations capable of accounting for some of the distinctive properties of the texts which emerge as their end product.

While all of the readings collected here exemplify such approaches to the production contexts of popular fictions, they have also been selected with other purposes in view: first, to illuminate some of the differences between the production contexts for film and television; second, to afford the opportunity for comparisons to be drawn between British and American production contexts for both film and television. They also share a concern to theorize the role of intentions – of scriptwriters, directors and producers – in the production process, but without seeking to privilege any of these positions or to confer upon their occupants the sovereign status of authors.

The first two readings are thus concerned with the institutional constraints regulating series production in British and American television. Both, moreover, examine series which have acquired a reputation for 'quality television'. In 'Send-up: authorship and organization', John Tulloch and Manuel Alvarado consider how the specific institutional space occupied by *Doctor Who* within the programming strategies of the BBC enabled it to combine an interest in innovation with a concern for ratings success in ways which allowed it to bridge the divide between popular and serious drama which characterizes most television output. Tulloch and Alvarado are also concerned with the factors allowing for the elasticity of the *Doctor Who* text: that is, its ability to accommodate the 'signatures' of different writers and producers and yet still subordinate these – albeit not always without tension – to the institutional identity of the series. Paul Kerr is likewise concerned to explain how, in the quite different context of American television, a particular company – MTM Enterprises – has been able to acquire such a consistent reputation for high quality, socially relevant drama and comedy over a period of more than a decade. Established in 1970 to produce television programmes on a commission basis for the American network system, MTM Enterprises has an impressive list of successful series to its credit: *The Mary Tyler Moore Show, Lou Grant, Hill Street Blues*. In examining the production context for the first of these, Kerr seeks to establish the basis for the MTM style not only in the ethos and organization of the company but in the specific set of broader conditions prevailing within American television at the time, and especially the changing pressures of advertisers interested in targetting higher income audiences.

In the course of his discussion, Kerr cites a remark of

Edward Buscombe's which has often served as a summary of the major lacunae of studies of particular film studios:

> What seems to be lacking is any conception of the relations between the economic structure of a studio, its particular organization and the kinds of films it produced. For if there is such a thing as studio style it should be possible to provide some explanation of how it was formed. (p. 333)

Both John Ellis's study of Ealing Studios in the postwar period and Paul Kerr's discussion of the B *film noir* output of such studios as RKO over a roughly similar period are mindful of the difficulties to which Buscombe points here and seek to chart a way out of them. Yet, while both incorporate a rich complexity of determinations into their analyses of these production contexts, their emphases are, ultimately, different. In Ellis's account – which ranges across the available technology, the conditions of the cinema industry in Britain, the division of labour within Ealing Studios – the crucial organizing role is ultimately assigned to the world-view and values of the elite core of Ealing writers, producers and directors. Kerr, too, assigns considerable importance to such considerations: indeed, he regards the B *film noir* as the product of an attempt to produce an oppositional aesthetic and style within American cinema. The stress in his account, however, falls on the particular conditions prevailing within the system of film exhibition at the time in allowing the B *film noir* to flourish as an economically viable, if subordinate branch, of the film industry.

17
Send-up: authorship and organization
John Tulloch and Manuel Alvarado

> *Doctor*: I am asking you to help yourself. Nothing will change round here unless you change it. . . .
> *Gaudry:* It's crazy talk. Rebellion? Who would support you?
> *Doctor*: Given the chance to breathe clean air for a few hours they might. Have you thought of that?
> *Mandrell*: What have we got to lose?
> *Doctor*: Only your claims.
> *Bisham*: Well put, Doctor!
> *Doctor*: (smiling) Oh, it was nothing. I have a gift for the apt phrase.

Tom Baker's pastiche of Marx in 'The Sun Makers' is actually in calling on the oppressed to throw off their (tax) 'claims'. This kind of 'apt phrase' as comic 'in-joke' became Baker's signature as the fourth Doctor – especially during the three years when *Doctor Who* was produced by Graham Williams. It was comedy relying on a certain privileged information. . . .

This was a feature of the Williams/Baker years which the next producer, John Nathan-Turner (who was production unit manager under Williams) particularly disliked, complaining that the use, for instance, of the *Doctor Who* production office telephone number for a computer in one story was a private joke which was lost on the majority of the audience. 'I think that some of those mythical stories are terrific. But if you are going to do them, I really think you've not got to be tempted by a sort of in-joke of the whole thing.'[1] . . . Graham Williams disagreed. 'After all, for those who knew it, it would mean something; for those who didn't, it wouldn't detract anything. . . .'

The disagreement over audiences and dramatic values between Williams and Nathan-Turner itself raised quite dramatically the ways in which an institution like *Doctor Who* can vary according to different production and professional practices. This chapter will look at ways in which variations within professional ideology materially affect production practices; and further, at ways in which professional values that are ostensibly identical can themselves be inflected differently according to pressure from within and outside the television industry.

Intertextuality and audience space

Orwell's and Huxley's science fiction dystopias provided Williams's 'The Sun Makers' with the story of a society dominated by a rapacious 'Big Brother' who controls everybody's movements by means of omni-present cameras, and keeps them timid with specially manufactured gas as he collects his oppressive taxes. A different SF coding was laid over these by director Pennant Roberts, who recast the dystopic themes visually and dramatically in reference to Fritz Lang's classic science fiction film, *Metropolis*. The visual drama of Leela about to be steamed alive by the Collector in a half-cylindrical, transparent chamber was borrowed from Lang's laboratory scene where Rotwang reproduces the unconscious Maria in an identical chamber. The revolt of underground workers against their capitalist masters is also taken directly from *Metropolis*, as is the image of workers grappling desperately with the clock-like dials of machines out of control.

The direct motivation for the story was far more pragmatic: writer Robert Holmes's temporary annoyance with his tax man. Intentional comment of this kind does not, of course, provide the meaning of a programme in any simplistic way. Even where producers are aware of them, they are very quickly recoded according to the professional values of good drama, appropriate television, and so on. External references like these, however, help locate the programme both in terms of its institutional need for the novelty-within-continuity, and its perceived audience, and therefore its notion of the appropriate level at which to negotiate the SF genre.

> *Williams*: You couldn't, I don't think, go into the Orwellian side of that monolithic society as much as Orwell did. Nor did we want to. It was enough that there was the overburdening of tax. And that depression provided us with the villain of the piece. Everything else was a mere device to tell that story. And so one used the taxation system instead of common-or-garden slavery. You could substitute slavery for it quite easily, and it wouldn't make a scrap of difference to the story.
> *Tulloch*: Some of my students felt it was markedly politically oriented.
> *Williams*: Well, it was. But it wasn't party-politicized.
> *Tulloch*: No, but as a system – like a capitalist system?
> *Williams*: Well, taxation, I think, extends beyond the capitalist system – because the Government has to be paid for. You could say it was a classically Roman civilization with as much force as you could say it was an American, British or German civilization. I think that drawing attention to the fact of a society that has allowed its aims to become so confused that taxation is an end in itself rather than a means of providing services for the entire community is no bad achievement in a popular science fiction programme. . . .

Williams's attitude to politics in *Doctor Who* – 'a fair and accurate depiction of the circumstances' while avoiding 'party politicizing' – represents the media ideology of balance and neutrality.[2] However, there is a good deal more to professional ideology than the question of political balance, as Williams's reply indicates.

First, there is the question of promoting difference within continuity in a television institution conceived as 'serious' as well as popular. The 'Orwellian' theme inflects the programme in terms of serious SF, yet is itself transmitted via the Holmes signature as a light-hearted rebuke of any system which has lost sight of its democratic function. . . .

Secondly, there is the question of tailoring the programme to implied audiences. Williams was concerned to keep social comment as a 'side issue' of the 'action-thriller adventure' because he felt that there was a 'bedrock audience loyalty' of between six and eight million viewers 'which we should feed and take notice of'. Other references – to politics, to serious SF, to classic cinema, to history, to myth and so on – were designed to 'grab on the wing' another audience in order to build *Doctor Who*'s following from the six million bedrock to anything up to fourteen million, which Philip Hinchcliffe had achieved with 'Ark in Space'. In one respect the programme worked for narrative unity and coherence by relegating such references to what Nathan-Turner called 'in-group' asides, and Williams called audience 'bonuses'. Alternatively, the programme has always – and especially in the Williams era – made its appeal to audience 'sophistication' by means of an allegorical mode of address.

The reason for the common, but differently valued, use by fans and students of the terms 'pantomime' and 'slap-stick' for the Williams era – despite his own apparent intentions – has a lot to do with the very overt emphasis on allegory and intertextuality in some of his shows. Basically allegory, as a mode that works at two levels – a literal one, complete in itself where the drama is enacted, and a metaphorical one, carrying a 'message' – is ideal for *Doctor Who*, since it should allow both the strong sense of narrative designed by producers for the bedrock audience and the 'intellectual suggestiveness' required for the 'bonus' audience.

The double meaning implicit in allegory has to be indicated by some device to alert the target reader/viewer. In *Doctor Who* this is often done by a play on names and parallel situations. Sanders (the name already recalling 'films of Empire') puts on a pith helmet in 'Kinda', a tale of 'Raj' type militarism and imperialism; there is a reference to Troy in 'The Armageddon Factor', as the miniaturized Doctor, concealed inside K-9, enters the enemy's lair to rescue his princess; and an allusion to 'Morton's Fork' in 'The Sun Makers', a tale of a quasi-monarchical capitalist who exploits the people through a rapacious tax collector. . . .

However, whether or not intertextuality operates semantically for some audiences, all producers of *Doctor Who* agree that it must not operate in contradiction to the authenticating and rhetorical conventions of the 'bedrock' audience. For them any intertextural reference in *Doctor Who* must be re-tied to the fictional world in so far as its foregrounding devices have (as in the 'Ark in Space' example) a direct relevance to the dominant generic and narrative values of the programme.

Intertextuality in *Doctor Who* is, quite apart from any semantic function it might have, also a mode of address. Even at the most simplistic level – of recognition of references to Greek myth, Shakespeare, the Bible, history, Lang's *Metropolis*, 'specialized' sciences, etc. – the programme seeks to establish a 'complicit' relationship with its audience, which is much closer to the conventions of theatrical vaudeville than to those of dramatic 'realism'. In the case of the tertiary educated audience – a significant target group for *Doctor Who* – these 'double meanings' (where the 'allegorical' reference is in fact to another 'high art' text or to an entire mode, such as melodrama) can have as much to do with the pleasure derived from the text as its 'scary' dramatic qualities have for a younger audience or its *intra*-textual references have for fans.

> *Peter Holland*: Part of the way the programme *does* appeal to me now, is the trendy, sophisticated 'get the reference' game . . . when the Doctor come to the cave in 'Kinda' and says, 'Such stuff as dreams are made of' I thought, when I saw them playing chess, straight away of

Ferdinand and Miranda playing chess in *The Tempest*. Now whether I want to take that further and say, 'this is a sort of *Tempest* story' I don't know yet. But those sort of references are planted for me to pick up quite deliberately. They are looking for an audience that will get the reference.

Nathan-Turner (who produced 'Kinda') was happy to use the Shakespearian or other 'bonuses' provided they did not weaken the drama. Williams's sin against the programme – in the eyes of other producers, directors and fans – was his tendency to signify other texts (whether high art, melodrama or pantomime) too overtly, to make *Doctor Who* (through the use of John Cleese in 'City of Death') into, as Ian Levine put it, 'a slap-stick *Fawlty Towers* in space' – or in our terms to destroy *Doctor Who* as allegory by destroying its basic story. . . .

Intertextual references are, however, the site and stake of a much larger target audience than the 'sophisticated' – for Williams nothing less than the entire audience above the 'bedrock'. In the first place, Williams quickly began to orientate the programme beyond the young children he was instructed to address.

> *Williams*: We discovered that very much the largest single sector of our audience was between 26 and 36, and almost as large a segment was between 36 and 46. So the adult audience very much outnumbered the children – which was our gut reaction to start with. We thought it was *terribly* dangerous to start playing down to what we would imagine kids would want . . .

In 'The Sun Makers' the references to *Metropolis* – as well as references to 'gangster' torture conventions – were designed for the 'great big audience of people who actually do enjoy the visual medium nowadays' (such as the audience for 'classic' movies) and who, like the *Doctor Who* fans but on a wider front, could pick up and enjoy 'buff' references. Indeed, Williams's entire 'audience beyond the bedrock' conception was built up on this notion of popular but sophisticated intertextual reference.

> *Williams*: What I *did* take as my barometer, more consciously than anything else I think, were the book stands. Because I used to make an investigation almost every week, by going around the popular book stalls . . . and seeing what paperbacks were shifting – across the board, not just science fiction – and then paid attention to what science fiction was going . . . You could see waves coming and going: of interest in yukky violence, in big business, in family sagas, in historical romances . . . I'd say, OK. Well, is there anything there that we can do? No, we can't do sickly romance. It's not our bag really, so we'll just have to forget that strand . . . Yukky violence isn't our bag either. *But* that sort of historical romance, yes . . . we can work that in some way. . . . I reckoned that if people were committed enough to go out and buy the book, then they were likely to be committed enough to notice what was going on in the programme. And it is for *that* sort – if you like, the book-buying public – that we aimed the little one-offs, the little asides that we were talking about. . . .

Parody and drama: space 'send-up'

. . . In Williams's last season as producer, under the impact of Doug Adams as script editor, the 'parody' signature became still more ambitious. Whereas Williams was happy enough to see in Duggan (the 'spoof' detective of 'The City of Death') a simple 'send-up' of *Bulldog Drummond*, Adams began to question the conventions of popular television 'realism'. For instance, the trivialization of the Daleks in Adams's first story as script editor, 'Destiny of the Daleks' (1979), was a humorously logical comment on *Doctor Who*'s commitment to 'plausibility' and 'realism'. When the Doctor tells the Daleks that if they really are the master race of the universe they should follow him up a rope ladder, and then later immobilizes a Dalek by throwing his hat over its antenna before rolling it down a corridor to destruction, he is doing no more than pointing to the extreme implausibility of these ball-bearing monsters for anything other than the most unsophisticated child audience.

This, however, drew attention to the bare bones of the action drama – and demystified the show's most venerable villains which angered the fans on the grounds of continuity as well as 'realism'. Philip Hinchcliffe had recognized the problem of their implausibility, but his response was to enfold the Daleks as horrifically as possible within his 'Gothic' signature in 'Genesis of the Daleks'. 'The great problem with those Daleks stories is not to make them silly. David Maloney directed that one, and he worked extremely hard to make the Daleks powerful – you know, so that they are not just idiots running around . . . You can't dwell on those Daleks. You've really got to edit them together and make them more powerful and make them more menacing than they are by the way you shoot it.'

Hinchcliffe's attitude to the Daleks was very similar to that of the fans, who recognized – and objected to – the Daleks being turned into 'bumbling idiots' as early as 'The Chase' in 1965. As fan Paul Mount wrote:

> With Dennis Spooner as story editor many of the preceding serials of the second season had possessed a lighter, less tense air than those of the first season under David Whittaker. This trend continues noticeably with 'The Chase'. The old adage 'familiarity breeds contempt' is temptingly applicable to the Daleks in this adventure. During their first two serials they had been taken totally seriously, as objects of horror and destruction. It appears that the only logical step to take now is to debase them a little – ridicule them and turn them into objects of fun. The Daleks . . . are thwarted at every turn; outwitted by the faster-thinking, faster-moving humanoids of the story and made to look like lumbering fools at almost every opportunity. Yet the magic of it is that, at the end of it all, the Daleks retain their dignity – their charisma and genius carrying them through the excesses of the plot.[3]

So, despite their 'silly, spluttering and coughing sounds . . . spoiling the effect' of the drama in places, the Daleks retained their dignity and the narrative its tension – which is not what the fans thought of Graham Williams's 'Destiny of the Daleks'. Working with Douglas Adams as script editor in this 1979 story, Williams's conditions of production were quite different from Verity Lambert's when working with Dennis Spooner in 1965, and the coding of 'comedy' was consequently quite different. . . .

Mrs Whitehouse: the space for comedy

When Graham Williams took over as producer of *Doctor Who* it was at the forefront of critical attention from Mary Whitehouse's National Viewers' and Listeners' Association. The liking of Gothic Horror by the former producer, Philip Hinchcliffe, and his script editor, Robert Holmes, had led to the public criticism of 'Genesis of the Daleks', 'The Brain of Morbius', 'The Seeds of Doom' and 'The Deadly Assassin' (1976). 'The Talons of Weng Chiang' (1977) came in for special abuse for its racism, violence and sexuality. This was the high point of a long-term campaign against *Doctor Who* for its 'corrupting' influence in de-sensitizing children to violence. For Mrs Whitehouse, 'strangulation – by hand, by claw, or obscene vegetable matter – is the latest gimmick, sufficiently close up so that they get the point. And just for a little variety, show the children how to make a Molotov Cocktail.'[4] The response of the BBC was to prohibit easily imitated methods of violence from the programme, and to discourage the portrayal of horror through everyday household objects. Teddy bears or dolls which turned into monstrous aliens, and death – or the suggestion of death – by means of scissors, 'garotting or slicing with razors', were henceforth consciously avoided. . . .

Williams took the Whitehouse attack very seriously. 'The violence and the pretty ladies – one was very

conscious that the microscope was there, that the spot-
light was on us.' Williams felt that the poor audience
figures at the beginning of his period as producer were
directly attributable to the Whitehouse-inspired public
debate about *Doctor Who* in the press, Parliament and
in letters to the BBC Board of Governors. . . . The turn
to comedy was 'entirely, directly' related to the Whitehouse attack. 'It was replacing the violence . . . that was
a very, very major part of the thinking.' Hence
Williams's new signature of 'suspense following light
relief' was established, 'because in a thriller situation, if
you can't have the nasties, it's a vacuum – you've got to
put something in there'. Another influence was the
massive success of *Star Wars*.[5]

> *Williams*: I was up against it, because my boss was
> saying, 'What are we going to do about *Star Wars* coming
> out, and *Star Trek* coming back?' And my point of view
> was that we didn't have the money or the expertise to do
> it. Neither did *they* have our – I thought it was a British
> – television strength, which is in building and creating –
> writing, acting, directing – character, and pretty quirky
> character at that. And again, all this, as you can see,
> added up to the humour and that sort of treatment. If we
> didn't go for the hardwear, we had to go for something.
> And we went for character. Then if you're going to have
> character, you can't have people just talking to each
> other. You could either play it very doom-laden, and
> weighty and pompous, or you could have people who
> took themselves very seriously but the Doctor doesn't
> have to take them seriously as well.

The terrain had been prepared for the arrival of Douglas
Adams.

Meta-space and realism: 'The City of Death'

Tom Baker had been consistently witty under his first
producer, Philip Hinchcliffe. But there the humour had
been incorporated as part of the discourse of human
spontaneity within the Gothic mode. For example, in

'The Masque of Mandragola' the Doctor says, 'Had a hard day in the catacombs' as, playing with his yo-yo on the underground altar, he is approached slowly and ominously from behind by the frighteningly masked and cowled space villain. Hinchcliffe's mixture of the fearsome and comic in stories, where men take on the appearance of robots ('The Robots of Death') or sprout tendrils like plants ('The Seeds of Doom'), and where the Doctor can laugh in the face of these excrescences and parodies of the human form, was genuinely in the tradition of the grotesque; a laughter at cosmic fear which promotes relief and anxiety together.[6]

What enabled Baker to 'go over the top' in the Williams era was the conjuncture of the new (Whitehouse induced) comedy coding with the arrival as script editor of Douglas Adams. Adams (with his favourite SF writers, Kurt Vonnegut and Robert Sheckley) was part of the movement of modernist (or 'meta') SF which, as Ebert describes, 'acquires its narrative force from laying bare the conventions of science fiction and subverting its transparent language of mimesis and believability. Instead of using a language which is only a means for achieving other ends, such as telling an appealing and suspenseful story, it employs a self-reflexive discourse acutely aware of its own aesthetic status and artificiality. Not only language but also other components of fiction such as 'character', 'plot' and 'point of view' are handled with aesthetic self-consciousness in a manner that makes it impossible to take them for anything but what they actually are: created literary characters, made-up plots and so forth.'[7] . . .

As Ebert has explained, the development of 'modernist' SF has derived in part from attempts to 'energize' the stale, 'automized' and no longer effective conventions of the genre. When Doug Adams argued that his intention was not to 'send up' *Doctor Who* but rather to critique its stale 'aliens seek to rule the universe' SF theme, he was drawing on this meta-SF tendency, which came to be seen by his critics as self-reflexive because

generically (rather than in terms of *Doctor Who* itself)
that is what it was.

At the same time, Adams was never a pure 'modernist': certainly not in *Doctor Who* where he was
consciously adhering to television's 'realist' discourse of
'plausible' motivation. 'I wasn't so keen on something
just being a spoof or parody of something else. I thought
"All right, we'll take an element from something, but
then actually build it solidly into the story, so that
whatever aspects we decide to give this character actually
become embedded in the story and become part of the
way the story is worked out." If something's there just
for the sake of poking fun at something else, I think it's
dull, it's boring.' . . .

Thus in 'The City of Death' the trajectory of the
narrative is conventional, as the Doctor acts to stop the
Jaggeroth's attempt to prevent the birth of humankind.
But the defeat of the villain is by means of one punch to
the jaw from a detective, who is a parody of the 'hard-
boiled dick' genre. As Brooke-Rose comments, this kind
of ironic treatment of conventions of popular 'realist'
fiction – in 'The City of Death' of the heroic human
action of SF via parody of the detective genre – consists
of the humorous use of generic clichés in a kind of
knowing wink to the reader/viewer. In this case it
worked outside the institutional continuity of the
programme, and hence was a wink which *Doctor Who*
fans clearly did not enjoy.

'The City of Death', in fact, belongs to what SF writer
Robert Sheckley calls the 'most venerable of all' the
perennially popular science fiction sub-genres, 'The End
of The World'. In his edited compilation, *After the Fall*,
Sheckley plays on the end of the world theme with satiric
and whimsical levity: 'Although we will not go so far as
to call it a laughing matter, still, it does seem that the
destruction of ourselves and everything we hold dear
could be considered with some levity, especially since we
are only reading about it rather than undergoing it.'[8]

In 'City of Death', Adams produced an 'upbeat end of

the world story' of that kind. He intersperses the horror with laughter, for instance: the running joke about art 'authenticity'; the introduction of a pastiche American, the 'hard-boiled dick' Duggan who, in contrast to the Doctor's wit and logic, tries to counter every situation with a punch; and, most memorably, by the brief insertion of John Cleese and Eleanor Bron. In the last episode the Doctor, Romana and Duggan rush frantically back to the Tardis to try to reach the Jaggeroth ship before the Count. As they reach the gallery the Tardis is being contemplated by two art critics, played by Cleese and Bron:

> *Cleese*: For me the most curious thing about the piece is its wonderful a-functionalism.
> *Bron*: Yes – I see what you mean. Divorced from its function and seen purely as a work of art, its structure of line and colour is obviously counterpointed by the redundant vestiges of its function.
> *Cleese*: And since it has no call to be here the art lies in the fact that it is here.

(The Doctor and his companions rush past them and enter the Tardis. The door closes and, with the critics still contemplating it, the Tardis dematerializes.)

> *Bron*: (now staring at the empty gallery space left by the vanished Tardis): Exquisite. Absolutely exquisite. (Cleese nods sagely in agreement, and with a gesture signifies 'superb').

This interlude is very carefully tied into the narrative by Adams in a number of ways. First, by re-presenting the discourse about art 'authenticity'. Secondly, by continuing the interplay of 'up-beat' levity and dramatic horror, placed as it is between the frantic chase and the final defeat of the Count. Moments before there had been some humour at the Doctor's inability to catch a Parisian taxi to take him back to the Tardis and the beginnings of time. Adams believes this tension between comedy and horror heightened the drama, 'The story . . . was worked out in a considerable amount of detail, and actually held a terrifying idea at the bottom of it.' Hence Adams inserted the taxi scene, quickly followed by the art critics. 'The Doctor rushes through on his terrible, urgent mission, dematerializes, and the critics – just to demonstrate the fact that they couldn't even begin to understand the level of problem with which they are confronted – don't even realize that anything strange has happened. They just think it is part of the artistic experience.' Thirdly, despite the absurd intervention of Cleese and Bron, their appearance, like the rest of the story, is coded for 'realism'. It was important to Adams that the incident should be motivated realistically, as well as dramatically: 'The thing about the way the Doctor works is that there should always be a fierce logic behind what he does. Now logic can sometimes appear to be absolutely manic. So, for instance, I thought, "Now he's landed in Paris at the beginning of the story, where would he hide the police box?" Because we tend to forget, you see, the fact that he's still wandering around in this police box, which tends to be taken for granted – and if you operate strictly within the context of the stories, people shouldn't be taking this for granted. So, I thought, "where's he going to park it in Paris? All right, he'll park it in a modern art gallery where he hopes it will go unnoticed."'

Adams solved his problem far more innovatively and 'realistically' in 'The City of Death' than many other writers, who either tend to ignore the problem or else place the incoming Tardis in some disused quarry from where the Doctor walks to his adventure. In doing so, Adams plausibly motivated the appearance of his art critics. Hence Adams maintained the 'realist' motivation which has remained unchanged since the first episode of *Doctor Who*, even though its coding has varied – from the hermeneutic 'mystery' coding of Totters junkyard to the 'upbeat' humour of the Parisian art gallery.

Graham Williams nominated 'The City of Death' as his favourite production during his three years at the helm of *Doctor Who*. His successor as producer, John

Nathan-Turner, however did not like it, complaining of Williams's tendency to 'undergraduate humour'. . . .

It was quickly clear from the discussion that Nathan-Turner's 'adventure' values were as 'realist' as Adams's – dense characterization (the Doctor was to be vulnerable as well as knowing, humorous as well as serious), audience identification, traditional narrative designs of 'lack', suspension and resolution – and yet that he also saw himself as rejecting the direction on the Williams/Adams period and 'getting back' to the 'true' traditions of the programme which had been disturbed by a period of 'send up'. . . .

Nathan-Turner's tendency to run together 'undergraduate' and 'childish' humour as undesirable was determined by his concern not to undercut the audience's suspension of disbelief:

> *Tulloch*: The Williams era was very melodramatic, and yet it seemed to me to be sending up the melodrama. I thought that it might actually be oriented towards not just a 'silly' audience, but in fact a more sophisticated one which actually liked that play on melodrama. Now, is that reading something into it that wasn't there?
> *Nathan-Turner*: No, I think it probably was there, and I just think that that undercuts the drama. I mean, that's my own personal feeling – and it is why I have cut it out. You can't have a villain that cracks jokes in *Doctor Who*. And we did have one. Once again, it seems as though I'm knocking the previous regime, and I suppose I am in a way – we did have villains who cracked jokes. I don't think the Doctor as a character can take them seriously, and the viewer as part of the audience can get involved successfully, if the baddies crack jokes.

Nathan-Turner's insistence on traditional 'adventure' and audience identification led him to disapprove of the Cleese/Bron episode in 'The City of Death' as something inserted and drawing attention to itself. 'When somebody walks on for thirty seconds which the audience spends saying, "Oh look! It's John Cleese", or "It's John whatisname – er, oh, you know, the man from *Fawlty*

Towers, blah, blah, blah'', you've lost a scene! Either they're in it or they're not.' . . .

From this dispute among *Doctor Who* professionals, two things are particularly clear. First, that Nathan-Turner, Adams and his producer Graham Williams all justified their inflections of the programme in terms of dominant 'professional' values – that is, in terms of 'good drama', 'plausibility' and 'realism'. But that secondly, each oriented this justification in a different way according to his particular professional interests. John Nathan-Turner understood 'drama' in terms of the roots of the programme itself – a return to something it had once been and had 'lost' in the Williams era, a respect for the institution of *Doctor Who* as a series and for its 'continuity', which endeared him to the fans. Graham Williams rejected the 'Oh yeah, that's a real gas – carry on and trip over the carpet as you go out' caricature of his era by Nathan-Turner, and himself justified the comedy in terms of cinema's most recognized 'auteur' – Hitchcock. 'We felt, in the classic sense, that comedy relief sets up the tragedy. Thus we hoped – and Hitchcock uses the same thing to wonderful effect – to cut the ground from under your feet before you take the moment of tension. . . . To provide a cliffhanger, we've already said to the audience, "It's OK folks, only a gas . . . it's only a giggle", and then suddenly it's for real.'

Douglas Adams tried to orient the programme in the 'comedy of character' direction of 'complex' drama, and as a writer appealed to literature's most exalted 'auteur':

> You should never, by introducing a gag, undermine the tension of what's going on . . . A particular dramatic device Shakespeare used, which I think is one of the most fantastically impressive pieces of theatre imaginable, is that in *Macbeth* when the worst has happened . . . Duncan has been murdered by Macbeth. It's a terrible crime against nature and you've got Macduff there at the gates – banging on the castle gates trying to be let in. It's a moment of terrific tension, terror; and at that moment you suddenly get this comic character coming on stage –

the character of the Porter, telling jokes about French tailors . . . At the moment of highest tension – and not to undermine the tension but in fact to key it up still further – you bring in a moment of humour.

Given the TV industry background of Nathan-Turner and Williams and the Cambridge 'Eng. Lit.' one of Adams, their respective legitimating references are not particularly surprising. The question is, how do the conditions of production of *Doctor Who* allow 'high art' and 'serious drama' interventions to take place at all – since it is undoubtedly these which permit a whole range of critical (and pleasurable) readings to take place. . . .

Television is a terrain in which a limited space for 'authorship' may be negotiated, but always in terms of already existing discursive practices (such as *Play of the Month* and 'serious' SF) and material practices (of production and reception) inside and outside the institution of the BBC.

High art and mass entertainment: the space for authorship

There was a certain appropriateness in the Parisian 'Art' context of 'The City of Death', with its play on notions of artistic 'authenticity' and criticism, since Tom Baker's 'bohemian' look – his features concealed behind a wide-brimmed hat and a scarf – had been based on a portrait by Toulouse Lautrec. However, there was another way in which the production drew on 'Art'. In *The Hitch Hiker's Guide to the Galaxy*, Arthur Dent attempts to save his life by his reference to the monstrous Vogon's poetry: 'Interesting rhythmic devices . . . which contrives through the medium of the verse structure to sublimate this, transcend that, and come to terms with the fundamental dichotomies of the other.'[9] This passage, which clearly draws on Adams's particular cultural competence in 'Lit. Crit.' (whose academic discourse he is, among other things, satirizing), is extremely similar to Bron's 'Art' discourse in 'The City of Death'.

Both fuse the satiric and dramatic in comparable ways within the narrative of events. And, further, they both draw playfully on recognizable 'academic' discourses designed to appeal to the large number of adult viewers with considerable 'intellectual capital' – the tertiary educated audience of *Doctor Who* and *The Hitch Hiker's Guide to the Galaxy*. These are audience members who might be expected to watch programmes about art, in which the views that Bron and Cleese only slightly parody could well be expressed. At the same time the satire works – through the effect of 'actor as text' – via a recognizable tradition of television comedy represented by John Cleese and the 'arty/intellectual' image of Eleanor Bron (as carried by films such as *Women in Love*). Audience members with this particular cultural 'competence' are perfectly capable of appropriating these effects and of being articulate about them in discussion of the programme. What this represents is the curious admixture of popular ratings orientation with high art seriousness and style which marks some British television institutions. And *Doctor Who*'s ability to cross that institutional interface between 'serious' and 'popular' is a central reason for its successful incorporation of many different audience groups.

In addressing this issue of British television's mixture of 'artistic' and 'popular', Graham Murdock has pointed out that analysts of the role of the writer in television drama have tended to start either from the notion of 'authentic' and 'creative' authorship, or from the notion of the craftsman utterly enmeshed within the cramping restriction of a ratings-oriented industry. . . .

. . . By the time that television got underway in the mid-1950s . . . the major ideological and institutional divisions within the cultural industries were already firmly established, and television drama was obliged to accommodate to them. In pursuit of maximum audiences, the popular series and serial took over the performer orientation of Hollywood and the entertainment industry. From the titles onwards (*Dixon, Quatermass, Callan, Lillie*) the whole form of presentation, explicitly invited viewers to identify with the central characters and to get involved with their dilemmas week by week. In contrast, single play production derived its ethos primarily from the 'serious' theatre and worked from the beginning with the ideology of authorship.[10]

As a popular series, *Doctor Who* is inescapably wedded to ratings and stardom. And yet the 'popular/serious' opposition is clouded by two considerations: the origins of the programme as 'educational' as well as 'entertaining', and 'adult' as well as 'children's' drama, so that a considerable 'serious' audience has been built up over the years; and more importantly, by the fact that SF as genre challenges the 'popular/serious' interface of the culture industries.

As a long-running series, always on the look-out for novel stories, the programme does incorporate the possibility of authorship, and on occasion the theme itself can refer to the 'art versus craft' debate. . . .

In Adams's case, precisely because the suspension of disbelief itself was questioned, the personal signature was widely recognized and resented by many. Adams's 'meta-SF' comedy of character, and Bailey's 'Ursula Le Guin' interiorized drama tended to appropriate a space for authorship in terms of the 'serious creativity' formula.

On the other hand, there is a space for authorship, which, quite unlike the obtrusive creativity approach, is appreciated by fans because (like genre authorship) it works within and expands the mythology of the institution. Here authorship is seen to be closer to the craftsman dimension, yet creativity is perceived in the degree to which conventions are adjusted and recirculated for the obvious pleasure of millions. Jeremy Bentham writes that 'Robert Holmes's belief that the series is always at its best when its sources are showing is evident from his *Doctor Who* story, "Spearhead from Space", which plagiarises *Quatermass* to the detail. However, borrowing previously used ideas and converting them into the *Doctor Who* genre has been a practice used in the programme since the

Daleks merged together two of H.G. Wells's immortal creations, namely, the Morlocks and the Martian Fighting Machines. The appeal of any *Doctor Who* serial has always been judged by how well it carries over to the millions watching on their television screens. By that token, Robert Holmes need have no worries.'[11] Here the sense is of the continued expansion (but never breaching) of the mythology of the programme as institution. . . .

For fans like Bentham the 'auteur' quality of Holmes is his constant renewal and recreation of the programme's *originating* tensions between science fiction and history, fantasy and realism, space and time, morality and humour.

Typical of genre approaches to 'creativity', Bentham finds Holmes's signature in his ability to re-combine already existing elements in ways which are at the same time transformations of the programme. 'Witty' aphorisms are approved of in Holmes – Bentham likes the lines in 'Carnival of Monsters': 'No vapourization without representation' and 'If you can't stand the cold, stay out of the freezer' – but only because they are combined with a deep seriousness about the 'genre' and its conventional suspension of disbelief. . . .

The central accusation by fans of Graham Williams was that he 'didn't care', and Bentham discussed his 'un-forgiveable' Romana regeneration sequence in 'Destiny of the Daleks' in relation to the careful 'generic' continuity established by Holmes. Hence the programme's return (after the Williams era) to encouraging authorship-within-continuity and within 'generic mythology' is supported by the most serious fans. On the other hand, the same fans also draw a distinction between the programme and 'American high gloss ratings television which *Doctor Who* isn't'. Jeremy Bentham and Ian Levine distinguish between the 'ideas', 'character' and 'ingenuity' of *Doctor Who* on the one hand and the 'plastic', 'identical' and 'totally ineffectual' American '35 mm film gloss' of *Fantastic Journey, Buck Rogers* and *Battlestar Gallactica*.

So that, even while 'star' orientation is a strong (and

probably increasing) feature of *Doctor Who*, its sense of itself as a peculiarly 'British' and 'quality' show works (through the duplicity of science fiction as both 'serious' and 'mass') to blur the conventional 'high/low' culture interface. . . .

It is arguable that not only the 'English' quirkiness of the Doctor but also the frequent replacement of the star has laid stress on the *idea* of the character (and the 'liberal' perspectivism he has always stood for) rather than on the star persona itself. . . .

Even at its most ratings conscious *Doctor Who* continues to encourage this distinction of 'character' and 'innovation' in overt contrast to American SF. It is clear that Nathan-Turner was keen to uphold the 'quality' reputation of the series, and continued to encourage philosophical debate and literary references providing that they did not 'get in the way' of the pace of the show. . . .

Because science fiction has a legitimated 'serious' dimension, and because of the self-consciously 'British quality' aspect of *Doctor Who* the programme inhabits a site across the margins of the dual production system that Murdock describes. 'Logopolis' pleased both the fans through its 'in-house' references to the history of the programme and the more serious SF audience with its commitment to scientific ideas. While certainly working within the 'ethos of entertainment which promises excitement and emotional engagement rather than intellectual challenge'[12] (and Doug Adams rejected 'Logopolis' for its lack of 'realistic' motivation), it is arguable that the space for authorship which the programme leaves open can *both* provide (on occasion, and always tightly circumscribed) the intellectual provocation and ideological challenge (as for instance in Barry Letts's 'The Green Death') which Murdock argues is institutionally the preserve of 'serious' drama, *and* the 'generic' innovation which serious fans see in the work of Robert Holmes. The intention of the programme – and it is a conscious one – is to blend the two without the obtrusiveness of taking authorship – as in the case of Doug Adams – 'over the top'.

Notes

1 Unless otherwise stated all quotations are from interviews with the authors.
2 On this issue see Hall, S., Connell, I. and Curti, L. (1976) 'The unity of current affairs TV', *Working Papers in Cultural Studies*, no. 9, pp. 51–94; Golding, Peter, 'Media professionalism in the third world', in Curran, James *et al.*, (eds) (1977) *Mass Communication and Society*, London: Edward Arnold, pp. 291–308. For an analysis of professional ideology in relation to fictional forms, see Tulloch, John (1982) *Australian Cinema: Industry, Narrative and Meaning*, Sydney: Allen & Unwin, pp. 101–21.
3 Mount, Paul, 'The Chase', *Doctor Who: An Adventure in Space and Time*, London: Cybermark, Serial R, p. 5.
4 Cited in Tracey, Michael and Morrison, David (1979) *Whitehouse*, London: Macmillan, p. 85. . . .
5 There is some debate as to whether K-9 was a spin-off from *Star Wars*' domesticated robots. John Nathan-Turner, production unit manager in the Williams period, and partly responsible for K-9 becoming a regular in the series, insists that 'we were first'.
6 See Thompson, Philip (1972) *The Grotesque*, London: Methuen, and Bakhtin, Mikhail (1968) *Rabelais and his World*, Cambridge, Mass.: MIT Press, cited in Thompson, John O. (ed.) (1982) *Monty Python: Complete and Utter Theory of the Grotesque*, London: British Film Institute, pp. 13–14, 17–19, 42–3.
7 Ebert, Teresa L. (1980) 'The convergence of postmodern innovative fiction and science fiction', *Poetics Today*, 1 (4): 93.
8 Sheckley, Robert (1980) *After the Fall*, London: Sphere, p. vii.
9 Adams, Douglas (1979) *The Hitch Hiker's Guide to the Galaxy*, London: Pan, p. 55.
10 Murdock, Graham (1980) 'Authorship and organisation', *Screen Education*, 35 (summer): 27.
11 Bentham, Jeremy (1979) *Amazing Journeys*, London: Doctor Who Appreciation Society, p. 26.
12 Murdock, op. cit., p. 29.

18
The making of (the) MTM (show)
Paul Kerr

To the casual observer, the success of a sitcom series
featuring a small-screen star like Mary Tyler Moore
might seem unsurprising and thus undeserving of analysis
or explanation. Similarly, the emergence and expansion
of one more independent production company in the
billion dollar business that is American network television seems, on the surface at least, less than noteworthy.
This essay, however, argues that the success of MTM
Enterprises as a production company and of *The Mary
Tyler Moore Show* as a television series were far from
predictable and were indeed predicated on a coincidence
of developments both inside the television industry and
in the broader stream of American life. The aim of this
article, therefore, is to replace both MTM and *The Mary
Tyler Moore Show* in the historical context out of which
they emerged in 1970. It attempts, in other words, to
diagnose the conditions of existence of MTM and thus to
try and unpack – without resort to either reflection
theory or simple studio-as-auteurism – the relations
between the mode and moment of production and the
product.

In the 1960s Mary Tyler Moore had been a popular
television performer, particular well-loved for her role as
Laura Petrie, the wife of the Dick Van Dyke character in
The Dick Van Dyke Show, which she came to after a

series of lesser late 1950s roles (notably as 'sexy' secretary Sam in *Richard Diamond, Private Detective* – in which she only ever appeared from the waist down – and as Happy Hotpoint, an anthropomorphic advertising gimmick for a washing machine).

Then, in April 1969, CBS reunited her with Dick Van Dyke in a television special entitled *Dick Van Dyke and The Other Woman*. When the show garnered the kind of critical respect and audience approval that several recent Van Dyke vehicles had all too visibly lacked CBS seems to have concluded that perhaps *The Dick Van Dyke Show*'s prestige and popularity weren't entirely attributable to the talents of its male lead. In September 1969 Mary Tyler Moore was offered a multi-million dollar deal by CBS to star in a series of her choice of (initially) thirteen episodes. Furthermore, the network were willing to offer an on-air guarantee without benefit or pilot or pre-testing. Her manager, Arthur Price, and her then husband, Grant Tinker (at that time a programming executive at 20th Century-Fox-TV) were apparently pleased to be able to steer the star back to the medium where her talents were best appreciated and perhaps best suited. According to *Rolling Stone*:

> At Tinker's urging she went with the CBS offer which was a multi-million dollar deal that allowed them to set up their own company – MTM Enterprises – and retain partial ownership of this and subsequent productions as well as creative control.[1]

The precise details of this deal have never been made public – indeed, MTM remains a privately held company in every sense – but the general practice of network/ independent production company relationships at this time was for the network to commission programmes from programme producers for an agreed licence fee. This licence fee was paid in return for a licence allowing the network to screen these programmes twice (i.e. to include repeat rights) and thus functioned as a sort of rental. The licence fee system originated as a way of ensuring that both networks and production companies profited, but by the beginning of the 1970s for reasons outlined below licence fees could no longer always be relied on even to cover production costs. . . .

The other side of this deal was that CBS granted the new company and the proposed programme an unusual degree of creative autonomy, as we shall see. By October 1969 *Variety* was announcing CBS's signing of Mary Tyler Moore and confidently predicting its significance for the forthcoming season. Under the headline, in *Variety*'s very own vernacular, 'CBS Inking of 3 New (Old) Stars Seen As Tipoff That Rube Image May Be Shucked In Next 2 Years' was a detailed diagnosis of the network's present ills and presumed remedies:

> The batch of Nielsen-proof stars just locked up by CBS – Andy Griffith and Mary Tyler Moore for next season and Dick Van Dyke for '71–'72 – shapes as significant in several respects. One is that the web is making fewer development pilots these days. Another is that, stemming from this, program development costs are trimmed. And third, if suspicions of some insiders turn out to hold water, could be that the new additions to its star stable could be the opening move in de-ruralizing the currently heavy down-on-the-farm flavor of its sitcom profile.[2]

The 'rube-shucking' strategy was a consequence of changes in audience measurement by the A.C. Nielsen Company which in turn were related to changes in the attitudes to consumers on the part of television advertisers (for whom, ultimately, the Nielsen ratings are measured). Traditionally, Nielsen ratings had been determined in a pretty strictly quantitative manner to indicate the size of an audience tuned in for (rather than actually watching) a particular network at a particular time. This figure, supplemented by audience 'diaries', is calculated on the basis of a random sample of 1200 homes which function as a 'cross-section' of TV viewers nationally. In the 1960s advertisers occasionally requested breakdowns by age and by sex but the data were interpreted and indeed intended for relatively straightforward quantitative calculations; slots were sold to advertisers on the basis of the size of the audience anticipated to be watching at that time. At the end of the 1960s, however, the then trailing network, NBC, began stressing the importance of the demographic composition of the total and even argued that the demographic parts could, thus calculated, be more important than their aggregate sum. At NBC the champion of this new approach was Paul Klein, who was then the network's vice-president in charge of audience measurement.

The extent to which this represented a dramatic reversal of CBS's previous strategy can perhaps be illustrated by reference to one series. In April 1969, the same month that Dick Van Dyke and Mary Tyler Moore were reunited in a CBS special, CBS cancelled a series called *The Smothers Brothers Comedy Hour*. Far from being one of the rural-based sitcoms, however, this was a controversial series which seemed particularly able to attract just the sort of young, sophisticated, urban viewers which the new season rhetoric was already promising. Furthermore, it even contained 'relevant' material; too relevant as it turned out – the series' political satire over such issues as racism and the Vietnam war proved too much for the CBS corporate stomach.[3] It also shared with another contemporary comedy series, *Rowan and Martin's Laugh-In*, a cynical self-consciousness abut television itself which was rapidly to become a prime-time staple. One critic, David Marc, has attributed the advent of this sort of humour in the late 1960s to two factors.[4] First, the adulthood of the first generation of 'television babies'; and second, the impact of what he calls 'electric shadow memory comedy' of the escalation of alternative technologies to broadcasting; alternatives such as syndication, satellite, cable and cassettes, all of which would need stockpiles of such material to fill out their product but all of which would need to take a new attitude to such material in order to 'distinguish' themselves as 'alternatives'. . . .

Meanwhile, as the months of planning the 1970–1

season passed, a number of additional changes were taking place. And one of these was to sound one of the first warnings to the networks of the 'narrowcast' future which Marc was later to point to. Between the 3rd and the 8th April 1970, for instance, the annual convention of the National Association of Broadcasters was held in Chicago. 1970 was in fact the fiftieth anniversary of American broadcasting, but the anticipated celebrations were slightly marred by worries about the imminent destruction of network hegemony by the unleashing of a technological monster. Since the majority of NAB membership was made up of local station owners and operators and their staffs there was considerable concern over the potentially damaging inroads into their advertising revenues (and profits) which the new media might forge. According to industry critic Les Brown, the fear most commonly expressed at the conference was that cable in particular might prove itself capable of:

> fractionalizing the television audience. . . . Television had always had a horizontal audience, playing to what was considered to be the mass taste. Cable's deed might well turn out to be to turn the stations into vertical entities, each addressing itself to a specific audience, whether white-collar, blue-collar, ethnic, suburban, teenage, geriatric, or whatever.[5]

Here perhaps is one key to Paul Klein's shift from the rhetoric of 'mass taste' to that of 'quality demographics' and specifically addressed programming. Another, of course, was NBC's better standing in terms of the latter criteria than the former.

The following month another conference was held. The sixteenth annual CBS-TV Affiliates Conference took place on the weekend of 5–6 May. (Each of the three networks is affiliated to local stations across the States as well as being entitled by Federal Communications Commission regulations to own and operate five such stations of its own in the largest markets.) This year, CBS Network President Robert Wood was announcing a new strategy for the network in spite of its place at the head of the Nielsen ratings. Perhaps surprisingly, the network had taken the decision to drop six very popular and long-running series from their schedules for the 1970–1 season. Wood argued that the network saw no point in:

> stringing along with those shows that might still deliver respectable ratings for another season even though we had concluded, reluctantly, that they had no long term future on our schedule. . . . Neither past performance nor present popularity is sufficient any longer to guarantee future pulling power. . . . The days are gone in programming when we can afford to be imitative rather than innovative. We have to hold the audiences we have; we have to broaden our base; we have to attract new viewers of every generation, reflecting the educated and sophisticated in American life, people who live in every part of the country. We are taking a young, fresh, new approach to programming. The rookies are going to be given their chance.[6]

Beneath the inflationary rhetoric a number of quite material changes were being hinted at here, confirming *Variety*'s predictions of the previous autumn. The following month Wood appointed Fred Silverman as Head of Programming at CBS and the latter swiftly learnt that the network was under intense pressure through their sales department from advertisers who wanted them to 'think demographically'. Wood himself had worked his way up in the CBS hierarchy after serving as a manager of a CBS owned and operated station and he knew that some of their top-rating series nationally actually performed poorly in the top urban markets where the O&Os [owned and operated stations] were located. They decided to drop some of those series, since the large audiences they still undoubtedly attracted were simply top-heavy with viewers who had little disposable income or were too young, too old or too far from the cities to be able to spend it. . . .

Meanwhile television advertising was itself changing

radically. It was, after all, the advertisers who were behind the changes in the Nielsen demographic categories. And this in turn related to the demise of the sponsorship system in the 1960s. The end of the single sponsor per programme system and the advent of magazine style advertising on television returned television programming to the complete control of the networks. And this, in turn, reopened the networks to the possibility of anti-trust action. And, as the number and frequency of commercial interruptions increased almost exponentially, the very form of programming and particularly of programme flow began to change. Instead of making programmes which would complement particular products – and particular groups of consumers – magazine style advertising necessitated the selling of separate 'slots' and a number of critics perceived an accompanying 'overcommercialization' of the programmes themselves.[7]

Meanwhile, after several years of heated debate, the FCC finally decided to ban cigarette advertising from the small screen from 1 January 1971. When this decision was announced in 1970 there was considerable panic in the industry. The tobacco business brought television an estimated $220 million revenue in 1970 out of a gross income of $3 billion. In the following year, the three networks lost some 12 per cent of their total advertising revenue as a result of this ban and, in order to readjust their profits, the networks extended their control over programming and froze their fees to independent producers.[8] But with 12 per cent of their revenue to make up, the networks necessarily turned to new advertisers to fill their empty prime-time slots. At first they were simply forced to lower their rates. In the final three months of 1970 (the very months of *The Mary Tyler Moore Show*'s launch) the networks' advertising sales fell by nearly 4 per cent. Total pre-tax profits for the three networks in 1970 were just over $50 million – $43 million less than the previous year.[9] CBS in particular were determined to cope with this crisis. Firstly they reduced their overall programming budget by 15 per cent in February 1971, though this ploy was too late to have affected *The Mary Tyler Moore Show*. Rather earlier, however, they decided to cut back on commissions – restricting first commitments to a maximum of thirteen episodes and, where possible, eliminating the pilot stage of series development. *The Mary Tyler Moore Show* was to benefit from both these economies. Indeed, the first thirteen episodes of the series were commissioned without pause for a pilot and a 24-episode season was eventually produced where in previous years 36 episodes had been the practice. With advertising revenue continuing to fall, CBS came up with an additional strategy in their bid to win new advertisers:

> To lure new customers, especially advertisers with small budgets, CBS cut the minimum amount of time they could buy from one minute to thirty seconds. . . . By early March [1971] a herd of advertisers stampeded the networks. They spent more than 100 million dollars in a two-week period, prompting ABC, CBS and NBC to raise their rates by 25 per cent. . . .[10]

Taken together these developments in television advertising also had their effect on the formation and strategy of MTM. In response to (some would say recuperation of) the women's liberation movement the advertising world belatedly began to recognize the existence of working women, of women as consumers with disposable incomes, of women, that is, who weren't simply being perceived as 'housewives' (who were considered to be already well served by day-time soaps). And this recognition in turn revealed a new realm of the audience and of the advertising world for the networks. . . . The relationship between the advertisers' newfound ambitions – and audiences – and the new CBS strategy should not be underestimated. In 1969 a Virginia Slims cigarette advertisement with the slogan 'You've Come A Long Way, Baby' was screened regularly in prime-time. In September 1970 an article with the same title appeared in *TV Guide* launching *The Mary Tyler Moore Show*.[11] The article's subtitle also reflected this attention to changes in advertising: 'Happy Hotpoint is now Mary Tyler Moviestar.' But 1970 was also the year that the FCC decided to ban cigarette advertising from television. And although the ban didn't actually come into force until 1 January 1971 the participating advertisers in the first episode of *The Mary Tyler Moore Show* included Proctor and Gamble and Miles Labs – just two of the firms previously primarily associated with day-time programming who were tempted into prime-time by the exile of cigarette ads, the consequent cheapness of commercial slots, and the new Nielsen-led demographic emphasis on target audiences, specifically women aged 18–49.

All these factors reinforced the networks in their decision literally to disenfranchise one section of its audience to the benefit of another. And the disenfranchized sector was composed, predictably enough, of very young viewers, older viewers and viewers who were either too poor or too rural to be considered a priority by the advertisers. Ironically, they were doing just that in order to be able to produce programmes which could boast some sort of 'relevance', some sort of relationship to the real world and its social problems – the kind of problems, in other words, experienced by the very young, the old, the poor and the unprivileged. . . .

Creating the show

The Mary Tyler Moore Show evolved from a deal between CBS and Mary Tyler Moore. The deal was made, or at least announced, in September 1969. The first episode of the series was transmitted in September the following year. In that twelve-month period the series developed through a number of concepts to a treatment and then to a first draft and ultimately final draft script. The central characters were also fleshed out in this period. But at the same time as this process was taking place, as WJM Minneapolis was becoming a palpable fiction, so too was MTM Enterprises becoming a material fact. In September 1969, the same month that the CBS-Mary Tyler Moore deal was announced, 20th-Century-Fox launched a new series entitled *Room 222* which went on to win an Emmy as Outstanding New Series at the end of its first season. *Room 222* was produced by Gene Reynolds (who was later to become co-creator of *Lou Grant*), created by James L. Brooks and scripted by Brooks and another young writer, Allan Burns. If this article has avoided attributing authorial responsibility for the series until now that is only a consequence of how often the prevailing conditions of the industry (and of America) in 1969–70 have been written out of the account of the series' genesis. There can be no doubt that between them Brooks and Burns were crucial to the creation of *The Mary Tyler Moore Show* and thus to the existence of MTM Enterprises. Nor, however, can there be any doubt that without MTM Brooks and Burns would probably never have produced work of the durability they did. . . .

Tinker, Price and Moore together decided to invite Brooks and Burns to come up with a series concept for them:

> All I had to start them off was the premise of Mary being single and 30 and living in Minneapolis – which on the face of it is a pretty dull thought. I just told them to go away and create.[12] . . .

At this stage, according to Burns:

> We hadn't even met Mary yet. What trust she had in Grant to let him put two total strangers in sole charge of re-launching her career. A good thing she wasn't in on some of our first sessions. Boy, did we come up with some lousy ideas. Like Mary was going to be a leg person for a gossip columnist. Mary was going to play the field dating two guys simultaneously – which one will get her? Then we latched on to Divorce and we knew we had a winner. Every writer in town had a divorce story on the

drawing board. But we had the lady it would work with.[13]

Elsewhere Burns has described in rather more detail the process by which they came up with the concept which they took back to Tinker, Price and Moore and, ultimately, CBS:

> It's a very mild idea: a single girl working in a television newsroom in Minnesota doesn't sound too scintillating and it was not our original concept. Our original idea, frankly, I thought was better than that, at least to get us going. It had been our observation, and not ours alone, that a divorce on TV was something that should be done. Up to then it hadn't been. . . . We thought it was damn well time to do it. We backed it up with lots of reasons and Mary liked the idea. We did not have the TV newsroom concept at the time. We had her working at a newspaper as a stringer for a columnist. We were really entering on the idea of divorce as being something that was interesting. This was just on the cusp of the women's movement, it not having become really full-blown yet. We might not feel it necessary today to explain why a woman at age thirty-one is not married but at that time . . . we thought it was necessary to explain. We didn't want to make her one of those girls like Doris Day who didn't seem to have any age.[14]

Burns has elsewhere admitted that:

> It tells you a little bit about our own lack of awareness of the women's movement at that time, which was just starting, but our feeling was that if a girl was over thirty and unmarried there had to be an explanation for such a freak of nature as that.[15]

CBS rejected the divorce premise, and, having failed to persuade MTM to sack Brooks and Burns, the latter were granted extra time to come up with a rewrite. The new concept had Mary Richards as an unmarried, thirtyish, career woman on the rebound from a failed four-year affair. Perhaps significantly for debates about 'authorship' and 'creativity' in television the network's request for a rewrite had positively propelled Brooks and Burns toward the premise for which they became famous. As Allan Burns has put it, 'As it turns out a career woman of thirty is a more radical concept than a divorce.'[16] Furthermore, the revision encouraged Brooks and Burns to extend their focus from Mary Richards herself (her personal life as a divorcee on the one hand, her isolated professional life as a stringer for a gossip columnist on the other) to two specific situations – one her apartment, the other an office. And this, in turn, led to the integration of Mary into a much larger than originally anticipated ensemble cast. Finally, the necessity to replace the 'relevant' issue of divorce with another fashionably topical situation may well have contributed to the dropping of the stringer concept and its replacement with that of a television newsroom which could capitalize on both Brooks's own experiences in a TV newsroom and on the continuing controversies about news practices during the Nixon presidency. . . .

The new premise for the series, therefore, had Mary Richards living in Minneapolis. The first episode dramatized her 'backstory', her move from small-town Minnesota, the break up of her affair, and the search for a new apartment and a new job in a new city. The apartment is in a boarding house run by Phyllis Lindstrom, but another tenant, Rhoda Morgenstern, also wants it. Thus two of the series' running characters are swiftly introduced. Mary then hurries off to an interview with a TV newsroom editor, Lou Grant, for a job which she gets. The episode ends with the former fiancé, a medical intern, arriving to try and tempt Mary back to him, but his entreaties are interrupted by a drunk Lou Grant stumbling into her apartment.

Once the new outline was agreed MTM could, literally, go into business. Brooks and Burns were left not only to script the series but also to set up the company. As James Brooks has described it:

In television I was really lucky because at the time I was coming in they were beginning to give the inmates the run of the asylum and writers were getting control of their shows and being called executive producers and having total control and I was the beneficiary of that. At MTM this really flowered because when we started at MTM – Allan Burns and myself – we hired the businessmen, we hired the accountants. I don't think that's happened before or since, where writers call an accountant and interview them.[17]

Elsewhere, Brooks has explained how they proceeded:

We hired a secretary, who became one of our best friends, and a writer. We hired a best friend we had in common for our first producer, Dave Davis. And then we hired the business people. The business people did everything we said because Grant Tinker said 'Do what they say.' We decided to make it a writers' shop and a place where writers would have a lot of say-so, so our friends who are writers came in and they felt good.[18]

Both Burns and Tinker point to the series' status as three-camera comedy (shot on film not tape but recorded with three cameras in front of a live audience and subsequently edited down to a fluid master) as being responsible for the decision to hire writer-producer teams at MTM. According to Burns:

It was Tinker's idea to make us a team. I think that doing that kind of show, a three-camera show, is so demanding, that teams are almost a necessity; it's just tremendously hard to do them alone.[19]

Tinker agrees:

MTM was founded on writers. Brooks and Burns being the first two, and then others joined us later and these people became writer-producers. It's particularly important in three-camera comedy, which is evolutionary, from the Monday script read round the table till the Friday night we shoot it, that the people who are involved should all be writers. That's what they are doing all week, re-writing the show as things don't work, or they see they can improve it.[20]

This goes some way to explain the existence of the writer-producer hyphenate in American television and its particular prominence at MTM and the other independent companies specializing in sitcom launched at the same time. Unlike American cinema where, for all the debates about authorship, directors can exercise a considerable degree of creative autonomy, American television belongs to the producer.

Allan Burns has explained why this is the case and how precisely it inflected the structure and strategy of (The) MTM (Show). Burns argues that because, in television, the producer's authority is total and because it is writers who conceive projects rather than directors, the nature of network assembly lines makes the writer-producer a particularly privileged executive. Although writer-producers had existed in the 1950s and 1960s, they really only came of age in the industry in 1970 when the FCC's Financial Interest ruling and Department of Justice anti-trust action against the networks accelerated the emergence of small independent production companies – several of which were actually spun off from the networks. Burns is convinced that the continued presence of one writer-producer throughout a series elevates them above the roles of directors and individual episode writers, both of whom are usually only freelance, and so devolves to them, if only by default, the creative control of programme production.[21]

Nevertheless, Brooks, Burns and the series itself needed a director. Indeed, without one they couldn't even begin to cast the series. Jay Sandrich, the son of RKO director Mark Sandrich, had previously worked on such successful series as *I Love Lucy, The Danny Thomas Show, The Dick Van Dyke Show, Get Smart* and *He and She* in a career which involved a gradual climb from second assistant to director, with a brief but frustrating detour as a producer. Jay Sandrich takes up the story:

I got a call from Grant Tinker who I had known peripherally when I was doing *The Dick Van Dyke Show* and they were starting a new show called *The Mary Tyler Moore Show* and they were looking for a director. They had talked to a few other directors and for one reason or another they were not available. Grant and Mary had liked *He and She* and they offered me the show. At this point there was no cast and there was only an idea for the show – there wasn't even a script. I had met Jim and Allan and they seemed like really nice gentlemen. I said to Grant 'I do not want to commit myself to one series and then have it cancelled (as *He and She* had been) and all those heartaches, so I'll do the first three shows and if I like it I'll come back.' By that time I'd seen three or four of the scripts and I was reading writing the like of which I'd never seen. It was different, it was situational, it was not jokey as I had been used to. None of us were sure how it was going to work.[22] . . .

As Sandrich points out, the first episode did not test well with audiences and, in the absence of an on-air commitment from CBS, it seems likely that the series would never have got on the air. Sally Bedell quotes some of the sample audience's responses to the first episode in her book *Up The Tube*. Apparently the Mary Richards character was perceived as something of 'a loser', Rhoda was considered 'too abrasive' and Phyllis was simply condemned as 'not believable'. When Mike Dann was replaced by Fred Silverman as Head of Programming *The Mary Tyler Moore Show* was hastily rescheduled from its initial slot on Tuesdays just before the rural comedy *Hee Haw* to a Saturday night slot previously occupied by the hayseed series *Green Acres*. This time it was scheduled immediately after another new series, *Arnie*, a blue collar comedy about an ethnic worker suddenly promoted to an executive position – both symptom and symbol of the overall CBS strategy. The following January (1971) another series, Norman Lear's *All In The Family*, was launched and when it too transferred to Saturday night CBS's schedule was secure for the new look: 8.00: *All In The Family*; 8.30: *Funny*

Face; 9.00: *The New Dick Van Dyke Show*; 9.30: *The Mary Tyler Moore Show*. *Funny Face* was a sitcom which borrowed more than a little from the success of *The Mary Tyler Moore Show*, its single working woman protagonist also working in TV, this time in commercials. *The New Dick Van Dyke Show*, similarly, returned its star to a TV setting, this time in the guise of a talk show host for a local station in Phoenix, Arizona.

Where *Arnie, Funny Face* and even *The New Dick Van Dyke Show* differed from *The Mary Tyler Moore Show* was, among other things, in the latter's emphasis on the ensemble nature of the comedy and its consequent unwillingness to elevate Mary Richards into the only area of interest. (This in turn was to pay off later for MTM when they were able to spin off characters from the show into their own series.) Grant Tinker has described the series, somewhat incompletely, as being 'about a single woman getting along by herself and for herself in our society'.[23] But in fact, by the late 1960s successful series were rarely if ever 'about' single individuals in this way. Just as the Western at the end of that decade had developed a ranch family variant of its traditional lone gunslinger format, so too sitcoms had found families a useful way of spreading the workload and multiplying potential protagonists, thus increasing the identification figures for a show at the same time as hedging its demographic bets. As Grant Tinker puts it:

> At one time in television Jackie Gleason could sit out there and practically do it all by himself. But by the 1970s the attention span of the viewers had shortened. They were spoiled. You had to come at them from all directions to keep their attention. An ensemble could do that.[24]

Whether or not we accept Tinker's verdict that the move to ensemble was simply a response to the audience's shrinking attention span, the character ingredients of *The Mary Tyler Moore Show* are illuminating, both as textual difference and as demographic bait. Mary, Rhoda, Phyllis and Lou – to name only the most familiar characters from the series – all offered specific pleasures as distinctive personalities, specific images as identification figures, or comic butts; together they 'represented' network demographics in the new Nielsen categories.

In fact, much of *The Mary Tyler Moore Show*'s success has been attributed to its coincidence with the crisis of the nuclear family and the impact of the women's movement, in much the same way that *All In The Family* has been associated with changing liberal attitudes toward race and racial equality. But then that 'coincidence', after all, was very much intended by CBS and by the independent production companies they commissioned to fill the ideological vacuum they perceived. *The Mary Tyler Moore Show*, for instance, was a dramatic departure from the three female stereotypes that dominated prime-time comedy programming in 1970. The three dominant types were the zany incompetent, immortalized by Lucille Ball; the passive housewife, personified by Donna Reed and in her previous prime-time role Mary Tyler Moore herself as Laura Petrie; and the dumb blondes and brunettes that accompanied the male stars of some of the older shows, like Ellie May in *The Beverly Hillbillies*. (In film studies these three stereotypes have been 'fleshed out' theoretically as the screwball, the virgin mother and the eroticized/exoticized sex object.) If the screwball was the most obvious option for a sitcom it was by no means an easy identity to write in to the new 'realist' comedy. And Mary Tyler Moore had herself already played the other two roles on television – as Happy Hotpoint the housewife's friend, as husky-voiced, long-legged but head- and body-less Sam, and, of course, as Laura Petrie – perfect wife and mother. In a way, though, it was Mary Tyler Moore's association with such stereotyped roles that enabled the Mary Richards character to appear so utterly and dramatically to escape them and to evolve as a 'real' woman. Though she had a screwball side, she was never as nuts as Rhoda or Phyllis; though she was attractive and interested in men she was never as man-hungry as

Rhoda, as faddish as Phyllis or as sex-obsessive as Sue Anne Nevins, WJM-TV's Happy Homemaker (a mockery of the Hotpoint role?). In fact, she had a rather straight-laced and conventional set of values.

The strategy of the series, then, was to steer a middle way between the 'thoughtless' acceptance of the conventional female role and the equally 'thoughtless' rejection of it. But if, in the real world beyond the small screen, this seems no more than a hedge-sitting compromise, on television itself it meant a great deal more. As Brooks remembers it:

> We began with the character, Mary Richards, who believed *Father Knows Best*. She was brought up in middle America, had done everything right and had not been prepared for an adulthood where there would be problems. Mary began to evolve almost immediately. I mean our timing was very fortunate, the way the women's movement started to evolve. So not only our ideas, but what was happening in society began to appear in the show.[25] . . .

The MTM house-style

The moment and manner of (The) MTM (Show)'s emergence – the political, economic and ideological conditions of its existence, including the televisual conditions – has clearly left its mark on subsequent structures and strategies, both economic and aesthetic. As Edward Buscombe has noted in an essay on Warner Brothers in the 1940s, 'studio style is a term which occasionally crops up in film criticism, but in a loose kind of way.'[26] In television criticism, whether journalistic or academic, it crops up even less often and even more loosely. Nevertheless, Buscombe's conclusions about the applicability of the 'studio style' approach to American cinema seems equally pertinent to the analysis of American network television. . . . His most substantive point, however, is that, as far as extant analyses of studio style are concerned:

What seems to be lacking is any conception of the relations between the economic structure of a studio, its
particular organization and the kinds of films it
produced. For if there is such a thing as studio style it
should be possible to provide some explanation of how it
was formed.[27]

Before going on to try and provide some explanation of
my own, it is necessary to ask whether such a style is
indeed discernible across the relatively broad range of
MTM's output and over the decade and a half of the
company's history.

Journalistically (both in the trade press and among
critical periodicals) and among MTM staffers themselves
there certainly seems to be an assumption that MTM has
a house style and that that style is comedy. Thus Howard
Rosenberg described MTM as the 'House That Comedy
Built'.[28] And thus, in 1977, MTM's then president,
Grant Tinker, admitted 'We're sort of typecast. Our
label is comedy.'[29] But 1977, as outlined in my chapter
on *Lou Grant* and *Hill Street Blues*, was a watershed
year for the company and indeed, by 1980, Tinker was
announcing ' . . . we've begun to get rid of that label of
comedy and do other things.'[30] The 'other things' that
Tinker had in mind were not only non-comic series (like
Lou Grant, The White Shadow and later *Hill Street
Blues*) but also TV movies, mini-series, variety specials.
And it was in 1977 that MTM set up a subsidiary, MTM-
AM, to develop day-time programming.

Furthermore, even the sitcoms themselves resist easy
categorizing. While television comedy since the 1960s
at least has tended to be bracketed under the umbrella
of 'sitcom' Brooks, Burns and Tinker have refused
that term, preferring to describe (The) MTM (Show)
style as 'character comedy'. In a recent interview in
Film Comment, James Brooks noted that, 'When
somebody called *Mary* a sitcom, we'd be furious. We
weren't doing sitcom. We knew what sitcom was. We had
done sitcom. We were doing character comedy.'[31] Similarly, when quizzed about MTM's stylistic specialization

Grant Tinker responded:

> I think of it as character comedy. In the case of *Lou
> Grant* and to a somewhat lesser extent *White Shadow* and
> *Hill Street*, it is character drama. You are telling a story,
> for sure. That's important, but the shows are peopled by
> characters who are credible and carefully developed, and
> whose interrelationships are valid and consistent.[32]

In an interview for this book, Jay Sandrich offered his
own brief definition of the MTM style:

> The MTM style is essentially good writing, sophisticated
> writing, and trying to present adult fare. Casting actors
> who could do comedy rather than comedians. Trying to
> maintain a certain reality.[33]

Writer-producer Jerry McNeely, who was recruited into
MTM's creative stable in the mid-1970s, echoes
Sandrich's verdict on the company's preferred aesthetic
mode – realism, sophistication, 'quality' – all, of course,
arguable terms. But McNeely goes on to attribute their
presence in MTM programmes to a particular industrial
strategy:

> MTM is a company that was built on Grant Tinker's
> determination to let creative people have some freedom.
> Now of course that freedom was limited to what MTM
> wanted to have their company name connected with [but]
> I never experienced any serious resistance to things I
> wanted to do, certainly nothing I would call interference.
> MTM is a quality company – they want to do good televi-
> sion and they're willing to take some chances . . . [34]

It is the slippage here between 'quality company' and
'good television' that seems to point to a link between
the MTM style as a business and the style associated with
the programmers. . . . Of course, the 'quality' of the
acting and the writing – so often applauded by those
inside and outside of MTM – are 'mutually reinforcing'.
Because the scripts are good, MTM is able to attract some
of television's most talented performers to their shows,
and because those performers are series regulars, the

company can continue to attract top writers. Ironically, however, these very qualities (so reminiscent of the alleged strengths of British television), both of which contribute so much to what MTM refer to as 'character comedy' (and, later, 'character drama') have led to a stylistic quality which is often considered to be the antithesis of well-written, well-acted TV – its status as tele*vision*. For while an emphasis on 'realistic' character rather than on silly situations necessitates skilled performances and well-crafted, witty scripts – where sitcoms could rely on slapstick and farce – it also led to a character-motivated rather than just-another-part-of-the-furniture role for the camera. Freed from the limited visual grammar of the studio, the MTM style would eventually include the employment of fluid tracks and long takes that would be the envy of many theatrical films (and which, ironically, were entirely absent from MTM's one feature film to date, *A Little Sex*, whose sitcom characters simply failed to motivate any motion pictures).

To a certain extent, of course, such 'quality' is always in the eye of the beholder. In another sense, though, it is also a marketable commodity, a hallmark or corporate calling card which helps to distinguish MTM product from its competitors for the benefit of networks, advertisers, critics and audiences alike. And while there is undoubtedly a rhetoric related to this quality there is also a very real ambition to aim higher than other independent producers in the television marketplace. MTM, in other words, has often aimed to ensure that its 'beholders' have higher levels of disposable income than many other sectors of the audience and many other companies. Thus Grant Tinker's suggestion that 'I think there's a connection between how high you set your sights and the resultant programs';[35] and thus the conclusion of sociologist Paul Espinosa, who sat in on early script conferences of *Lou Grant*:

The producers of the *Lou Grant* show see themselves as producing a different kind of product; this notion of differentiation is a major motif in the discourse of production. From top management down to members of the crew, the show is talked about as though it were different from, superior to, better than, and more intelligent than other television shows.[36]

And once again, the cast and crew of *Hill Street Blues* – which at the end of its first season won more Emmys than any other weekly series in American television history – have often been quoted as determined to end the series if they felt that its quality was slipping. Robert Wood, one-time CBS President and now an independent producer in his own right, has said of MTM:

They're not slicing bologna over there. Damn it, they're class, real craftsmen. Pound for pound there's no company better than MTM. I think they'd rather fold up than put on a piece of crap.[37] . . .

MTM: 'the quality factory'

In spite of such changes of personnel and of programme strategy over the years, MTM retains its reputation as a reliable supplier of quality product. Indeed, industry commentators who have worked at MTM or with MTM all appear to agree on the company's superiority to the competition both as a producer and, more simply, as a place to work, a company, an ensemble of its own. James Brooks, for instance, has described MTM as a Shangri-La;[38] Robert Wood – ex-CBS executive and now an independent producer in his own right – has called it the Tiffany's of television,[39] while Jay Tarses compared it to an Algonquin Round Table.[40] This reputation rests in turn on a tradition of attracting and not interfering with top creative talent but instead making them their own producers. Thus Brooks described MTM as 'a writers' shop' and Tinker himself termed it 'an artists' company':[41] 'People do the shows without edict from us . . . The kind of people we like to attract wouldn't come here if we tried to legislate.'[42]

The 'relative autonomy' afforded creative personnel at MTM seems to be based on and secured by the smallness of the company. Indeed, one aspect of MTM in which the economic and organizational structures of the company clearly intersect with each other (as well as with its aesthetic structures) is in MTM's size. At the time of Rosenberg's profile of the company in 1981 the full-time staff was estimated at no more than twenty and Tinker was quoted as admitting:

> We're wilfully small. There is a kind of optimum level at which we run best and at which I feel connected to things, and that's about where we are now. If we have four shows on all the time, that is optimum. Five is okay, even six may be okay but beyond that it might feel too impersonal, and I wouldn't feel connected. And below four, you begin to lose people you don't want to lose.[43]

By 1983, however, the *New York Times* could comment that:

> The company now has 300 full time employees scattered through four buildings on the CBS-20th Century-Fox studio complex. Where there were three vice-presidents five years ago, there are now nine.[44]

What had happened? It is difficult to judge just how important Tinker's departure – to head NBC – and his replacement by Arthur Price has been. Certainly, the shift towards drama series with 60-minute episodes shot on film and the move away from 30-minute sitcoms often made on tape took place in this period. Thus it is that while to the staff members who had worked with the company since its beginnings – predominantly in sitcoms – MTM appeared to have grown too large, to others it still seemed to offer just the right intimate, friendly atmosphere it had been championed for in the early 1970s. James Brooks, for instance, has recalled that:

> In [those] days MTM was small, especially in relation to what it is now. I had real control over my work as producer . . . I left MTM when its size precluded the

luxury of intimacy in work.[45] . . . at a certain point the idea of giving the creative part of the staff that kind of autonomy became absolutely impossible for business reasons.[46] It went from intimate to large to very big. The Shangri-La had to end at a certain size. Going from three shows to four shows makes a difference. Suddenly cost control becomes very important. [And this, in turn, leads to] a subtle shift from creative people to business people.[47]

Brooks's feelings about this shift are echoed by director Jay Sandrich in an interview recorded for this book:

> As the studio grew bigger and bigger they started doing more and more shows and what happened to MTM from the creative people's point of view was that the businessmen started taking over. What made it worthwhile for all of us was Grant Tinker – probably the best executive I've ever worked with – he always had an open door for those of us who started with him, always sided with his creative people; never said: 'the network wants', always said 'what do you want?' Unfortunately, from my point of view, Jim's point of view and Ed and Stan's point of view, a man who was essentially the production manager started getting too much authority, because when you are that large an organization you sometimes will make compromises for money and it was no longer the same family operation it had been.[48]

Jay Tarses, who left MTM with his partner Tom Patchett in 1980, seconds Sandrich's verdict: 'It's changed from a good solid mom-and-pop company where everyone knows everyone to a factory. It started to get huge, out of hand.'[49] Even Allan Burns, the only one of the first writer-producers still at MTM, admits to these changes with some nostalgia: 'We were all friends in the early days, but now there are so many faces I don't recognize.'[50] Tinker himself, however, disagrees with this diagnosis strongly:

> If you visited *Hill Street* and spent a little time hanging around the set, you would have a feeling of 'Boy, these people are really loving what they're doing.' They have

that same sense of excitement and pride that the people who did [*The*] *Mary* [*Tyler Moore Show*] had several years ago, because they know they're doing something that is superior to most other television.[51] . . .

The recurrent complaints about the alleged erosion of a 'good solid mom-and-pop company where everyone knows everyone' and its replacement by a faceless corporation may or may not paint an accurate picture of the changes that have taken place at MTM since 1970. More interestingly perhaps, they illuminate the importance which the ideology of 'the family business' seems to have played in the minds of MTM's creative personnel. Similarly, rhetoric about the 'handicraft' nature of production (in some cases only nostalgia for those comedies recorded in front of an audience in an era now dominated by location film drama) and the creative community of 'interlocking friendships' which MTM-alumni so cherish seems curiously consistent with the settings of a number of their shows, each with its own real and/or surrogate work-family. Indeed, the characteristic MTM mixture of professionalism, ethics and either domestic life or a domesticated public sphere seem not only to apply to *The Mary Tyler Moore Show* but also to such later series as *Lou Grant* and *Hill Street Blues*.

Complaints like those reprinted above reiterate the familiar litany of criticisms levelled at the culture industry and at attempts to produce art on an assembly line. Such critics argue – and have done since Adorno – that industrial production and aesthetic production, art and business, are quite simply incompatible. If this is an unexceptional argument to come across in the work of the Frankfurt School, however, it is rather more surprising to find it expressed quite so regularly and eloquently by those who work in the heart of the culture industry, American network television. And this illuminates how MTM's own compromise between 'family business' and multi-media corporation is not a concealment of the latter under the ideology of the former but rather a very material compromise between the two, a compromise which provided the space within which (The) MTM (Show) could function and even flourish – both as a business and as a series of fictions. Just as *The Mary Tyler Moore Show* is a product not only of the creative talents of Brooks, Burns, Sandrich and Mary Tyler Moore and her co-stars but also of MTM, so MTM itself is a product not just of the combined talents of Miss Moore, Arthur Price and Grant Tinker but of a moment in American television history. And that moment has exercised its own momentum on the 'television formation' of MTM, both as a 'house' and as a 'style'.

Notes

1 Varmeulen, Michael (1980) 'Mary Tyler Moore', *Rolling Stone*, 13 November, p. 50.
2 *Variety* 1 October 1969, p. 35.
3 Spector, Bert, 'A clash of cultures: the Smothers Brothers *vs* CBS Television' in O'Conner, John E. (ed.) (1983) *American History/American Television*, New York: Frederick Ungar.
4 Marc, David (1984) *Demographic Vistas*, Philadelphia: University of Pennsylvania Press, p. 165.
5 Brown, Les (1971) *The Business Behind The Box*, New York: Harcourt Brace Jovanovich, pp. 161–3.
6 'CBS-TV affiliates strike a harmonious chord', *Broadcasting*, 11 May 1970.
7 For a fuller discussion of this system see Brown, op. cit., p. 65. For a book length study of the subject see Barnouw, Erik (1978) *The Sponsor: Notes on a Modern Potentate*, New York: Oxford University Press.
8 For an excellent account of the network reaction to losses in advertising revenue and the threat of anti-trust actions, see Edgerton, Gary and Pratt, Cathy (1983) 'The influence of the Paramount decision on network television in America', *Quarterly Review of Film Studies*, 8 (3) summer.
9 Bedell, Sally (1981) *Up The Tube*, New York: Viking Press, p. 51.
10 ibid., p. 54.
11 *TV Guide*, 19 September 1970. The article's 'Happy Hotpoint' subtitle referred back to the eras of sponsorship and sexism as if they were both things of the past. *The Mary Tyler Moore Show* was to create its own equivalent, the Happy Homemaker, and later MTM was to begin to court corporate sponsors back into prime-time.

12 *TV Guide*, 8 February 1975, p. 32.
13 ibid., p. 32.
14 Newcomb, Horace and Alley, Robert S. (1983) *The Producer's Medium*, New York: Oxford University Press, p. 220.
15 Gitlin, Todd (1983) *Inside Prime Time*, New York: Pantheon Books, p. 214. Eventually, *The Mary Tyler Moore Show* was to involve Lou Grant's divorce from his wife Edie. Later, *Rhoda* dramatized the divorce of its protagonist from her husband Joe, and the female reporter in *Lou Grant*, Billie Newman, was also a divorcee. Furillo, the lieutenant at the centre of *Hill Street Blues*, was already divorced from his wife Fay at the outset of the series.
16 Newcomb and Alley, op. cit., p. 198.
17 Unpublished interview with Shelia Johnstone in London, 13 March 1984.
18 'Dialogue on film', *American Film*, June 1980.
19 Newcomb and Alley, op. cit., p. 213.
20 ibid., p. 226.
21 ibid., p. 209.
22 Interview with Jay Sandrich conducted in 1983.
23 Bedell, op. cit., p. 66.
24 ibid.
25 Newcomb and Alley, op. cit., p. 219.
26 Buscombe, Edward, 'Walsh and Warner Brothers', in Hardy, Phil (ed.) (1974) *Raoul Walsh*, Edinburgh: Edinburgh Film Festival.
27 ibid., p. 52.
28 Rosenberg, Howard (1981) 'Above the Crowd: Grant Tinker's MTM', *Emmy*, spring.
29 Sklar, Robert (1980) *Prime Time America*, New York: Oxford University Press, p. 86.
30 Rosenberg, op. cit., p. 24.
31 Turan, Kenneth (1984) 'On His Own Terms', *Film Comment*, April.
32 Newcomb and Alley, op. cit., p. 227.
33 Interview with Jay Sandrich conducted by Tise Vahimagi.
34 Interview with Jerry McNeely conducted by Tise Vahimagi.
35 Newcomb and Alley, op. cit., p. 226.
36 Espinosa, Paul (1982) 'The audience in the text: ethnographic observations of a Hollywood story conference', *Media, Culture and Society*, 4 (1) January.
37 Rosenberg, op. cit., p. 24.
38 Brooks, James (1980) 'Dialogue on film', *American Film*, June.
39 Rosenberg, op. cit., p. 24.
40 ibid., p. 25.
41 ibid.
42 ibid.
43 Rosenberg, op. cit., p. 29.

44 *New York Times*, 22 May 1983.
45 Newcomb and Alley, op. cit., p. 208.
46 *American Film*, June 1980.
47 Rosenberg, op. cit., p. 29.
48 Jay Sandrich, interview with Tise Vahimagi.
49 Rosenberg, op. cit., p. 29.
50 Newcomb and Alley, op. cit., p. 211.
51 ibid., p. 227.

19
Made in Ealing
John Ellis

. . . Film texts are the product of three determinants; it is only by excavating these determinants that it is possible to show the way in which (the 'extent' to which) it is seized by the dominant ideology, and therefore the progressive potential of its alternative readings.

Any film text is first the product of the entire history of the cinema (its system of production, distribution and exhibition) down to the present, inasmuch as this history is written into the technology available. However, this technology is 'demanded *and exploited* in the conjuncture of particular economic and ideological conditions,[1] its limits and potential are those of the dominant ideology. This technology is therefore directed towards the containing of contradictions within the realist mode; to the current ideas of entertainment; 'to the renewal of the world as it is from within, i.e. according to the current fashion' (Walter Benjamin).

The second area of determination begins to open out progressive areas within (and sometimes in conflict with) the space of technology. This is the specific organization of production which creates the text. The character of the process by which ideas are generated; the different emphases given to the stages of pre-production, shooting and post-production; the different control that groups have over these stages and that of exhibition and distribution; all these develop a text whose relation to the dominant ideology is uneasy, strained in some way. . . .

The third area of determination is that of the beliefs of the group controlling production. Their aesthetic and social ideas determine the way in which conflict is resolved. This is the area of the relative freedom of the individuals whose work creates and sustains the structure of determinations in which they are caught. Their freedom is (necessarily) constructed from a field of possibilities: the form of comedy is one such field whose strengths and limitations are already established, even if (as in Ealing's case) they are used in a relatively new way. This play of freedom and determinations is as true for the social beliefs of the film-makers, both in that they belong to the middle class, and to a certain fraction of that class (the possessors of 'cultural capital'); and in the ways in which their particular beliefs lead them to adopt, in their film-making, the position of a different class. This is Ealing's situation: a group of conventionally educated intellectuals, through a certain liberal-radicalism, come to make films about, and for, 'the people', whom they think of as the lower levels of the petty bourgeoisie. . . .

Ealing and the industry

. . . After the War, Rank set out on a major programme of production expansion, backed by Lord Rank's extensive capital in flour-milling. The aim was to break into the American and world market, setting up distribution companies and buying chains of prestige cinemas in the US, Canada, South Africa, etc. . . . It was in this atmosphere of immense and costly expansion and experimentation . . . that Balcon concluded an exceptional finance and distribution deal with Rank:

> Negotiations were skilfully conducted by Reg Baker and eventually an agreement was concluded which gave Ealing complete production autonomy and independence, circuit release for Ealing films, favourable distribution terms,

and approval of the terms on which our films were booked to cinemas.[2] . . .

Thus Ealing became an independent company tied into one of the dominant forces in the industry: they were engaged in a distinctive and innovatory form of film-making which at the same time fulfilled enough of the industry's basic requirements to make them a safe gamble, a prized commodity. . . .

The cinema industry gave Ealing a certain definition of its task. Regular cinema programmes were about three hours long, with a second and first feature. Vast amounts of capital have been invested in this pattern of entertainment, and to deviate from it is still very difficult, as the fate of short films has shown. At that time, second features were considered only as quota quickies to be made for the lowest legal cost (£7,500 for a 60-minute film). An enterprise like Val Lewton's at RKO, exploiting the artistic independence afforded by B-features, was financially impossible in England. Instead, Ealing had to concentrate on first features, with a pre-defined technical standard, costing and length. The length was about eighty to ninety minutes (increasing towards the end of the period in question), and the cost ranged from £100,000 to anything over £350,000 for big spectaculars. Ealing's costs were between £120,000 and £200,000, with the comedies averaging about £160,000, which places them at the upper end of the average price range. . . . This choice of costing was dictated by the availability of finance, and by the fact that a certain number of films had to be made to ensure continuing profitability. Balcon says:

> Profits and losses were important, of course, but our object at Ealing was to expend certain money on making a programme of films, and to get rather more money back on the selling of that programme so that it turned itself over. We felt that we would come out on top over a programme of films: it's inevitable that certain films make losses.[3]

Thus though Ealing's aims were not directly commercial, the commercial structure of the industry imposed certain basic definitions on the studio so that a pattern of making about five films a year emerged. But the difference between Balcon's Ealing and the pattern of production under Basil Dean (1931–9) was that all films were regarded as on the same level artistically. Dean had subsidized the prestige productions (mostly adaptations of stage plays) with a programme of immensely popular 'low' comedies starring Gracie Fields and George Formby. But in Balcon's words:

> We did not manufacture films at Ealing, we produced films. The only things we took into account were the things that we ourselves wanted to do. We felt that if we believed in them strongly enough, then we would carry that belief through to an audience.

Charles Barr has shown clearly that Ealing's aim was to project a certain idea of Britain.[4] The exact historical and aesthetic nature of this aim, both during its progressive moment after the War and in its more uncertain drift in the 1950s, is outlined below. This freedom did not go beyond certain constraints, but these were felt to be natural and normal by the film-makers (this being precisely their power). Massive investments of human energy and capital had normalized a certain number of the potentials of film. These were expressed in the exhibition in the film theatres of a certain kind of entertainment programme, but also in the very equipment which the film-makers used.

Studio technology

Technology is not a neutral force in filming: it contains in its very construction basic assumptions about the ideological purpose of film. Therefore the history of film is not a history of technological development carried on in a back room by scientists dedicated to the perfection of the medium. It is a history in which technological development is itself tailored to the needs of the dominant ideology. In the late 1940s and early 1950s, it was becoming possible for films of adequate technical quality to be made completely outside the studio. Ealing's films were not studio-bound, but with the exception of *Whisky Galore*, none were completely location films. The realism needed by Ealing was not that of the *nouvelle vogue* or even of Italian neo-realism, it was much closer to the traditional studio-filming of pre-war British and American films. Ealing did not abandon the studio; they even engineered their location work so that it would preserve as many as possible of the features of studio work. There were several reasons for this: much capital was invested in the studio and its equipment (the studio itself was sold for £467,000); much technical skill was invested in studio production methods; the technology for location shooting was developed slowly as a result of these large investments (it accelerated when the contraction of the cinema market and the demands of television dictated cheaper productions); and finally the kind of realistic surface needed could be achieved in the studio as easily as on location.

The normal equipment available at the time illustrates this complicated interplay of technological development, the material demands of capital, ideological constraints and the learnt techniques of film-makers.[5]

Studio cameras were bulky, blimped and sophisticated. Technological development had been directed towards three aims: to produce a camera that had a constant speed of twenty-four frames a second and silent running (the demands of the realist sound film); a camera that was rock-steady to avoid an unstable image; and a lens which reproduced as nearly as possible the subjective effect of an individual watching a scene, eliminating the 'distorting' parallax effects of 'true' perspective. Cameras were normally mounted on a tripod as tall as an average man, completing the effect of recreating the monocular perspective of a spectator watching a real scene. Tripod mounting was assumed in several cameras:

the Mitchell Standard and the Newall (made by a Rank subsidiary) used a focusing system through a side-mounted telescope, with the camera tipped side-ways on its tripod to put this in the position of the lens. The requirements of sound shooting also imposed heavily on the design of cameras: the Mitchell Standard, the Vinten Everest and Normandy all had motors synchronized only for twenty-four frames per second. Studio cameras that could shoot fast or slow motion were the exception rather than the rule. These cameras were also blimped, muffled, so that the sound of the mechanism was not picked up by the recording equipment, with the result that they weighed about 150 pounds. To move them therefore became a major operation: a tracking shot required either a trailer with pneumatic wheels or tracks. British studios, in contrast to most others, had no curved tracks. In short, to get a complicated camera movement 'right' (smooth, even, unobtrusive) required several takes. As this tended to slow down shooting and to increase costs, directors and cameramen tended to avoid such movements. Thus the accumulated determinants written into the cameras produced a tendency towards a cinema where fluid camera movements were replaced with fluent and complex cutting. . . .

The development of camera shutter speed, film negative stock and studio lighting had all been directed towards increasing the range of contrasts available on black-and-white film, and thus the illusion of depth and flawless surface of the image. Film stock and printing were both directed towards high contrast, non-grainy pictures; shutter speeds on studio cameras varied from around 1/50th second to 1/900th second (the Eyemo was fixed at 1/54th second); a studio lighting style had been developed also to give the illusion of depth (physical and thus psychological). The conditions of studio lighting, with its large range of contrasts, were difficult to reproduce on location. Thus Ealing's overall shooting style tended to compromise between the two: a bland lighting style was adopted in the studio (because the renunciation of certain possible effects connoted 'documentary'); highlighting and spotlighting were used sparingly, creating a rather flat picture which seems almost drab in comparison with the chiaroscuro effects of the Hollywood *film noir* (*Double Indemnity*) or the deep focus film (*Mrs Miniver*), but approximates closely to that obtained by current TV lighting procedures. In return, location shooting was approximated to the studio: the street in *Passport to Pimlico* was built on a bombsite as a set. This made possible a certain amount of control of the lighting effects. . . .

This matter of lighting . . . illustrates the complicated interplay of determinants on the form of a text, and on the practice of film-making. . . .

Organization of production

Charles Barr's articles on Ealing Studios have already dealt with the specific history of Ealing, built as the first sound studio in England by Basil Dean, and originally planned to be double its eventual size: Balcon attributes this shortfall to the unsuccessful stock-market flotation of 1931. Barr also contrasts the different production methods adopted by Dean and Balcon, as well as charting the various influences on Balcon's method of production and the distinctive forms of Ealing's post-war product. The influences he traces are those of Dean himself; of Balcon's previous career; of the 1930s documentary movement; and of the war situation. Equally important is Barr's demonstration of the way in which production under Balcon was stabilized with a large staff of directors, associate producers, editors and cameramen etc. under permanent contract; as well as the way in which promotions were made internally. Barr tabulates the Ealing careers of this tight group, and provides detailed information (on which I draw heavily) about the previous and subsequent lives of major figures.

This gives a picture of a creative elite in the studio: at any time there were about eight directors, eight associate producers and half a dozen scriptwriters who formed the nucleus around whom projects grew. Other people with a major influence on the eventual shape of the films were the senior editors (a pool of about six); the cameramen, of whom three or four were on permanent contract (Douglas Slocombe for seventeen years, Otto Heller for the last three years); and the art directors. In all, the creative elite numbered about fifty out of the staff of 400.

Whereas normal union rates were paid to the majority of the staff, this 'top echelon of creative people', as Balcon calls them, accepted substantially lower salaries than was normal:

> During the war and immediately afterwards we were prepared to work not attaching too much importance to what we earned. But during the 1950s I think that the studio was showing slight signs of fragmentation: temptations must have been coming from other people. The agents fastened on to Ealing and our personnel, and they'd get offers from all directions. (Balcon)

T.E.B. Clarke, the scriptwriter of seven of the comedies, describes one such approach. After his Academy Award for *The Lavender Hill Mob*, he was approached by 'a well-known Hollywood actor lately turned producer' who wanted some spare-time uncredited writing work:

> In the absence of a written contract he was ready to pay me cash in advance. At this he snapped open his attache case; it was packed with five-pound notes. . . . I forget how long I hesitated, but I can still recall the look of scornful pity on that familiar face at my ultimate refusal.[6]

Clarke's loyalty to Ealing is graphically demonstrated by this, but it is a loyalty which he looks back upon with a little regret:

> During my sixteen years at Ealing I dealt personally with all renewals of my original contract. Astonishing as it seems now, it was considered rather caddish for anyone on the creative side to employ an agent, who doubtless

would have gained one better terms than one managed to get oneself. Today when I reread some of the clauses in those contracts which I had cheerfully accepted, I gasp over my humility and the fidelity to Ealing that caused me to disregard all enticements from the outside world.[7] . . .

Preproduction

The most important work is done before and after a film goes on the floor.[8]

Those sixteen or seventeen people sitting at the huge round table over their cups of tea did not really fit into the usual conception of a 'directors conference' at all. . . . The atmosphere was friendly and informal.

And yet, almost all the producers, directors and script-writers of Ealing Studios were gathered around that table in one of the periodically held studio conferences in which views are exchanged in all frankness, and future plans discussed without the air of secrecy so common to many studios, particularly when different production teams are working at the same time. . . .[9]

This is a description of the Round Table, the fortnightly meeting of the creative elite at which the studio schedule was decided. Proposals were brought in at a very early stage of development (as one-page treatment), and discussed, rejected or sent for further work. Most of the films originated in the script department or in the ideas of other staff; about 20 to 25 per cent were made from novels (like *Whisky Galore*) or from stage successes (like *The Man in the White Suit* from a play by Roger Macdougall, Mackendrick's cousin) . . .

Generally, ideas came from within the group and were discussed at the Round Table:

Gradually at these meetings a programme would be developed. Hal Mason took charge of all the physical aspects of production, and as a story was built up, I would begin to book the various artists. In this way the studio programme became more definite as the scripts themselves developed. (Balcon)

Script development was carried out not just by the script department, but by the interested parties who were to become associate producer or director. For instance, *Hue and Cry*, originally thought up by Cornelius, its eventual producer, was developed by Clarke and taken up by Crichton:

> 'Corny' had in mind a picture based on what might be called the freemasonry among boys, all of them participants in that life of semi-fantasy exclusive to boyhood. . . . 'I want to aim,' he said, 'at a sort of situation that only boys are really competent to handle. I'm completely vague about what it could be, except that it should have a snowball effect – one boy getting his three or four pals interested, they in turn roping in other boys at the places where they work, until eventually we have a tremendous chase or round-up with boys from all over London taking part.'

Clarke was assigned to develop this:

> My fifteen-page story outline was well received by Cornelius; it also appealed to Charles Crichton, who saw a film emerging from it that he would like to direct. The outline and our joint enthusiasm brought us Balcon's blessing, though it was impressed on us that our comedy was obviously going to be unconventional and thus a risky venture, which meant it *must* – the word was stressed beyond mere italics – be made on a low budget.[10]

This acceptance meant that the film was given a provisional place in the production programme. Already at this stage the project was gathering a team. Directors came to a film in a variety of ways: as Crichton here; as Hamer at the very beginning of *Kind Hearts and Coronets* when Michael Pertwee first broached the idea; as Frend to *A Run For Your Money* by a simple desire to direct comedy. From this detailed outline, a draft script was written. At this point, the final acceptance or rejection took place; if accepted the film was allocated its place in the production programme, and was destined to be made: Balcon could remember no rejections or abandoned projects after this point. This was about six months before the film was due to take the floor, and a team of staff was created around the original collaborators. An art director was appointed (often someone still working on another project); and a cameraman from the pool who did the screentests from which a cast was assembled. At the same time an editor was allocated from the pool, and the composer of the music hired. Finally the production manager and assistant to director joined. By this stage the details of production had emerged, and the first-draft shooting script had been completed. Then as the preceding project took the floor, leaving ten to twelve weeks to go, the detailed costing and calculations of shooting time were begun. These were carried out in discussion with the Production Department, and at the same time the script was examined in detail by Balcon and by Angus Macphail, the Script Department Head, for 'points of characterization, dialogue, motivation and clarity of development'. Most scripts went through about four drafts before the final shooting script was completed. At this stage the team was fully assembled; it consisted of the people who would follow the film through all its stages, whereas those working under them only saw the stage they were immediately concerned with. This constitutes the basic division of labour, dividing collaborators from ordinary workers. . . .

Production

. . . The use of the studios in late 1950 [early] 1951 is shown below:

1950	MAIN STAGES	STAGE ONE
Oct.	Shooting *Pool of London* (one stage) *Lavender Hill Mob* set building; shooting begins mid-month	Tests for *The Man in the White Suit*

Nov.	Extra shooting *Pool of London* (one stage)	Tests for *The Man in the White Suit* and *Secret People*
	Main shooting *The Lavender Hill Mob*	
Dec.	*Lavender Hill Mob* ended for Christmas	Tests for *Secret People*
	Set building for *The Man in the White Suit*	

1951

Jan.	*Man in the White Suit* shooting
Feb.	
Mar.	Final shooting *The Man in the White Suit*
	Set building for *Secret People*
Mar. 15	*Secret People* shooting begins
April	*Secret People* main shooting
	Extra work on *The Lavender Hill Mob* and *The Man in the White Suit* after location shooting
May 31	*Secret People* ends

Pool of London needed extra shooting, so it occupied a stage whilst *The Lavender Hill Mob* was being shot. The result was certain restrictions on space, so *The Lavender Hill Mob* took ten weeks rather than the eight probably planned. At the same time, screentests were taking place on the small Stage One for the next two productions. *The Man in the White Suit* took ten weeks in the studio, and Dickinson's *Secret People* eleven. Balcon refers to both Mackendrick and Dickinson as being somewhat slower than average. Scenes were not shot in sequence, but according to the dictates of studio space. As sets were not up for all of the shooting, care had to be taken to get satisfactory shots, and a certain amount of covering material for emergencies. This also increased the shooting time, since only the roughest rehearsals could be made before the sets were available. So two functions had to be fulfilled before shooting: shots had to be lined up, and the scene correctly lit (a certain amount of pre-lighting was done). Stand-ins were used for the main actors here; then the actors themselves rehearsed on the set. Finally, several takes were made. This meant that an average of two minutes' screen time a day could be shot. . . .

This method of shooting dictates the style of the films. At this point the accumulated technological and human determinants are finally expressed in the film. The difficulty and length of time needed to make panning shots are evident. The nature of the studio, its equipment and its schedules therefore dictated a style of filming that tended towards short takes and preferred static to moving camera shots. . . .

With a shooting style determined to this degree, it was possible for directors to take over each other's projects: Balcon mentions the help that Crichton gave Mackendrick in the editing of certain parts of *Whisky Galore*; the editor Truman taking over *Passport to Pimlico* when Cornelius was ill for a time; and Hamer taking over *The Cruel Sea* when Charles Frend had appendicitis. But the directors did not 'control' projects: the actors (notably Alec Guinness) had a certain liberty in moulding their roles, although their general character was already dictated by which actor was chosen; the camera crew participated in the composition of the shots and the lighting. A good performance drew applause from the technicians. Asked about the degree of participation by the floor staff, Balcon replied:

> This is a very interesting question. I wouldn't pretend that I had any contact with the scene-painters: that depended on the individual units, and I can't pretend that too much of that happened. I think the director would discuss his scripts with his cameraman, his writer, the editor, his set-designer and people like that. . . . Though there were some exceptions, by and large a director wouldn't go all the way along the line discussing anything.

The viewing of the rushes provided the main opportunity for such intervention:

There was an arrangement with the union, by which the whole unit used to give up part of their lunchtime to see the film. It depended on the director, but if they had any sense they invited the whole of the working unit to see the rushes. It was voluntary, but a good unit always did go to see their work.

Asked if there was any free comment in these sessions, Balcon replied: 'I dare say, amongst themselves. It didn't come my way.' It seems that the actual participation was not great. . . .

Postproduction

This stage consists of editing and dubbing, the preparation of the publicity and the treatment by the distributors. Editing took place in parallel with the shooting. Having seen the rushes, the editor matched sound to vision, and began to build up a first assembly of the film. At this stage, he was independent of the director, but in daily contact with Balcon. After shooting had finished, the complete rough cut was viewed by the director and the editing then took place in collaboration. The music (already composed) could not be recorded until the final cut had been made, and was timed exactly. It was played at Ealing's recording studios by the New Philharmonic conducted by the flamboyant resident supervisor of music, Ernest Irving, a strict traditionalist. The role given to music was usually secondary and supportive: in the comedies it was rarely used to convey emotions. . . .

The postproduction stage took about five months. Cutting from the editor's first assembly took about four weeks. This rough cut was then shown and discussed with Balcon, and the final cut took about three more weeks. The censor was shown a print early, without the music track. . . .

Once the completed negative had been sent to Rank's General Film Distributors, the film was virtually out of Ealing's control. But their agreement with Rank ensured an easy passage for the films: Rank could not re-edit them, and had to release them as first features. Ealing films were assured national distribution. The studio retained control of publicity, however. Here there was a conscious attempt to create a public image for the studio. Several graphic artists were employed to make a distinct style of poster, and at one time or another men like John Piper, James Fitton, Edwin Bawden and John Minton designed poster campaigns which contrasted strongly with the usual Rank Organization artwork.

Rank released the films about eighteen months after they had been originally entered into the schedule: the release dates for the films mentioned above were: *Pool of London*, February 1951; *The Lavender Hill Mob*, June 1951; *The Man in the White Suit*, August 1951; *Secret People*, February 1952. Thus the release dates were up to six months after the films had been completed, and a year after shooting had been concluded. Hence it was possible for an Ealing film to be released into a political and social climate fairly close to that in which it had been conceived.

The preceding sections have examined in detail the institutional frameworks in which the film-makers worked. Already certain limits and a definite style of film-making are emerging from these determinants, which are at once determinants of technology and of technique. The whole framework is used by people in certain relationships who hold certain conscious and unconscious beliefs about the nature of their specific task and the society of which that is a part. The rest of this article will examine these relationships and beliefs.

Relations of production

Ealing had four distinct kinds of employees, and they formed four different social groups both inside and outside the studio. The first were the permanent salaried workers: the directors, scriptwriters, senior editors,

cinematographers, etc. They were on long-term contracts, a rare thing in the industry even then, and
exchanged job security for lowish salaries. Under them
were the permanent wage-workers, the studio technicians, film cutters, secretaries, etc. There were also two
groups of temporarily employed workers: those paid
salaries like composers, outside scriptwriters, leading
actors, and those paid wages, like the minor roles and
extras, technical advisors etc.

Within the studio, a fairly close working relationship
evolved. Everyone was addressed by Christian name or
nickname:

> The practice is common, of course, throughout the
> cinema – even more so in the theatre; and it is a good one
> is so far as it expresses, or helps to create, a genuine
> camaraderie of endeavour. It can be overdone: the prop
> man on the floor of *Quartet* who invited the author to
> 'have a cup of tea, Somerset' was certainly going too far.
> But at Ealing the habit comes naturally. In the words of
> a critic, 'its films, one feels, are made by a family for the
> family.'[11]

. . . Though this kind of atmosphere was often
remarked on by commentators, Ealing's team still
preserved the normal relations of production of any
studio: a top echelon of creative artists and a large number
of employees whose effect over the shape of projects was
very limited. In other words, the studio was liberal rather
than radical, progressive rather than revolutionary. . . .

Also symptomatic of the real situation is the way in
which Balcon's 'we' constantly shifts from the whole 400
employees to the senior group of fifty.

This differentiation is reflected in the way the different
groups related outside the studio. Here also there was
little interchange. The creative elite used to go to the pub
across the green, the Red Lion, to discuss the state of
play in the studio. Balcon rarely went: 'I largely used to
leave them to themselves in the evening; so they could
tear me to pieces if they wanted to, and get it off their
chests and come back the next morning.' Meanwhile the

average studio-floor worker used to 'toddle off back to his semi' in the words of a BBC news cameraman who now uses the studio. . . .

Realism

> *Hue and Cry* had a quality of reality, in addition to its fun, that the public were now prepared, even eager, to accept.[12]

Ealing Studio's post-war productions were innovatory within realist cinema. The films were recognized as fresh and new, and yet at the same time were easily watched and enjoyed by the mass audience. This is because their innovations preserved many of the fundamental methods of classic cinema (preserved them as part of the unconscious practice of the film-makers): they shifted the terrain of, but did not alter, the basic aim of realism, that of showing the world as it 'naturally' appears to be. Within the cinema, this means a use of language which seems to be invisible, natural, but in fact has its own history, and is also massively sustained as natural by its perpetual repetition through the dominant modes of both news and entertainment. . . . This language is not the expression of a society and its inhabitants in the process of their social construction; rather, it shows characters who are full and finished, living as the centre of the social totality. This carries with it a certain mode of watching, which confirms the viewer's own idea of him/herself as a coherent entity; that is, as the subject for the ideological formations which make up the text. This process is a complex and double-sided one of recognition and misrecognition. It is recognition in that the viewer's idea of self does actually correspond with the representation, and thus in this sense the representation contains an element of 'truth'. It is misrecognition in that this practice of recognition instantly puts the subject into an already-defined situation; he is inserted into a given structure, a structure which, in Jacques-Alain Miller's words, 'puts in place an experience for the subject that it includes'. Thus the representation of the consistent and finished character confirms the viewer in his position as subject for ideological formations. And this is the effective role of ideology: it exists to produce this category of subject in order to reproduce the relations of production.

But this is not a monolithic process: it may be that this mode of inscription is an impossible one for a revolutionary art, but it is itself fissured and full of contradictions. In any film, the complicated process of recognition–misrecognition takes place in a context where a narrative form is being used to pose certain real (ideologically defined) problems and to reach some resolution or reintegration of their conflict. It is possible for real social problems to be posed in this mode, and this was Ealing's purpose: to make the real world seem worth living in. The very way in which this purpose is posed shows that it is open at once to a reactionary tendency (that of social control), and a progressive tendency (that of showing as full individuals those people who had previously been denied any real individuality: the lower middle and working classes). . . .

This method of filmic narration is very similar to the classic Hollywood use: a highly developed shooting and editing style which nevertheless appears natural. This was already inscribed into the very technology that Ealing used, and the techniques which were applied to its use. But it would have been possible, using even this equipment, to have made greater stylistic innovations. However, this did not suit the purpose of the people working at the studio, and their use of specifically cinematic language only refused certain techniques in order to make the whole fiction seem super-real and concerned with one concrete situation.

Their innovations were principally on another level, not that of the specifically cinematic language used, but that of the languages brought in from outside. . . . The 'freshness' of Ealing's realism lies in the way in which lower-middle-class and even working-class styles and experiences were introduced into the filmic discourse, not for parody, or as objects of concern for the main characters (the form of Saville's *South Riding*, seen as progressive in 1938), but as people who can act and whose actions are a fit subject for fiction. *Screen* has called Hamer's *It Always Rains on Sunday* 'one of the few worthwhile films about working-class London',[13] and it was Balcon's project to show 'real people'. There were also attempts to portray a social totality within the narrative form, either in the omnibus films like *Train of Events*, or in the numerous films about cohesive social groups: *Passport to Pimlico, Whisky Galore, The Titfield Thunderbolt*, etc. This portrayal of the 'lower orders' was paralleled by a new way of signifying 'this is real' in each shot: no longer is the background there merely as an ever-present connotation of 'carefree luxury' as it is in *The Philadelphia Story* and many other Hollywood social comedies; nor is it that of 'romantic history' as in *Les Enfants du Paradis*. The background had to carry part of the signification 'this is real life'. Two quotations open out into a definition of how this process worked and how it was experienced. The first is from the *Evening Standard* review of *Passport to Pimlico*: 'The studio sets never carry the fresh conviction of the camerawork actually done in the East End' (28 April 1949), and the second from Balcon a few months before:

> The thought struck me when reading a critic's appreciation of a new film in which he praised 'the newsreel effect' of the camera work. Where are we going, then, with this overinsistence on realism? If we are going to rely on camerawork faking the effect of actuality filming in order to create an on-the-spot illusion of realism, if the employment of amateur actors is done not for reasons of necessity or *faute de mieux* but, again, for an artificial effect of realism ('Look, dear, you can see he's a *real* soldier because he obviously can't *act* for toffee!') then what is to happen to the film as an art form? Surely, we shall be back again to the original revolt of the artist in films against the mechanical literal eye'.[14]

The illusion of reality in this particular kind of realist film is guaranteed by photographing real objects, rather than a studio art director's remoulding of objects. It provides a different kind of 'language'; no longer is the controlled, stylized poverty of the image supplied by the great art directors of 1930s Hollywood quite enough to guarantee the illusion. A sufficiency of non-doubled objects and people (things present but not 'speaking', like servants, the poor, and blacks, as well as chairs and chandeliers), a sufficiency which defined 'reality' in these films now gives way to a new sufficiency, that of the more elaborate casualness of real life, where objects have the appearance of having been used, and people of having a biography. This biography may not be spoken in the narrative, but it is there, spoken in their appearance and style of acting. . . .

Comedy

Ealing's comedy, the kind of film with which the studio is most popularly identified, fits into this natural assumption of film as the language of the real. There seem to be two kinds of comedy: first that which is aware of language and works by deconstructing and recombining it, the comedy of gags, of illogicality and incongruity; and second that which rests on a natural language and instead deals with social disruption. The first is that of a Tashlin or a Chaplin, the second that of Ealing or of a Preston Sturges. The distinction cannot be rigidly maintained, as elements of each appear in the other: Ealing comedies all use various gags. Chaplin's comedies all had a social edge which the passage of time and idolatry has only served to blunt. But it is a distinction which is fruitful: Paul Willemen has convincingly demonstrated that Tashlin's films are 'intricate networks of quote, parodies, pastiches, satires' which function through the combination of elements by 'addition, subtraction, multiplication, juxtaposition, condensation etc.' He argues that the formal quality of

these gags is their dominant feature; although the codes
which are combined together are those of the normal
social discourse, the way they are disrupted is more
important than their social implications.[15] . . . The kind
of disruption of language identified with Tashlin is not
present in Ealing work: there are hardly any gags like the
one he contributed to the Marx Brothers' *Casablanca*,
where a cop finds Harpo leaning against a wall and asks
sarcastically if he's propping the building up; Harpo
nods, and when the cop angrily pulls him away, the
building collapses. The nearest equivalent is the sequence
in *The Lavender Hill Mob* where the gang melt down the
gold and each shot of each action is accompanied by a
radio news bulletin full of puns about gold/melting-
down/towers/escape. Here, the whole gag submits to
and furthers the logic of the narrative (on one level it is
another way of disguising the massive temporal discon-
tinuity involved). It is not enjoyed, in other words, for
its demasking of language as the Tashlin gag is: there it
has no narrative function whatsoever. Gags are used in
the Ealing comedies in this way in order to show that
they are comedy, so it is the films which seem most to
evade this label (e.g. *The Man in the White Suit*) that
have the most comic routines. . . .

Ealing comedy rather belongs to the type which deals
with the disruption of social reality, something that is
often defined as the safe playing-out of 'base urges': the
enactment of desires that are not socially sanctioned.
This applies as much to hatreds and utopian desires as
it does to sexuality: comedy is the space in which these
motivations can be revealed and played through. This
produces a disruption of the surface tranquillity of
existence, and this disruption is sometimes expressed in
the disruption of codes that produces laughter, in unexpected twists and logical incongruities etc. But the basis
of this kind of comedy is the way in which it deals with
feelings which are not quite socially sanctioned. The
outer edges of this space are defined by the limits of
subversion: comedy which 'gets too close to the bone' is

that which deals with desires which cannot be integrated. Then it transgresses into the area of the other, the area of experience which is totally excluded from civilization at that particular moment. Comedy has to effect some kind of reconciliation between the desires it deals with and the society which these desires are disrupting. . . . comedy is progressive in that it reveals the partially repressed areas, the areas of unease, tension, guilt, of potential change, but in the end it has to effect, in the reading preferred by the film-makers, some kind of re-integration. Yet this can be an uneasy confirmation of traditional values even within the preferred reading. In the readings of a corporate or oppositional class this integration can be lost or ignored. . . .

Ealing's comedy style was new in that it dealt with the utopian desires of the lower middle class rather than its resentments. Certainly, resentment played a part in the working of the comedy ('Who hasn't wanted to kick the bureaucrat in the pants' wrote Balcon), but it was not its main emphasis. Rather this style dealt with the consequences of that resentment when it was played through; these consequences were the release of subterranean values. These values, and their playing-out in a specific area in a limited amount of time, constitute the 'fantasy', the affectionate 'whimsicality' often noted in the Ealing comedies. They are values which are felt to be lacking in lower-middle-class life, either denied or under historical pressure. The expression of these fringe values, the ideals of community which tend to be denied by the facts of a competitive, status-conscious middle-class life, produce the more progressive comedies. Hence in *Passport to Pimlico*, resentment about rationing produces an expression of the utopian desires for a self-regulating independent community; in *Whisky Galore*, it is the compensatory 'golden age' dream of an anarchic self-governing community before the arrival of the more individualistic present. These values are expressed through the disruption of the social order, a disruption that is made possible by certain resentments. Hence also the aspirations for a different class status are expressed, in *The Lavender Hill Mob* through robbery and in *Kind Hearts and Coronets* through murder. The more reactionary comedies spring from the regret for those ideals which are seen as being swept aside by the forces of history; it becomes a more nostalgic and sentimentalizing comedy, best shown in *The Titfield Thunderbolt*.

The expression of these values is only possible because of an initial disruption – hence Balcon's definition of the comedies as 'real people in impossible situations'. Impossible not because they lead to stalemate, but because they cannot occur. The situation makes comedy possible, whether it be a sudden discovery that disrupts (*Passport to Pimlico, The Man in the White Suit*), or the encroachment of outside interests and powers (*Whisky Galore, The Titfield Thunderbolt, Barnacle Bill*). The result is what Durgnat and Balcon both call 'anarchistic', precisely because it expresses the shadowy desires and aspirations at the margins of bourgeois thought. This definition differentiates Ealing comedy from that of the Boulting Brothers (who made *Lucky Jim* after Ealing rejected it). Balcon, making the comparison, says: 'Our comedies were done with affection . . . in a sense the Boulting comedy had a sharper edge to it, and was unkinder'. The Boultings tended to deal with satire and class conflict; Ealing dealt with aspirational, utopian comedy, and so substantively only with one class. The idea of affection links the impetus with the idea of the acceptable disruption of established beliefs and institutions. Balcon is firm about the limits of Ealing's willingness to show the shortcomings of the State or of morality: 'Barnacle Bill might defy the Whitehall planners, but Michael Balcon told Ken Tynan he could never make a film which profoundly criticized such British institutions as the army.'[16] This is paralleled by T.E.B. Clarke's account of how one night he was arrested for breaking in when he'd forgotten his key:

'Says he wrote *The Blue Lamp*,' the man on the beat concluded. . . . 'Then aren't you the same one that wrote *The Lavender Hill Mob* – the film that takes the piss out of the police?' The frying pan had given way to the fire. I had to admit it. 'Just a bit of good-humoured fun' I equivocated. 'Now don't you play it down! – it was great. . . . It's a long time since I enjoyed a picture like that last one of yours. Just what was needed – somebody to take the piss out of the job!' I knew then that I really had reason to feel proud, for I had not let my old force down.[17]

This demonstrates exactly how little resentment was thought to be permissible amongst the studio staff, no matter how radical they might be in private. But from this kind of restriction a different kind of comedy was created, one which dealt more with aspirations, what the reviewers called 'fantasy'.

A multitude of logical incongruities are born from the initial disruptions that give rise to the comedies. The gags and routines are secondary to this, and as the comedies lose their social impetus (and a large part of their popularity) the gags become predominant, most obviously in *Who Done It*, a playing through of stereotyped slapstick situations. Mostly however, the comedy is born out of the complicated negotiations between the established order and the disruptive forces. This determines the diverse amusements of Holland suddenly thinking of himself as gangleader (*The Lavender Hill Mob*); of Pemberton calling for law and order when he had explicitly rejected it only the night before (*Passport to Pimlico*); of Louis's cool justification of his multiple murders (*Kind Hearts and Coronets*); of the mutual incomprehension of the Scots and businessmen in *The Maggie* where neither can understand how the others can be so stupid, because they use different logics.

The basis of the comedies lies in the way that they play out the fringe ideals and subterranean values of the class to whom their preferred meaning is directed. The comedies are, therefore, amusing rather than to be laughed at out loud. It is a fond amusement, the recognition of these utopian ideals and shadowy values when they are played out in a limited space. The disruption of the normal order is possible so long as its expression is always local, localized in a specific place for a specific length of time for a well-defined group of people. The recognition has to be within these limits for it to be acceptable and not too disturbing. But for audiences with a different class background from that of those who sympathies lie with the preferred reading, these values and ideals have a different weight. They may already find a considerable degree of expression, as with the ideal of community, which is the normal mode of behaviour in an organic working-class community. The comedy then takes on a different character. It is no longer a comedy of fantasy but of fact; it is no longer a comedy in which, for a short time, recognition of the shadowy areas of belief can be expressed, but a comedy where normal ways of behaving are shown and are causing disruption and defiance of those who do not behave that way. So the weight of defiance in *Passport to Pimlico* or *Whisky Galore* is very different for working-class and middle-class audiences. For one it is fantasy, whimsy; for the other it is an expression of real potential.

Social and political ideas

> By and large we were a group of liberal-minded, like-minded people. I don't know if anyone was terribly politically involved, we were film-makers: it was our life, it was our total life. (Balcon)

'Real people in real situations' is not simply proposing a certain kind of cinematic style, it is equally a social proposal: the people shown have to have convincing psychologies and belong to a recognizable class. A complicated set of ideas about both cinematic technique and social relevance is impacted into this one idea because it was not the habit of film-makers at this time to reflect overall about what they were doing. The issues were thought through in terms of an instinctual response to specific problems, so cinematic realism emerged as transparent precisely because it was not thought of as language, but as the efficient duplication of the real. The same process is found with social ideas. Balcon has evident difficulty in thinking of the films in terms of their class position; he is much more used to seeing them in terms of the 'idea' they express, as shown in his interpretation of *The Man in the White Suit*:

> The relationships of management and labour are not dealt with in depth. It's more concerned with the question of processes, and the search for a synthetic substitute; it bears a relationship to that kind of research today.

Mackendrick sees the film in more psychological terms:

> I'd like to make another 'hysterical comedy' like *The Man in the White Suit*, which is my favourite film. A man lives in a social group. This group seems normal and he abnormal. Little by little you realize that it is *he* who is full of good sense. In a psychotic world, neurotics sometimes seem normal.[18]

Similarly, T.E.B. Clarke writes of *Passport to Pimlico* in terms of its comic idea rather than of the type of people involved.[19] The concern of the studio staff was to elaborate the entertainment rather than to give a social view. So the latter was not thought through consciously, it was a matter of what 'felt right', and what the staff sympathized with. Balcon gives a basic statement of their class position:

> If you think about Ealing at those times, we were a bundle . . . (I'm not saying this in any critical sense), we were middle-class people brought up with middle-class backgrounds and rather conventional educations. Though we were radical in our points of view, we did not want to tear down institutions: this was before the days of Marxism or Maoism or Lévi-Strauss or Marcuse. We were people of the immediate post-war generation, and we voted Labour for the first time after the war; this was our

mild revolution. We had a great affection for British institutions: the comedies were done with affection, and I don't think we would have thought of tearing down institutions unless we had a blueprint for what we wanted to put in their place. Of course we wanted to improve them, or to use the cliché of today, to look for a more just society in the terms that we knew. The comedies were a mild protest, but not protests at anything more sinister than the regimentation of the times. I think we were going through a mildly euphoric period then; believing in ourselves and having some sense of, it sounds awful, of national pride.

Elsewhere he has described his own background as 'Gladstonian liberal' from a 'respectable but impoverished family'. The idea of liberalism covers two related political tendencies, both of which are evident in Ealing's staff. The first is that of the nineteenth-century Liberal Party, an uneasy alliance of progressive political forces, the backbone of whose support was the Nonconformist petty bourgeoisie. It was the party of peace, prosperity, free enterprise and decency. One of its basic tenets was tolerance, the ability to see both sides of the question, an attitude which informs the preferred reading of *The Man in the White Suit*. Growing from this during the twentieth century was the liberalism of the generation after Balcon's, that of most of the studio staff. They experienced early in adult life the effects of the depression and the rise of fascism. The reaction to these conditions amongst the liberal intelligentsia was a certain radicalism, a radicalism which had not developed during the earlier period of labour militancy immediately after the First World War. It was a radicalism born out of humanitarianism, a response to a failure of the system rather than a challenge to it. Its most concrete expression was a commitment to the Republicans in the Spanish Civil War: Ivor Montagu, Sid Cole and Thorold Dickinson were all in the unit which made *Behind the Spanish Lines* and *Spanish ABC* in 1938. Dickinson was also on the 1937 ACT delegation to Russia. The pro-Spanish-

Republican spirit pervaded the GPO film unit, as Cavalcanti shows in the *Screen* interview.[20] The limits of this radicalism are demonstrated by the post-war careers of these people: there was an acute suspicion of the left as somehow dehumanized (the product of Stalinism), which led Dickinson to make *Secret People*, viciously condemning a group which attempts to assassinate a fascist dictator. It also leads to comments like Balcon's 'Ivor Montagu was a great character, no doubt a member of the Communist Party, but he was the sweetest, nicest, gentlest man that ever happened.' Balcon's own attitude to political affiliations is that they were none of his business so long as they stayed outside the studio:

> Mary Kessel used to sell the *Daily Worker*, but we had an arrangement with her that she would sell it outside the studio gate and not inside. This was the kind of atmosphere, it was much milder. There was Baynham Honri, our technical supervisor, and another technician, Eric Williams, who were arch-Tories, but the men used to pull their legs.

Almost all of the studio staff had come from comfortable middle-class backgrounds, qualitatively different from the lower-middle-class one they portray. Many had had some form of higher education: Hamer, Clarke, Crichton and Frend at Oxbridge; Mackendrick and Relph at art colleges; Cornelius, from South Africa, went to Max Reinhardt's academy in Berlin and to the Sorbonne. Others were from theatrical backgrounds: Dearden, Holt, Relph. Most of them participated in the radicalization of the intelligentsia in the 1930s, and voted Labour in 1945. There was certainly a more political atmosphere during the War; asked whether the senior staff participated in the swing from Labour in 1950, Balcon replied: 'I wouldn't have been particularly conscious of it at that time. One was obviously conscious of it during the War because one talked of the world that one had to face in post-war times.' This radicalism consisted of a rejection of the anarchic capitalism identified with the depression in favour of a State-regulated system; also, in the arts, it leaned towards the portrayal of 'real people', a tendency marked in the cinema by rejection of what Hollywood was supposed to stand for. But film-makers of this class background and with the demands of entertainment to fulfil conceived of 'the people' in a very distinct way, not as factory workers, an amorphous mass with whom they had little or no contact, but as that more public echelon of shopkeepers and clerks, the petty bourgeoisie. These were people who were easy to observe unobtrusively (Anderson recounts how they sat in the Soho café that was the model for the café in *Secret People* 'observing the clientele'), and were known to be familiar to the whole audience. But this in itself is not enough to explain the concentration on the petty bourgeoisie: it is also a concentration on the point of exchange rather than the place of production: as Charles Barr put it, 'the small catering establishment' is a 'social melting-pot' which occurs very frequently in British films.[21] This is precisely because the point of exchange is the only point in capitalist society where social relationships are expressed. . . . This means that the only point in the social process at which individuality is fully expressed is at the point of exchange; to express psychology and to show individuals, entertainment will be biased towards this class and this area when it wants to show 'the people'. Unencumbered by such an impulse, it can go ahead and show those sections of society whose wealth makes it possible for them to develop their psychological processes to the full. This was the drift of Hollywood in the 1930s, a drift which Balcon and others explicitly rejected because of the war. The multitude of difficulties in showing the process of work and maintaining the demands of entertainment and psychological development at the same time are well known. The only Ealing film to attempt this leans heavily on the moment of exchange for its justification: the stalemate in *The Man in the White Suit* that makes the invention unacceptable is the result of the endless circulation of exchange; if everlasting products were made, this system of always-expanding reproduction of need would be short-circuited. There would be nothing for the workers to do, and no more return on capital. In this film as well, although the setting is industrial, there is still no portrayal of workers working. The only work-process shown is the individualized process of bosses and researchers. Workers are not individuals in as much as their work deprives them of individuality and therefore of 'dramatic interest'.

Thus the concentration of Ealing's films on the lower middle class is a result of a complex of factors. The first is biographical: the majority of the film-makers were born into middle-class families, many strongly imbued with old-fashioned liberalism, which expressed the class interest of the emergent lower sections of the bourgeoisie. They were of the generation which passed through the depression and was radicalized by it, producing a desire to show 'the people' in films. Both personal knowledge and the demands of entertainment narratives confirmed them in the choice of this class fraction as the area of interest. The development of Ealing comedy is closely linked to the complex history of this class fraction since the War. Balcon agreed with the identification of this interest, but was extremely hesitant about calling it a conscious attitude:

> I suppose that we resented the fact that everybody had treated what you call the lower middle class as types; and I think we attempted to treat them, oddly enough, as human beings. . . . I think we probably found them easier to deal with.

The Ealing creative elite, themselves members of the middle echelons of the middle class, came to make films in sympathy with lowest strata of that class.

This sympathy is expressed in a certain moral attitude: 'Nothing would induce us to do anything against the public interest just for the sake of making money.' This is at once a personal and a political morality: it refuses any infringement of the national moral norm, or that moral norm which is assumed to be national, and at the same time refuses any contradiction of the demands of the state. No real revolution can be advocated, and no serious criticism of national institutions of power (judiciary, army, parliament, etc.), except that which is sanctioned by comedy. But it is in the role of women that Ealing's strict morality was and is most remarked upon. There have been many films which have seen the police as a natural force for good in society as do all Ealing films, but few studios that have consistently dealt with women in such a restrictive way. Most criticism of Ealing's morality, however, equates the role of women with that of sex, e.g. Bryan Forbes's 'Sex was buried with full military honours at Ealing' (*Evening Standard* review of *Hollywood, England*). But the matter of sexuality is only the most visible manifestation of the petty-bourgeois idea of femininity. Women are seen as the repositories of moral values, and it is therefore no accident that they are less in evidence in the comedies than in the serious dramas, as even Balcon will admit. Since comedy involves the infringement of ideals and accepted structures, it is possible for men to be involved, but not women. This is equally evident in matters of property as of sexuality. The robbery films (*The Lavender Hill Mob* and *The Ladykillers*) are remarkable for the lack of women: the old lady in *The Ladykillers* is the single exception, and her importance lies precisely in the way that she is inviolable, a moral absolute. Equally in *Whisky Galore* the women are marginal to the actions; in *Kind Hearts and Coronets* the action concerns Louis's prevarication over which woman he wants as his, or rather his attempts to possess both. It is the standard ploy of 'men act, women appear', a widespread attitude which is more a product of patriarchal than of capitalist society. But it is an attitude which has a different form in the different material and ethical fields in which it is expressed. So the petty-bourgeois ideal is that of the 'little woman', the woman who exists as an ignorant housekeeper and spiritual comfort. It is a matter of the particular way in which the separateness of work from home, and of the privacy of the home come to be dealt with. In short, it is a matter of the cultural space of a particular class fraction, and the available modes of subjectivity for women within it. As petty-bourgeois roles are defined in terms of a 'private life' rigidly isolated from social life, attitudes towards sexuality (the private acts at the heart of private life) best define the available range of attitudes. Not mentioning anything that goes on within 'the sanctity of marriage', anything of the details of either personal life or of sexuality, are attitudes more typical of a petty-bourgeois mentality. . . .

Notes

1 Heath, Stephen (1974) *Cambridge Review*, autumn.
2 *Michael Balcon Presents . . . A Lifetime in Films*, p. 154.
3 All quotations from Sir Michael Balcon, unless otherwise stated, are from an interview with the author in August 1974.
4 See *Screen*, 15 (1 and 2), spring and summer 1974.
5 The bulk of the technical information for this section has been taken from Bomack, R.H. (1950) *Cine Data Book*, London: Fountain Press.
6 Clarke, T.E.B. (1974) *This Is Where I Came In*, London: Michael Joseph, p. 182.
7 ibid., p. 181.
8 Balcon in a BFI summer school paper, 1945.
9 Koval, Francis, *Sight and Sound* Festival Special, 1951, p. 8.
10 Clarke, op. cit., pp. 155–6.
11 Anderson, Lindsay (1951) *Making a Film*, London: Allen & Unwin, p. 159.
12 *Michael Balcon Presents . . .* , p. 159.
13 *Screen*, 13 (2) summer 1972: 51.
14 *Saraband for Dead Lovers*, p. 11.
15 See Willemen, Paul (1973) *Frank Tashlin*, Edinburgh Festival, p. 125.
16 Durgnat, Raymond *Mirror for England*, London: Faber, p. 38.
17 Clarke, op. cit., p. 169.
18 Interview in *Positif*, 92, 1968.
19 Clarke, op. cit., pp. 159–61.
20 *Screen*, 13 (2) summer 1972.
21 *Screen*, 15 (1) spring 1974: 117.

20
Out of what past? Notes on the B *film noir*

Paul Kerr

Ever since the publication of Borde and Chaumeton's pioneering *Panorama du Film Noir Américain* in 1955, there has been a continuing dispute about the genre's precise cultural sources and critical status.[1] In their attempts to provide *film noir* with a respectable pedigree, subsequent studies have cited not only cinematic but also sociological, psychological, philosophical, political, technological and aesthetic factors amongst its progenitors. What they have not done, however, is to relate these general – and generally untheorized – notions of 'influence' to the specific modes of production, both economic and ideological, upon which they were, presumably, exercised; in this case, those structures and strategies adopted by certain factions within the American film industry over a period of almost two decades. . . .

This article, then, taking its cue from the oft-cited specificity of *film noir* as a genre, will attempt to relate it not to the general American social formation (as some species of 'reflection'), nor to a monolithically conceived film industry, but rather to particular, relatively autonomous modes of film production, distribution and exhibition in a particular conjuncture. What follows, therefore, is an exploratory rather than an exhaustive analysis of the reciprocal relation which obtained between *film noir*'s primary determinants – the economic and the ideological. . . . This analysis attends in particular to the relatively autonomous and uneven development of the B *film noir*, a category constituted, I will argue, by a negotiated resistance to the realist aesthetic on the one hand and an accommodation to restricted expenditure on the other. . . .

Towards a definition

Before a discussion of such suggestions can legitimately begin, however, some kind of critical consensus about these 'practices' and the period in which they were pursued is needed. The authors of the *Panorama* focus their own analysis on those films produced between 1941 and 1953 but more recent critics have broadened these bounds somewhat to include films made from the beginning of the 1940s (and sometimes even earlier) until the end of the following decade. If we employ the more elastic of these estimates and allow an additional – and admittedly arbitrary – margin at the beginning of the period, we may be able to reconstruct at least some of the industrial determinants of the genre. Furthermore, several critics have tried to demonstrate that *film noir* comprises a number of distinct stages. Paul Schrader, for example, has outlined 'three broad phases' for the genre: the first lasting until about 1946 and characterized by couples like Bogart and Bacall and 'classy' studio directors like Curtiz; the second spanning the immediate postwar years, when shooting began to move out of the studios and into the streets; and the third and final phase in which both characters and conventions alike were subject to extraordinary permutations. Perhaps film history will ultimately explain the industrial underpinnings of such 'sub-generic' shifts as well as the primary determinants and eventual demise of the wider genre itself.[2] Until then, whether the period of *film noir* production is relatively easily agreed upon or not, the volume of that production is decidedly more difficult to ascertain. This is due, to some degree at least, to the primacy of the economic and relative autonomy of the ideological instances of the *film noir*. Equally important is its controversial status as a genre at all, since it is usually defined in terms of its style rather than – as most genres are – in relation to content, character, setting and plot. . . .

Despite such difficulties, it still remains possible to offer at least an outline of the genre's defining characteristics.[3] Primarily, *film noir* has been associated with a propensity for low key lighting, a convention which was in direct opposition to the cinematographic orthodoxy of the previous decade. In the 1930s the dominant lighting style, known as high key, had been characterized by a contrast ratio of approximately 4:1 between the light value of the key lamp on the one hand and the filler on the other. *Noir*, with a considerably higher range of contrasts, is thus a *chiaroscuro* style, its low key effects often undiffused by either lens gauzes or lamp glasses – as they certainly would have been in conventional high key style. Instead, *noir* sets are often only half or quarter lit, with the important exception of those brief sequences in the '*blanc*' (that is, 'normal') world which are sometimes employed as a framing device at the beginning and end of the narrative. Otherwise, shooting tends to be either day-for-night or night-for-night and the main action has a habit of occurring in shadowy rooms, dingy offices, overlush apartments and rainwashed streets. In such settings both actors and decor are often partially obscured by the foregrounding of oblique objects – shutters and bannisters, for instance, casting horizontal or vertical grids of light and dark across faces and furniture. Meanwhile, the arrangement of space within the frame is often equally irregular, both in regard to its occupation by actors and props as well as to the width and depth of focus. This can lead to a 'discomposition' of the image (and consequent disorientation of the spectator) in terms of the neo-classical conventions of composition generally used and, indeed, reinforced by Hollywood. These kinds of disorientation can be accentuated by the use of 'perversely' low and high camera angles (a perversity defined entirely in relation to contemporary realist criteria) and the virtual elimination of those other staples of realism, the establishing long shot and the personalizing close-up. In fact, the latter is often used ironically in the *film noir* in soft focus treatment of male villainy (signifying feminine decadence) whilst women, the conventional 'objects' of such attention, are often photographed in harsh, unflattering and undiffused light with wide angle distorting lenses. Such an emphasis on unconventional camera angles and lighting set-ups, however, is often achieved at the (literal) expense of camera movement and classical editing. A number of other realist conventions, including the shot-reverse-shot alternation of points of view and the 180 degree rule, are also occasionally infringed by the *film noir*.[4] Finally, there is a great deal of reliance on such fragmented narrative structures as the flashback, which lend an additional sense of inevitability to the plot and helplessness to the characters. Hitherto, most definitions of the genre have more or less rested at this point, tending to ignore that plot and those characters. One recent critic, however, has assembled what he calls a 'rudimentary working prototype' of characteristic content for *film noir* along the following lines:

> Either because he is fated to do so by chance, or because he has been hired for a job specifically associated with her, a man whose experience of life has left him sanguine and often bitter meets a not-innocent woman of similar outlook to whom he is sexually and fatally attracted. Through this attraction, either because the woman induces him to it or because it is the natural result of their relationship, the man comes to cheat, attempt to murder or actually murder a second man to whom the woman is unhappily or unwillingly attached (generally he is her husband or lover), an act which brings about the sometimes metaphoric but usually literal destruction of the woman, the man to whom she is attached and frequently the protagonist himself.[5]

This schematic summary of *film noir* will have to suffice for our purposes here, if only as a result of the extremely tentative account of the genre's determination outlined below.

The coming of the B feature

The B film was launched as an attempt by a number of independent exhibitors to lure audiences back into their theatres at a time of acute economic crisis in the industry. Along with the double bill these independents had already – by the beginning of the 1930s – introduced lotteries, live acts, quizzes, free gifts and several other gimmicks in order to build up bigger audiences and, at the same time, keep those patrons they already had in their seats a little longer, so boosting both box-office takings and confectionery sales whilst re-legitimizing admission prices. The double bill, however, had the additional – and, as it proved, crucial – advantage of enabling independent exhibitors to accommodate their programme policies to the majors' monopolistic distribution practices (such as blind selling and block booking) and allowing them to exhibit more independent product at the same time. Of the 23,000 theatres operating in the United States in 1930, the five majors (MGM, RKO, Fox, Warners and Paramount) either owned or controlled some 3,000 – most of that number being among the biggest and best situated of the first-run theatres; these 3,000 theatres, though comprising less than 14 per cent of the total number then in operation, accounted for nearly 70 per cent of the entire industry's box-office takings that year. This left the independents with some 20,000 theatres in which to screen what were either second-run or independent films. By the end of 1931 the double bill, which had originated in New England, had spread its influence on programme policy right across the country, establishing itself as at least a part of that policy in one-eighth of the theatres then in operation. In 1935, the last of the majors to adopt double bills in their theatres – MGM and RKO – announced their decision to screen two features in all but two of their theatres. By 1947, the fraction of cinemas advertising double bills had risen to nearly two-thirds. In normal circumstances, of course, any such increase in the volume of films in exhibition would have led to a similar increase in the volume of film production but this was not the case. Overproduction by the majors since the advent of sound had accumulated an enormous backlog of as yet unreleased material. It was not, therefore, until this reservoir of ready-made second features had been exhausted that it became necessary to set up an entirely new mode of film production – the B unit.

While those units within the vertically integrated majors virtually monopolized the independent exhibition outlets a number of B studios established to meet the same demand were compelled to rely on the so-called States Rights system, whereby studios sold distribution rights to film franchises on a territorial basis. Lacking theatre chains of their own, several independent production companies were forced to farm out their product to a relatively unknown market. Monogram and Republic did eventually set up small exchanges of their own in a few cities and their main rival, PRC, even acquired some theatres of its own in the 1940s but the distinction between such venues and those owned by the majors should not be forgotten. Certainly, the producers of the B films themselves would have been acutely aware of the kind of cinemas in which the bulk of their products would have been seen and this may have been as influential a factor in B film production as the picture palaces undoubtedly were for the As. Mae D. Huettig, for instance, has described how Los Angeles's eleven first-run theatres exhibited 405 films in the year 1939/40 of which only five were the product of independent companies, all but one of that five being shown at the bottom of a double bill.[6] Wherever such double bills were programmed, however, few exhibitors could afford the rentals of two top quality (i.e. top price) products at the same time. The double bill, therefore, was a combination of one relatively expensive A film and one relatively inexpensive B, the former generally deriving from the major studios and costing, throughout the 1940s, upwards of $700,000 and the latter being produced by low budget units at the same studios as well as by several B studios, at anything less than about $400,000. In general, the A feature's rental was based on a percentage of box-office takings whilst the Bs played for a fixed or flat rental and were thus not so reliant on audience attendances figures at all – at least, not in the short term. In the long term, however, these B units would be compelled to carve out identifiable and distinctive styles for themselves in order to differentiate their product – within generic constraints – for the benefit of audiences in general and exhibitors in particular.

In most cases the B *film noir* would have been produced – like all Bs – on a fixed budget which would itself have been calculated in relation to fixed rentals. In illustrating the effects such economies exercised on these Bs I have restricted reference, as far as possible, to one large integrated company, RKO, and one small independent company, PRC.[7] At the beginning of the decade the budgets of RKO's most important production unit in the B sector were approximately $150,000 per picture; at PRC, several years later, most units were working with less than two-thirds of that amount. To take two examples: Val Lewton's films at RKO had tight, twenty-one-day schedules whilst Edgar G. Ulmer's at PRC were often brought in after only six days and nights. . . . Props, sets and costumes were kept to a minimum, except on those occasions when they could be borrowed from more expensive productions, as Lewton borrowed a staircase from *The Magnificent Ambersons* for his first feature, *The Cat People*. . . .

Night shooting, of course, was an obvious and often unavoidable strategy for getting films in on short schedules as well as fully exploiting fixed assets and economizing on rentals. (It also suited those employees who sought to avoid IATSE overtime bans.) Mark Robson, an editor and later director in Lewton's unit, has recalled that 'the streets we had in *The Seventh Victim*, for instance, were studio streets and the less light we put on them the better they looked.'[8] Similarly, expensive special effects and spectacular action sequences were generally avoided unless stock footage could be borrowed from other films. This 'borrowing' became known as the 'montage' and involved the use of 'a series of quick cuts of film'. As Grinde has explained,

> You can't shoot a first-rate crime wave on short dough, so you borrow or buy about twenty pieces of thrilling moments from twenty forgotten pictures. A fleeing limousine skids into a street-car, a pedestrian is socked over the head in an alley, a newspaper office is wrecked by hoodlums, a woman screams, a couple of mugs are slapping a little merchant into seeing things their way. And so on until we end up on a really big explosion.[9] . . .

The exploitation of borrowed footage and furniture was only really possible as long as films were still being shot inside the studios. Until the middle of the 1940s location shooting was extremely rare and even independents like Monogram and PRC had their own studio facilities. As fixed and variable costs began to escalate at the end of the war, however, production units were encouraged to go out on location and this practice was extended by the prolonged studio strikes of 1945–47. In 1946, the abolition of block booking encouraged the appearance of a number of small studio-less independent production companies and these also contributed to the 'street' rather than 'studio' look in the latter half of the decade. Constraints at both the production and distribution ends of the industry meant that the running length of Bs fluctuated between about fifty-five and seventy-five minutes; raw footage was expensive, audiences had only limited amounts of time and, of course, exhibitors were keen to screen their double bills as many times a day as possible. In 1943 the government reduced basic allotments of raw film stock to the studios by 25 per cent and once again it was the B units which were hardest hit. Consequently 'montages' became even more common. Casts and crews on contract to B units were kept at a manageable minimum, so prohibiting plots with long cast lists, crowd scenes and complicated camera or lighting set-ups. Similarly, overworked script departments often produced unpolished and occasionally incoherent scripts. (Film titles were pretested with audiences before stories or scripts were even considered.) Despite such drawbacks, however, the B units, throughout the 1940s and as late as the mid-1950s, employed the same basic equipment as their big budget rivals, including Mitchell or Bell and Howell cameras, Mole Richardson lighting units, Moviola editing gear and RCA or Western Electric sound systems. Such economies as B units practised, therefore, were not related to fixed assets like rents and salaries but to variable costs like sets, scripts, footage, casual labour and, crucially, power.

RKO's production of *noir* Bs seems to have been inaugurated in 1940 with the release of Boris Ingster's extraordinary *Stranger On The Third Floor*. The studio had emerged from receivership at the end of the previous decade – a period of some prosperity for the other majors – to make only minimal profits of $18,604 in 1938 and $228,608 in 1939. In 1940 the studio lost almost half a million dollars and began to augment its low budget policy with B series like *The Saint* and *The Falcon*. It was not until 1942, however, when RKO plunged more than two million dollars into debt that the trend towards the B *film noir* became really evident. . . . It was at this point that Val Lewton was brought to the studio to set up his own B unit. Within the limitations I have outlined, as well as the generic constraints of having to work in the 'horror' category, Lewton's unit, and others like it, were accorded a degree of autonomy which would never have been sanctioned for more expensive studio productions.[10] At PRC the situation was rather different. The company had been formed in March 1940 by the creditors of its predecessor, the Producers' Distributing Corporation, and with the cooperation of the Pathé Laboratories. The new Producers' Releasing Corporation had five separate production units and the Fine Arts Studio (formerly Grand National). At first the emphasis was on comedy and westerns; PRC produced forty-four films, mostly in these genres, in the 1941/42 season. By 1942, however, PRC had acquired twenty-three film exchanges and with the replacement of George Batchelor by Leon Fromkess as production head, there was an increased diversification of product. While most units concentrated on comedies and musicals, others began to turn out cut-rate westerns and crime thrillers. It was also in 1942 that Edgar G. Ulmer began work for the studio. Allowed only about 15,000 feet per picture, Ulmer's unit, like Lewton's, economized with stock footage (as in *Girls in Chains* PRC 1943) and minimal casts and sets (as in *Detour* PRC 1946).

Artistic ingenuity in the face of economic intransigence is one critical commonplace about the B *film noir* (and about people like Lewton and Ulmer in particular). Against this, I have suggested that a number of *noir* characteristics can at least be associated with – if not directly attributed to – economic and therefore technological constraints. The paucity of 'production values' (sets, stars and so forth) may even have encouraged low budget production units to compensate with complicated plots and convoluted atmosphere. Realist denotation would thus have been de-emphasized in favour of expressionist connotation (in *The Cat People* RKO 1942, for example). This 'connotative' quality might also owe something to the influence of the Hays Office, which meant that 'unspeakable' subjects could only be suggested – *Under Age* (Columbia 1941), although concerned with the criminal exploitation of young girls, could never actually illustrate that exploitation. Similarly, compressed shooting schedules, overworked script editors and general cost cutting procedures could well have contributed to what we now call *film noir*.

Nevertheless, an analysis of *film noir* as nothing more than an attempt to make a stylistic virtue out of economic necessity – the equation, at its crudest, of low budgets with low key lighting – is inadequate: budgetary constraints and the relative autonomy of many B units in comparison with As were a necessary but by no means sufficient condition for its formation. It was, I have suggested, constituted not only by accommodation to restricted expenditure but also by resistance to the realist aesthetic – like the B film generally, it was determined not only economically but also ideologically. For instance, the double bill was not simply the result of combining any two films, one A and one B, but often depended on a number of quite complex contrasts. *The Saint in New York*, for example, was billed with *Gold Diggers in Paris, Blind Alibi* with *Holiday*. According to Frank Ricketson Jr, the tendency of both distributors and exhibitors was to ensure that

> Heavy drama is blended with sparkling comedy. A virile action picture is mated with a sophisticated society play. An all-star production is matched with a light situation comedy of no-star value. An adventure story is contrasted with a musical production.[11] . . .

Stylistic generation

Meanwhile, the monopoly structure of the industry – which had been initially, if indirectly, responsible for the B phenomenon – was being challenged. In May 1935 the Supreme Court voted to revoke Roosevelt's National Industry Recovery Act (under which *A Code Of Fair Competition For The Motion Picture Industry* had more or less condoned the industry's monopoly practices) on the grounds that it was unconstitutional. Opposition to motion picture monopolies was mounting, not only among the independent companies but also in the courts and even in Congress itself. Finally, in July 1938, the Department of Justice filed an Anti-Trust suit against the majors, United States versus Paramount Pictures Inc. *et al.*, so launching a case which was to reach the Supreme Court a decade later. In the suit the majors were accused of separate infringements of Anti-Trust legislation but, in November 1940, the case was apparently abandoned; in fact it was merely being adjourned for the duration of hostilities, the government being unwilling to provoke Hollywood at a time when the communications media were of such crucial importance. The suit was settled out of court with the signing of a modest Consent Decree, the provisions of which included an agreement by the majors to 'modify' their use of block booking, to eliminate blind selling and to refrain from 'unnecessary' theatrical expansion. Most important of all the Decree's requirements, however, was the majors' agreement to withdraw from the package selling procedures which had compelled independent exhibitors to screen shorts, reissues, serial westerns and newsreels with their main features. The last provision expanded the market for low budget production almost overnight. Whereas at the end of the 1930s there had been very few independent companies, by 1946 (the year in which block booking was finally abolished) there were more than forty. The Anti-Trust Commission never entirely dropped their case against Hollywood, however, and finally, in 1948, the five fully integrated companies were instructed to divest themselves of their theatrical holdings. Paramount was the first to obey this ruling, divorcing its exhibition arm from the production/distribution end of its business in late 1949. RKO followed in 1950, 20th-Century-Fox in 1952, Warner Bros. in 1953 and MGM in 1959. Rather ironically, the divorce meant the demise of many independent studios which had thrived on providing films for the bottom half of the bill; quite simply, low budget productions could no longer be guaranteed fixed rentals in exhibition. Consequently, one of the first casualties of divorcement was the double bill. The majors cancelled their B productions and the independents were forced to choose between closure and absorption. In 1949 PRC was absorbed by Rank and transformed into Eagle Lion;

the following year it ceased production altogether and merged with United Artists. In 1953 Monogram became Allied Artists Pictures Corporation and began to operate an increasingly important television subsidiary. Republic, whose staple product had always been westerns and serials, was finally sold to CBS in 1959 and became that network's Television City Studio.

It was thus between the first filing of the Anti-Trust suit in 1938 and the final act of divorcement in 1959 that the B *film noir* flourished. Obviously, however, the trend towards media conglomerates and away from simple monopolies was by no means the only 'political' determinant on cinematic modes in that period, a period which witnessed American entry into the war, the rise of McCarthyism and a series of jurisdictional disputes in the labour unions.[12] During the Second World War the international market for American films shrank drastically and the domestic market expanded to take its place. By 1941, the cinemas of continental Europe, where the majors had earned more than a quarter of their entire box office in 1936, were no longer open to American distributors. Even in Britain, where most cinemas remained open throughout the war and where attendance actually rose from a weekly average of nineteen million in 1939 to more than thirty million in 1945, the Hollywood majors were unable to maintain even prewar profits. The introduction of currency restrictions severely limited the amount that American distributors could remove from the country; thus, only half their former revenues – some $17,500,000 – were withdrawn in 1940 and only $12,900,000 in 1941. Meanwhile, however, American domestic rentals soared from $193,000,000 in 1939 to $332,000,000 in 1946. By the end of the war, average weekly attendance in the US was back at about 90,000,000, its prewar peak. As the majors' profits rose, the volume of their production actually fell: having released some 400 films in 1939 the big eight companies released only 250 in 1946, the balance being made up by a flush of new B companies. This geographically – but not economically – reduced constituency may have afforded Hollywood the opportunity to take a closer look at contemporary and specifically American phenomena without relying on the 'comfortable' distance provided by classic genres like the western or the musical. That 'closer look' (at, for instance, urban crime, the family and the rise of corporations) could, furthermore, because of the national specificity of its audience and as a result of the 'dialectic' of its consumption (within the double bill), employ a less orthodox aesthetic than would previously have been likely.

The aesthetic orthodoxy of the American cinema in the 1940s and 1950s was realism and so it is necessary to relate cinematic realism to the *film noir*. Colin MacCabe has suggested its two primary conditions:

(1) The classic realist text cannot deal with the real as contradictory.
(2) In a reciprocal movement the classic realist text ensures the position of the subject in a relation of dominant specularity.

These two conditions, the repression of contradiction and the construction of spectatorial omniscience, are negotiated through a hierarchy of narrative discourses:

> Through the knowledge we gain from the narrative we can split the discourses of the various characters from their situation and compare what is said in these discourses with what has been revealed to us through narration. The camera shows us what happens – it tells the truth against which we can measure the discourses.[13]

Elsewhere MacCabe has restated this notion quite clearly: 'classical realism . . . involves the homogenization of different discourses by their relation to one dominant discourse – assured of its domination by the security and transparency of its image.'[14]

It is this very 'transparency' which *film noir* refuses; indeed, Sylvia Harvey has noted that 'One way of looking at the plot of the typical *film noir* is to see it as a struggle between different voices for control over the telling of the story.' From that perspective, *film noir* represents a fissure in the aesthetic and ideological fabric of realism. Thus,

> Despite the presence of most of the conventions of the dominant methods of film-making and storytelling, the impetus towards the resolution of the plot, the diffusion of tension, the circularity of a narrative that resolves all the problems it encounters, the successful completion of the individual's quest, these methods do not, in the end, create the most significant contours of the cultural map of *film noir*. The defining contours of this group of films are the product of that which is abnormal and dissonant.[15]

Gill Davies, on the other hand, has suggested that such 'dissonance' can quite comfortably be contained by the 'weight' of generic convention.

> The disturbing effect of mystery or suspense is balanced by confidence in the inevitability of the genre. Character types, stock settings and the repetition of familiar plot devices assure the reader that a harmonious resolution will take place. This narrative pattern pretends to challenge the reader, creates superficial disorientation, while maintaining total narrative control. . . .[16]

In terms of *film noir*, however, I would argue that the 'surplus' of realist devices catalogued by Harvey and Davies indicates an attempt to hold in balance traditional generic elements with unorthodox aesthetic practices that constantly undermine them. *Film noir* can thus be seen as the negotiation of an 'oppositional space' within and against realist cinematic practice; this trend could only be effectively disarmed by the introduction of a number of stock devices derived from other genres (such as melodrama or the detective story). It is not an object of this article, though, to gauge the degree to which that resistance was or was not successful. Rather, its task is to begin to establish those historically contemporaneous strands of realism – Technicolor, television and the A film – against which any such resistance would necessarily have defined itself.

Television and Technicolor

In 1947 there were only 14,000 television receivers in the United States; two years later that number had risen to a million. By 1950 there were four million and by 1954 thirty-two million. In the face of such swiftly escalating opposition and as a consequence of the impending demise of the double bill (in the aftermath of the Anti-Trust decision), several of the smaller studios began renting theatrical films for television exhibition and even producing tele-films of their own. Thus, in 1949, Columbia formed a subsidiary, Screen Gems, to produce new films for and release old films to the new medium. In 1955, the first of the five majors, Warner Bros., was persuaded to produce a weekly ABC TV series, to be called *Warner Brothers Presents*, based on three of that studio's successful 1940s features: *King's Row* (1941), *Casablanca* (1944) and *Cheyenne* (1947). It is perhaps worth pointing out that *Cheyenne* was the only one which lacked elements of the '*noir*' style and also the only one to enjoy a mass audience; indeed it was ultimately 'spun off' into a seven-year series of its own while the other two 'thirds' of the slot were quietly discontinued. In December of 1955 RKO withdrew from film production altogether and sold its film library to a television programming syndicate; two years later, the old RKO studio itself was in the hands of Desilu, an independent television production company owned by ex-RKO contract player Lucille Ball and her husband Desi Arnez. In fact, Lucille Ball's comedy series *I Love Lucy* had been the first 'filmed' (as opposed to live) series on American television; it was only dislodged from its place at the top of the ratings by another filmed series, *Dragnet*. The latter, characterized by high key lighting, sparse shadowless sets and procedural plots, was to provide a model for television crime fiction for more than two decades. It is particularly ironic, therefore, to note that *Dragnet* derived from a 1948 B *film noir* produced by Eagle Lion, *He Walked By Night*, a film which contains what is perhaps the most dramatically *chiaroscuro* scene ever shot in Hollywood. In 1954 Warner Bros. released a cinematic spin-off from the series, again called *Dragnet*, but this time without a trace of the stylistic virtuosity which had characterized its cinematic grandparent. (The fact that this film proved unsuccessful at the box office, far from invalidating my thesis about the relationship between television and the *film noir*, actually corroborates my account of the different 'spaces' occupied by the discourse of realism in television and the cinema.) Very simply, the low contrast range of television receivers meant that any high contrast cinematic features (like *films noirs*) were inherently unsuitable for tele-cine reproduction.

If *film noir* was determined to any degree by an initial desire to differentiate B cinematic product from that of television (as A product was differentiated by colour, production values, 3D, wide screens and epic or 'adult' themes), as, too, its ultimate demise relates to capitulation to the requirements of tele-cine, that 'difference' can also be seen as a response to the advent of colour. The first full-length Technicolor feature, *Becky Sharp*, was released in 1935 (by RKO), and its director, Rouben Mamoulian – one of the few professionals in favour of colour at that time – has described in some detail the aesthetic consensus into which the new process was inserted:

> For more than twenty years, cinematographers have varied the key of lighting in photographing black-and-white pictures to make the visual impression enhance the emotional mood of the action. We have become accustomed to a definite language of lighting: low key effects, with sombre, heavy shadows express a sombrely dramatic mood; high key effects, with brilliant lighting and sparkling definition, suggest a lighter mood; harsh contrasts with velvety shadows and strong highlights strike a melodramatic note. Today we have color – a new medium, basically different in many ways from any dramatic medium previously known. . . . Is it not logical,

therefore, to feel that it is incumbent upon all of us, as film craftsmen, to seek to evolve a photodramatic language of color analogous with the language of light with which we are all so familiar?[17]

Mamoulian's implicit appeal to a 'logic of the form' might well have impressed some of the 'creative' workers associated with A film productions but it is unlikely to have been heard sympathetically among employees of the Bs. Indeed, the advent of colour actually exacerbated the situation he had outlined: the Technicolor process demanded 'high key effects, with brilliant lighting and sparkling definition' as a very condition of its existence. It is, therefore, hardly surprising that a cinema of 'low key effects, with sombre heavy shadows' flourished in counterpart to it. Furthermore, the films actually employing Technicolor were often characterized by exotic locations, lavish sets, elaborate costumes and spectacular action sequences (generally of the musical or swashbuckling variety) and so fell into an expanding group of 'colour-specific' genres – westerns, musicals, epics, historical dramas, etcetera – leaving melodramas, thrillers, and horror films to the lower budgets of black and white. Finally, in 1939 the really decisive blow for the industrial endorsement of colour was struck by the unprecedented success of *Gone With The Wind*. However, wartime economic and technological restraint frustrated much further movement to colour for several years – as it also postponed the rise of television – and perhaps the very 'dormancy' of the Technicolor phenomenon in those years encouraged people engaged in and/or committed to black and white to continue to experiment. . . .

I would like, finally, to suggest that it was, specifically, the absorption of a colour aesthetic within realism which generated the space which *film noir* was to occupy. Indeed, just as the advent of radio in 1924 had provoked a cinematic trend away from realism until it was reversed in 1927 with the coming of sound to the cinema, so while colour originally signified 'fantasy' and was first appropriated by 'fantastic' genres, it too was soon recuperated within the realist aesthetic. Compare, for instance, the realist status of black and white sequences in *The Wizard Of Oz* (1939) and *If* (1969). The period of this transition, the period in which the equation between black and white on the one hand and realism on the other was at its most fragile, was thus the period from the late 1930s – when television, Technicolor and the double bill were first operating – to the late 1950s, when television and colour had established themselves, both economically and ideologically, as powerful lobbies in the industry, and the double bill had virtually disappeared. That period, of something less than twenty years, saw the conjunction of a primarily economically determined mode of production, known as B film-making, with what were primarily ideologically defined modes of 'difference', known as the *film noir*. Specific conjunctures such as this – of economic constraints, institutional structures, technological developments, political, legal and labour relations – are central to any history of film; they represent the industrial conditions in which certain representational modes, certain generic codes come into existence. . . .

Notes

1 Borde, Raymond and Chaumeton, Etienne (1955) *Panorama du Film Noir Americain*, Paris: Les Editions de Minuit. I use the term genre in this article where others have opted for 'subgenre', 'series', 'cycle', 'style', 'period', 'movement', etc. For a recent discussion of critical notions of (and approaches to) *film noir*, see Damico, James (1978) '*Film noir*: a modest proposal' in *Film Reader 3*, Evanston.

2 For a useful contribution to the historical debate see Buscombe, Edward (1977) 'A new approach to film history', *Film Studies Annual*.

3 Much of the stylistic detail in this outline is indebted to Place, J.A. and Peterson, L.S. (1974) 'Some visual motifs of *film noir*', *Film Comment*, January.

4 For further examples of such infringements see Marshall, Stuart (1977) '*Lady in the Lake*: identification and the drives' in *Film*

Form, 2 (2); Heath, Stephen (1975), 'Film and system: terms of analysis' in *Screen*, 16 (1 and 2) spring/summer; Thompson, Kristin (1977) 'The duplicitous text: an analysis of *Stage Fright*' in *Film Reader 2*; Thompson, Kristin (1978) 'Closure within a dream: point-of-view in *Laura*' in *Film Reader 3*.

5 Damico, op. cit., p. 54.

6 Heuttig, Mae D. (1944) *Economic Control of the Motion Picture Industry*, Philadelphia.

7 Producers' Releasing Corporation: for information on this see McCarthy, Tod and Flynn, Charles (eds) (1975) *Kings of the Bs*, Dutton; Miller, Don (1973) *B Movies*, Curtis Books; Miller, Don (1978) 'Eagle Lion: The Violent Years' in *Focus on Film*, 31, November.

8 Mark Robson interviewed in *The Velvet Light Trap*, no. 10.

9 Grinde, Nick (1946) 'Pictures for Peanuts' in *The Penguin Film Review*, no. 1, August (reprinted London: Scolar Press, 1977, p. 44).

10 For information on the Lewton unit see Siegel, Joel (1972) *Val Lewton, The Reality of Terror*, London: Secker and Warburg/British Film Institute. For further detail on RKO see the special issue (no. 10) of *The Velvet Light Trap*. On production in general see Fernett, Gene (1973) *Poverty Row*, Coral Reef.

11 Ricketson Jr., Frank (1938) *The Management of Motion Picture Theatres*, New York, pp. 82–3.

12 For one account of the effect of these pressures on the cinema, see Kelly, Keith and Steinman, Clay (1978) 'Crossfire: a dialectical attack' in *Film Reader 3*.

13 MacCabe, Colin (1974) 'Realism and the cinema: notes on some Brechtian theses', *Screen*, 15 (2) summer: 10–12.

14 MacCabe, Colin (1976) 'Theory and film: principles of realism and pleasure', *Screen*, 17 (3) autumn: 12.

15 Harvey, Sylvia (1978) 'Woman's place: the absent family of *film noir*' in Kaplan, E. Ann (ed.) *Women in Film Noir*, London: British Film Institute, p. 22.

16 Davies, Gill (1978/9) 'Teaching About Narrative', *Screen Education*, 29, winter: 62.

17 Mamoulian, Rouben (1941) 'Controlling color for dramatic effect' in *The American Cinematographer*, June, and collected in Koszarski, Richard (ed.) (1976) *Hollywood Directors 1941–1976*, New York: Oxford University Press, p. 15.

Section 6
Reading

Introduction

Pierre Bourdieu has argued that the principles regulating popular judgments of taste are informed by a logic of the concrete, showing a marked preference for 'plots that proceed logically and chronologically towards a happy end' and for 'simply drawn situations and characters' rather than for 'ambiguous and symbolic figures'.[1] Above all, though, Bourdieu suggests that popular taste is characterized by its preference for participation, for emotional and moral involvement in the lives and situations depicted in fictional works. As such, Bourdieu argues, these principles of taste are not merely different from those of the 'high aesthetic' which govern responses to officially sanctioned works of art – principles which demand a withdrawal from the concrete particularities of the content of the work of art in order to arrive at an abstracted and disinterested appreciation of its formal qualities – but their exact opposite. These differences are perhaps most sharply revealed in the very different forms of appreciation that are manifest when objects of popular taste fall under the judgement of those trained in the high aesthetic:

> This popular reaction is the very opposite of the detach-
> ment of the aesthete, who, as is seen whenever he
> appropriates one of the objects of popular taste (e.g.,

Westerns or strip cartoons), introduces a distance, a gap
– the measure of his distant distinction – *vis-à-vis* 'first-
degree' perception, by displacing the interest from the
'content', characters, plot, etc., to the form, to the
specifically artistic effects which are only appreciated
relationally, through a comparison with other works
which is incompatible with immersion in the singularity of
the work immediately given.[2]

Some critics have argued that Bourdieu overdraws this
distinction in polarizing the relations between these two
aesthetics. Nonetheless, the argument serves a useful
purpose here in underlining the fact that works of
popular fiction may be differently received and interpreted according to the principles of taste and criteria of
value which inform the judgments and preferences of
different communities of readers and viewers. Nor are
these the only factors which affect the reception of works
of fiction. Recent work in reception theory has drawn
attention to a complex multiplicity of factors influencing
the processes through which texts are interpreted, made
sense of, used and integrated into the social practices of
different social groups: the different cultural codes and
competencies of different class and ethnic communities;
the role of practices of reviewing in pre-interpreting texts
for readers; the systems of inter-textuality which provide
the cultural horizon within which particular texts are
interpreted in specific contexts and, finally, the specific
social settings – of home and family or the more public
space of the cinema – in which reception is located.

The readings comprising this section illustrate a range
of the different conditions and pressures which organize
the reading of popular fictions. The first two essays offer
interesting commentaries on the issues Bourdieu introduces in demonstrating the ways in which the reception
of popular texts may be aestheticized just as, contrary-
wise, texts invested with a high cultural status may be
subjected to quite different interpretations and evalua-
tions by popular audiences. It is this latter process that
interests Neil Harris in 'The operational aesthetic'. From

the very outset, Poe's detective stories have been systematically ambiguous with regard to their placing in relation to the categories of literature and popular fiction. Influencing Baudelaire just as much as Conan Doyle, they have come to be counted among the founding texts of literary modernism. Yet they were also very popular with American readers of magazine fiction – the context in which they were originally published. Harris attributes this popularity to the influence of a distinctive aesthetic within the extended reading public of mid-nineteenth-century America, one which rated highly a technical interest in puzzle-solving to which Poe's stories appealed. Harris persuasively argues that the original reception of Poe's stories was regulated by a broader culture which, by no means confined to literature, was also manifest in the popular fascination with the tricks and antics of such legendary showmen as P.T. Barnum.

If Harris's discussion casts valuable light on an episode in the cultural history of Poe's stories which has been eclipsed by their subsequent installation as important works in the literary canon, Jacqueline Rose is concerned with the opposite process: the aestheticization of a text, *Peter Pan*, which ordinarily circulates under another heading than that of art – in this case, that of children's fiction. However, in examining the variety of material forms in which the text of *Peter Pan* has been produced and circulated, Rose's concerns go beyond those of considering the literary values this text has accumulated to encompass the ambiguous – and dubious – ideological investment in, and aestheticization of, the figure of the child which has accompanied these processes.

In 'Figures of Bond', Tony Bennett and Janet Woollacott exhibit a similar concern with the diverse social and material forms in which 'the same texts' may be circulated, often with profound consequences for the ways in which those texts operate ideologically in different contexts of reception. Taking the James Bond novels and films as their primary points of interest, they show how other texts – such as fanzines and men's magazines –

have functioned as 'textual shifters' in relation to these primary texts, altering the horizons within which they have been read with perceptible consequences for the positions they have occupied in relation to ideologies of class, nation and gender. In view of these considerations, Bennett and Woollacott are led to suggest that popular fictional texts do not have fixed ideological meanings or effects but function rather 'as pieces of play within different regions of ideological contestation, capable of being moved around differently within them' (p. 428).

Finally, in 'Television and gender', David Morley turns his attention to the crucial role of gender in organizing the frameworks in which television is interpreted and used. In 1985, Morley conducted a research project consisting of extended, unstructured interviews with eighteen families. The originality of the inquiry consisted in the members of the families being interviewed together, rather than separately. Morley decided on this interview format partly because many people typically watch television as members of families, and partly because he particularly wanted to discover how television is used as an occasion for constructing and organizing social relations within the home. While the interviews ranged freely across many topics, the excerpts selected here summarize some of Morley's more salient findings concerning the different cultures of use and expectation which characterize male and female orientations toward television. His findings lend vivid support to the arguments Tania Modleski advances in accounting for women's interest in soap operas. They also provide a startling demonstration of the degree to which control over the television set can become a matter of key concern within the structure of domestic power relations.

Notes

1 Bourdieu, Pierre (1984) *Distinction: A Social Critique of the Judgement of Taste*, London: Routledge & Kegan Paul, p. 32.
2 ibid., p. 34.

21
The operational aesthetic

Neil Harris

At the end of August 1843, New York newspaper advertisements announced a 'Grand Buffalo Hunt, Free of Charge', to take place on a Thursday afternoon in Hoboken. A Mr C.D. French, 'one of the most daring and experienced hunters of the West', had captured the animals near Santa Fe at considerable risk to life and limb. Strong fences would protect the public from the savage beasts, who would be lassoed and hunted as part of the entertainment. What the newspaper advertisements did not say was that the buffaloes were feeble, docile beasts, hardly capable of movement, much less of violence. Barnum had purchased the herd for several hundred dollars when he saw it earlier that summer in Massachusetts and had stowed it away for several weeks in New Jersey. Knowing that the spectacle might not be all the audience anticipated, Barnum wisely decided to make admission free. What he did not disclose was an arrangement with the ferryboat owners who would transport the public from Manhattan to New Jersey; his profits were to come from a percentage of the fares.

The great day finally arrived, and boatloads of spectators crossed to New Jersey. There were to be several shows, and by the time the first batch of spectators had seen the hunt, a second batch was passing them on the Hudson. The returnees called out from their boats that the hunt – a debacle in which the frightened animals fled to a nearby swamp – was the biggest humbug imaginable. Instead of being disappointed, however, the expectant audience, in the words of a witness, 'instantly gave three cheers for the author of the humbug, whoever he might be.'

Barnum told the whole story in his autobiography. He understood that American audiences did not mind cries of trickery; in fact, they delighted in debate. Amusement and deceit could coexist; people would come to see something they suspected might be an exaggeration or even a masquerade. Any publicity was better than none at all, and if the audiences did not get all they anticipated, they had a pleasant outing in New Jersey for the price of a boat ride.

The principle of the Hoboken Hunt – the national tolerance for clever imposture – was one Barnum relied on again and again in his early museum days. As he was building up his cabinet of natural curiosities, he couldn't resist making his exhibits a bit more enticing than literal truth permitted. In the 1840s museum visitors could examine the wooden leg that Santa Anna had lost on a Mexican battlefield, captured, presumably, by American troops; a woolly horse, supposedly brought back by John Fremont from the Rocky Mountains; and a mass of other spurious but colourfully described oddities. . . .

Barnum's success was so great and so long-lasting, everywhere but in the South, that there had to be more to it than the simple collection of curiosities on which other entrepreneurs had already given up. To explain it, at least two questions must be answered. First, why were Americans apparently so credulous, why could they be fooled so easily, why did they flock to see mermaids, woolly horses, and other anatomical monstrosities that seem in later days to be so patently false? Why did they accept commonplace objects – wooden legs, articles of clothing, minerals and weapons – as sacred relics associated with famous men and historic events? And second, why did Americans *enjoy* watching shows and visiting exhibits that they suspected might be contrived, why did they flock to witness impostures that they knew about? In other words, why the apparent naïveté about deception, and why the pleasure in experiencing deception after knowledge of it had been gained?

These questions are related to a larger issue, for P.T. Barnum was not the only entrepreneur to fool Americans in the early nineteenth century. Ever since Washington Irving and James K. Paulding had published *Salmagundi; or, The Whim-Whams and Opinions of Lancelot Langstaff, Esq.*, in 1807–8, New York City had been popularly known as Gotham, the legendary town of fools, and the name appeared to have some basis in fact. In the three decades before the Civil War, New York was the setting for several tremendous hoaxes that Barnum had no hand in. One of the most memorable became known as the Moon Hoax, an episode engineered by Richard Adams Locke of the *New York Sun*.

The *Sun* had been founded in 1833 by Benjamin H. Day as a penny daily. It concentrated on human interest stories, and Day was one of the earliest practitioners of what would become an established tradition in American urban journalism. Readers of the *Sun* discovered, in the summer of 1835, that the internationally known British astronomer Sir John Herschel had gone to the Cape of Good Hope to experiment with a new and powerful telescope. The articles, supposedly reprinted from the *Edinburgh Journal of Science*, went on to say that Herschel's success had been beyond his wildest dreams, for with the telescope he had managed to penetrate the secrets of the moon. And Herschel's discoveries were far more interesting, or at least more astounding, than the actual voyage that would be made over a century later. The moon, it turned out, contained trees, oceans, pelicans, and most exciting of all, winged men. The *Sun* 'quoted' Herschel's minute description. 'I could perceive', he wrote, 'that their wings possessed great expansion and were similar in structure to those of the bat, being a semi-transparent membrane expanded in curvilineal divisions by means of straight radii, united at the back by the dorsal integuments.'

This was, to be sure, hard reading, and so was the extremely detailed description of the telescope's design. The *Sun* sold its papers madly, however, and while running the article reached a circulation of almost twenty thousand, larger, it asserted, than any daily newspaper in the world. Thousands of Americans believed the story absolutely, and there followed some of the rituals that seem inevitably to be born of these jokes. Some Baptist clergymen immediately began prayer meetings for the benefit of their unconverted brethren in the moon. A number of scholars at Yale went over the material to substantiate the accuracy of the episode. At last, to much general embarrassment, Locke confessed his authorship, and the discoveries turned out to be an important chapter not in the history of natural science but in the history of hoaxing.

Having achieved one success, the *New York Sun* did not rest on its laurels for too long. In 1844 the same newspaper relayed astonishing news from South Carolina. Mr Monck Mason had crossed the Atlantic in his balloon, the *Victoria*, making the voyage from England to America in seventy-five hours. Once again, the description was careful. The size and weight of the flying machine were specified, and so was the design of the screw, 'an axis of hollow brass tube, eighteen inches in length, though which, upon a semi-spiral inclined at fifteen degrees, pass a series of steel-wire radii, two feet long, and thus projecting a foot on either side'. The technical analysis could not be matched by anything so astonishing as moon men, but the newspaper dispatch did celebrate the joys of flying over water: 'The immense flaming ocean writhes and is tortured uncomplainingly. The mountainous surges suggest the idea of innumerable dumb gigantic fiends struggling in impotent agony. In a night such as is this to me, a man *lives* – lives a whole century of ordinary life – nor would I forego this rapturous delight for that of a whole century of ordinary existence.' This marvellous conquest of nature could not last as long as the Moon Hoax, alas, because it took only a short time to establish contact with the Charleston post office and find that no Atlantic crossing had taken place. It was all the product of the fertile imagination of Edgar Allan Poe.

Poe himself, in 'Diddling Considered as One of the Exact Sciences', noted the prevalence of deception on both a large and a small scale. 'A crow thieves; a fox cheats; a weasel outwits; a man diddles.' The successful diddler was ingenious, audacious, persevering, original, and entirely self-interested. Poe described some of the successful variations. A camp meeting would be held near a free bridge. 'A diddler stations himself upon this bridge, respectfully informs all passers-by of the new county law which establishes a toll of one cent for foot passengers, two for horses and donkeys, and so forth and so forth. Some grumble but all submit, and the diddler goes home a wealthier man by some $50 or $60 well earned.' This scene was not the product of Poe's imagination but actually took place, one of the innumerable devices by which Americans tricked each other. . . .

A full explanation for the effectiveness of the pranksters must take account of the advanced technical and material conditions of American life. By the 1830s and 1840s portions of the United States were as advanced in those areas as any part of the Old World; innovations like the railroad and the telegraph were greeted with enthusiasm and constructed with rapidity. American mechanics and toolmakers competed with European rivals. There was widespread interest in and support for scientific progress. Physical improvement had become inextricably connected with the genius of American civilization. Visiting the United States in the 1830s, Harriet Martineau was fascinated by the Moon Hoax. She argued, however, that its success was misleading. Americans learned of real scientific advances more quickly than they were taken in by frauds. In any other nation, she went on, the Moon Hoax would have fooled a far larger proportion of the population than in America, because Americans were becoming scientifically educated and alert to the possibilities and varieties of technological change.

In emphasizing American scientific literacy Harriet Martineau got hold of the right issue, but from the wrong end. American experience with science and technology was crucial to the hoaxing attempts, but this experience led not to less credulity but to more. A vital factor in the success of the hoaxes was national skepticism itself. Men accustomed to examining the truth or validity of every person, idea, object or act presented to them – as Americans proverbially were – became easy targets for pseudoscientific explanations, for detailed descriptions of fictional machinery, for any fantasy that was couched in the bland neutrality of a technological vocabulary. Men priding themselves on their rationalistic, scientific bent, familiar with the operation of novel machines, aware of the variety of nature, tended to accept as true anything which seemed to work – or seemed likely to work. The coming of steam, of railroads, of telegraphs indicated the futility of declaring anything impossible or incredible. Nothing mechanical was beyond the range of Nature's imagination. . . .

Not only was the predisposition to accept the mechanically probable or the organically possible a result of changing technology and the growth of natural science, it was also a peculiarly patriotic position in Jacksonian America. At a time when the advantages of a common school education were being extolled by reformers, when the common sense of the average citizen was proposed as a guarantee for the republic's future, many avid democrats assumed that any problem could be expressed clearly, concisely and comprehensively enough for the ordinary man to resolve it. Secret information and private learning were anathema. All knowledge was meant to be shared. Contemporary pamphleteers delighted in ridiculing experts and specialists; the expert turned out frequently to be a pedantic ignoramus, easily fooled himself; the learned doctor was often a victim of scientific nonsense and deserved to be overruled by intelligent laymen. 'When *doctors* disagree', Barnum had phrased it in his mermaid advertisement, then it was up to ordinary men to decide for themselves. . . .

Technological progress and egalitarian self-confidence combined to make many Americans certain of their own opinions – and so, easy prey for the hoaxers. And these traits were supplemented by the sheer exhilaration of debate, the utter fun of the opportunity to learn and evaluate, whether the subject was an ancient slave, an exotic mermaid, or a politician's honour. Barnum's audiences found the encounter with potential frauds exciting. It was a form of intellectual exercise, stimulating even when literal truth could not be determined. Machinery was beginning to accustom the public not merely to a belief in the continual appearance of new marvels but to a jargon that concentrated on methods of operation, on aspects of mechanical organization and construction, on horsepower, gears, pulleys and safety valves.

The language of technical explanation and scientific description itself had become a form of recreational literature by the 1840s and 1850s. Newspapers, magazines, even novels and short stories catered to this passion for detail. Manuals on almost every conceivable activity poured forth from American presses. . . .

Nowhere was the zest for operational description better satisfied than in the sea novels that figured prominently on American reading lists of the Jacksonian era. The complexity of the great sailing ship, the varied activities of the crew, the complex task of coordinating the rapid raising and lowering of the sails to meet the challenges of weather and position, formed a staple for the novelists. . . .

The novels of Herman Melville contained, in addition to the depiction of sailing and harpooning operations, immense and erudite discussions of anatomy, geology, and physiology. Floods of data, anecdotes, measurements, whaling lore, manipulated more skillfully by

Melville than by any contemporary writer, overwhelmed the reader in his passage through the book. Such detail satisfied the same relish for acquiring knowledge that led to travel literature, how-to-do-it manuals, and almanacs of useful information.

This delight in learning explains why the experience of deceit was enjoyable even after the hoax had been penetrated, or at least during the period of doubt and suspicion. Experiencing a complicated hoax was pleasurable because of the competition between victim and hoaxer, each seeking to outmanoeuvre the other, to catch him off-balance and detect the critical weakness. Barnum, Poe, Locke and other hoaxers didn't fear public suspicion; they invited it. They understood, most particularly Barnum understood, that the opportunity to debate the *issue* of falsity, to discover how deception had been practiced, was even more exciting than the discovery of fraud itself. The manipulation of a prank, after all, was as interesting a technique in its own right as the presentation of genuine curiosities. Therefore, when people paid to see frauds, thinking they were true, they paid again to hear how the frauds were committed. Barnum reprinted his own ticket-seller's analysis. 'First he humbugs them, and then they pay to hear him tell how he did it. I believe if he should swindle a man out of twenty dollars, the man would give a quarter to hear him tell about it.' . . .

There is one final reason why American audiences responded to Barnum's techniques and so enjoyed practical joking. The practice of humbugging solved some special problems of the mass sensibility, problems particularly acute in America, where cultural ambitions outstripped cultural achievements. Concentration on whether a particular show, exhibit, or event was real or false, genuine or contrived, narrowed the task of judgment for the multitude of spectators. It structured problems of experiencing the exotic and unfamiliar by reducing that experience to a simple evaluation.

Many Americans, however much they admired and

respected the realm of art, feared its mysteries. They were uncomfortable encountering masterpieces because they could neither analyse nor justify their reactions. Art exhibitions, when they were organized with theatrical settings and sentimental appeals – Hiram Powers's sensationally popular 'Greek Slave', for example – were crowded with onlookers. And patriotic appeals aided the art unions of the forties and fifties in distributing thousands of lithographs of landscapes and genre paintings. But these were, on the whole, exceptional experiences. No great public galleries existed for the public to stroll through, no historic buildings featured ancient murals and statuary. Instead, paintings and sculpture stood alongside mummies, mastodon bones and stuffed animals. American museums were not, in the antebellum period, segregated temples of the fine arts, but repositories of information, collections of strange or doubtful data. Such indiscriminate assemblages made artistic objects take on the innocent yet familiar shape of exhibition curiosities. Contemplating a painting or a statue was not so different from studying Napoleon's cane or wood from Noah's ark; in every instance, a momentary brush with a historical artefact stimulating reflections on its cost, age, detail and rarity.

The American Museums then, as well as Barnum's elaborate hoaxes, trained Americans to absorb knowledge. This was an aesthetic of the operational, a delight in observing processes and examining for literal truth. In place of intensive spiritual absorption, Barnum's exhibitions concentrated on information and the problem of deception. Onlookers were relieved from the burden of coping with more abstract problems. Beauty, significance, spiritual values, could be bypassed in favour of seeking what was odd, or what worked, or was genuine. . . .

But it was in American fiction that the taste for exposure and problem-solving most convincingly appeared. The pre-eminent practitioner of the art was Edgar Allan Poe, with his famous studies of criminal detection. This period witnessed the birth of the modern detective story, and in C. Auguste Dupin, the hero of 'The Purloined Letter', 'The Murders in the Rue Morgue' and 'The Mystery of Marie Roget', Poe created one of the archetypes of detective fiction, the detached, powerful, analytic intellect who solved crimes of the greatest mystery by logical method and intensive empathizing. In 'The Murders in the Rue Morgue' Dupin proves even before he discovers the evidence that the true killer of two women in a Paris apartment had to be an orangoutang, and much of the story deals with the steps which lead him to this conclusion. Poe begins the tale by apostrophizing the analytical intellect: 'As the strong man exults in his physical ability, delighting in such exercises as call his muscles into action, so glories the analyst in that moral activity which Disentangles. He derives pleasure from even the most trivial occupations bringing his talent into play. He is fond of enigmas, of conundrums, hieroglyphics; exhibiting in his solutions of each a degree of acumen which appears to the ordinary apprehension praeternatural.' This was also a description of the person who delighted in the competitiveness of Barnum's exhibitions, who sought to measure his wits against a master hoaxer, who enjoyed the intellectual exercise of disentangling the true from the false, the spurious from the genuine.

Reason alone, to be sure, was insufficient for the great detective. In 'The Purloined Letter' the Paris police, 'persevering, ingenious, cunning and thoroughly versed in the knowledge which their duties seem chiefly to demand', fail to discover a stolen document they know to be in the hands of a government minister. Dupin is more successful because he measures the minister as a man and a mind before deciding what he could have done with the letter. The police consider only 'their *own* ideas of ingenuity; and, in searching for any thing hidden', refer 'only to the modes in which *they* would have hidden it'. When the cunning of the felon differs from their own, the felon foils them. 'They have no variation of principle in their investigations.' Problem-solving of the highest sort, then, was not simply a rarefied strategy of logical rules; it demanded insight into personality and character, a knowledge of the ways of the world, a willingness to burrow into the temperament of other men and uncover the springs of action that push them forward. Dupin, like Barnum, never made the mistake of assuming that all men would reflect his tastes and proclivities; he acted only after observation and generalization permitted him to categorize the possibilities and vary his techniques.

Poe's artistic intentions, certainly, were complex, and his tales of mystery touched on interests not directly related to the operational aesthetic. Yet his stories exerted an immediate appeal and enthralled his readers because of their controlled problems; his audience joined with the protagonist to discover the intricacies of the puzzle and enjoyed the lengthy expositions that demonstrated the true facts. In the popular 1845 edition of Poe's tales, Evert A. Duyckinck, the editor, selected the three detective stories as part of his total of twelve, leaving out others that Poe considered among his best. For many, Poe's mystery tales actually came to symbolize mental training, and they served this use even in political campaigning.

In 1860, shortly before the presidential election, William Dean Howells wrote a brief but influential campaign biography of Abraham Lincoln. Howells faced the problem of proving that this little-known western lawyer, poorly educated, with few intellectual pretensions, was really quite intelligent, and equal to the burdens of the office he sought. Howells turned to Lincoln's reading habits to make his point. Having a mathematical bent of mind, he wrote, Lincoln was naturally pleased 'with the absolute and logical method of Poe's tales and sketches, in which the problem of mystery is given, and wrought out into every-day facts by processes of cunning analysis'. In the isolation of the rural Midwest men could sharpen their wits by studying the clever reasoning of C. Auguste Dupin. Lincoln allowed no year to go by without reading some Poe, added Howells to clinch his argument.

Poe's fascination with cryptography also satisfied the taste for problem-solving. In various issues of *Alexander's Weekly Messenger* for 1840, and in the summer of 1841 in *Graham's Magazine*, Poe published a series of ciphers with some solutions to them. Wide public interest was aroused, and readers sent codes in for Poe to solve. In a three-month period in 1840, fifteen articles on ciphers appeared in *Alexander's* and thirty-six ciphers were published or referred to. Poe did not explain his methods at this point, but waited until he published 'The Gold Bug'. Here, W.K. Wimsatt, Jr., has written, 'in dramatized form, with the romantic adjuncts of invisible ink, a golden scaraboeus, a skull and a buried treasure', Poe revealed his method of translating ciphers, 'for which fireside cogitators have long awaited. It was a master stroke of selling strategy', stimulating the interest of readers with tempting glimpses of cryptographic methods, but satisfying them only in his finished tale. That Poe's analysis contained important errors was less important than the impression he made on his contemporaries as a man of great analytical power, whetting their appetite for its continual demonstration. . . .

22
Peter Pan and the commercialization of the child
Jacqueline Rose

. . . There is one question asked by children which is almost as hard to answer as where babies come from and that is how money is *made*. How can you explain to a child how you make something which always comes from somewhere or somebody else? Perhaps it is because of this difficulty, and not just because of the seeming insatiability of children's demands, that we so often resort to insisting that 'money doesn't grow on trees'. We could try saying simply that money doesn't *grow* at all. But it does. It accumulates according to processes that are often as invisible to us as to children. Making money, like sex, is another one of those always mystified processes which then gets converted into a childhood taboo – which might be another reason why it is so difficult to trace its movements, other than symptomatically, in the history of literature for the child.

Peter Pan, as has already been mentioned, accumulated vast sums of money. But whereas we could see that money (its quantity) as helping us to define the value of *Peter Pan* (just what is it worth?), instead it only makes it more obscure. One look at the extent of the commercialization of *Peter Pan* is enough to establish that we do not really know what we are talking about when we refer to *Peter Pan*. In its history to date, *Peter Pan* has stood for, or been converted into, almost every conceivable (and some inconceivable) material forms: toys, crackers, posters, a Golf Club, Ladies League, stained glass window in St James's Church, Paddington, and a 5,000-ton Hamburg–Scandinavia car ferry. As if only too aware of the infinite convertibility of their gift, the Great Ormond Street Hospital asks in contracts (Legitimate Stage Rights, Musical in Arena Production Rights, Animated Cartoon Rights, Live Motion Picture Rights, Puppet Rights and Television Rights) for a percentage on merchandise which is double that on producer's profits.

Peter Pan is, therefore, more than *one* – it is repeated, reproduced, revived and converted in a seemingly endless spiralling chain. But it is seen to represent *oneness*. And that oneness conceals the multiplicity of commodities, the accumulation of money, and the non-identity of the child audience and reader to whom it so awkwardly relates. In the case of the play, we have seen the easy confusion, or conflation, of child-spectacle, child-performer and child-audience – the idea of the third allowing us to gloss over the more insistent and difficult reality of the first two. In the book trade, we are dealing not only with the relative homogeneity of an upper-middle-class audience which finds the most perfect image for its own self-identity in the child, but with different markets and different readers. And these differences make all the more apparent the mystification which we perpetuate whenever we take as a simple point of reference the idea of *a* book for *the* child. We can start with the crudest level of value – the price of the book, that is, its own declaration of what it is worth.

In *The Bookseller* for August 1981, a new edition of J.M. Barrie's *Peter Pan and Wendy* is advertised for £7.95. It appears in the advertisement section for the over-fives along with gift books which include Kay Nielsen's illustrated edition of *The Fairy Tales of Hans Christian Andersen*. This last book is priced at £6.95, the same price as the other collection of Hans Christian Andersen fairy tales which is advertised. The fact is worth noting only because these books (with *Peter Pan and Wendy* at the fore) are conspicuously the most expensive books on the page. In 1979, an advertisement in the *Peter Pan* programme of His Majesty's Theatre, Aberdeen, offered Eleanor Graham's retelling of *Peter and Wendy* at £3.95, and a facsimile of the 1921 edition at £7.95: 'to mark the centenary of the birth of Mabel Lucie Attwell and the 75th anniversary of *Peter Pan*'s first appearance a special gift edition containing Sir James Barrie's full length story together with Mabel Lucie Attwell's original illustrations has just been produced'. As is the case in the theatre, when *Peter Pan* appears, it carries with it the weight (and the price) of its history. *Peter Pan* can be retold (£3.95), or else it can be issued as a prized relic of publishing history (£7.95), and relics are worth their weight in gold.

Peter Pan was in this sense a relic before it started. First published as *Peter Pan in Kensington Gardens* in 1906 in an 'Edition de luxe', it belonged to the category of collector's items, first editions and important works, which already included a number of books problematically identified with a child audience, such as Andrew Lang's *Green Fairy Book* of 1893 and Arthur Rackham's first big illustrated *Rip Van Winkle*, which had been published in 1905. These books presented the 'best' of publishing – they were the 'leading items' of artistic production.[1] Barrie's book was oversubscribed, and reviewed in the Fine Art and Archaeology sections of *The Athenaeum* (December 1906) and *The Book Monthly* (December 1906). This is where *Peter Pan* first appears as a book – a children's book only to the extent that these venerated archaeological treasures were classics which had already been (although not originally), or else were on the point of being, associated with, and then given to, the child.

A gift can be an aggressive act. Marcel Mauss, the anthropologist, has described communities which exchange gifts of gradually ascending value in order to drive their opposite number into economic collapse.[2]

Children's gift books are better seen as belonging some-where between a bribe and a demand – a bribe of the purchasing adult and a demand on the receiving child. John Newberry's first book for children was advertised in 1744 as a guarantee of strength, health, virtue, wisdom and happiness in the receiving child (a tall order).[3] One of the chief ways of ensuring the circulation of children's books has been their use as prizes, with the book as a reward for a correctness which it is intended to encourage. In my school, prizes had to be selected from a fixed list of books (presumably in case we all went wild). According to the historians of children's fiction, it was the late Victorians who turned the use of children's books as prizes into a 'standard trade'.[4]

The period when *Peter Pan* was first produced as a book shares with the last three decades of this century its expansiveness in the field of children's books. In the first half of the nineteenth century, booksellers redefined themselves as 'publishers', establishing themselves as what could be recognized as the British book trade by the second half of the century. In the last three decades of the twentieth century, children's books have once again become (after a comparative lull) a 'major field of publishing and international exchange'.[5] The value of these glossy books of the late nineteenth century, of which Barrie's text was one, can therefore be seen as the celebration of an expanding industry, the spectacle-on-paper of a growing financial concern. Books, no less than theatre, were part of a visual display in which children offered up some of the richest potential for the trade. The late nineteenth-century child was 'grist to the mill' of the miscellaneous bookseller.[6] In 1896, *The Bookman* added a special section on children's books to its Christmas Supplement on illustrated books which, together with popular magazines and fairy tales, were the most commercially viable products of the market. The fairly tale was, therefore, good business first; the idea of children's books came second. The confused association between children and fairies reproduces itself in the commercial history of children's books, and continues to this day. Writing on the recent expansion in output of children's books, Naomi Lewis talks of the popularity of 'books about children or fairies; or both'.[7]

In his Appendix to the 1982 edition of Darton's *Children's Books in England*, Brian Alderson lists as the main factors in the late nineteenth-century publication of children's books: the private consumption of books in the home, the establishment of the prize, the beginnings of children's book criticism, and the expressiveness of a writer like Beatrix Potter, 'the uncompromising story-teller, knowing that *her* way is the way that the story needs to go and that the children will follow her'.[8] Alderson lists these features in order to demonstrate that the new freedom in children's writing started in the late nineteenth century, as a corrective to Darton's belief that the main breakthrough came later (with the appearance of *Peter Pan*). There is an irony in this (the perverseness, as Alderson puts it, of associating freedom in children's literature with the moment when it becomes an object of investigation by adults). For what this list offers is children's literature as an uncompromising, newly self-conscious, self-promoting and self-commenting material concern ('children *will* follow'). The freedom of children's literature seems to lie somewhere between the freedom of a market economy and *Peter Pan*.

In this context, the heavy commercial promotion of *Peter Pan* becomes more than an incidental factor of its history. It reveals both how marketable the child was for the book trade, and the gap which could in fact hold between this reality and something which might finally reach its destination as literature for children. Hodder and Stoughton, who published *Peter Pan*, were not children's publishers, but Barrie was one of their most successful and heavily promoted writers, and they had their own publicity journal, *The Bookman*, which was started in 1891 (this was exactly the time when the publicity journal was castigated by booksellers for its commercialization of the trade). The advance promotion

for *The Little White Bird* included a half-page advertisement in *The Publisher's Circular* which announced that
it was to be 'the greatest success of the season'.[9]
Between 1903 and 1911, *The Bookman* produced no less
than seven portfolios and supplements on *Peter Pan*. The
1905 Christmas number, for example, with a Barrie
photograph on the cover and a supplement of photographs from the play, had reached a 200 per cent
premium on its original price by November 1906 (*Peter
Pan* already a 'collector's item'). It was on the back of
this that *Peter Pan in Kensington Gardens* was issued in
the following year.

The publication of *Peter Pan in Kensington Gardens*
therefore had very little to do with a child reader. Rather
it illustrates just how far the child had become one of the
chief fantasies – object of desire and investment – of the
turn of the century publishing trade. Thus its publication
has been taken to show that children were now considered 'worthy of loveliness, not to say aesthetic
luxury'[10] – as if they could assimilate into themselves,
and render innocent (again), the more glaring commercial
realities of the trade.

Luxury is never a neutral concept. In the world of
children's books, it signals both class and excess ('the
well-to-do classes almost forced their offspring into a
surfeit')[11] – not so much an achievement, or consumma-
tion, as the beginnings of a divide. If *Peter Pan in Kensington Gardens* was indeed eloquent of 'child
glorification', then that eloquence and its associated
value had its reverse image in contemporary complaints
about the debasement of literary value and the cheapen-
ing of literary taste. The advent of the cheap (seven
pence) reprint was seen by its critics as leading to the
overproduction and general devaluation of fiction:
'Fiction, like every other article, should have a fixed
value'.[12] This already shows the volatile and contradictory nature of ideas of literary value at this time. But, in
relation to children's fiction, the importance of the cheap
reprint lies in the fact that it was associated by its critics

with the development of a new child reader – not the receiver of the Christmas gift, but the child who was emerging from the recently compulsory elementary schools. The overproduction of fiction meant, by implication, an overproduction of the educated child:

> Quantity not quality – is that what is now demanded in a reprint? Every year thousands of new readers are being sent forth by the Board Schools, and naturally they are first attracted to books by what may be called the 'story interest' of these. But by-and-by the same readers evolve a minority who take a deeper critical interest in what they read. That then is the road which leads to a scholarly reprint, and so, ultimately, its fortunes are secure.[13]

Only a minority (the argument anticipates F.R. Leavis) can ultimately ensure the value (and the price) of books.

The idea that there was a sudden expansion of literary output to encounter the new literacy is now thought to be mistaken. The point here, however, is that *commercially* the child did not form a homogeneous market. When *Peter Pan* was written, that market was divided between the child *recipient* of the Christmas gift and the child *reader*, the former the object of a new and increasing commercial attention (aesthetic luxury and value), the latter the displaced focus of anxieties about the commercial and literary effects on the book trade of the changing educational policy of the state (overproduction, devaluation).

Thus the question of what children were reading carried the weight of anxiety about literary degeneration and cultural decay. 'Blood and thunder' stories were a 'menace to juvenile civilisation';[14] they were rubbish ('What Boys Do Read – the Need for Stemming a River of Yellow Rubbish'),[15] and were leading to a decay of the infantile mind: 'when our books are bought as rubbish, sold as rubbish, and received as rubbish, it is perhaps natural for anyone to suppose that they are read and written in the same spirit'.[16] The objection was as much to the form in which these books appeared (papers rather than bound books) as it was to the content of the stories.

In the attacks on the quality of this literature, it was compared with the contemporary music hall, with the complaint that the better books by Verne, Henty, Reed and Kingston normally associated with boys' literary culture were now only bought by parents and their friends. The distinction between the two different types of child reader was, therefore, a distinction between a classic children's literary culture still largely dominated by the adult market (literary tradition) and the emergence of an autonomous children's literature which was being negatively identified with aspects of working-class culture. The 'cheapness' ascribed to the latter clearly went beyond the question of price, since the same journals which criticized the development of cheap boys' fiction were simultaneously praising the new technology of the three-colour process which made it possible to produce colour illustrated books for children at a lower price than before. This new gift book was not *cheap*, it was *natural* ('The New Gift-Book, the Arrival of Naturalness and the Three-Colour Picture')[17] – as 'natural', that is, as the comfort of the nursery which this new gift book mirrored back to itself: 'Now the nursery is getting what it most likes, a mirror of itself'.[18]

The Peter Pan Picture Book published at five shillings by Bell in 1907, probably falls into this category of the cheaper colour illustrated book for children.[19] Unlike *Peter Pan in Kensington Gardens*, it was listed as a children's book by *The Book Monthly* when it was published in 1907, and again in a new edition at three shillings and sixpence in 1911, to the exclusion of J.M. Barrie's *Peter and Wendy* which was published that year.

In this context, the circulation of *Peter Pan* (it has by now been published in every conceivable price range), and its value, take on a new meaning – that of a wholly generalized concept of culture which cannot see the divisions on which it rests. The aestheticization, the glorification, the valuing of the child – to which its first publication so eloquently bears witness – act as a kind of cover for these differences, of reader and address, differences which manifest themselves in the very physical substance of the book. If we look at the children's book market, its identity falls apart, exposing the gaps between producer (writer), distributor (bookseller or publisher), purchaser (parent, friends and/or children) and the consumer (ideally, but only ideally, the child). These spaces, missed meeting points, places of imposition, exploitation (or even glorification of the child) are not entirely different in kind from those which characterize other aspects of the literary life of our culture. They are not exclusive to the world of children's books. But there is something about the totality, the oneness, of *Peter Pan*'s status as a myth which makes them appear as an affront – the affront, for example, of claiming, as I would, that J. M. Barrie never wrote a version of *Peter Pan* (on stage or on paper) for children.

I would say that the responses of children to *Peter Pan* (for responses there have undoubtedly been) can in no sense be deducted from its material success (great as this, equally undoubtedly, has been); but that this success, and the corresponding status of *Peter Pan*, say something about the fantasies which our culture continues to perpetuate – about its own worth, its future and its traditions – through the child. That the child serves above all as a fantasy in all of this is given perhaps most clearly in the image of the little girl with twisted knees and head thrown back in ecstasy, an image off which we read that a fragment of our cultural history still survives; or else in the image of the beautiful book, the imprint or insignia of a value which, at the beginning of the century at least, we could still see as infinitely expanding throughout the world.

One of the strongest weights which *Peter Pan* carries is something which I would call the aesthetic mode – a system of values attaching to language and literature which we tend to take for granted, and whose very universality serves to close off the divisions in culture of the type which I have described in this chapter in relation to children's literature. A week after Barrie died in 1937, the *Times Literary Supplement* published a long article in which the question of *Peter Pan*'s survival drew onto itself the whole question, not just of Barrie's survival as a dramatist, but of what – in general – *can* survive, of what *is* endurance, perpetuity and eternal worth. This worth, defined by the article as true literature or literature as truth, finally dispenses with the present, with what might be the responsibility now. Because if *Peter Pan* survives, we all survive, and the problem of the present, and its difficulty, no longer has to be asked:

> No dramatist has ever been more perilous to criticism than Barrie within a week of his death . . . when everything has been said of the technical adroitness, the darting humour, the narrative skill of his other plays, the problem of Barrie's survival remains the problem of *Peter Pan*; and this not by any means because he is to be recognised as a 'one-play' dramatist but because what will cause his other plays to endure, if anything does, is that element of fantasy, or, as some would have it, of the seer, in them which in *Peter Pan* has its most concentrated expression. . . . If *Peter Pan* is fashionable sentimentality . . . then the whole of Barrie's theatre is refused its major claim. But if *Peter Pan* is in the succession to *Cinderella*, if it is not a Christmas pantomime but one of those stories that embody and perpetuate the intuitive wisdom of childlike humanity, then Barrie's work will be in flower when all the 'intellectual and social forces' of our time, Ibsen, Strindberg or Shaw, have vanished even from the encyclopedias. *Peter Pan* is, in this sense, the greatest of all critical gambles . . . The problem may be grappled a little more closely if we are prepared to grant that the test of validity in any work of art is its realism *on its own plane*. Whether it makes a contribution to contemporary thought is not relevant; whether it represents superficial experience, past or present – whether or not it is 'like' something that its audience recognises – is not relevant; whether it is moral, immoral, or non-moral is not relevant. The test is that an artist has not polluted his own imagining, whether naturalistic,

fantastic or mystical, with stuff borrowed from others or from a different self, and that, having thus preserved the purity of his idea, he has stuck fearlessly for the whole truth – that is the essence of it.

It is upon this ground – that it blinks its own truth – that those who condemn *Peter Pan* must justify their criticism . . . It is possible to point to the continuing vitality of the play during a quarter of a century, to remember what delight many – but not all – children have in it, and to say:— 'This is work which, in fact, confounds your analysis. You may prove a thousand flaws in it, but still it goes on. It goes on because its audiences are unaware, as Barrie himself was unaware, that it is spiritual autobiography.

'To them the confusions, the contradictions, the avoidances that you complain of resemble the inconsequence of their own dreams, and the thing before their eyes has the quality of a legend that they are making up for themselves.' If this be true, it means that Barrie had the power which is much greater than that of story-telling of compelling successive generations to invent his story afresh, to tell it to themselves and in their own terms – that is to say, he was able not merely to instruct or entertain but to impregnate the collective mind of his audience. And if he did, indeed, possess this power, which is precisely the power of the great fairy-tales, criticism may as well throw its pen away, for then he is immortal by election and there is no more to be said about it.[20]

If, therefore, *Peter Pan* survives, it is because there is a realm of literature which stares unblinkingly at the truth, which strides over flaws and inconsistencies, over the intellectual and social forces of our time, straight into the collective mind of its audience. 'Intuition', 'wisdom', 'truth' and the 'childlike humanity' of the collective – these are all terms which have appeared together before. What is different here is the way that they are assimilated to a concept of the *literary* as truth (the whole truth) – staring unblinkingly and, I would say, blinded by the feat. In this context, that *Peter Pan* should end up at the Barbican is fitting in another sense. For it fulfils the wish which I have often seen expressed that *Peter Pan* should at last be freed from the wrong connotations of infancy (mere childishness) and into the upper reaches of our cultural life ('the intuitive wisdom of childlike humanity'),[21] by being interpreted by a director such as Peter Brooke or performed at the National Theatre as a wholly serious play.[22] . . .

Notes

1 *The Bookman*, January 1906, p. 150.
2 See Mauss, M. (1954) *The Gift: Form and Function of Exchange in Archaic Societies*, London: Cohen and West.
3 See Newberry, J. (1744) *A Little Pretty Pocket Book* (facsimile edition M.F. Thwaite, London: Oxford University Press, 1966).
4 Darton, F.J.H. (1932) 'The youth of a children's magazine', *Cornhill*, May. Reprinted as Appendix 4 to Darton (1982) *Children's Books in England, Five Centuries of Social Life* (edited by Brian Alderson), Cambridge: Cambridge University Press, p. 322.
5 Lewis, Preface to Kirkpatrick, D. (ed.) (1978) *Twentieth-Century Children's Writers*, London: Macmillan, p. vii.
6 *The Bookman*, December 1891, p. 105.
7 Lewis, Preface to Kirkpatrick (1978), p. vii.
8 Appendix to Darton, op. cit., p. 328.
9 *The Publisher's Circular*, 15 November 1902, p. 539.
10 Darton, op. cit., p. 311.
11 ibid., p. 311.
12 *The Bookman*, June 1909, p. 636.
13 *The Book Monthly*, February 1906, p. 292.
14 Darton, op. cit., p. 311.
15 *The Book Monthly*, 4 September 1910, pp. 883–5.
16 *Guardian*, 2 May 1900.
17 *The Book Monthly*, January 1907, pp. 223–38.
18 ibid., p. 224.
19 Published by O'Connor and Woodward, 1907.
20 *Times Literary Supplement*, 26 June 1937, pp. 469–70 (front page feature).
21 *Guardian*, 23 December 1977.
22 Eric Shorter in the *Daily Telegraph*, 6 December 1979.

23
Figures of Bond
Tony Bennett and Janet Woollacott

'I am very much a Domino sort of girl myself. A fun-loving extrovert. Whatever it is I am doing I enjoy doing it – loving, driving, riding, shopping, travelling, even cooking.'

As alluring as all of Fleming's girls are, there is always some masculine trait about them . . . 'Even so', says Claudine, 'they are essentially feminine, the ultimate in modern, emancipated woman.'

'They can live without a man doing everything for them because they are independent. They like to decide their future destinies for themselves. They are highly sexual – but only with men worth their loving. They are free, you see, completely free. I may be married, but I feel I am like this. I am free. I always have been. I always will be.'[1]

So said Claudine Auger, who played Domino Vitali in *Thunderball*, reported in a 1965 fanzine. A decade later, in a *TV Times* feature, she is quoted again on the subject of 'the Bond girl':

I think a woman needs to feel the strength of a man to acknowledge his superiority. The fact that young men today are not strong is basically the fault of women who dress to look like boys. A woman should always keep her femininity. I like the Bond girls because they are free, they make love easily and they are on equal terms when it comes to intelligence. But they are essentially feminine.

I married an older man because he knew what life was about. And he married me because I have a feminine body. I would not dare to put on the trousers unless I was going horse-riding or hunting.[2]

Both passages typify the ways in which the figures of actresses and actors have been constructed and made to stand in relation to the Bond films. Functioning as simulacres for either Bond or 'the Bond girl', their lives, views and preferences have been made to mimic the fictional world of Bond in order that that world might appear not entirely fictional. Life is thus modelled on fiction in order that fiction, in appearing to reflect real life, might also serve as a model for it. However, the differences between the two passages are equally noteworthy. In the first, the concept of the 'essentially feminine' is articulated to the 'emancipated woman' of the early 1960s whereas, in the second, it functions as a sign of women's necessary subordination to men, limiting the possible scope of women's emancipation in specifying the 'laws of nature' it must respect.

This shift is symptomatic of the general change in the ideological currency of Bond and 'the Bond girl' between the early 1960s and the 1970s as the emphasis moved away from the construction of new and relatively more independent forms of gender identity and sexuality, for women as well as for men, towards the placing of women – already 'too greatly emancipated' – back into a 'properly subalterned' position in relation to men. As we have seen, this was one of the major transformations associated with the Bond films of the 1970s. It is all the more interesting, therefore, that the occasion for the second interview with Claudine Auger was the first television screening of the Bond films produced in the 1960s. In thus being activated for consumption via a different construction of 'the Bond girl', their relations to ideologies of gender and sexuality were, at least tendentially, reordered in being brought into line with the specific network of ideological concerns which the figures of Bond and 'the Bond girl' served to condense and articulate in the 1970s.

This example nicely illustrates our purpose in this chapter, to examine the various 'texts of Bond' which, in contributing to the expanded reproduction of the figure of Bond, have also played their part in remodelling that figure culturally and ideologically. In doing so, we shall relate our discussions to a number of more general concerns.

First, we shall consider the active part such texts play in organizing and reorganizing the social and ideological relations of popular reading. They function, in effect, similarly to the way in which criticism functions regarding the consumption of texts classified as 'literary' or, more generally, as being of serious cultural value. However, they do so by different means. In the case of valued texts which circulate under the name of an author, Foucault argues, criticism normally organizes their reading by constructing the author as the issuing source of their meaning.[3] Popular reading is more typically organized in accordance with different interpretative principles. Here, to put the point in terms of Foucault's formulations, the figure to which a text is made to point and which serves as a support for its meaning is not one which is outside and precedes it (the author), but one which is simultaneously outside and within it (the actor/actress as a cypher for the character portrayed). The result, in the case of the 'texts of Bond', has been the construction of a series of micro-narratives in which the 'real' biographies, views, tastes and preferences of Sean Connery and Roger Moore and the various actresses who have played opposite them have filled out and been filled out by the figures of Bond and 'the Bond girl'. These micro-narratives have thus run alongside and adjacent to the Bond novels and films, complementing them by means of a seeming mimesis whilst in fact actively organizing their consumption in particular ways.

While differently organized, however, such texts have effects similar to those produced by the functioning of criticism. In the case of texts classified as 'literary', criticism constitutes a series of bids and counter-bids concerning the inter-textual, ideological and cultural references which are to prevail in animating reading practices in a particular context. It is by the operation of this system of bids and counter-bids that a text is kept alive in history, yet always as other than just 'itself' since, in the process, its relations to history are constantly rewritten. In like manner, the 'texts of Bond' we are concerned with here have functioned as 'textual shifters', drawing the Bond novels and films into the orbit of activity of the different sets of ideological and cultural concerns that have been articulated around the figure of Bond at different points in time.

The implications of these considerations are far-reaching. A part of our concern in this study has been to study the Bond novels and films not as completed givens but in the light of the incessantly mobile reordering of the relations between them. One consequence of doing so is to call into question the assumption that the relations between a text classified as fiction and ideology can be determined, in an essentialist way and once and for all, purely by an examination of its internal formal properties. By considering the ways in which what we have called 'textual shifters' have located the Bond films and novels within different spheres of ideological action – or within the same spheres of ideological action, but placed in different and even contradictory relations to them at different points in time or within different reading formations – it will be possible to show that the question of the 'ideological effects' of the Bond films and novels cannot be resolved abstractly. Indeed, properly speaking, they have never had such effects but have rather functioned as pieces of play within different regions of ideological contestation, capable of being moved around differently within them. . . .

Textual shifters

While the ideological preoccupations discernible in the

'textual shifters' bearing most directly on the popular reading of the Bond novels and films have been fairly consistent in scope, their *relative weight* and *specific functioning* have varied considerably. We shall illustrate this by examining the changing function of the ideology of competitive individualism as articulated in relation to the figure of Bond, and by tracing some of the shifts in the representations of sexuality associated with Bond and 'the Bond girl'.

Jerry Palmer has argued that the distinguishing characteristic of the thriller genre consists in its organization of the relations between the values of amateurism and bureaucratic rigidity and, mediating between the two, those of professionalism in its 'combination of improvisation and programming'.[4] In the case of the Bond novels, Palmer suggests, Bond thus mediates between the values represented by 'the girl' and the villain. 'The girl' (sometimes) represents the values of amateurism in the sense that her actions are ineffective against the organized conspiracy of the villain and likely, moreover, to make life more difficult for the hero: Tilly Masterton's attempt to avenge her sister's death, for example, results in both Bond and Tilly being captured by Goldfinger. At the other extreme, the villain embodies the principle of planning carried to excess: he puts into operation a 'master plan', perfected down to the last detail, leaving no possible room for error or miscalculation. As a consequence, Palmer argues, the villain is 'often incapable of improvizing, and when a contingency that he has failed to foresee arises, he is completely lost'.[5] Bond combines the two virtues and, thereby, dissociates them from their negative aspects. A professional trained in his occupation, operating within a bureaucracy and, usually, with a back-up team, he none the less retains a capacity to improvise which usually turns the tables decisively in his contest with the villain. . . . In thus embodying an ideal blend of trained programming and improvisation, Palmer suggests, Bond constitutes an exemplary hero of capitalist competitive individualism constructed in opposition to the rigidities of communist totalitarianism.

It's true, of course, that the opposition between Bond's innovative professionalism and the dead hand of bureaucratic inertia played an important part in the constructions of Bond which predominated in the late 1950s. However, this came to be rather less important, in the early 1960s, than the way in which these qualities were made to stand for a new image of nationhood, fashioning, in Bond, the model for a new 'classless ruling class'. While the earlier, Cold War dimensions of these aspects of Bond's characterization were not entirely jettisoned, they typically survived only in muted and significantly modified forms. Connery's biography – the son of a Glaswegian van driver who made good, but solely through his own efforts and self-reliance, fighting his way to the top through a series of dead-end jobs and bit parts – was thus endlessly rehearsed, but usually with the effect of constructing these virtues in opposition to the allegedly morally sapping effects of welfare socialism, as part of a diagnostics of national decline, rather than in direct opposition to communist regimes.[6]

Christopher Brooker has commented on the widespread tendency, in the 1960s, to construe the period as a watershed marking a decisive break with the values of Britain's traditional Tory governing élite and those of 'old-fashioned' socialism.[7] Attributing the responsibility for the vicissitudes of Britain's post-war history to the contest between these two anachronistic forms of political and cultural leadership, Brooker argues that the tough, no-nonsense professionalism of a new meritocracy, recognizing no loyalties of class or any virtues other than those of ability, was widely regarded as heralding a new way forward for Britain. The key political figures in this respect were Heath and Wilson, the one portrayed as embodying the image of a modernized Toryism and the other, in shedding the shibboleths of socialism, as dragging a reluctant Labour Party into an age dominated by the 'white heat of science and technology'. In thus being grouped together, in spite of their different political philosophies, as exemplifying a critical temper opposed to the dodoism of tradition, Heath and Wilson served as representatives of a new 'spirit of the age'.

More immediately relevant to our concerns here was the operation of this discourse of modernization in the construction of new types of public heroes and heroines in the media, fashion, advertising and the cinema. Tracing the media's celebration of actors such as Terence Stamp, Michael Caine ('an anti-actor . . . exactly right for 1965 in his triumphant classlessness', according to a contemporary newspaper) and Connery himself, of novelists such as Len Deighton and John Braine and fashion designers like Mary Quant, Brooker contends that the result was to foster an image of a young, talent-based, classless, untraditional, anti-Establishment cultural élite which respected only dedicated professionalism and not birth or privilege. Something of the flavour and legacy of this period is captured in John Boorman's introduction to M.F. Callan's *Sean Connery: His Life and Films*:

> There is no bitterness about his [Connery's] deprived childhood. He looks upon it as an enriching experience. He suffered the customary humiliations of the British class system, but today moves up and down classes with tolerance and, above all, without modifying his own behaviour . . . I believe that Connery touches us because he personifies the best qualities that came out of the post-war upheavals in Britain. The reform of education, the busting of the BBC's monopoly, and so on allowed a lot of new talent to flourish . . . Connery is an archetype of what was best in those times. And that is his power. But like all archetypes, he also represents something timeless. His persona reaches back and touches a tradition in British life. I can best define that by suggesting characters that he could play better than anyone else:

> CAPTAIN COOK   TOM FINNEY
> THOMAS HARDY   W.G. GRACE

ISAMBARD BRUNEL   KEIR HARDY
                     DRAKE[8]

The shift in the signifying currency of the figure of Bond which resulted from its insertion in this discourse of modernization amounted to little less than an ideological *volte face*. Whilst, initially, Bond had supplied a point of fictional reference in relation to which an imperialist sense of nation and nationhood could be symbolically refurbished, he was now made to point in the opposite direction – towards the future rather than the past. Functioning as a figure of modernization, he became the very model of the tough, abrasive professionalism that was allegedly destined to lead Britain into the modern, no illusions, no holds-barred post-imperialist age, a hero of rupture rather than one of tradition. Or rather, as Boorman suggests, a hero of rupture *and* tradition, heralding a brighter future by recalling the virtues of a doughtier, more valiant and socially inclusive tradition of Englishness which could be opposed to the cloying and restrictive foibles of the Establishment.

This shift in Bond's ideological currency, while chiefly attributable to the first cycle of Bond films, was not limited to these or to their influence on the ways in which the novels were read. It was also discernible in the classificatory and contextualizing practices brought to bear on the 'texts of Bond'. One of the most telling examples of this was provided by the first edition of the *Sunday Times Colour Supplement*, published in 1962. Titled 'A Sharp Look at the Mood of Britain', its purpose was to discern the currents which had allegedly been slumbering within Britain and which, on the brink of awakening, were said to embody a strongly throbbing new sense of national purpose. The 'evidence' for this consisted of six articles on 'people who represent today' – an airline pilot, Jimmy McIlroy of Burnley Football Club, Peter Blake, Alan Little (a sociology lecturer), Sebastian de Ferranti and Mary Quant. Although from different walks of life and backgrounds, these were all portrayed as belonging to the same 'classless class', new leaders, committed to professionalism and efficiency, slicing through tradition like a knife through butter. Alan Little, for example, was described as follows:

> Dr Alan Little is 27 and a sociologist. A milkman's son from Liverpool with a brother at Trinity, Cambridge, he is married to a doctor, earns slightly more than £1,000 a year and lives in a Span house in Beckenham. . . . In his way he is typical of something new asserting itself in the life of Britain's Universities. . . . Men like him spell the death of the comfortable, feline, cloistered world which dons are supposed to inhabit. At Oxford or Cambridge, the donnish ideal that still lingers is that of the inspired amateur. By contrast, Little is a tough and highly dedicated professional. . . . And, during the last few years, men like him have been quietly setting the pattern for a new type of donnish society. . . . They live in a dispersed, classless society of their own and seem to value the universities for the freedom they have to probe society wherever it is most vulnerable.[9]

The final item in the supplement was a new Bond short story, specially written for the occasion, presenting Bond as a figure ranged alongside the exemplary biographies constructed in the preceding items, a mythic encapsulation and 'capping' of the discourse of modernization.

It might, of course, be argued that the Cold War construction of Bond's competitive individualism should be regarded as its 'true' or 'essential meaning', subsequently distorted in being adapted to a new set of ideological concerns. . . . There is, however, nothing to be gained in representing the relations between these readings such that one is privileged as 'truth' and the other devalued as 'distortion'. The most that can be established is that the novels served as a basis for one set of meanings when hooked into a particular set of ideological and cultural coordinates and for another set of readings when uncoupled from those coordinates and connected to new ones.

The same is true of the way the figure of Bond has functioned in relation to ideologies of gender and sexuality. The key 'textual shifters' in this respect have consisted in representations of the relations between Bond and 'the Bond girl'. Apart from varying between the early 1960s and the 1970s, these relations have also been differently constructed according to whether the envisaged readership has been male, female or mixed. Throughout all periods, the position of an implied male reader has predominated, and necessarily so, since any discussion which accepts the terms of reference suggested by the phrase 'the Bond girls' is committed to constructing female gender identities and forms of sexuality in relation to the norms of masculinity supplied by the figure of Bond.

The discourse of 'liberation' which governed representations of 'the Bond girls' in the early 1960s would thus be more accurately described as a discourse of female adjustment. A component of the discourse of modernization, the new set of identities it constructed for women was defined in relation to the requirements of a liberated male sexuality. Representations of 'the Bond girl', in portraying her as the subject of an independent and free sexuality, served only to make her instantly and always available – but only for men. 'They are women of the nuclear age', Terence Young argued, 'freer and able to make love when they want to without worrying about it'.[10] From a male point of view, this constituted a strategic and selective 'liberation' of women – free only in the areas (bed) and respects (sexuality) that 'liberated man' required. Moreover, the freedom of 'the Bond girl' was conceived as essentially masculine in form; she was, in fact, Bond's *alter ego*, fashioned in his image. As Luciana Paluzzi, who played Fiona in *Thunderball*, described her part: 'Yes rather like a female Bond in a way. She lives like he does. She's 100 per cent feminine – but able to do things men do.'[11]

The ideal represented by 'the Bond girl' in this period thus consisted of a harmonious blend of tradition, defined in female terms, and modernity, defined in male terms. Although sexually 'liberated', her sexuality, in being represented as merely the female equivalent of a promiscuous male genital sexuality, was devoid of any disturbing threat of otherness. At the same time, she was still 'essentially feminine', still knew 'her place', a place defined in relation to men and to the phallus. Here's Connery again, constructing for himself/Bond the role of Big Prick of the phallic order:

> All feminine women are mobile, adaptable. To be temperamentally mobile is to be like a wheel. The person at the hub is fixed, stable. The person at the end of the spoke goes round the hub. Such a person is mobile, adaptable. One of the first reactions of a mobile person is to cross the legs – men as well as women. If you are attracted to someone, you sit like this' – he leaned forward, knees apart, hands outstretched.[12]

In sum, 'the Bond girl' of the 1960s disconnected female sexuality from traditional female gender identities, preserving these latter virtually intact (although adding to them the requirement of competence in outdoor and physical pursuits) whilst articulating the former to male defined norms of genital sexuality. In essence, her sexuality was the product of a licensed distribution of phallic attributes from men to women. Since the 1970s, this licensed adjustment of traditional norms of female sexuality has given way before an obsessive concern to effect a redistribution of phallic attributes back from women to men. Publicity posters for the Bond films of this period thus typically represented the relations between Bond and 'the Bond girl' in the form of a contest between two rival sources of phallic power and authority.

The poster for *For Your Eyes Only*, read from an anxious male perspective, is a case in point. The foreground is dominated by the buttocks and legs of a girl clad in swimming wear and seen from the rear. She stands with legs astride, the relations between her two feet – clad in high-heeled shoes – and her crotch form a triangle with the crotch forming the apex. Her right hand holds a cross-bow, sprung for action and armed with an arrow, pointing to the ground. Bond is framed within the triangle formed by the girl's legs and crotch. Diminished by the girl's domination of the foreground – his head is level with her knees – Bond is placed directly below the girl's crotch, gun in hand with his gaze directed anxiously not to the viewer or to the girl's face but to her crotch. Outside the triangle formed by the girl's legs, a variety of action scenes from the film are depicted – a car chase, an underwater sequence, etc. The 'adventure' elements of the plot are thus relegated to the margins of the composition, a series of escapades which have a distinctly Boy's Own flavour compared with the central challenge which Bond has to respond to: restoring the symbolic order of the phallus by 'outgunning' the girl whose phallic power threatens to overwhelm him.

In earlier posters, by contrast, the contest between Bond and the girl was more usually portrayed as in the process of being resolved, or as already having been resolved, in Bond's favour. In the posters for the first cycle of Bond films, the subordination of women takes the form of a fetishization of the body of the hero. Typically, the image of Connery/Bond predominates, his phallic authority represented by fetishistic symbols of male power. The girl or girls are usually portrayed as significantly smaller than Connery/Bond, and adopting positions of dependency and subservience in relation to him. The poster for *Thunderball* (1965) portrays Connery/Bond kneeling in a wet-suit with one knee up and a loaded spear-gun pointing up vertically from between his thighs. He is surrounded by four women, kneeling or lying before him, a sea of swooning and dependent femininity belittled by the preponderance of his physical presence. The poster for *Live and Let Die* (1973) strikes a more shrill and anxious note. It consists of five playing cards bevilled towards the viewer so that the central one is larger than the rest. The women portrayed in the frames of each of the two cards on either side of the central card are thus perspectivally diminished by the figure of Moore/Bond emerging from the central card, breaking its frame, with gun to cheek. A piece of flame-spurting artillery juts from between his thighs with a girl placed astride it.

Such shifts in time in the signifying currency of Bond and of 'the girl' are rather less important than the differences between the ways in which that currency has been manifested, and contested, in 'textual shifters' aimed at different groups of readers. The cult of Bond has thus been explicitly attacked in women's magazines. *Nova* published a hard-hitting article by Mordecai Richler who attributes Bond's popularity to a regressed formation of male sexuality, locked into the pre-Oedipal phase in its inability to recognize the otherness and autonomy of female sexuality.[13] However, this is the only piece of an explicitly analytical and critical nature that we have come across in women's magazines. More typical was the attempt to puncture the illusionism of the Bond films in a 1979 *Woman's Own* feature on 'Glamour Girls in Bondage'. This consisted mainly of interview material with a series of minor starlets who take the lid off the way the glamour of 'the Bond girls' is carefully contrived and produced, and discuss the personal problems which arise from their surrendering control over their bodies to the studio. The editorial comment mobilizes this shared and secret 'inside knowledge' against the gullibility of the male viewer:

> As far as giving shape and form to thousands of male fantasies is concerned, the creators of the James Bond films have got it right. . . . The girls in Bondage follow a set formula: it doesn't matter if a girl's blonde or brunette, so long as she displays evenly tanned skin (no knicker elastic marks, please). It's a 'plus' if the script places her on the opposing side, as the tool of the current arch enemy, for then gentleman James can knock her around a little, thus allowing her pneumatic breasts to bob about ever so slightly. . . . And Mr Average Man in the cinema will love them all, too. He will never know of

the hours spent in Make-up, the specially designed clothing that went into the making of a Bond girl. Nor will he guess at the other problems arising from the transformation. Everything will be perfect in 007's fantasy land – even if it isn't in real life.[14]

However, these are exceptions. More typically, features on 'the Bond girls' – whether in the popular press or in magazines aimed at a mixed or a primarily female readership – have been complicit with the general currency of Bond, underwriting its effects rather than opposing them. In some cases, it is true, contradictory tendencies have coexisted, but usually within a definite order of priority. In 1977, for instance, the *Sunday People*, in an article on the production of *The Spy Who Loved Me*, noted that while 'Bond has become the ultimate sex symbol . . . few of his screen heroines share the same feelings about him'. Britt Ekland, who played Mary Goodnight in *The Man with the Golden Gun*, is thus quoted to the effect that she considered Bond 'a total male chauvinistic pig'. All of this, however, is placed within the context of an exemplary tale which, in the case of *The Spy Who Loved Me*, put 'the Bond girl' in her place even before filming had started:

> Barbara Bach, latest of a beautiful line of Bond girls, feels she is a liberated enough creature of the 1970s not to wear a bra. But when she turned up on the set of the new James Bond epic, *The Spy Who Loved Me*, there was a shock for this russet-haired American beauty.
> 'Go and buy a bra', she was politely but firmly told.[15]

However, even this limited degree of variability is in marked contrast to the part played by the figures of Bond and 'the Bond girl' in the constructions of sexuality in men's magazines. These have exhibited a consistent pattern throughout the various moments of Bond's career, falling into two broad categories. First, articles on the technological gadgetry associated with the Bond films have typically articulated male sexuality to the ability to harness and control the power of machinery.

The following commentary on Bond's Aston Martin DB5 in *Thunderball*, although taken from a fanzine intended for general circulation, aptly illustrates the way in which Bondian machinery has thus been 'phallomorphized': 'A twist of the key sets the motor bursting into powerful throbbing life. It is then that you realise that here is a machine that separates the men from the boys.'[16]

However, photo-essays of 'the nudest Miss Bond' variety in men's soft-porn magazines have arguably been more influential. 'You will never', according to the *Sunday People*, 'ever see an 007 girl in the nude.' The justification for this view was provided by Cubby Broccoli: 'Nudity would destroy Bond's career. His image must be clean cut. We can't risk offending his massive family audience in any way.'[17]

A little while later, Barbara Bach was featured in both semi and total nudity in *Playboy*, photographed in various poses of crouching subordination before Moore/Bond, the inevitable gun in hand. Timed to coincide with the release of *The Spy Who Loved Me*, the feature was clearly a promotional stunt, a requirement of Bach's contract rather than a piece of freelance work. *Playboy* has regularly carried features of this type as has *Penthouse* and, in Britain, magazines like *Mayfair, Men Only* and *Rex*.[18] Their function is clear. The film of *For Your Eyes Only* ends as 'the girl', turning to Bond, drops her towel from her shoulders, saying, to Bond: 'For your eyes only.' We look on this scene alternately from behind 'the girl', so that we see Bond looking, and from behind Bond, but with his body shielding that of 'the girl' from our view, so that we may only imagine but do not see what Bond looks at. This is typical of the way the Bond films end, with Bond, in possessing 'the girl', being placed in a position of vision and power withheld from the spectator. The films thus produce a scopophilic drive which is always stopped tantalisingly short of its object. Photo-essays featuring 'the Bond girls' 'as never seen before' realize the scopophilic expectations engendered by the films in placing the male reader in a position of dominant specularity, inscribing him in the place of Bond in subordinating 'the girl' to his controlling gaze. They complete the work of the narrative in carrying it to a point of visual fulfilment that is impossible within the constraints of the requirements imposed by the family entertainment film.

Nor, according to Michael Denning, is it entirely a coincidence that the first edition of *Playboy* was published in the same year as *Casino Royale* (1953). In his extremely stimulating discussion of the Bond novels, Denning suggests that their role – and that of the Bond phenomenon more generally – in relation to the reformation of sexuality is best understood when they are viewed in relation to the narrative code of the era of mass pornography which *Playboy* inaugurated.[19] Denning argues that the Bond novels construct imperialist and racist ideologies by means of a narrative code of tourism through which the strange and exotic locations of peripheral societies are represented as the object of Bond's Western, metropolitan look. Similarly, he argues that 'the girl' is put into place within a new system of sex and gender relations via the narrative code of pornography in which Bond's 'licence to kill' is less important that his 'licence to look'. Just as the narrative code of tourism represents peripheral societies as objects of spectacle, so the narrative code of pornography codes women as the object of a voyeuristic look; these two systems of looking – the western look and the male look – being privileged in being combined with the secret look of the spy. Denning supports this analysis by drawing attention to the many sequences in the Bond novels in which, much as in the films, 'the girl' is made the object of the reader's look through the relay of Bond's look – the appearance of Honeychile Rider on the beach at Crab Keys, for instance.

The details of this analysis are of less concern to us here than the more general point it illustrates. Denning is less concerned to distil the meaning of the Bond novels than he is to understand the ways in which they operated, within a broader set of inter-textual relations, to promote a genuine shift in sexual practices and a reconstitution of sexuality which continued to subordinate and oppress women, but in ways tailored to the requirements of a mass consumer capitalism. Bond, as bearer of the 'licence to look', becomes the key exemplar of a 'licence to consume' – foreign sights, women, cars, cigarettes and liquor – thus furnishing a model for the reformation of human capacities appropriate to an economic system which requires obedient and diligent consumers as well as willing producers.

In his *Visible Fictions*, John Ellis argues that the function of the various types of film publicity we have considered in this section is to construct a 'narrative image' of the individual film concerned, a promise of a particular type of pleasure which will attract the public to see the film.[20] They may also subtly determine the nature of the film the public sees. Kier Elam has argued that dramatic reviews function in this way:

> The review sets up, before the event, a secondary and explicit frame of a 'metalinguistic' kind (i.e. parasitic on the object 'language', the performance) which will determine the decodification to a greater or lesser extent, depending on the credence given by the spectator to the critic's judgment.[21]

Film publicity posters, fanzine articles, interviews with stars, promotional stunts, etc., function in much the same way. It needs to be borne in mind, however, that the forms of publicity brought to bear on films may vary through time and from one context of reception to another and that, thereby, the 'same text' may be differently constituted as a text-to-be-read as a result of its insertion within differently organized social and ideological relations of reading. . . .

To put this point more forcibly, this means not merely that the same Bond film may be liable to be read differently in different contexts of reception. Our argument is not that every 'spectator's interpretation of the text is in effect a new construction of it according to the cultural and ideological disposition of the subject'. Rather, it is that what we have called 'textual shifters'[22] function, alongside the other components of a reading formation (systems of inter-textuality, the institutional practices which bear on the formation of reading competencies, etc.), to organize *the relations between texts and readers*. They do not act solely upon the reader to produce different readings of 'the same text' but also act upon the text, shifting its very signifying potential so that it is no longer what it once was because, in terms of its cultural location, it is no longer where it once was. . . .

Of course, consideration of such 'textual shifters' is not, in itself, a sufficient account of 'the role of the reader' or a substitute for it. None the less, their role in structuring the social and ideological relations of reading – producing texts for readers and readers for texts – is of considerable importance. Much previous debate on the question of reading has deadlocked on the opposition between the view of the text as dictating its readings and the view that readers are able to mobilize cultural resources which enable them to read against the grain of the text or to negotiate its meanings in particular ways. Our purpose has been to displace the terms of this dispute by suggesting that neither approach takes sufficient account of the cultural and ideological forces which organize and reorganize the network of inter-textual relations within which texts are inserted as texts-to-be-read in certain ways by reading subjects organized to read in certain ways. The relations between texts and readers, we have suggested, are always profoundly mediated by the discursive and inter-textual determinations which, operating on both, structure the domain of their encounter so as to produce, always in specific and variable forms, texts and readers as the mutual supports of one another. . . .

Notes

1 'The Bond girls', in *James Bond in Thunderball*.
2 Passingham, K. (1975) 'The gorgeous girls of James Bond', *TV Times*, 23 October, p. 27.
3 See Foucault, M. (1979) 'What is an author?', *Screen* 20 (1) spring.
4 Palmer, J., 'Thrillers: the deviant behind the consensus', in Taylor, I. and Taylor, J. (eds) (1973) *Politics and Deviance*, Harmondsworth: Penguin, p. 142.
5 ibid., p. 140.
6 See the interview with Connery in *Playboy*, November 1965, and Lewin, D., 'Sean Connery – the screen's James Bond', in *James Bond in Thunderball*.
7 See Brooker, C. (1969) *The Neophiliacs: A Study in the Revolution in English Life in the Fifties and Sixties*, London: Collins.
8 See Callan, M.F. (1983) *Sean Connery: His Life and Films*, London: W.H. Allen, pp. 1–2.
9 *Sunday Times Colour Supplement*, no. 1, 4 February 1962, p. 18.
10 Cited in 'What happened to the Bond girls?', *Telegraph Sunday Magazine*, 17 September 1978, p. 10.
11 *James Bond in Thunderball*.
12 'Sean Connery takes apart the blood, guts and girls man', in Lane, S. (ed.) (1965) *For Bond Lovers Only*, London: Panther, p. 30.
13 See Richler, M. (1970) 'Ian Fleming: a voice for little England', *Nova*, January.
14 *Women's Own*, 30 June 1979.
15 *Sunday People*, 26 June 1977.
16 *James Bond in Thunderball*.
17 *Sunday People*, 26 June 1977.
18 The following are examples of features of this type: 'James Bond's girls', *Playboy*, November 1965; 'The girls of Casino Royale', *Playboy*, February 1967; '007's oriental eyefuls', *Playboy*, June 1967; '8 Bond beauties', *Playboy*, July 1979; 'Stella, Bond's black beauty', *Mayfair*, 9 (5); 'Uncovered: James Bond's lotus-flower girl', *Mayfair*, 8 (7); and 'The Bond girls – vintage '73', *Rex*, 9.
19 See Denning, M. (1987) *Cover Stories: Narrative and Ideology in British Spy Thrillers*, London: Routledge & Kegan Paul.
20 See Ellis, J. (1982) *Visible Fictions. Cinema: Television: Video*, London: Routledge & Kegan Paul, chapter 2.
21 Elam, K. (1980) *The Semiotics of Theatre and Drama*, London: Methuen, p. 94.
22 ibid., p. 95.

24

Television and gender

David Morley

. . . I would first like to make some general points about the significance of the empirical differences which my research revealed between the viewing habits of the men and women in the sample. As will be seen below, the men and women offer clearly contrasting accounts of their viewing habits – in terms of their differential power to choose what they view, how much they view, their viewing styles and their choice of particular viewing material. However, I am not suggesting that these empirical differences are attributes of their essential biological characteristics as men and women. Rather, I am trying to argue that these differences are the effects of the particular social roles that these men and women occupy within the home. Moreover, as I have indicated, this sample primarily consists of lower middle-class and working-class nuclear families (all of whom are white) and I am not suggesting that the particular pattern of gender relations within the home found here (with all the consequences which that pattern has for viewing behaviour) would necessarily be replicated either in nuclear families form a different class or ethnic background, or in households of different types with the same class and ethnic backgrounds. Rather, it is always a case of how gender relations interact with, and are formed differently within, these different contexts.

However, aside from these qualifications, there is one fundamental point which needs to be made concerning the basically different positioning of men and women within the domestic sphere. It should be noted that in the earlier chapters of this book there was much emphasis on the fact that this research project was concerned with television viewing in its domestic context. The essential point here is that the dominant model of gender relations within this society (and certainly within that sub-section of it represented in my sample) is one in which the home is primarily defined for men as a site of leisure – in distinction to the 'industrial time' of their employment outside the home – while the home is primarily defined for women as a sphere of work (whether or not they also work outside the home). This simply means that in investigating television viewing in the home one is by definition investigating something which men are better placed to do wholeheartedly, and which women seem only to be able to do distractedly and guiltily, because of their continuing sense of their domestic responsibilities. Moreover, this differential positioning is given a greater significance as the home becomes increasingly defined as the 'proper' sphere of leisure, with the decline of public forms of entertainment and the growth of home-based leisure technologies such as video, etc. . . .

When considering the empirical findings summarized below, care must be taken to hold in view this structuring of the domestic environment by gender relations as the backdrop against which these particular patterns of viewing behaviour have developed. Otherwise we risk seeing this pattern as somehow the direct result of 'essential' or biological characteristics of men and women *per se*. As Charlotte Brunsdon has put it, commenting on research in this area we could

> mistakenly . . . differentiate a male – fixed, controlling, uninterruptible – gaze, and a female – distracted, obscured, already busy – manner of watching television. There is some empirical truth in these characterisations, but to take this empirical truth for explanation leads to a

theoretical short circuit . . . Television is a domestic medium – and indeed the male/female differentiation above is very close to the way in which cinema and television have themselves been differentiated. Cinema, the audiovisual medium of the public sphere [demands] the masculine gaze, while the domestic (feminine) medium is much less demanding, needing only an intermittent glance. This, given the empirical evidence . . . offers us an image of male viewers trying to masculinise the domestic sphere. This way of watching television, however, seems not so much a masculine mode, but a mode of power. Current arrangements between men and women make it likely that it is men who will occupy this position in the home.[1] . . .

Power and control over programme choice

Masculine power is evident in a number of the families as the ultimate determinant on occasions of conflict over viewing choices ('we discuss what we all want to watch and the biggest wins. That's me. I'm the biggest', Man, Family 4). More crudely, it is even more apparent in the case of those families who have an automatic control device. None of the women in any of the families use the automatic control regularly. A number of them complain that their husbands use the channel control device obsessively, channel flicking across programmes when their wives are trying to watch something else. Characteristically, the control device is the symbolic possession of the father (or of the son, in the father's absence) which sits 'on the arm of Daddy's chair' and is used almost exclusively by him. It is a highly visible symbol of condensed power relations (the descendent of the medieval mace perhaps?). . . .

F2 Daughter: 'Dad keeps both of the automatic controls – one on each side of his chair.'
F3 Woman: 'Well, I don't get much chance, because he sits there with the automatic control beside him and that's it . . . I get annoyed because I can be watching a

programme and he's flicking channels to see if a programme on the other side is finished, so he can record something. So the television's flickering all the time, while he's flicking the timer. I just say, "For goodness' sake, leave it alone." I don't get the chance to use the control. I don't get near it.'

F15 Woman: 'No, not really. I don't get the chance to use the automatic control. I leave that down to him. It is aggravating, because I can be watching something and all of a sudden he turns it over to get the football result.'

F9 Daughter: 'The control's always next to Dad's chair. It doesn't come away when Dad's here. It stays right there.'

F9 Woman: 'And that's what you do [her husband], isn't it? Flick, flick, flick – when they're in the middle of a sentence on the telly. He's always flicking it over.'

F9 Man: 'The remote control, oh yes, I use it all the time.' . . .

Interestingly, the main exceptions to this overall pattern concern those families in which the man is unemployed while his wife is working. In these cases it is slightly more common for the man to be expected to be prepared to let other family members watch what they want to when it is broadcast, while videotaping what he would like to see, in order to watch that later at night or the following day – given that his timetable of commitments is more flexible than those of the working members of the family. Here we begin to see the way in which the position of power held by most of the men in the sample (and which their wives concede) is based not simply on the biological fact of being men but rather on a social definition of a masculinity of which employment (that is, the 'breadwinner' role) is a necessary and constituent part. When that condition is not met, the pattern of power relations within the home can change noticeably.[2]

Styles of viewing

One major finding is the consistency of the distinction between the characteristic ways in which men and women describe their viewing activity. Essentially the men state a clear preference for viewing attentively, in silence, without interruption 'in order not to miss anything'. Moreover, they display puzzlement at the way their wives and daughters watch television. This the women themselves describe as a fundamentally social activity, involving ongoing conversation, and usually the performance of at least one other domestic activity (ironing, etc.) at the same time. Indeed, many of the women feel that to just watch television without doing something else at the same time would be an indefensible waste of time, given their sense of their domestic obligations. To watch in this way is something they rarely do, except occasionally, when alone or with other women friends, when they have managed to construct an 'occasion' on which to watch their favourite programme, video or film. The women note that their husbands are always 'on at them' to shut up. The men can't really understand how their wives can follow the programmes if they are doing something else at the same time.

F2 Man: 'We don't talk. They talk a bit.'
F2 Woman: 'You keep saying sshh.'
F2 Man: 'I can't concentrate if there's anyone talking while I'm watching. But they can, they can watch and just talk at the same time. We just watch it – take it all in. If you talk, you've missed the bit that's really worth watching. We listen to every bit of it and if you talk you miss something that's important. My attitude is sort of go in the other room if you want to talk.'

F5 Man: 'It really amazes me that this lot [his wife and daughters] can talk and do things and still pick up what's going on. To my mind it's not very good if you can do that'
F5 Woman: 'Because we have it on all the time it's like

second nature. We watch, and chat at the same time.'

F18 Woman: 'I knit because I think I am wasting my time just watching. I know what's going on, so I only have to glance up. I always knit when I watch.'

F15 Woman: 'I can generally sit and read a book and watch a film at the same time and keep the gist of it. If it's a good film it doesn't bother me. I'm generally sewing or something like that.'

F9 Man: 'I like to watch it without aggravation. I'd rather watch on my own. If it's just something I want to watch, I like to watch everything with no talking at all.'

F9 Woman: 'Every now and again he says, "Ssshhh shut up." It's terrible. He comes in . . . from a pool match and he'll say, "Shut up, please shut up!"'

F9 Man: 'You can't watch anything in peace unless they're all out. Half the time they start an argument and then you've missed easily twenty minutes of it . . . usually the catchphrase which you've got to listen to to find out what's going to happen in the programme. Sometimes I just go upstairs. It's not worth watching.'
. . .

Charlotte Brunsdon, commenting on this and other research in this area, provides a useful way of understanding the behaviour reported here. As she argues, it is not that the women have no desire ever to watch television attentively, but rather that their domestic position makes it almost impossible for them to do this unless all the other members of the household are 'out of the way'.

> The social relations between men and women appear to work in such a way that although the men feel OK about imposing their choice of viewing on the whole of the family, the women do not. The women have developed all sorts of strategies to cope with television viewing that they don't particularly like. . . . However, the women in general seem to find it almost impossible to switch into the silent communion with the television set that characterises so much male viewing. Revealingly, they often speak

rather longingly of doing this, but it always turns out to require the physical absence of the rest of the family.[3]

Again we see that these distinctive viewing styles are not simply characteristics of men and women as such but, rather, characteristics of the domestic roles of masculinity and femininity.

Television related talk

Women seem to show much less reluctance to 'admit' that they talk about television to their friends and workmates. Very few men (see below for the exceptions) admit to doing this. It is as if they feel that to admit that they watch too much television (especially with the degree of involvement that would be implied by finding it important enough to talk about) would be to put their very masculinity in question (see the section on programme type preference below). The only standard exception is where the men are willing to admit that they talk about sport on television. All this is clearly related to the theme of gender and programme choice and the 'masculinity/femininity' syllogism identified there. Some part of this is simply to do with the fact that femininity is a more expressive cultural mode than is masculinity. Thus even if women watch less, with less intent viewing styles, nonetheless they are inclined to talk about television *more* than men, despite the fact that the men watch more of it, more attentively.

F1 Woman: 'Actually my mum and my sister don't watch *Dynasty* and I often tell them bits about it. If my sister watches it, she likes it. And I say to her, "Did you watch it?" and she says no. But if there's something especially good on one night – you know, you might see your friends and say, "Did you see so and so last night?" I occasionally miss *Dynasty*. I said to a friend, "What happened?" and she's caught me up, but I tend to see most of the series. Marion used to keep me going, didn't she? Tell me what was happening and that.'

F2 Man: 'I might mention something on telly occasionally, but I really don't talk about it to anyone.'

F5 Woman: 'At work we constantly talk about *Dallas* and *Dynasty*. We run them down, pick out who we like and who we don't like. What we think should happen next. General chit-chat. I work with quite a few girls, so we have a good old chat. . . . We do have some really interesting discussions about television [at work]. We haven't go much else in common, so we talk a lot about television.'

F6 Woman: 'I go round my mate's and she'll say, "Did you watch *Coronation Street* last night? What about so and so?" And we'll sit there discussing it. I think most women and most young girls do. We always sit down and it's "Do you think she's right last night, what she's done?" Or, "I wouldn't have done that," or "Wasn't she a cow to him? Do you reckon he'll get . . . I wonder what he's going to do?" Then we sort of fantasise between us, then when I see her the next day she'll say, "You were right," or "See, I told you so."'

F16 Woman: 'Mums at school will say, "Have you seen any god videos?" And when *Jewel in the Crown* was on, yes, we'd talk about that. When I'm watching the big epics, the big serials, I would talk about those.'

F8 Daughter: 'I like to watch *Brookside*, it's my favourite programme . . . 'cause down the stables everyone else watches it – it's something to chat about when we go down there . . .'

F17 Man: 'If we do talk, it'll be about something like a news programme – something we didn't know anything about – something that's come up that's interesting.'

F18 Woman: 'I'll talk about things on telly to my friends. I do. I think it is women who talk about television more so than men. I work with an Indian girl and when *Jewel in the Crown* was on we used to talk about that, because she used to tell me what was

different in India. *Gandhi* we had on video. She told me
what it was like and why that was interesting. Other than
that it's anything. She went to see *Passage to India* and
she said it was good, but it was a bit like *Jewel in the
Crown*.

F18 Man: 'I won't talk about television at work unless
there'd been something like boxing on. I wouldn't talk
about *Coronation Street* or a joke on Benny Hill, so
other than that, no.' . . .

The issue of the differential tendency for women and
men to talk about their television viewing is of
considerable interest. It could be objected that, as my
research is based on only respondents' accounts of their
behaviour, the findings are unreliable in so far as
respondents may have misrepresented their actual
behaviour – especially when the accounts offered by my
respondents seem to conflict with established survey
findings. Thus in principle it could be argued that the
claims many of the male respondents make about only
watching 'factual' television are a misrepresentation of
their actual behaviour, based on their anxiety about
admitting to watching fictional programmes. However,
even if this were the case, it would remain a social fact
of some interest that the male respondents felt this
compulsion to misrepresent their actual behaviour in this
particular way. Moreover, this very reluctance to talk
about some of the programmes they may watch itself has
important consequences. Even if it were the case that
men and women in fact watched the same range of
programmes (contrary to the accounts they gave me), the
fact that the men are reluctant to talk about watching
anything other than factual programmes or sport means
that their viewing experience is profoundly different from
that of the women in the sample. Given that meanings
are made not simply in the moment of individual viewing, but also in the subsequent social processes of discussion and 'digestion' of material viewed, the men's much
greater reluctance to talk about (part of) their viewing

will mean that their consumption of television material is of a quite different kind from that of their wives. . . .

'Solo' viewing and guilty pleasures

A number of the women in the sample explain that their greatest pleasure is to be able to watch 'a nice weepie', or their favourite serial, when the rest of the family aren't there. Only then do they feel free enough of their domestic responsibilities to 'indulge' themselves in the kind of attentive viewing which their husbands engage in routinely. Here we enter the territory identified by Brodie and Stoneman who found that mothers tended to maintain their role as 'domestic manager' across programme types, as opposed to their husbands' tendency to abandon their manager/parent role when viewing material of particular interest to them.[4] The point is expressed most clearly by the woman in F7 who explains that she particularly enjoys watching early morning television at the weekends – because, as these are the only occasions on which her husband and sons 'sleep in', these are, by the same token, the only occasions when she can watch television attentively, without keeping half an eye on the needs of others.

Several of these women will arrange to view a video or film with other women friends during the afternoon. It is the classically feminine way of dealing with conflict – in this case over programme choice – by avoiding it, and 'rescheduling' the programmes (often with someone's help in relation to the video) to a point where it can be watched more pleasurably.

F5 Woman: 'That's one thing we don't have on when he's here, we don't have the games programmes on because he hates them. If we women are here on our own – I love it. I think they're lovely . . . If I'm here alone, I try to get something a bit mushy and then I sit here and have a cry, if I'm here on my own. It's not often, but I enjoy that.'

F6 Woman: 'If I get a good film on now, I'll tape it and keep it, especially if it's a weepie. I'll sit there and keep it for ages – especially in the afternoon, if there's no one here at all. If I'm tired, I'll put that on – especially in the winter – and it's nice then, 'cause you sit there and there's no one around . . . We get those *Bestsellers* and put them together so you get the whole series together, especially if it's late at night. You're so tired – it's nice to watch the whole film together. We try and keep them, so of an afternoon, if you haven't got a lot to do, you can sit and watch them.' . . .

My findings in this respect are very clearly supported by Ann Gray's research. Gray argues that her women respondents do have definite preconceptions as to what constitutes a 'film for men' as against a 'film for women', and on this basis she also develops a typology of viewing contexts, for masculine and feminine viewing (jointly and separately) along with a typology of types of films and programmes 'appropriate' to these different viewing contexts. Her point is that quite different types of viewing material are felt to be appropriate to the different viewing contexts of the whole family together, male and female partners together, male alone and female alone. Moreover, she argues that among her respondents, women will only usually watch the kinds of material which they particularly like when their partner is out of the house (at work or leisure), whereas the men will often watch the material which they alone like while their partner is there – she simply would busy herself around the house, or sit without really watching.[5]

As Gray notes, women who are at home all day in fact have obvious opportunities then to view alone, but for many of them daytime television viewing is seen as a kind of 'drug' to which they feel, guiltily, that they could easily become addicted.

These comments bring us back to the issue already considered concerning the sense in which the home simply is not a sphere of leisure for women, and thus the ways in which their viewing is constrained by guilt and obligation. However, beyond these considerations there is another dimension which is perhaps even more fundamental. As Ann Gray expresses it, summarizing her research in this area, 'It is the most powerful member of the household who defines this hierarchy of serious and silly, important and trivial, which leaves women and their pleasures downgraded, objects and subjects of fun and derision, having to consume [the films and programmes they like] almost in secret.'[6]

What is at issue here is the guilt that most of these women feel about their own pleasures. They are, on the whole, prepared to concede that the drama and soap opera they like is 'silly' or 'badly acted' or inconsequential – that is, they accept the terms of a masculine hegemony which defines their preferences as having a low status. Having accepted these terms, they then find it hard to argue for their preference in a conflict (because, by definition, what their husbands want to watch is more prestigious). They then deal with this by watching their programmes, where possible, on their own, or only with their women friends, and will fit such arrangements into the crevices of their domestic timetables.

F3 Woman: 'What I really like is typical American trash I suppose, but I love it . . . All the American rubbish, really. And I love those Australian films. I think they're really good, those.'

F17 Woman: 'When the children go to bed he has the ultimate choice. I feel guilty if I push for what I want to see because he and the boys want to see the same thing, rather than what a mere woman would want to watch . . . if there was a love film on, I'd be happy to see it and they wouldn't. It's like when you go to pick up a video, instead of getting a nice sloppy love story, I think I can't get that because of the others. I'd feel guilty watching it – because I think I'm getting my pleasure whilst the others aren't getting any pleasure, because they're not interested.' . . .

Programme type preference

My respondents displayed a notable consistency in this area, whereby masculinity was primarily identified with a strong preference for 'factual' programmes (news, current affairs, documentaries) and femininity identified with a preference for fictional programmes. The observation may be banal, but the strength of the consistency displayed here was remarkable, whenever respondents were asked about programme preferences, and especially when asked which programmes they would make a point of being in for, and viewing attentively.

F6 Man: 'I like all documentaries . . . I like watching stuff like that . . . I can watch fiction but I am not a great lover of it.'

F6 Woman: 'He don't like a lot of serials.'

F6 Man: 'It's not my type of stuff. I do like the news, current affairs, all that type of stuff.'

F6 Woman: 'Me and the girls love our serials.'

F6 Man: 'I watch the news all the time, I like the news, current affairs and all that.'

F6 Woman: 'I don't like it so much.'

F6 Man: 'I watch the news every time, 5.40p.m., 6p.m., 9p.m., 10p.m., I try to watch.'

F6 Woman: 'I just watch the main news so I know what's going on. Once is enough. Then I'm not interested in it.'

F10 Man: 'I must admit I prefer more factual television. I enjoy some of the *TV Eye* series. We have just watched the *Trojan War* – that was brilliant. I enjoy series like that – like *Life On Earth* – wildlife programmes, and *World in Action* . . . I like to know about things because basically I am a working-class man and I like to know what is happening. I like to know what is happening to me personally . . . I do enjoy watching factual programmes. I think I would much rather watch a factual programme.' . . .

The argument also extends further. First, there is the

refrain among the men that watching fiction in the way that their wives do is an improper and almost 'irresponsible' activity, an indulgence in fantasy of which they disapprove (compare nineteenth-century views of novel-reading as a 'feminizing' activity). This is perhaps best expressed in the words of the couples in F1 and F6, where in both case the husbands clearly disapprove of their wives' enjoyment of 'fantasy' programmes.

F1 Woman: 'That's what's nice about it [*Dynasty*]. It's a dream world, isn't it?'
F1 Man: 'It's a fantasy world that everybody wants to live in, but that – no I can't get on with that.'

The husband in F6 takes the view that watching television in a way is an abrogation of civil responsibility.

F6 Man: 'People get lost in TV. They fantasize in TV. It's taken over their lives. . . . People today are coming into their front rooms, they shut their front door and that's it. They identify with that little world on the box.'
F6 Woman: 'To me, I think telly's real life.'
F6 Man: 'That's what I'm saying. Telly's taken over your life.'
F6 Woman: 'Well, I don't mind it taking over my life. It keeps me happy.'

The depth of this man's feelings on this point are confirmed later in the interview when he is discussing his general leisure pursuits. He explains that he now regularly goes to the library in the afternoons, and comments that he 'didn't realize the library was so good – I thought it was all just fiction'. Clearly, for him, 'good' and 'fiction' are simply incompatible categories.

Secondly, the men's programme genre preference for factual programmes is also framed by a sense of guilt about the fact that watching television is a 'second-best choice' in itself – in relation to a strong belief (not shared in the same way by the majority of women) that watching television at all is 'second-best' to 'real' leisure activity:

F4 Man: 'I'm not usually here. I watch it if there's nothing else to do, but I'd rather not. . . . In the summer I'd rather go out. I can't bear to watch TV if it's still light.'

F16 Man: 'I like fishing. I don't care what's on if I'm going out fishing. I'm not worried what's on the telly then.'

F11 Man: 'If it's good weather we're out in the garden or visiting people . . . I've got a book and a crossword lined up for when she goes out, rather than just watch the television.' . . .

Moreover, when the interviews move to a discussion of the fictional programmes that the men do watch, consistency is maintained by their preference for a 'realistic' situation comedy (a realism of social life) and a rejection of all forms of romance.

These responses seem to fit fairly readily into a kind of 'syllogism' of masculine/feminine relationships to television:

Masculine	Feminine
Activity	Watching television
Fact programmes	Fiction programmes
Realist fiction	Romance

Again, it may be objected that my findings in this respect exaggerate the 'real' differences between men's and women's viewing and underestimate the extent of 'overlap' viewing as between men and women. Certainly my respondents offer a more sharply differentiated picture of men's and women's viewing than is ordinarily reported by survey work, which seems to show substantial numbers of men watching 'fictional' programmes and equally substantial numbers of women watching 'factual' programmes.

However, this apparent contradiction largely rests on the conflation of 'viewing' with 'viewing attentively and with enjoyment'. If we use the first definition, then we can expect considerable degrees of overlap as between men's and women's 'viewing'. Once we use the second definition, the distinctions as between men's and women's preferred forms of viewing become much more marked. Moreover, even if this were not the case, and it could be demonstrated that my respondents had misrepresented their behaviour to me (offering classic masculine and feminine stereotypes which belied the complexity of their actual behaviour), it would remain as a social fact of considerable interest that these were the particular forms of misrepresentation which respondents felt constrained to offer of themselves – and these tendencies (for the men to be unable to admit to watching fiction) themselves have real effects in their social lives.

Further it could be objected that the fact that the respondents were interviewed *en famille* may have predisposed them to adopt stereotyped familial roles in the interviews which, if interviewed separately, they would not adhere to – thus again leading to a tendency towards misleading forms of classical gender stereotyping. However, this was precisely the point of interviewing respondents *en famille* – as it was their viewing *en famille* which was at issue, specifically in respect of the ways in which their familial roles interact with their roles as viewers. Accounts which respondents might give of their behaviour individually would precisely lack this dimension of family dynamics and role-playing.

More fundamentally, if one poses the issue as one in which 'real' behaviour (as monitored by survey techniques) is counterposed to 'unreliable' accounts offered by respondents, one runs the risk of remaining perpetually stuck at the level of external measurements of behaviour which offer no insight or understanding into what the observed behaviour means to the people concerned. Thus, monitoring techniques may seem to show that many women are 'watching' factual television (as measured in terms of physical presence in front of the set) when, as far as they are concerned, they are in fact paying little or no attention to what is on the screen (not least because it is often a programme which they did not themselves choose to watch), as revealed by their comments when asked to give their own accounts of their viewing behaviour. Moreover, it is only through viewers' own accounts of why they are interested (or disinterested) in particular types of programmes that we can begin to get any sense of the criteria they employ in making the particular viewing choices they do.

Notes

1 Brunsdon, Charlotte, 'Women watching television', paper to Women and The Electronic Mass Media Conference, Copenhagen, 1986, unpublished.
2 See Marsden, D. and Duff, E. (1975) *Workless: Some Unemployed Men and their Families*, Harmondsworth: Penguin, for more on these issues.
3 Brunsdon, op. cit.
4 Brodie, Jean and Stoneman, Lynda, 'Television's role in family interaction: a family systems perspective', *Journal of Family Issues*, June 1983.
5 Gray, Ann, 'Women and video' in Baehr, Helen and Dyer, Gillian (eds) (forthcoming) *Boxed In: Women and Television*, London: Routledge & Kegan Paul.
6 ibid.

Bibliography

I have not aspired to completeness in this bibliography. Rather, my purpose has been to provide a rough map of the field for the reader who wants to acquire some general bearings in the area. I have limited my attention largely to recent studies and, for the most part, to ones concerned with contemporary forms of popular fiction. The bibliography is also restricted to the themes explored in this collection. However, a brief list of relevant journals is provided for the reader who wishes to keep abreast of developments in the field more generally.

I Surveys, introductions and anthologies

(a) General

There are scarcely any introductory studies or collections concerned specifically with popular fiction in its literary, cinematic and televisual forms. However, a good deal of relevant material can be found in collections devoted to other topics.

Bennett, Tony, Mercer, Colin and Woollacott, Janet (eds) (1986) *Popular Culture and Social Relations*, Milton Keynes: Open University Press. (Contains essays on TV sitcoms and police series as well as on theoretical aspects of popular fiction.)

Bigsby, C.W.E. (ed.) (1976) *Approaches to Popular Culture*,

London: Edward Arnold. (Mainly general studies, but with some specific studies on television.)

Hall, Stuart and Whannel, Paddy (1964) *The Popular Arts*, London: Hutchinson. (Extensive range, and an important text in stimulating the development of popular fiction studies in Britain, although now a little dated.)

Lowenthal, Leo (1961) *Literature, Popular Culture and Society*, Englewood Cliffs, N.J.: Prentice Hall. (Mainly popular literature, but raises more general issues from the perspective of Frankfurt critical theory.)

Waites, Bernard, Bennett, Tony and Martin, Graham (eds) (1982) *Popular Culture: Past and Present*, London: Croom Helm. (Contains essays on science fiction, adolescent girls' magazines, British cinema and the James Bond novels.)

(b)   Popular literature

While it is customary to bemoan the fact that popular literature has received less attention than the literary canon, the secondary literature is in fact very considerable and detailed. Useful general starting points include:

Cawelti, J.G. (1976) *Adventure, Mystery and Romance: Formula Stories as Art and Popular Culture*, Chicago: University of Chicago Press. (The best general survey of the narrative formulae of popular fiction genres.)

Eco, Umberto (1979) *The Role of the Reader*, London: Hutchinson. (Eco's essays on Superman and the James Bond novels are classic examples of the structuralist approach to popular narratives.)

Humm, Peter, Stigant, Paul and Widdowson, Peter (1986) *Popular Fictions: Essays in Literature and History*, London: Methuen. (A collection of theoretically probing essays ranging widely across nineteenth- and twentieth-century popular literature.)

Moretti, Franco (1983) *Signs Taken for Wonders. Essays in the Sociology of Literary Forms*, London: Verso. (Contains a useful introduction as well as the essay 'Clues' and an interesting discussion of the figures of Dracula and Frankenstein.)

Pawling, Christopher (ed.) (1984) *Popular Fiction and Social Change*, London: Macmillan. (Ranges across science fiction, fantasy, thrillers and women's magazines. Includes a helpful introduction.)

Warpole, Ken (1984) *Reading By Numbers: Contemporary Publishing and Popular Fiction*, London: Verso. (Very condensed and politically focused account of the economics of popular fiction publishing and its influence on its main genres.)

(c)   Cinema and television

Perhaps the best general introduction to the theoretical concerns which have reanimated cinema studies since the 1960s is Cook, Pam (ed.) (1985) *The Cinema Book*, London: British Film Institute. Other useful surveys and anthologies include:

Bennett, Tony, Boyd-Bowman, Susan, Mercer, Colin and Woollacott, Janet (eds) (1981) *Popular Television and Film*, London: British Film Institute. (Contains a section on popular film and pleasure; essays on sitcoms, police series and TV drama.)

Bordwell, David and Thompson, Kristin (1979) *Film Art: An Introduction*, Reading, Mass.: Addison Wesley. (Very useful introduction to the major aspects of film – production, editing, sound, *mise-en-scène*, narrative – placed in a historical perspective.)

Ellis, John (1982) *Visible Fictions. Cinema: Television: Video*, London: Routledge & Kegan Paul. (Useful introduction to the institutional aspects of the cinema and the cinematic experience, as also of television – although the latter is treated less in its own right than in terms of its differences from cinema.)

Fiske, John and Hartley, John (1978) *Reading Television*, London: Methuen. (Useful overview of British television, although sometimes idiosyncratic.)

Kaplan, E. Ann (ed.) (1983) *Regarding Television. Critical Approaches – An Anthology*, Los Angeles: American Film Institute and University Publications of America. (Lively collection with a major focus on soap opera.)

MacCabe, Colin (ed.) (1986) *High Theory/Low Culture: Analysing Popular Television and Film*, Manchester: Manchester University Press. (Interesting individual contributions but a little lacking in focus as a collection.)

Masterman, Len (ed.) (1984) *Television Mythologies – Stars, Shows and Signs*, London: Comedia. (A collection of short essays spanning the full range of TV output with some studies of specific popular fictional genres.)

Newcomb, E. (1974) *Television: The Most Popular Art*, New York: Doubleday, Anchor Books. (Influential survey of the main genres of American television.)

Williams, Raymond (1974) *Television, Technology and Cultural Form*, London: Fontana. (A formative text with considerable influence on most major subsequent writings on television.)

II   Cultural technologies

Most of the sources cited in I above are relevant to the themes developed in section 1 of this collection – especially Ellis (1982) and Williams (1974). On cinema as a cultural technology, see the following:

(a)   Cinema

Chanan, Michael (1980) *The Dream that Kicks. The Prehistory and Early Years of Cinema in Britain*, London: Routledge & Kegan Paul. (A challenging account of the formation of British cinema encompassing economic, technical and cultural factors.)

De Lauretis, Teresa and Heath, Stephen (eds) (1980) *The Cinematic Apparatus*, London: Macmillan. (A collection of influential statements on the relations between technology, ideology and cinema.)

De Lauretis, Teresa (1984) *Alice Doesn't. Feminism, Semiotics, Cinema*, London: Macmillan. (Brings a feminist perspective to the debate. Deservedly highly regarded.)

Heath, Stephen (1981) *Questions of Cinema*, London: Macmillan. (A compilation of essays exploring the regulation of desire effected by the cinema; ambitious attempt to incorporate psychoanalysis into the concerns of film theory.)

Metz, Christian (1982) *Psychoanalysis and Cinema: The Imaginary Signifier*, London: Macmillan. (A formative text in proposing that cinema be investigated as a mental machinery. Very difficult, though.)

Neale, Steve (1985) *Cinema and Technology: Image, Sound,*

Colour, London: British Film Institute. (Perhaps the most accessible introduction to the area. Richly illustrated.)

(b) Popular literature

The relations between the development of the publishing industry and popular literature are explored in the following:

Altick, Richard D. (1957) *The English Common Reader: A Social History of the Mass Reading Public*, Chicago: University of Chicago Press. (Richly detailed and very informative.)

Davies, Tony (1983) 'Transports of Pleasure', *Formations of Pleasure*, London: Routledge & Kegan Paul. (Good on the connections between the social relations and the pleasures of nineteenth-century popular reading.)

James, Louis (1963) *Fiction for the Working Man, 1830–50*, Oxford: Oxford University Press. (Examines the transformation of the content and occasions of popular reading associated with the development of a mass publishing industry.)

Leavis, Q.D. (1932) *Fiction and the Reading Public*, London: Chatto & Windus. (Exhibits an inevitable high cultural bias, but remains an important and probing study.)

Vicinus, Martha (1974) *The Industrial Muse: A Study of Nineteenth-Century British Working Class Literature*, London: Croom Helm. (Similar focus to James.)

Williams, Raymond (1965) *The Long Revolution*. Harmondsworth: Penguin. (Important in placing the development of the publishing industry in a broader perspective.)

III Popular fiction and nationalism

Aldgate, Tony and Richards, Jeffrey (1986) *Britain Can Take It: The British Cinema in the Second World War*, Oxford: Blackwell. (Survey of the nationalizing rhetoric of the British film industry in the service of the war effort.)

Cultural Critique, 3, spring 1986. (Special issue on American representations of Vietnam.)

Dick, Bernard F. (1985) *The Star-Spangled Screen: The American Film in World War II*, Lexington: University Press of Kentucky. (Examines the role of Hollywood in the patriotization of America.)

Formations of Nation and People, London: Routledge & Kegan Paul, 1984. (A collection of essays providing a good general perspective on the relations between culture and nation.)

Gramsci, Antonio (1985) *Selections from Cultural Writings*, London: Lawrence and Wishart. (The sections on 'Language, linguistics and folklore', 'People, nation and culture' and 'Popular literature and journalism' are of special interest.)

Hurd, Geoff (ed.) (1984) *National Fictions. World War Two in British Films and Television*, London: British Film Institute. (Main focus is on retrospective representations of the war.)

McArthur, Colin (ed.) (1982) *Scotch Reels: Scotland in Cinema and Television*, London: British Film Institute. (Mainly concerned with film.)

Moran, Albert and O'Regan, Tom (1985) *An Australian Film Reader*, Sydney: Currency Press. (Essays and documents on the development of the Australian cinema.)

Tulloch, John (1981) *Legends on the Screen: The Australian Narrative Cinema 1919–1929*, Sydney: Currency Press. (Detailed study of the formative years of the Australian film industry.)

Turner, Graeme (1986) *National Fictions: Literature, Film and the Construction of Australian Narrative*, Sydney: Allen & Unwin. (Considers the forces shaping the development of an Australian narrative tradition in film and writing.)

Wilden, Tony (1980) *The Imaginary Canadian*, Vancouver: Pulp Press. (Innovative application of perspectives derived from psychoanalysis to the cultural aspects of nationalism.)

IV Feminist criticism

The literature here is now very considerable and growing almost daily. The following sources are therefore only some of the more obvious starting points.

(a) Literature

Coward, Rosalind (1984) *Female Desire: Women's Sexuality Today*, London: Paladin. (A work of general cultural criticism, but includes a section on popular fictions.)

Greene, Gayle and Kahn, Coppelia (eds) (1985) *Making a Difference: Feminist Literary Criticism*, London: Methuen. (Very little specifically on popular fiction, but a representative collection of the main schools of feminist literary criticism.)

Modleski, Tania (1982) *Loving with a Vengeance: Mass-produced Fantasies for Women*, New York and London: Methuen. (Contains chapters on romance and the gothic novel as well as soap-opera.)

Moi, Toril (1985) *Sexual/Textual Politics: Feminist Literary Theory*, London: Methuen. (Very accessible introduction to the different schools of feminist literary criticism.)

(b) Film and television

Baehr, Helen and Dyer, Gillian (eds) (1987) *Boxed In: Women On and In Television*, London: Routledge & Kegan Paul. (A much needed collection.)

Haskell, Molly (1973) *From Reverence to Rape: The Treatment of Women in the Movies*, New York: Holt, Rinehart & Winston. (Surveys the changing conventions governing the representation of women in American films from the 1920s to the 1960s.)

Kay, Karyn and Peary, Gerald (eds) (1977) *Women and the Cinema: A Critical Anthology*, New York: E.P. Dutton. (A wide ranging collection including some classics of feminist film theory.)

Kaplan, E. Ann (1983) *Women and Film: Both Sides of the Camera*, New York and London: Methuen. (Locates the work of independent feminist film makers against an examination of the classical and contemporary forms of Hollywood cinema.)

Kaplan, E. Ann (ed.) (1980) *Women in Film Noir*, London: British Film Institute. (A collection of studies examining the representations of women in specific *noir* films.)

Kuhn, Annette (1982) *Women's Pictures: Feminism and Cinema*, London: Routledge & Kegan Paul. (A very clear introduction to feminist debates in contemporary film theory.)

Kuhn, Annette (1985) *The Power of the Image: Essays on Representation and Sexuality*, London: Routledge & Kegan Paul. (A collection of consistently thoughtful and provocative essays.)

Rosen, Marjorie (1973) *Popcorn Venus: Women, Movies and the American Dream*, New York: Avon Books. (Examines the role of film in shaping ideals of femininity from the 1920s to the 1960s.)

Screen, 23 (3–4) September/October 1982. (Special double issue on sex and spectatorship.)

See also De Lauretis (1984) under II (a) above.

V Detective fiction

The literature on detective fiction is unusually rich and rewarding. The most interesting survey of the genre, and by a long shot, is Dennis Porter's *The Pursuit of Crime: Art and Ideology in Detective Fiction* (New Haven and London: Yale University Press, 1981) – exemplary in both the detailed knowledge of the form it exhibits and the probing yet open spirit of theoretical inquiry in which the examination is conducted. Other sources of interest include the following:

Cawelti, J.G. (1976) *Adventure, Mystery and Romance: Formula Stories as Art and Popular Culture*, Chicago, University of Chicago Press. (Useful in comparing detective fiction to other popular genres; especially interesting on the differences and similarities between the classical detective story and the 'hard-boiled' detective fiction of Chandler, Hammett and Spillane.)

Eco, Umberto and Sebeok, T. (eds) (1983) *Sign of Three: Dupin, Holmes, Peirce*, Bloomington: Indiana University Press. (A collection of essays devoted to examining the relations between the philosophies and methods of Poe's Dupin and Conan Doyle's Holmes and those of the American pragmatist Charles S. Peirce. Also covers the relations between detective fiction and medical semiotics.)

Ejxenbaum, B.M. (1971) 'O. Henry and the theory of the short story' in Matejka, L. and Pomorska, K. (eds) *Readings in Russian Poetics*, Cambridge, Mass.: MIT Press. (A representative of the Russian Formalist school of criticism, Ejxenbaum offers a taut analysis of the relations between the short story and the generic properties of detective fiction.)

Grossvogel, D.I. (1979) *Mystery and its Fictions: Oedipus to*

Agatha Christie, Baltimore: Johns Hopkins University Press. (Less concerned with detective fiction *per se* than with the use of similar devices – but to different effect – in the mainstream traditions of western literature. Contains interesting applications of Lacanian psychoanalytic perspectives.)

Jameson, Fredric (1970) 'On Raymond Chandler', *Southern Review*, 6 (1) spring. (Interesting on Chandler's style.)

Knight, Stephen (1980) *Form and Ideology in Detective Fiction*, London: Macmillan. (Focuses mainly on Poe and Conan Doyle and offers a provoking analysis of the relations of their works to nineteenth-century ideologies of individualism and rationalism.)

Murch, A.E. (1968) *The Development of the Detective Novel*, Westport, Connecticut: Greenwood Publishers. (Offers a detailed discussion of the development of detective fiction out of the eighteenth-century literature of crime. Consistently informative, but somewhat marred by a teleological view of the genre's development.)

Warpole, Ken (1983) *Dockers and Detectives. Popular Reading: Popular Writing*, London: Verso Editions. (Warpole's discussion of the genre contains few surprises; however, very informative on the reception of 'hard-boiled' detective fiction in Britain.)

Winks, R.W. (ed.) (1980) *Detective Fiction: A Collection of Critical Essays*, Englewood Cliffs, N.J.: Prentice Hall. (Contains many of the classic essays on the genre by Christie, Sayers, Auden, etc. G. Grella's 'the formal detective novel' is of particular interest.)

VI Production studies

(a) Cinema

Barr, Charles (1977) *Ealing Studios*, London: Cameron and Taylor. (The first major study of Ealing.)

Bennett, Tony and Woollacott, Janet (1987) *Bond and Beyond: The Political Career of a Popular Hero*, London: Macmillan; New York: Methuen Inc. (Contains a chapter on the making of *The Spy Who Loved Me*.)

Bordwell, David, Staiger, Janet and Thompson, Kristin (1985) *The Classic Hollywood Cinema: Film Style and Mode of*

Production, London: Routledge & Kegan Paul. (Very detailed; already established as a central text on the subject.)

Gomery, Douglas (1986) *The Hollywood Studio System*, London: Macmillan/British Film Institute. (Useful general account covering all the major studios.)

Rodick, Nick (1983) *A New Deal in Entertainment: Warner Brothers in the 1930s*, London: British Film Institute. (Discusses the place of Warner Brothers in relation to the Hollywood studio system. Focuses especially on gangster movies and history epics.)

Tulloch, John (1982) *Australian Cinema: Industry, Narrative and Meaning*, Sydney: Allen & Unwin. (A study of the Australian cinema in the 1920s and 1930s which relates the organization of the Australian film industry to the narrative structures of a selection of Australian films.)

(b) Television

Alvardo, Manuel and Buscombe, Edward (1978) *Hazell: The Making of a TV Series*, London: British Film Institute. (One of the first detailed studies of a British TV production context.)

Alvardo, Manuel and Stewart, John (1985) *Made for Television: Euston Films Limited*, London: British Film Institute. (Discusses the general place of Euston Films in relation to the organization of British commercial television, with detailed studies of *The Sweeny, Out, Fox, Minder, The Flame Trees of Thika* and *Widows*.)

Hobson, Dorothy (1982) *Crossroads: The Drama of a Soap Opera*, London: Methuen. (Examines a crisis moment in the history of *Crossroads* to unravel the contradictory pressures affecting production decisions.)

Feuer, Jane, Kerr, Paul and Vahimagi, Tise (eds) (1984) *MTM 'Quality Television'*, London: British Film Institute. (Examines the place of MTM Enterprises in American television and the characteristics of the MTM style. Includes detailed studies of *The Mary Tyler Moore Show, Lou Grant* and *Hill Street Blues*.)

Moran, Albert (1985) *Images and Industry: Television Drama Production in Australia*, Sydney: Currency Press. (Useful general survey of the organization of TV drama in Australia.)

Moran, Albert (1982) *Making a TV Series: The Bellamy Project*, Sydney: Currency Press. (Interesting as a study of a series which flopped.)

Paterson, Richard, 'The production context of *Coronation Street*', in Dyer, Richard *et al.* (1981) *Coronation Street*, London: British Film Institute. (A very condensed and illuminating account of the multiplicity of factors which define a TV production context.)

Tulloch, John and Alvarado, Manuel (1983) *Doctor Who: The Unfolding Text*, London: Macmillan. (A richly detailed account of the institutional constraints regulating the production of *Doctor Who*.)

Tulloch, John and Moran, Albert (1986) *A Country Practice*: 'Quality Soap', Sydney: Currency Press. (Considers the unusual relations of production characterizing the Australian series.)

VII   Reading

The question of reading and its determinants is addressed in many of the studies already mentioned. To specify these, in the order in which they are cited: Eco (1979) offers an uncompromisingly structuralist account of the role of the reader. Humm *et al.*: Paul O'Flinn's essay on the production and reproduction of *Frankenstein* is of special interest. Ellis (1982) explores the institutional factors and the role of contexts of reception in regulating reading practices in both film and television. Fiske and Hartley (1978) devote considerable attention to the regimes of reading associated with television, while Metz (1982) offers a theory of the psychoanalytic determinations of the position and responses of the cinematic spectator. Bennett and Woollacott (1987) consider varying readings of both the Bond novels and films, paying particular attention to the role of gendered reading formations in this regard. Hobson (1982) discusses audience reactions to *Crossroads* in some detail. Tulloch and Alvarado (1983) is interesting not only in its consideration of producers' and writers' calculations of their relations to their audiences but also in the significance it accords the views of fans.

Other relevant studies are itemized below:

(a) Literature

Eagleton, Terry *et al.* (1984) 'The "text in itself": a symposium', *Southern Review*, 17 (2). (Useful debate regarding the implications of readership studies for the status of the text in literary studies.)

Holub, Robert (1984) *Reception Theory: A Critical Introduction*, London: Methuen. (An accessible introduction to the various schools of reception theory currently influential within literary studies.)

Radway, Janice (1984) *Reading the Romance: Women, Patriarchy and Popular Literature*, Chapel Hill: University of North Carolina Press. (Offers a detailed examination of the reactions of a particular group of women readers to Harlequin romances. Extrapolates from these to consider the attractions of romance fiction for women more generally.)

Parry, Ann (1985) 'Reading formations in the Victorian press: the reception of Kipling, 1888–1891', *Literature and History*, 11 (2). (An examination of the factors moulding initial responses to Kipling's works.)

White, Michael (1982) 'Reading and rewriting. The production of an economic Robinson Crusoe', *Southern Review*, 15 (2). (Fascinating study of historical shifts in the reception of *Robinson Crusoe*.)

(b) Film

I am not familiar with any detailed studies of audience readings of particular films or popular genres. However, while this has not been a central area of inquiry within film studies, considerable attention has been paid to the factors which organize the expectations of cinema-goers and structure the position of the spectator. The titles addressing cinema listed under II above deal with questions of this kind. Work on the star system has also displayed a strong audience orientation. The following are of particular interest in this respect:

Dyer, Richard (1979) *Stars*, London: British Film Institute. (Interesting on Jane Fonda and Robert Redford.)

Dyer, Richard (1987) *Heavenly Bodies: Film Stars and Society*, London: British Film Institute. (Surveys the contradictory star currencies of Marilyn Monroe, Paul Robeson and Judy Garland.)

Ellis, John (1982) 'Star/industry/image', *Star Signs*, London: British Film Institute.

(c) Television

While audience research is fairly well developed in television studies, most studies have been concerned with the audience for television as a whole or with audience responses in the news/current affairs areas of TV output. There's very little dealing specifically with audience readings of TV's popular fictional genres. However, the following offer some useful starting points for the reader interested in acquiring some bearings in this area:

Blumler, J. and Katz, E. (eds) (1974) *The Uses of Mass Communications*, Beverly Hills: Sage. (A collection of essays representing the uses and gratifications approach to audience studies.)

Goodhart, G.J., Ehrenberg, A. and Collins, M. (1975) *The Television Audience: Patterns of Viewing*, Farnborough: Saxon House. (Empirical survey of viewing habits.)

Morley, David (1980) *The* Nationwide *Audience*, London: British Film Institute. (A theoretically ambitious study of the *Nationwide* audience which blends sociological considerations with the perspectives of semiotics and discourse analysis.)

Morley, David (1986) *Family Television: Cultural Power and Domestic Leisure*, London: Comedia. (A broader study which extends and revises Morley's earlier arguments. Especially interesting on the domestic contexts of viewing and the functioning of television in relation to power relations within the home.)

Pieppe, A., Emerson, M. and Lannon, J. (1975) *Television and the Working Class*, Farnborough: Saxon House. (Considers the relations between social class and the media via a study of manual workers' responses to television.)

VIII Journals

Popular fiction studies tend to be somewhat dispersed in terms of their journal locations. While varying in their foci from literary through media and feminist studies to general cultural criticism, the following journals frequently contain relevant material:

Cultural Critique: Telos Press, 431 East 12th Street, New York, 1009.

Feminist Review: 11 Carleton Gardens, Brecknock Road, London, N19 5AQ.

Genre: Department of English, University of Oklahoma, Norman, Oklahoma, 73019, USA.

Journal of Cultural Studies: Routledge, 11 New Fetter Lane, London EC4P 4EE.

Journal of Popular Culture: Bowling Green University, Bowling Green, Ohio.

Literature and History: School of Humanities, Thames Polytechnic, Wellington Street, Woolwich, London, SE18 6PF.

Media, Culture and Society, Sage Publications, 23 Banner Street, London, EC1Y 8QE.

New Formations: Routledge.

Screen: Society for Education in Film and Television, 29 Old Compton Street, London, W1V 5PL.

Signs. A Journal of Women in Culture: University of Chicago Press, Journals Division, P.O. Box 37005, Chicago, Illinois, 60637, USA.

Textual Practice: Routledge.

Index